Unlocking the Potential of Children: How Cardology Can Help You Nurture the Development of a Child's Authentic Self

Donna Webb, EdD

Niyati Publishing

This book is dedicated to my former students who unknowingly assisted me in developing a deeper understanding of cardology and the Destiny Card system.

Table of Contents

Introduction

Cardology is the study of the ancient science behind playing cards. It might help you to think of cardology as a merging of astrology and numerology. My journey with cardology began in 1990 when I was browsing through the Aquarian Age bookstore in Houston, Texas. It has been my experience throughout life that certain books reach out and speak to me and this occasion was no different. The book reaching out to me at this time was *Sacred Symbols of the Ancients: The Mystical Significance of Our Fifty-Two Playing Cards and their Amazing Connection with Our Individual Birthdays* (1947), written by Edith L. Randall and Florence Evylinn Campbell. From scanning the book, I learned that each person's birthdate was associated with a playing card like how one's birthdate determines one's zodiac sign. Using a chart from within this book I found my birthdate was associated with a Q♣ Birth Card. I went on to read the description of my Birth Card in wonderment as the personality traits affiliated with a Q♣ Birth Card resonated with me at a very deep level. And so, I simply had to purchase and read this book. Over the years, I have always looked back at that moment in my life as a prime example of how one small action can change one's life forever.

My cardology knowledge fast-tracked over the next several years by reading Robert Lee Camp's books, *Love Cards* and *Cards of Your Destiny*. Robert's books explained the ancient science behind playing cards in a clearer, more understandable manner. Camp not only described the personality traits of each Birth Card, but he also revealed how the behavior of each Birth Card would be influenced by yearly energies through movements of the planets and celestial objects in our solar system. The purpose of these energies is to teach life lessons and guide each person toward their destiny specific to their Birth Card. I was both intrigued and skeptical about this information. I felt driven to learn more about cardology and thought the best approach was to apply what I was reading to myself and the people around me. I asked and investigated many questions surrounding Birth Cards. How did the Birth Cards explain my strengths and weaknesses? How could I use knowledge of my own Birth Card and the current energies I was experiencing to make better choices in love, friendships, and work? How did the people around me express the energy portrayed in their Birth Card? How could I use my understanding of Birth Cards to relate to and interact with others? How could I use the yearly energies of my Birth Card to make goals for the future?

For me to have an inquisitive nature toward spiritual matters is not surprising given that my Birth Card is a Q♣. Q♣s are highly intuitive and receptive to spiritual knowledge. Often their spiritual knowledge aims to serve and nurture children. I embody the personality traits of my Birth Card well as I have been an educator all my life. While trained as an elementary school teacher, I ended up teaching mostly at the middle school level. Some of my friends have joked to me that I should adopt their teenage kids and return them when they reach their twenties. You see, all my life I found teaching teenagers to be wonderful! And, yes, I often found teaching them to be equally challenging! I turned to cardology in hopes of finding another tool to help me support students during challenging times. At the beginning of each school year, I would write each student's name and Birth Card on an index card. Then I would use the information about each child's Birth Card to better understand and interact with them. Let's consider a simple example. At the start of every school year, I set up seating charts. Over time, if I had two students who sat next to each other and would not stop talking or arguing, I would examine their Birth Cards. I would then examine the personality traits of their Birth Cards to remedy the seating issue and create a more harmonious environment. Finding success in small matters such as this encouraged me to apply knowledge of cardology in bigger and more challenging classroom situations. I truly believe my application of cardology helped me nurture and effectively educate thousands of children over the years.

At the time of writing this book, having completed a doctorate degree in education, I am in the position of a teacher educator. Simply put, I teach young adults to become teachers. Such a role enables me to pass along wisdom obtained from my many years of teaching. However, the sharing of my teaching wisdom felt incomplete without explaining how to nurture children by applying knowledge of cardology. This feeling in turn, played a key role in my desire to write this book. However, I would be remiss by not mentioning that I also owe credit to my spiritual guide, Danny. You see, from a young age I have sensed that I receive spiritual knowledge from a guide. To be affiliated with a spiritual guide is also considered an occurrence common for a Q♣. In yet another book written by Robert Lee Camp titled, *Exploring the Little Book of the Seven Thunders*, Camp stated, "I have known many Q♣, including my own mother, who talk to God and to whom God talks back, and to most of them it is perfectly natural. Those Q♣ that cultivate this gift will have a spiritual guide who is always present to help them." Beginning in the summer of 2019 and because my spiritual guide was prodding me, I began to write this book. The information contained within this book is a combination of my own research, advice from my spiritual guide, and personal interpretations formed by my own identity and life experiences. I pray you find this book beneficial in relating to and unlocking the wonders of the children in your life.

A Compelling Personal Reason for this Book
I began writing this book six months prior to the coronavirus pandemic impacting the United States. At that time, I felt simultaneously compelled and conflicted about the timing for this writing. My struggle had to do with being a junior faculty member at a university and actively submerged within the 'publish or perish' reality of academia. Writing this book would take away the time and effort I would otherwise direct at writing research articles. Why should I write this book at this specific time? Why the urgency? Those research articles were mandatory to write to gain tenure. Should I take that risk? After extensive reflection, I decided to divide my writing time in half, equally working on both endeavors. While doing so, I kept asking my spiritual guide to send me signs to indicate if I was or was not on the right track with this division of my time. Then, COVID-19 struck.

During the pandemic, like me, you may have been fascinated if you heard that the psychic, Sylvia Browne, had predicted this virus in a book written in 2008. Was there any truth to this? Being curious, I had to go directly to the source of this prediction. Reading Browne's book, *End of Days*, Browne wrote: "In around 2020 a severe pneumonia-like illness will spread throughout the globe, attacking the lungs and bronchial tubes and resisting all known treatments." Wow, I thought. This was so accurate. Not one to disregard context, I decided to read the whole book. Meanwhile, I admit the book contained many other predictions, some happening and some not. What surprised me, though, was that a different part of the book caught my attention. Browne explained that she wrote the book because she was experiencing her fifty-second and last incarnation. Hmmm. That comment was in tune with my understanding of cardology, in that a soul is destined to journey through and learn from 52 Birth Cards and therefore 52 life incarnations. Because Browne believed her current life was her soul's final incarnation, she explained that her book, *End of Days*, was her last chance to persuade people to save humanity. As the title of her book implied, Browne believed human life would end in the twenty-first century if people did not make changes. To assist the planet through such a change, Browne predicted more and more advanced souls would volunteer to incarnate during the most difficult of times. When I read that last piece, my purpose and urgency in writing this book became clear.

The coronavirus pandemic upended many of our lives and hijacked our sense of security toward the future. For me personally, the crisis forced me to hit a 'pause' button and reflect upon my priorities. One thing became clear to me – I needed to write this book and write it now. It could not wait. As a seasoned Q♣, I have learned to trust my own intuition. And my intuition was screaming at me to write this book! It was shouting that God (or the universe if that is your belief) is initiating a transformation for mankind. Such a transformation is to make things right that have been wrong for so long. My initial desire in writing this book was to share my insights on how the application of cardology could help adults nurture children toward their highest potential. When COVID-19 struck, my intuition revealed a broader purpose. Today's children are tomorrow's future. And there is hope for humanity's future because, as Browne predicted, advanced souls will be born to facilitate this change. Today's children will be instrumental in mankind's transformation. And our children need to be at the top of their game to lead this difficult work.

I am in no way a special person in holding these intuitions. There are many other people across the globe who share my insights. Poet and filmmaker, Tom Roberts, presented a similar viewpoint in a humorous YouTube video titled, *The Great Revelation*, that went 'viral' during the pandemic (okay, sorry for the pun). In his video, Roberts is reading a bedtime story to his child. The story begins by describing a society fixated on technology, consumption, and greed. Then, a virus strikes that causes people to hide away. Shocked by their new realities, people start to question life. The outcome was that humanity rediscovered what was most important to them, such as "clapping to say thank you" or "calling up their mums." When the pandemic was over, people changed. Their priorities changed. They did not want to return to the old ways of doing things. Instead, people found that caring for the earth, valuing relationships, and demonstrating acts of kindness were the right ingredients for the future. The story ends with Roberts telling his child, "Now lie down, and dream of tomorrow, and all the things that we can do. And who knows, maybe if you dream strong enough, make some of them come true." Like me, Roberts sees opportunity and optimism in mankind's future through the potential of our children.

A more compelling, but less publicized prophecy about humanity's future has been orally passed down from generation to generation among the indigenous peoples. In her 2018 published book, *Sacred Instructions: Indigenous Wisdom for Living Spirit-Based Change*, Sherri Mitchell revealed that the manifestation of this prophesy is happening right now. Because we are at the beginning of this process, Mitchell was encouraged by indigenous elders to share this knowledge with a larger audience, thus the writing of her book. What is this prophecy, you ask? According to Mitchell (2018, p. *xix*):

We are living in a time of exposure, where the light of truth is shining into all the dark corners of our lives. As a result, all that has been lurking in the shadows is now coming into sharp focus. Some of the things that this light is revealing are deeply disturbing; some are downright terrifying. This is causing many people to feel lost and hopeless, or completely overwhelmed by the amount of work that we are facing.

When I think of deeply disturbing events prior to the time of writing this book, expressions of "I can't breathe" and other truths brought to light through the Black Lives Matter movement come to mind. And the many collective voices that were shared through the Me-Too movement. And the pleas from residents of Standing Rock Indian Reservation who stood against the Dakota Access pipeline. As a science teacher educator, I am particularly alarmed by the plethora of research-based reports of the harmful effects of human activity on climate change. It is painful for me to observe the lack of response to these reports from our leaders. Why are we ignoring nature's signs, nature's call for help? Why are we ignoring or disbelieving the warnings of scientists? Sadly, in my opinion, I believe we humans have been distracted away from these issues by all manner of things such as our consumption of materialism, technology, and political divisions to name a few.

Mitchell goes on to explain why humans must change their ways. For centuries, humanity has been under the illusion that all living things are separate in the world. Mankind has disconnected from the earth. And now mankind is destroying itself through its division in thinking and beliefs. The purpose behind this "time of exposure" is to shed light on the tragic consequences of separation and push people toward awareness. To become aware that we must change. We must evolve. If we do not, the earth will protect itself by eliminating the source of its pain – us. The famous astrologer, Susan Miller, made a similar remark in an editorial about the coronavirus when she stated, "Our misuse of the earth's resources and lack of proper stewardship of our planet have led to an imbalance that encourages deadly viruses to surface." My heart and mind have opened to the fact that children are already leading humanity towards such a transformation. As I finalize the writing of this book, I look back at recent examples of this. For instance, do you remember watching teenagers from Marjory Stoneman Douglas High School in Parkland, Florida demand change after a mass shooting traumatized their community? They were so articulate and resilient in the face of such tragedy. Or perhaps you know the story of Malala Yousafzai. As a young girl living in Pakistan, Malala was outspoken about her and other girl's rights to an education. Even after receiving threats to her life, Malala stood her ground refusing to stay home from school. Tragically Malala was shot one day walking home from school. Not only did she survive being shot in the head, but she continued to advocate for her rights. Or perhaps you recall the Swedish activist, Greta Thunberg, who made the case to fight climate change in a Ted Talk. She was 16 years old at the time of her plea. Watching this talk, I marveled at Greta's poise, intellect, and maturity that appeared so advanced for someone her age.

These children and events are making more sense to me now. What is clear to me is that for humanity to evolve there must first be deconstruction. Structures and systems that are no longer serving the needs of the collective will need to break down before reconstruction can take place. This process of deconstruction will be hard and painful. The pain is necessary, though. Pain will be the world's guide. You see, pain reveals the areas in the world that need improvement. And the children of today like Greta as well as the children who will be born over the coming years are the advanced souls that Browne talked about. I believe they embody hope for the future. They will light up and guide humanity's journey through the challenging times ahead. They will lead us through a rebirth. Their work will not be easy. To thrive in such difficult times, our children need to be resilient. They also need to be made aware of their superpowers or higher personality traits inherent to their Birth Card. You see, each Birth Card possesses unique traits that can manifest across a spectrum of higher or lower expressions. Parents and adults caring for or working with children can help them become aware of these traits. More importantly, adults can nurture these children toward their higher traits. The Dalai Lama captured the advantages of this kind of notion well when he said, "With realization of one's own potential and self-confidence in one's ability, one can build a better world." I see this moment in time as an opportunity to create; to create a better way, a better world. My hope as I finish writing this book is that it can contribute even the smallest bit to helping children manifest their highest traits which in turn, can fast track them to reaching their highest potential. By achieving this state, I believe our children will decide to make the future better. They will take action to create a better world. They will create a world in which people embrace connection, love, and harmony between all living things. They will create a world in which people work together and demand solutions to political, environmental, and social justice issues.

Donna Webb, EdD

Chapter 1

History and Basic Overview of Cardology

The origin of cardology or the ancient science behind playing cards is an elusive subject. Chinese scholars believe the first reference of playing cards was by a Chinese writer in the 9th century who described others playing a game with paper tiles called *"yezi ge"* or the "leaf game." Unfortunately, there wasn't any historical documentation of such tiles to validate this belief. From China, playing cards are thought to have expanded to Egypt and Syria during the time of the Mamluk dynasty (1250 – 1517). It is from this period that researchers found the first historical evidence of playing cards. In 1931, Leo Mayer, a professor of Eastern Art and Archeology, discovered a nearly complete deck of Mamluk playing cards at the Topkapi Palace in Istanbul. Even though the discovered cards were dated to the 15th century, their design confirmed the existence of previously unearthed, but incomplete decks of cards that dated back to the 12th century. If you were to examine the Mamluk cards, you would be surprised to find how similar they are in structure to the playing cards we recognize today. The Mamluk deck consisted of 52 cards that entailed four suits, each composed of 10 numerical cards and three court cards. The four suits represented were swords, goblets, coins, and polo-sticks. It was not until the 14th century, and after arriving in Western Europe by way of people travelling along trade routes, that playing cards were modified to entail Hearts, Clubs, Diamonds, and Spades as the four suits. This modification was made to support playing a card game that involved the concept of knights and chivalry. In this game, the Hearts suit represented the church. The Clubs suit depicted husbandmen or farmers. The Diamonds suit personified vassals or subordinate people who owed fidelity to a superior person. And the Spades suit represented knights who were men of noble birth trained in military and chivalrous conduct. It was this Western European version of playing cards that made it to America by way of Spanish explorers.

By the 18th century and prior to the thirteen colonies declaring their independence, playing cards were extremely popular in British America. Historical records show that several of our Founding Fathers, including Ben Franklin and George Washington enjoyed games with playing cards. Native Americans adopted the use of playing cards as well, making their own version by painting symbols on deerskin. You may remember studying this time in American history from lessons during elementary or middle school. You likely learned that the Stamp Act was one of several controversies related to the cause of the Revolutionary War. Enacted in 1765 by the British Parliament, the Stamp Act taxed American colonists on all forms of printed materials. This included legal documents, newspapers, and playing cards among other things. Because playing cards was popular throughout all social and economic classes, this tax impacted a significant number of people. It is interesting that the anger toward the tax imposed upon all these printed materials including playing cards contributed to the colonist's reasons to fight for and gain America's independence.

What is even more interesting about this period in the history of America is that the Continental Congress voted for independence on July 2, 1776. Because the Declaration of Independence was adopted on July 4, 1776, people associate this date with America's birthdate. Yet, because the Continental Congress acted on July 2, I see America's true birthdate as July 2, 1776. This birthdate in turn makes America associated with a K♦ Birth Card. The personality traits of a K♦ Birth Card include a love of freedom, a desire for material accumulation, and the ability to rule through power in money and values. Sounds about, right? Keep reading, because you will soon learn that the birthdates for you, your friends, your children, and other family members are associated with playing cards. And these playing cards reveal amazingly accurate descriptions of the people they represent.

At this point, you may be asking: where did this interpretation of playing cards come from? Playing cards have only been used for games, right? In 1893, Olney H. Richmond published the very first book on the topic of cardology. His book was titled, *The Mystic Test Book or The Magic of Cards*. In this book, Richmond claimed playing cards were not invented for entertainment. Richmond explained that playing cards had an even earlier beginning than when they appeared in China. He stated they were invented by the Atlanteans, the people of Atlantis. Do you consider Atlantis to be a fictional place? There is historical evidence supporting the existence of Atlantis based upon the writings of the philosopher Plato. In 360 B. C., Plato wrote about an advanced community that disappeared into the sea after being impacted by a series of earthquakes and floods. He called this place Atlantis. Although some scholars believe Plato's description of Atlantis was more figurative than literal, other scholars continue to believe in Atlantis' existence. In fact, some 21st century researchers have pointed to the Spanish coast as being the submerged location of Atlantis.

Plato described the city of Atlantis as a place inhabited by people with advanced tools and knowledge. According to Richmond, one field of advanced study had to do with cardology. By observing structural patterns of planets and celestial objects in the universe and the effects these patterns had upon mankind, Atlanteans discovered some interesting secrets about the universe. And they captured this knowledge through playing cards. Why was this knowledge expressed in the form of playing cards and not written in words? Richmond explained that symbols were used for communication of this information because they could be understood "in all tongues and among all peoples." Richmond also noted that evidence of this knowledge was written into the Christian Bible. In the final book of the Bible, known as the Book of Revelations, the Apostle John described an angel that came down from heaven holding a *Book of Seven Thunders*. This book contained mysteries and secrets which Richmond explained had to do with every person's destiny. After giving voice to these secrets, the angel would not allow John to write the content down. Instead, John ate the contents, and the angel told him "He must prophesy again about many peoples and nations and tongues and kings." Shortly after this time, a group of people formed a secret order to record, seal, protect, and pass along the knowledge contained within the *Book of Seven Thunders* until such time as the order allowed its contents to be revealed. This order was called the Ancient Order of the Magi. In 1893, as the Grand Master of the Ancient Order of the Magi, Richmond was given permission to publish much of the book's secrets. What did Richmond publish? He wrote about the mystic and real meanings of playing cards, asserting they embodied God's lessons (or the universe's lessons if this aligns more with your beliefs). To be more specific, playing cards represented different *life lessons* or destiny paths God created for mankind.

Building on this series of historical events related to cardology, in 2015 MIT professor and cosmologist Max Tegmark published a book titled, *Our Mathematical Universe*, in which he claimed that everything in the universe – both living and nonliving things are part of a mathematical structure. Several prominent scientists have embraced Tegmark's perspective, particularly because no properties have been discovered that do not adhere to mathematical properties. Take for example something as simple as throwing a football in the air; and how it follows a mathematical and predictable path. Likewise, the complex way in which a living cell divides also follows a mathematical and predictable path. Tegmark went on to state that "humans are substructures living in a relational reality." Because the spiritual essence of every person's soul is part of the universe, this would suggest that each person's soul can be described and will behave in mathematical and predictable ways. Why not? Surely, to say that everything within the universe, every element within it, exists alongside all other elements solely by coincidence seems highly unlikely. As Einstein brilliantly stated, "God doesn't play dice with the universe." Tegmark's theory supports the idea that the lives of humans follow a mathematical and somewhat predictable path. I also find it interesting that Tegmark was born May 5, 1967, which makes him associated with an A♠ Birth Card – the card that represents cardology!

You may be thinking it is illogical for each person's exact path to be predetermined because each of us lives such different lives. You are correct in that free will must also be factored in as it plays a critical role in one's destiny. Hence, each person's path is shaped by a measure of both *destiny* and *free will*. In the Bible, Proverbs 16:9 reminds us of this, "In their hearts humans plan their course, but the Lord establishes their steps." God gave us free will so we could make choices and learn lessons along our life path. In addition, you have probably heard others say that God has a plan for each of us. As these statements point out, many people believe God created destiny paths or life lessons for mankind.

Cardology is based upon the concept of *reincarnation* or the idea that when a person's physical body dies, the person's soul continues to exist and begins a new life in a different physical body. The date on which a soul is born is associated with a Birth Card. This Birth Card activates lessons created by God that a soul will experience in its present life incarnation. Just as there are grades that humans experience in a specific order within an educational system, there exists chronological learning experiences for souls. The order of these lessons is based upon a Birth Card's *suit* and *number*. Souls progress through life incarnations beginning as Hearts, moving on to Clubs, then Diamonds, and finally as Spades. Heart cards are the youngest souls and Spades are the oldest souls. In addition, souls chronologically progress through learning experiences within each suit, beginning with lessons as an Ace and culminating with lessons as a King. And just as survival instincts like fight or flight are transferred from one life incarnation to the next, spiritual lessons learned from past lives are passed along subconsciously to further life incarnations.

Going back to *The Mystic Test Book or The Magic of Cards*, Richmond revealed the mathematical structure of God's life lessons for mankind. This structure was visually depicted in the 52 playing cards (or Birth Cards) that were organized into a specific pattern. Richmond called this pattern of Birth Cards *the Spiritual Spread*. At birth, a soul is assigned a Birth Card for their current life incarnation. Due to that Birth Card's position in the Spiritual Spread, a soul adopts a specific temperament and activates a sequence of life lessons by establishing a combination of 13 cards God created for one's life. This means a child born to a specific Birth Card will experience predestined events related to past lives and related karma. How a child responds to these life situations, especially environmental challenges, will form a child's higher and lower personality traits. Robert Lee Camp, an author of numerous books about cardology, called these sequences of life lessons the *Life Spread*. If you are familiar with astrology, this would be like a person's *Birth Chart*. A Birth Chart is a diagram that shows the exact positions of the Sun, Moon, and other planets in our solar system on the date and time of a person's birth. Astrologists believe these structures in our solar system produce and embed energies within a person at birth. Then, each year of a person's life, the universe conveys new energies through all its patterns of planetary and other celestial movements. These yearly movements or transits impact each person differently depending upon a person's unique Birth Chart. In Camp's books, these yearly energies for each Birth Card are accounted for in what he termed *Yearly Spreads*. It may help to think of these Yearly Spreads as energies that present each person with shorter-term lessons. Each person responds to these energies by freely making choices, thus creating their own reality and life that is unlike anyone else's. The entire system of spreads – Spiritual, Life, and Yearly Spreads – in totality are known as the Destiny Card system. You see, these spreads mathematically adjust to create life lessons for a soul based upon their Birth Card. In other words, the Destiny Card system represents the mechanism through which a person learns lessons during a life incarnation. It is not the intention of this book to describe or interpret the Yearly Spreads of the Destiny Card system (Instead, I would recommend reading Robert Lee Camp's books as he covers this topic quite thoroughly). Rather, this book focuses upon what the Destiny Card system can reveal about a child and how adults can leverage that knowledge to nurture a child.

The purpose of this book is to help children achieve their authentic and highest potential by sharing the knowledge of each Birth Card's destiny and life lessons with parents and other adults who care for or work with children. Put another way, this book is to help adults nurture children from a place of awareness. Gary Zukav, yet another author of spiritual writings, wrote in his book *The Seat of the Soul*:

> When the energy of the soul is recognized, acknowledged and valued, it begins to infuse the life of the personality. When the personality comes fully to serve the energy of its soul, that is authentic empowerment. This is the goal of the evolutionary process in which we are involved and the reason for our being.

As an educator for over 30 years and having worked with numerous parents and their children who are manifesting challenging behaviors, I know two things to be true. First, every child has the potential to manifest the higher traits associated with their Birth Card. Secondly, at their core, every parent wants what is best for their child. Parenting is difficult work, though. Some people struggle to effectively parent. Perhaps they model poor techniques learned from their own parents. These parents have good intentions but make mistakes that may be avoidable. Some parents are experiencing a difficult life incarnation of their own that impacts their parenting. This book not only describes the higher and lower personality traits of children associated with their Birth Card, but it also provides suggestions for how a parent or an adult working with children can nurture a child toward their higher traits. While this book is far from a panacea to solve all problems related to raising children, it serves as one additional tool to help adults understand and nurture a child's true nature and potential destiny. As Deepak

Chopra eloquently stated, "When you discover your essential nature and know who you really are, in that knowing itself is the ability to fulfill any dream you have, because you are the eternal possibility, the immeasurable potential of all that was, is, and will be." This is to say that when a child understands their true nature and destiny, they become further empowered to achieve their highest potential. And isn't this what we all want for our children – for them to be the best version of themselves?

Chapter 2

A Deep Dive into the Destiny Card System

Have you ever heard a person say, "I guess it wasn't in the cards for me?" The phrase "wasn't in the cards" means that some situation lacked the potential of happening. On the other hand, and along this same line of thought, if an occurrence is "in the cards," it is destined to become reality. Where did these expressions come from? The answer is simple – it came from the historical recognition that playing cards represent a mathematical system which reveals each person's destiny.

As explained in Chapter 1, everything in the universe is part of a mathematical structure. Remarkably, both the calendar and playing cards depict this mathematical structure and therefore share distinct similarities. Think of the four seasons; how they are divided in time across the calendar and how they represent important transitions on Earth. Now think of the four suits of Hearts, Clubs, Diamonds, and Spades as representing the four seasons of a soul's journey. Each suit has 13 cards, which is the same number of weeks in a quarter and the number of lunar cycles in a year. A deck of cards contains 12 court cards, known as Kings, Queens, and Jacks. These court cards depict the 12 months in a year. A deck also consists of 52 cards in total, just as there are 52 weeks in a year. If you have had the experience of playing cards for entertainment, you know each card is associated with a specific number. Aces are associated with the number one, twos with twos, threes with threes, and so on. Likewise, court cards equate to numbers. Kings are equal to 13, queens are equal to 12, and Jacks are equal to 11. If you multiple each card's numerical value by four (representing the four suits), you get another connection to the calendar. For example, an Ace equates to one. One times four equals four. A Queen equates to 12. Twelve times four equals 48. Continue in this same manner with all 13 cards and then add all those numbers together. What number do you get? You get 364. But wait — let us not forget the Joker. The Joker's value is one and one quarter. Now, we are at 365 1/4, which is exactly the number of days in a year! This connection between the calendar and playing cards is not a coincidence.

The way the Destiny Card system works is that each day of the year is associated with a Birth Card. Each respective Birth Card reveals God's destiny path or life lessons for the person born on that date, regardless of the year in which they are born. The purpose of these life lessons is to help a soul achieve *spiritual enlightenment*. And spiritual enlightenment is attainable for all souls, not just the souls well known for their spiritual leadership, such as The Dalia Lama, Eckhart Tolle, or Deepak Chopra to name a few. But achieving spiritual enlightenment is no easy task and it does not happen in one lifetime. To achieve spiritual enlightenment each soul must experience and learn from 52 different life paths. Essentially this means part of God's plan is that we reincarnate from Birth Card to Birth Card learning the lessons inherent to each Birth Card. The best a soul can achieve in a single lifetime is to achieve *spiritual growth*; to become self-aware, authentically express one's personality traits and learn the life lessons of their current Birth Card. If a soul does not accomplish this, they will need to repeat these life lessons by repeating the same Birth Card in a different lifetime. Think of it like God's way of making a soul repeat a grade just like a child being held back in school to repeat a grade if they failed to meet the related requirements. At this point, you may be asking: What are the requirements or life lessons for each Birth Card?

A person's purpose, gifts, and current life lessons are determined by two distinct energies of one's Birth Card that combine to form a synergy of personality traits. These two energies are: 1) the suit of the Birth Card (Heart, Club, Diamond, or Spade), and 2) the number affiliated with the Birth Card (one through 13). Together the suit and number of a Birth Card establish a unique temperament and personality traits that can manifest as *higher* or *lower expressions*. These higher and lower expressions of traits play a significant role in a person's life lessons. Remember a soul's objective for a current life incarnation is to achieve spiritual growth. Spiritual growth is a sum game of one's actions, that is, of manifesting their higher and lower traits. It may be helpful to consider these traits on opposite sides of a continuum with varying degrees of middle ground or more moderate expressions. Throughout a lifetime, a person can manifest higher and lower traits and any frequency in between. When the sum of manifestations leans toward a higher expression of traits, a person is learning their current life lessons. On the other hand, when the sum of manifestations leans toward a lower expression of traits, a person is not learning their life lessons. As noted earlier, every person has free will. Every day individuals make choices as to how they are expressing their traits. Of course, every person makes mistakes from time to time. In a weak, stressful, or fearful moment a person can temporarily manifest a lower trait. The point is that we are to learn from those mistakes. Learning from mistakes and choosing higher traits equates to spiritual growth. Continued and significant mistakes made may result in bad karma to deal with in the next life incarnation. Failure to learn lessons over many life incarnations will negatively impact a soul's ultimate journey toward spiritual enlightenment. Because the suit and number of a Birth Card are the key to a person's life lessons, let's look more closely at each of these elements.

Suits and Their Personality Traits in a Birth Card
As previously mentioned, the suit of a Birth Card designates one of two energies that contribute to a person's purpose, gifts, and life lessons. When a person manifests the higher traits of their suit, they tend to feel joy and internal satisfaction. On the other hand, when a person manifests the lower traits of their suit, they tend to feel imbalance and dissatisfaction within their life. And keep in mind that a person can manifest varying degrees of middle ground expressions. Let's consider the traits of each suit, keeping in mind the four suits reflect the four seasons of a soul's journey.

Birth Cards of the Hearts suit represent spring, the first season of the year and the time of beginnings as nature awakens. Flowers begin to bloom, and adult animals give birth to their young. As a Birth Card, Hearts represent the youngest souls and so their life lessons are at the beginning of their journey toward spiritual enlightenment. It is common knowledge that the Heart is a symbol of love. Throughout their lifetime, a person born a Heart suit will direct their energies toward *love* and *relationships*. As such, a person associated with a Heart Birth Card retains gifts and experiences life lessons around love and relationships. When these individuals manifest the higher traits of their Heart suit, they demonstrate love, kindness, and compassion. They build healthy relationships and develop self-love. A person associated with a Heart Birth Card discovers their greatest joy comes when they develop and sustain loving relationships. If a

Heart Birth Card chooses the lower traits of their suit, they exhibit lust, self-indulgence, drama, and/or suffer from poor self-esteem. The ruling planets of Hearts are Venus and Neptune.

Birth Cards of the Clubs suit represent summertime, when living things optimize growth. Similarly, man achieves growth when gathering knowledge. Being born a Club suit represents the second season in which a soul journeys on its path toward spiritual enlightenment. A person born as a Club Birth Card will direct their energies toward *developing their intellect*. As such, a person associated with a Club Birth Card carries gifts and experiences life lessons in their ability to communicate and absorb information. When these individuals manifest the higher traits of their Club suit, they demonstrate creativity, curiosity, and being well informed. They communicate responsibly with others. These individuals discover the greatest joy comes when they master the acquisition and communication of knowledge. On the other hand, when a person born with a Club Birth Card reinforces the lower traits of their suit, they tend to be argumentative, negative, or anxious. They may spread gossip or develop mental health issues. The ruling planets of Clubs are Mercury and Mars.

The next season is autumn, the time of harvest. Birth Cards of the Diamond suit represent autumn well because Diamonds symbolize money, and harvest is the time when we benefit from nature's pay off. Yet, Diamonds also symbolize values and the third stage of a soul's journey toward spiritual enlightenment whereby a person accumulates and reinforces values. This process of growth is like what happens in nature, too. Trees stop the food-making process and shift to consolidating their energy. We see this when their leaves begin to change color. Soon the leaves lose their value, and trees let them go. In turn, Birth Cards with the Diamond suit direct their energies toward *what is valued*. As such, a person associated with a Diamond suit possesses gifts and experiences life lessons around money and values. When these individuals manifest the higher traits of their Diamond suit, they discover the greatest joy comes when they use what they accumulate to empower and give to others. However, working from the lower traits of their suit, a person born a Diamond Birth Card exhibits greed, selfishness, entitlement, and poor self-worth. The single ruling planet of Diamonds is Jupiter.

The last season is winter, represented by the Spade suit. In winter, many living things transform. Cranes migrate south in search of warmer temperatures. Foxes change their appearance to blend in with their new surroundings. Bears slow down their metabolism and hibernate in dens. Some living things die. Transformation into winter is not an easy process. Spades likewise require challenging lessons to transform as the soul is in its final series of life incarnations to achieve spiritual enlightenment. Spades experience transformational lessons by having to make sacrifices in love, health, money, and work. As the oldest souls, Spades utilize all the lessons learned from their past lives as Birth Cards of other suits to tackle the challenges in their current life. Throughout their lifetime, a person born a Spade Birth Card directs their energy toward *health* and *work* matters. As such, a person associated with a Spade suit retains gifts and experiences life lessons around health and work to achieve spiritual awakenings, the ultimate transformation of all. When these individuals manifest the higher traits of their suit, they demonstrate hard work, self-discipline, humility, and wisdom. On the other hand, when a person born a Spade suit manifests the lower traits of their suit, they are judgmental, inflexible, and unsympathetic to the emotions of others. In work, they may act like bullies or struggle with work and life balance. Some may manifest health problems. The ruling planets of Spades are Saturn and Uranus.

9

Numbers and Their Personality Traits in a Birth Card

The number affiliated with a Birth Card provides additional information about a person's purpose, gifts, and life lessons in their present life incarnation. Most people are familiar with the idea that numbers occur in patterns. Is there any significance to the numerical order of the Birth Cards? Yes, there is significance! Life lessons occur in *learning progressions*. In education, learning progressions is a term used by curriculum planners to describe how the learning of topics is spread out in such a way that is age appropriate. In a similar way, the Destiny Card system utilizes learning progressions as a soul experiences lessons in two ways: 1) within a soul's current life incarnation, and 2) across a soul's numerous life incarnations.

Have you ever experienced situations in life where you or someone else seemed to be repeating the same unhealthy pattern? These situations indicate learning progressions are at play within a person's current life incarnation. Over one's lifetime, specific energies come about that help a given Birth Card to learn life lessons. And just as educational lessons become increasingly challenging, we learn life lessons in more challenging ways as we age. The lessons get harder. If we do our homework and learn each lesson or even part of it at a younger age, the lessons later become more manageable. If we rebel against the lessons from the onset, the related problems become elevated, and the lessons become more challenging the next time around.

Learning progressions also exist across life incarnations. Remember, souls reincarnate and chronologically experience God's lessons beginning as Aces and graduating up to Kings. And these lessons progress in complexity and difficulty along each card's suit. For example, if you read the traits of a 4♥ and Q♥, there are similarities. Both cards nurture the people around them. While both cards experience lessons in love and relationships, a 4♥ experiences easier lessons than a Q♥. One life lesson for a 4♥ is superiority. They have fortunate and easy childhoods. This shapes their perspective. They have a hard time understanding unbalanced emotions in others. When others make poor decisions in times of instability, a 4♥ can be critical of them. A Q♥ also nurtures others, but their relational lessons are harder. One life lesson for a Q♥ is to learn the importance of setting boundaries in relationships. They need to balance their own needs and the amount of nurturing they give to others. All Queen's rule and therefore hold an added responsibility of service to others. For a Q♥ such service manifests as love and care for those around them. On one level this sounds easy. It is not. You see, a Q♥ often feels responsible for others. When people they care about feel unbalanced and make poor decisions, they empathize and feel a need to fix the situation. They think their love and care should heal the pain. They may overly nurture others. When their nurturing does not fix a person, emotional heartache often results, and they blame themselves. Indeed, the life lessons of a Q♥ are more challenging than the lessons of a 4♥.

As previously mentioned, a person's current life lessons are related to their Birth Card's traits and how they may manifest them as higher and lower expressions. Also remember, just as the suit of a Birth Card is associated with higher and lower traits, the same is true for the number of a Birth Card. The table on the following page describes the basic traits associated with each Birth Card number as well as the possible higher and lower expressions of these traits.

Card Number	Basic Traits	Higher Expressions	Lower Expressions
1 **(Aces)**	Seeker Self-discovery Ambition Activity	Leader Passionate Courageous Initiator	Selfish Impulsive Lack staying power Aggressive
2	Cooperation Sharing Balance Partnership	Congenial Diplomatic Supportive Collaborative	Whiner Fearful Subservient Dependent
3	Creative Curious Variety Sociable	Multitasker Humorous Optimistic Artistic	Indecisive Worrisome Intolerant Scattered
4	Solid Practical Security Dependable	Constructive Organized Protective Loyal	Undemonstrative Stubborn Fixed Insecure
5	Change Action Travel Versatile	Adaptable Thrive in ambiguity Independent Progressive	Restless Commitment issues Attention issues Moody
6	Status-quo Peace Stability Harmony	Good mediator Responsible Patient Mission-oriented	Not proactive Lazy Static Unforgiving
7	Spiritual Challenges Extra-sensory Wisdom	Philosophical Reflective Devoted Sensitive	Melancholy Skeptical Worrisome Chase rainbows
8	Power Charm Philanthropy Organized	Expansive Leader Magnetic Steadfast	Bully Opportunistic Egotistical Inflexible
9	Universal Obstacles Endings Letting go	Giver Transformative Broad-minded Intuitive	Negative Selfish Idealistic Co-dependent
10	Success Rewards Completion Self-made	Leader Hard worker Tenacious Achiever	Impatient Selfish Unscrupulous Obsessive
11 **(Jacks)**	Inventive Youthful Unisex Fun	Artistic Dramatic Playful Inspirational	Liar Immature Irresponsible Con Man
12 **(Queens)**	Feminine Motherly Teacher Receptive	Service-oriented Intuitive Good judgement Nurturing	Lazy Passive Passive-aggressive Hard to please
13 **(Kings)**	Masculine Ruler Master Responsible	Leader Sympathetic Wise Powerful	Fiercely independent Antagonistic Tyrant Arrogant

In scanning the table of Birth Card numbers and their basic traits, you may have noticed some gender-related words. These words only show up in the court cards (Kings, Queens, and Jacks). For instance, a basic trait for a King is the word *masculine*. This means all Kings, regardless of gender, have masculine energy. As an example, I have a female friend who is a K♦. She has worked in the military and served on two Gulf tours. She has expressed that she feels more comfortable working with males, does not get along with dramatic females, and has more male than female friends. You see, each court card manifests distinct gender traits despite the biological gender of the person. This means that all Queen Birth Cards, regardless of gender, carry *feminine* aspects. Interestingly, Jacks have the word *unisex* as a basic trait. They do not fit the mold of their biological gender and can be non-binary, where they may identify across a variety of gender identities or have a fluctuating identity.

A Birth Card's number and its related traits only provide part of the story. Remember a person's purpose, gifts, and life lessons inherent to each Birth Card are the result of two interacting energies: the suit and number of the Birth Card (see Figure 1). The traits associated with a Birth Card's suit form a synergy with a Birth Card's number. Let's consider this synergy by examining the 9♥ Birth Card and a person experiencing life lessons related to it. The Destiny Card system tells us several things about a 9♥ Birth Card. Based upon the suit of this card, a 9♥ experiences life lessons around love and relationships. The number Nine adds several basic traits for a 9♥ that may be expressed in higher or lower ways. Using the table above, one would find the basic traits associated with the number Nine are: universal, obstacles, endings, and letting go. Combining the traits of the number Nine with the traits of a Heart suit would suggest a 9♥'s purpose and gifts revolve around universal love and an expansive capacity to give to others. Their challenging life lessons often involve a great emotional loss or ending related to love.

Figure 1:

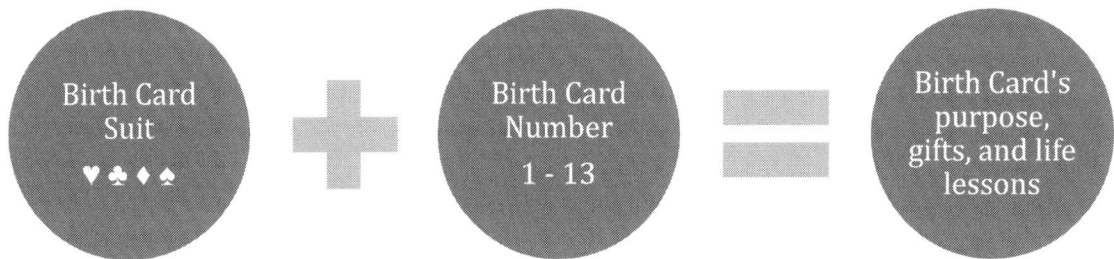

Birth Card Suit ♥ ♣ ♦ ♠ + Birth Card Number 1 - 13 = Birth Card's purpose, gifts, and life lessons

I am sure you are wanting to know the suit and number of your own Birth Card and the children in your life. Below is a table that provides you with birth dates and their associated Birth Cards.

Birth Cards Table

	Jan	Feb	Mar	Apr	May	June	July	Aug	Sept	Oct	Nov	Dec
1	K♠	J♠	9♠	7♠	5♠	3♠	A♠	Q♦	10♦	8♦	6♦	4♦
2	Q♠	10♠	8♠	6♠	4♠	2♠	K♦	J♦	9♦	7♦	5♦	3♦
3	J♠	9♠	7♠	5♠	3♠	A♠	Q♦	10♦	8♦	6♦	4♦	2♦
4	10♠	8♠	6♠	4♠	2♠	K♦	J♦	9♦	7♦	5♦	3♦	A♦
5	9♠	7♠	5♠	3♠	A♠	Q♦	10♦	8♦	6♦	4♦	2♦	K♣
6	8♠	6♠	4♠	2♠	K♦	J♦	9♦	7♦	5♦	3♦	A♦	Q♣
7	7♠	5♠	3♠	A♠	Q♦	10♦	8♦	6♦	4♦	2♦	K♣	J♣
8	6♠	4♠	2♠	K♦	J♦	9♦	7♦	5♦	3♦	A♦	Q♣	10♣
9	5♠	3♠	A♠	Q♦	10♦	8♦	6♦	4♦	2♦	K♣	J♣	9♣
10	4♠	2♠	K♦	J♦	9♦	7♦	5♦	3♦	A♦	Q♣	10♣	8♣
11	3♠	A♠	Q♦	10♦	8♦	6♦	4♦	2♦	K♣	J♣	9♣	7♣
12	2♠	K♦	J♦	9♦	7♦	5♦	3♦	A♦	Q♣	10♣	8♣	6♣
13	A♠	Q♦	10♦	8♦	6♦	4♦	2♦	K♣	J♣	9♣	7♣	5♣
14	K♦	J♦	9♦	7♦	5♦	3♦	A♦	Q♣	10♣	8♣	6♣	4♣
15	Q♦	10♦	8♦	6♦	4♦	2♦	K♣	J♣	9♣	7♣	5♣	3♣
16	J♦	9♦	7♦	5♦	3♦	A♦	Q♣	10♣	8♣	6♣	4♣	2♣
17	10♦	8♦	6♦	4♦	2♦	K♣	J♣	9♣	7♣	5♣	3♣	A♣
18	9♦	7♦	5♦	3♦	A♦	Q♣	10♣	8♣	6♣	4♣	2♣	K♥
19	8♦	6♦	4♦	2♦	K♣	J♣	9♣	7♣	5♣	3♣	A♣	Q♥
20	7♦	5♦	3♦	A♦	Q♣	10♣	8♣	6♣	4♣	2♣	K♥	J♥
21	6♦	4♦	2♦	K♣	J♣	9♣	7♣	5♣	3♣	A♣	Q♥	10♥
22	5♦	3♦	A♦	Q♣	10♣	8♣	6♣	4♣	2♣	K♥	J♥	9♥
23	4♦	2♦	K♣	J♣	9♣	7♣	5♣	3♣	A♣	Q♥	10♥	8♥
24	3♦	A♦	Q♣	10♣	8♣	6♣	4♣	2♣	K♥	J♥	9♥	7♥
25	2♦	K♣	J♣	9♣	7♣	5♣	3♣	A♣	Q♥	10♥	8♥	6♥
26	A♦	Q♣	10♣	8♣	6♣	4♣	2♣	K♥	J♥	9♥	7♥	5♥
27	K♣	J♣	9♣	7♣	5♣	3♣	A♣	Q♥	10♥	8♥	6♥	4♥
28	Q♣	10♣	8♣	6♣	4♣	2♣	K♥	J♥	9♥	7♥	5♥	3♥
29	J♣	9♣	7♣	5♣	3♣	A♣	Q♥	10♥	8♥	6♥	4♥	2♥
30	10♣		6♣	4♣	2♣	K♥	J♥	9♥	7♥	5♥	3♥	A♥
31	9♣		5♣		A♣		10♥	8♥		4♥		Joker

Did you find your own Birth Card or the Birth Card of a child close to you? What do you think are the personality traits of these Birth Cards? If deciphering the combined synergy of traits for a single Birth Card seems overwhelming, do not worry. I did the work for you! In Chapters 4 through 18, I describe each Birth Card, beginning with Aces and ending with the Joker. I explain each Birth Card's purpose, gifts, life lessons, and personality traits that can manifest as higher and lower expressions. Most importantly, I describe these elements in the context of childhood behaviors and offer tips on how to navigate them specific to a child's Birth Card. I go on to provide research-based educational strategies to help adults nurture any child to their highest potential. But, before going to Chapters 4 through 18, bear with me a little further. You need to understand one more important dimension to the Destiny Card system. You see, each Birth Card represents a child's *internal identity*, and as such, reflects the main purpose, gifts, and life lessons a child is to experience. While a Birth Card is designated by the date a child is born, that same date assigns another card to a child: a *Planetary Ruling Card*. A child's Planetary Ruling Card assigns additional purpose, life lessons, and traits they have at their disposal to use in life due to the influence of the zodiac sign ruling their Birth Card. Let's explore this concept deeper in the following section.

Zodiac Signs and Their Influence for a Birth Card

When you include the date February 29th during a leap year, there are 366 days in a year. Obviously, with 52 different Birth Cards, some dates within a year share the same Birth Card. Out of the 366 days, Hearts account for 52 days, Clubs for 133, Diamonds for 131, and Spades for the remaining 49 days. But wait – you may have noticed that all those numbers add up to 365. The last day of the year, December 31st, is associated with the Joker Birth Card. The Joker is the *wild card* and the individual possessing it randomly assigns itself a Birth Card, that is, any Birth Card. All of this is to say that the zodiac sign that a person is born under will be an additional energy influencing the identity and life lessons of a specific Birth Card.

If you share a Birth Card with someone else who has a different birth date, similarities exist between you. This is because a person's Birth Card represents their inner and true nature. However, you may also notice variations between individuals with the same Birth Card who were born on different dates. Let's look at an example. The 6♦ Birth Card appears 11 times within a calendar year. A 6♦ born under the sign Cancer has some similar traits as a 6♦ born under the sign Leo because these individuals share the synergy of a Diamond and a Six. Being a Six Birth Card provides the trait of stability, while being a Birth Card within the Diamond suit means the person holds gifts and experiences life lessons around money and values. Yet, these two 6♦s with different birthdates also have different traits from each other because they are ruled by different signs of the zodiac. Leos are prideful, and so a 6♦ under this sign tends not to remain in a job that does not pay well. On the other hand, a 6♦ under the sign of Cancer tends to be more caring, sensitive, and fixed in their careers. Unlike a Leo 6♦, they will stay in a lower paying job so long as they believe they are helping to improve the welfare and happiness of others.

Remember one's Planetary Ruling Card provides additional traits a person can tap into and externally express. Think of these traits as a mask or persona a person wears, though, not the person's true nature. For example, my father was born on June 17. His Birth Card was a K♣, and his Planetary Ruling Card was a J♦. My father told me stories of how friends during his teen years thought while he was musically gifted, because he was too playful and irresponsible, he would never amount to anything. Those playful and irresponsible traits speak to his J♦ Planetary Ruling Card. My father said he developed this façade in response to being teased by male classmates, who called him a sissy because he was a soloist in a boys' choir. In other words, he borrowed traits from his J♦ Planetary Ruling Card to influence how he was perceived by others. Yet his inner identity was a K♣. K♣ are responsible leaders. When he became an adult and embraced his true nature, he played trombone and formed his own orchestra business which he led successfully for many years. Manifesting mastery of musical knowledge and becoming a responsible leader was his highest potential inherent to his K♣ Birth Card.

Now let's consider one remaining aspect of a person's Planetary Ruling Card. In astrology, some people are described as being born on a *cusp* date. What does this mean? It means that a person was born on a date when the sun was leaving one zodiac sign and entering another. Because the exact time of this movement varies from year to year, people born on the same cusp date but in a different year may or may not be ruled by the same zodiac sign. To account for this difference, the Destiny Card system assigns two Planetary Ruling Cards to people born on the cusp. For example, if you were born on April 21, your Birth Card is a K♣. Your Planetary Ruling Card is a 4♦ or a 4♥. Everyone born on the cusp should consider the traits of each Planetary Ruling Card and decide which one fits them best. As a further note, in astrology, it is common knowledge that those born under the zodiac sign of Scorpio are complicated individuals. A fascinating element of the Destiny Card system is that it recognizes this aspect of Scorpios by associating them with two Planetary Ruling Cards. My son, having been born on October 30th is a 5♥. Because he is a Scorpio, he possesses two Planetary Ruling Cards: 9♥ and 9♦. As such, he has an even greater assortment of masks he can wear from day to day. No wonder Scorpios are known to be hard to read!

Use the following tables below to look up Birth and Planetary Ruling Cards for yourself and the children in your life. Then, before moving to Chapters 4 through 18 to read the descriptions of specific Birth and Planetary Ruling Cards, please continue by reading Chapter 3. In Chapter 3, I explain a step-by-step process to help adults apply knowledge of the Destiny Card system to nurture children to their authentic and highest potential.

Birth and Planetary Ruling Card Tables

January Birth Cards and Planetary Ruling Cards

	BC	PRC		BC	PRC
1	K♠	5♣	17	10♦	5♥
2	Q♠	K♣	18	9♦	4♥
3	J♠	10♦	19	8♦	10♠
4	10♠	7♦	20	7♦	2♥
5	9♠	4♣	21	6♦	A♥ or A♦
6	8♠	3♣	22	5♦	K♣
7	7♠	4♦	23	4♦	10♣
8	6♠	3♥	24	3♦	9♣
9	5♠	K♥	25	2♦	10♦
10	4♠	A♦	26	A♦	7♣
11	3♠	J♣	27	K♣	6♣
12	2♠	10♣	28	Q♣	7♦
13	A♠	9♣	29	J♣	4♥
14	K♦	8♣	30	10♣	10♠
15	Q♦	7♣	31	9♣	4♣
16	J♦	6♣			

February Birth Cards and Planetary Ruling Cards

	BC	PRC		BC	PRC
1	J♠	8♠	16	9♦	4♦
2	10♠	5♠	17	8♦	5♣
3	9♠	2♦	18	7♦	K♥
4	8♠	3♠	19	6♦	A♦
5	7♠	2♠	20	5♦	K♠ or J♦
6	6♠	A♣	21	4♦	8♦
7	5♠	K♦	22	3♦	9♠
8	4♠	Q♦	23	2♦	8♠
9	3♠	9♦	24	A♦	5♦
10	2♠	8♦	25	K♣	6♠
11	A♠	9♠	26	Q♣	5♠
12	K♦	6♦	27	J♣	4♦
13	Q♦	5♦	28	10♣	5♣
14	J♦	6♠	29	9♣	2♦
15	10♦	3♣			

March Birth Cards and Planetary Ruling Cards

	BC	PRC		BC	PRC
1	9♠	J♠	17	6♦	Q♦
2	8♠	9♥	18	5♦	J♦
3	7♠	8♥	19	4♦	8♦
4	6♠	Q♣	20	3♦	9♠ or 7♦
5	5♠	6♥	21	2♦	8♠ or 6♦
6	4♠	5♥	22	A♦	K♣
7	3♠	7♠	23	K♣	4♦
8	2♠	K♠	24	Q♣	3♦
9	A♠	2♥	25	J♣	2♣
10	K♦	4♠	26	10♣	3♥
11	Q♦	Q♠	27	9♣	K♥
12	J♦	Q♥	28	8♣	10♥
13	10♦	3♠	29	7♣	J♣
14	9♦	2♠	30	6♣	10♣
15	8♦	3♦	31	5♣	7♥
16	7♦	K♦			

April Birth Cards and Planetary Ruling Cards

	BC	PRC		BC	PRC
1	7♠	J♦	16	5♦	9♦
2	6♠	8♦	17	4♦	6♣
3	5♠	9♠	18	3♦	7♦
4	4♠	8♠	19	2♦	6♦
5	3♠	5♦	20	A♦	3♣ or 5♥
6	2♠	6♠	21	K♣	4♦ or 4♥
7	A♠	5♠	22	Q♣	5♠
8	K♦	2♦	23	J♣	7♠
9	Q♦	3♠	24	10♣	K♠
10	J♦	2♠	25	9♣	2♥
11	10♦	A♦	26	8♣	4♠
12	9♦	K♣	27	7♣	Q♠
13	8♦	A♣	28	6♣	Q♥
14	7♦	9♣	29	5♣	A♠
15	6♦	10♦	30	4♣	J♠

May Birth Cards and Planetary Ruling Cards

	BC	PRC		BC	PRC
1	5♠	9♣	17	2♦	8♣
2	4♠	10♦	18	A♦	5♥
3	3♠	7♠	19	K♣	4♥
4	2♠	6♣	20	Q♣	5♣ or 10♠
5	A♠	7♦	21	J♣	7♠ or 9♦
6	K♦	4♣	22	10♣	K♠ or 8♦
7	Q♦	3♣	23	9♣	9♠
8	J♦	4♦	24	8♣	6♦
9	10♦	A♥	25	7♣	5♦
10	9♦	2♣	26	6♣	6♠
11	8♦	3♥	27	5♣	3♦
12	7♦	J♥	28	4♣	2♦
13	6♦	10♥	29	3♣	3♠
14	5♦	J♣	30	2♣	K♣
15	4♦	8♥	31	A♣	Q♣
16	3♦	7♥			

June Birth Cards and Planetary Ruling Cards

	BC	PRC		BC	PRC
1	3♠	9♥	16	A♦	Q♦
2	2♠	8♥	17	K♣	J♦
3	A♠	7♥	18	Q♣	10♠
4	K♦	6♥	19	J♣	9♦
5	Q♦	5♥	20	10♣	8♦
6	J♦	4♥	21	9♣	9♠
7	10♦	8♠	22	8♣	6♦ or J♠
8	9♦	7♠	23	7♣	9♥
9	8♦	K♠	24	6♣	8♥
10	7♦	5♠	25	5♣	10♠
11	6♦	4♠	26	4♣	6♥
12	5♦	Q♠	27	3♣	5♥
13	4♦	2♠	28	2♣	7♠
14	3♦	A♠	29	A♣	3♥
15	2♦	J♠	30	K♥	2♥

July Birth Cards and Planetary Ruling Cards

	BC	PRC		BC	PRC
1	A♠	3♦	17	J♣	Q♠
2	K♦	K♥	18	10♣	Q♥
3	Q♦	A♦	19	9♣	J♥
4	J♦	K♣	20	8♣	J♠
5	10♦	10♥	21	7♣	9♥
6	9♦	J♣	22	6♣	8♥
7	8♦	10♣	23	5♣	10♠ or 5♣
8	7♦	7♥	24	4♣	4♣
9	6♦	8♣	25	3♣	3♣
10	5♦	7♣	26	2♣	2♣
11	4♦	4♥	27	A♣	A♣
12	3♦	5♣	28	K♥	K♥
13	2♦	4♣	29	Q♥	Q♥
14	A♦	A♥	30	J♥	J♥
15	K♣	2♣	31	10♥	10♥
16	Q♣	A♣			

August Birth Cards and Planetary Ruling Cards

	BC	PRC		BC	PRC
1	Q♦	Q♦	17	9♣	9♣
2	J♦	J♦	18	8♣	8♣
3	10♦	10♦	19	7♣	7♣
4	9♦	9♦	20	6♣	6♣
5	8♦	8♦	21	5♣	5♣
6	7♦	7♦	22	4♣	4♣ or 2♦
7	6♦	6♦	23	3♣	3♣ or 3♠
8	5♦	5♦	24	2♣	K♣
9	4♦	4♦	25	A♣	Q♣
10	3♦	3♦	26	K♥	K♦
11	2♦	2♦	27	Q♥	10♣
12	A♦	A♦	28	J♥	9♣
13	K♣	K♣	29	10♥	10♦
14	Q♣	Q♣	30	9♥	7♣
15	J♣	J♣	31	8♥	6♣
16	10♣	10♣			

September Birth Cards and Planetary Ruling Cards

	BC	PRC		BC	PRC
1	10♦	8♠	16	8♣	6♦
2	9♦	7♠	17	7♣	5♦
3	8♦	K♠	18	6♣	6♠
4	7♦	5♠	19	5♣	3♦
5	6♦	4♠	20	4♣	2♠
6	5♦	Q♠	21	3♣	3♠
7	4♦	2♠	22	2♣	K♣ or J♦
8	3♦	A♠	23	A♣	Q♣ or 10♠
9	2♦	J♠	24	K♥	6♥
10	A♦	Q♦	25	Q♥	8♦
11	K♣	J♦	26	J♥	9♠
12	Q♣	10♠	27	10♥	8♠
13	J♣	9♦	28	9♥	5♦
14	10♣	8♦	29	8♥	6♠
15	9♣	9♠	30	7♥	5♠

October Birth Cards and Planetary Ruling Cards

	BC	PRC		BC	PRC
1	8♦	3♥	17	5♣	A♠
2	7♦	J♥	18	4♣	J♠
3	6♦	10♥	19	3♣	9♥
4	5♦	J♣	20	2♣	J♦
5	4♦	8♥	21	A♣	10♠
6	3♦	7♥	22	K♥	6♥
7	2♦	8♣	23	Q♥	8♦ or K♠ & 5♣
8	A♦	5♥	24	J♥	9♥ or 2♥ & 2♦
9	K♣	4♥	25	10♥	A♥ & 3♠
10	Q♣	5♣	26	9♥	Q♠ & K♠
11	J♣	7♠	27	8♥	Q♥ & A♣
12	10♣	K♠	28	7♥	J♥ & K♦
13	9♣	2♥	29	6♥	J♠ & 10♦
14	8♣	4♠	30	5♥	9♥ & 9♦
15	7♣	Q♠	31	4♥	8♥ & 8♦
16	6♣	Q♥			

November Birth Cards and Planetary Ruling Cards

	BC	PRC		BC	PRC
1	6♦	10♦ & 5♥	16	4♣	8♣ & 8♠
2	5♦	9♦ & 4♥	17	3♣	7♣ & 7♠
3	4♦	6♣ & K♠	18	2♣	4♥ & 6♠
4	3♦	7♦ & 2♥	19	A♣	5♣ & 5♠
5	2♦	6♦ & A♥	20	K♥	4♣ & 4♠
6	A♦	3♣ & Q♠	21	Q♥	K♠ & 5♣
7	K♣	4♦ & Q♥	22	J♥	2♥ & 2♦
8	Q♣	3♦ & J♥	23	10♥	A♦
9	J♣	2♣ & 2♠	24	9♥	J♣
10	10♣	3♥ & 3♦	25	8♥	10♣
11	9♣	K♥ & J♠	26	7♥	9♣
12	8♣	10♥ & Q♦	27	6♥	8♣
13	7♣	J♣ & J♦	28	5♥	7♣
14	6♣	10♣ & Q♣	29	4♥	6♣
15	5♣	7♥ & 9♠	30	3♥	5♣

December Birth Cards and Planetary Ruling Cards

	BC	PRC		BC	PRC
1	4♦	6♠	17	A♣	3♦
2	3♦	5♠	18	K♥	2♦
3	2♦	4♠	19	Q♥	3♥
4	A♦	3♠	20	J♥	K♥
5	K♣	2♠	21	10♥	A♦ or Q♦
6	Q♣	A♠	22	9♥	J♣ or 9♦
7	J♣	K♣	23	8♥	8♦
8	10♣	A♣	24	7♥	9♠
9	9♣	K♦	25	6♥	6♦
10	8♣	10♦	26	5♥	5♦
11	7♣	9♦	27	4♥	6♠
12	6♣	8♦	28	3♥	3♦
13	5♣	7♦	29	2♥	2♦
14	4♣	6♦	30	A♥	3♠
15	3♣	5♦	31	Joker	
16	2♣	4♦			

Chapter 3

How to Use this Book

The feelings that come with being a parent or someone who works closely with children may be likened to how one feels swimming along the shoreline of a highly energetic ocean. The experience entails extreme highs and lows. At times one feels relaxed and present in the joyous moment. At other times one feels like they are barely treading water. And, of course, there are a lot of feelings happening in between! Having over 30 years of teaching experience, mostly at the middle school level, I certainly have experienced many of my own varying degrees of feelings working with children.

Nurturing children is difficult work. And most adults would agree that the preteen and teen years are the most challenging to work through and parent. I jokingly refer to children at these ages as the *hormonally challenged*. It is a time when a child is struggling to develop *autonomy*. According to psychologists, autonomy is a person's capacity to self-direct their feelings, decision-making, and actions. Parents recognize this as a time when their child desires more independence and pushes the limits of their freedom. As such, it is often a time when children make mistakes and exhibit poor behaviors. As an educator I have witnessed countless parents become emotional when they learn their child was misbehaving. Their emotion, in turn, can evolve into an assortment of reactions including excuses, contrition, guilt, and blaming others to name a few. Throughout my years as a teacher, I realized these reactions were likely due to a common parenting misperception; *that their child's behavior was a direct reflection of them and their parenting*. If their child was described as bad, then this implied they were a bad parent. Granted, poor parenting can impact a child's behavior and mental health, and I am not minimizing the trauma some children can experience from it.

In my opinion, the root cause of a child's misbehavior is that they are exploring the lower personality traits associated with their Birth and Planetary Rulings Cards. These lower traits are part of a child's life lessons; and these lessons are needed for a child to spiritually grow. My hope in explaining this is that adults should not be too quick to blame themselves when they are working with children who are expressing challenging behaviors. Rather, they should try as best as possible to separate their emotions from the problems they are trying to guide a child through. They should also view the challenging behavior as an opportunity for growth for this child. And I believe adults should use the Destiny Card system as one additional tool to help guide a child through their challenging behavior and toward their highest potential. At this moment, you likely have two burning questions:

1. How can the Destiny Card system help me nurture the development of a child's authentic self and highest potential?
2. How can the application of the Destiny Card system support me in guiding a child through challenging behaviors?

Before answering these two questions, let's explore what modern psychologists have to say about the development of a child's personality and how the Destiny Card system fits into this process. Most psychologists agree that each child is born with a unique temperament or predisposed mental, physical, and emotional traits. As a child experiences certain situations in life, including environmental challenges, how they respond to these situations forms character patterns. Over time, specific character patterns are reinforced and become integrated within a child's temperament. A child's unique personality evolves through this process. The choices a child makes especially matter during the first five to eight years of life; a time known as the *formative years*. Psychologists agree the formative years are the most critical in terms of child development.

The Destiny Card system aligns well with this view of personality formation. When a child is born, they are associated with a Birth and Planetary Ruling Card(s). These cards embed predetermined purpose, gifts, temperament, karmic people, events, and life lessons. A child's temperament or behavioral tendencies represent the higher and lower traits described in Chapter 2. Because children are learning boundaries around who they are and how they fit within the world, they can move back and forth along a continuum experimenting with their higher and lower traits. Children will likely vacillate along this continuum quite frequently as they respond to environmental situations, especially challenging ones. By asserting free will and making choices in life, a child will reinforce specific higher and/or lower traits. The most reinforced traits are often carried into adulthood. Therefore, childhood offers adults a time when they can be proactive – to facilitate a child navigating along their continuum of higher and lower traits, and to support them toward their authentic and highest potential.

Adults can use the Destiny Card system to nurture the development of a child's authentic self by learning about and supporting the true nature of a child based upon their Birth and Planetary Ruling Card(s). By learning the higher traits of a child's cards, an adult can act like a compass guiding them toward their highest expressions and therefore highest potential. In addition, knowledge of a child's temperament, personality, and life lessons can empower an adult to adopt communication and strategies that are targeted to nurture the child involved. By communicating with a child early on about the specific lower traits of their cards, an adult can help them explore their feelings, use reflection, and develop self-awareness. It is often through self-awareness that children can learn from their mistakes, build on their strengths, and make improvements in life. Guiding a child to develop self-awareness is key, but as we all know this is often a highly challenging task when dealing with an adolescent. Therefore, it is advantageous to incorporate the Destiny Card system into nurturing a child during their youngest years. The reason for this is, if a child consistently energizes lower traits, those traits can become reinforced and ingrained into their identity. This child will find it increasingly difficult as they get older to change their lower expressing identity. This also means an adult working with an adolescent may be dealing with lower traits that have been reinforced over many years. This is not to say an adolescent's traits are set in stone. If you are reading this book to help nurture an adolescent, please do not think it might be too late to do so. There are plenty of choices ahead for an adolescent that a nurturing adult can influence to reinforce higher traits. Adults in this situation must be realistic though – this process will likely take additional time and effort.

I know from personal experience in managing difficult situations with adolescents, I was more effective when I applied knowledge of the Destiny Card system. The system helped me deal with adolescents from a place of who they are; their true nature designated by their Birth and Planetary Ruling Card(s) and where they were at, possibly demonstrating lower traits. I embraced the higher traits of each child's cards as their potential, and I made sure to communicate these higher traits to them. Lastly, I used reflection in my communications with adolescents to help them draw meaning from their situations and encourage them to make better choices.

Let's consider a real-life example of how I applied knowledge of a child's Birth and Planetary Ruling Cards to navigate a challenging situation and nurture a child toward their highest potential. When I was a middle school science teacher, I taught a student who I will call Jessica. Jessica was not getting along with her lab partner. Jessica refused to give her partner any control during hands-on labs. She relegated her partner solely to writing down data and results. When her partner vocalized the unfairness of this, Jessica would get angry and extremely emotional. In turn, Jessica's partner shut down because of Jessica's behavior. Weeks of this behavior led Jessica's partner to tell me about the problem and ask for a new lab partner. And, of course, I referenced Jessica's Birth Card for an additional perspective on what was happening. Looking up Jessica's Birth Card, I found she was a 9♥. Understanding the difficult lessons of a 9♥ Birth Card, I was intentional about what questions I asked Jessica. In my private conversation with Jessica, I discovered she unexpectedly lost her father to a heart attack the previous school year. Such an event is one type of ending a 9♥ may experience to work out their life lessons. Clearly, Jessica was experiencing an ending due to being a Nine. And due to her being a Heart card, the ending was associated with a love relationship. This information led me to believe Jessica's lower expressing behavior was in response to feeling a lack of control in her life relative to having experienced such a traumatic loss.

Applying knowledge of Jessica's Birth Card allowed me to not only understand Jessica's behavior, but it also helped me guide her toward the higher expressions of her Birth Card. When communicating with a child I find it helpful to describe their higher traits as *superpowers*. I consider superpowers to be a child's most positive personality traits; those traits that hold the greatest potential to give purpose to one's life. In Jessica's case, I knew that compassion and strong interpersonal skills were higher traits of a 9♥ Birth Card. Clearly, Jessica was acting out of character. I also knew that the 9♥ Birth Card is named *The Global Giver of Love* because it is their destiny to share their compassion with a broader audience. Therefore, in my conversation with Jessica, I insisted she possessed a superpower – *compassion*. I gave Jessica specific examples of how I witnessed her compassionate nature. I also talked about how I knew of individuals who experienced trauma in their lives and then used their background to help others work through their own trauma. I emphasized to Jessica that she knew how it felt to feel despair, a loss, and uncertain in how to move forward in life. I implied those feelings may have caused her to make some mistakes, but this did not mean she was a bad person. Then, I encouraged Jessica to apply for a school position as a *peer mediator*. Peer mediators are school aged students who are trained to work with their peers to resolve disputes and behavioral problems within their school setting. I explained to Jessica that I believed she would listen compassionately to her peers who had been accused of making mistakes. I told Jessica that her loss and experience in managing feelings of grief could assist her in helping others. After hearing Jessica express interest in this position, I spoke to a school counselor about how Jessica's life experience would be an asset for such a position. Weeks later, Jessica was named as a school peer mediator. The following school year and months prior to attending high school, Jessica came to visit me. She thanked me for caring about her. In her excited talk about her future in high school, she mentioned how her experience as a peer mediator inspired a calling to help others. Jessica described further opportunities in high school through which she could explore her calling. Jessica was on the right path to achieve her highest potential!

At this point, you may be asking: How? Where do I start? Is there a proven procedure to implement this system with a child? In the following section, I offer a step-by-step process for applying knowledge of the Destiny Card system to maximize results in guiding a child toward their highest potential specific to their Birth and Planetary Ruling Card(s).

1. Find the child's Birth Card and learn about it.

Use the tables on pages 15 through 18 to look up the Birth Card of a child. Remember that the year of birth does not matter. Next, search through Chapters 4 through 17 to find the applicable pages of the Birth Card description. (Birth Card descriptions are in order beginning with Aces and ending with the Joker.) Read the related content and make notes particularly about the personality traits that ring true for the child involved. Each Birth Card description contains the following information:

a) How to Nurture the Temperament and Personality of a [Birth Card] Child – This section uses humorous anecdotes and relatable examples of child and adolescent behaviors to describe the temperament and several higher and lower personality traits associated with a specific Birth Card. To nurture a child toward a higher expression of traits, several parenting and teaching tips are suggested. In addition, this section focuses on several key lower traits tied to a child's most difficult life lessons. Because lower traits are challenging to manage, more content is offered on them to ensure a child is on track to reach their highest potential. These lower traits are not only described in detail, but they are also paired with specific strategies adults can implement to manage them. These targeted strategies are research-based and have been shown to be effective when used by educators and psychologists.

> **Note:** Does the description of the Birth Card of a child appear not to fit them? Any of the following three things might be going on. One, their birthdate isn't correct. Check their time of birth. This child might have been born just before midnight, but their birth certificate was written after midnight. Read the Birth Card associated with the date before this child's birth certificate date and see if that description fits them better. Another reason for an unfitting description may result from a child being medicated and/or if they are experiencing a mental health condition. If so, their outward appearance and behaviors may not be aligning with their inner soul or description of their Birth Card. Lastly, the child's true nature may be hiding behind their Planetary Ruling Card(s). In such cases, the child's Planetary Ruling Card(s) may describe them better.

b) Summary of Higher and Lower Personality Traits – This section provides key words associated with personality traits a child may manifest as higher or lower expressions given their Birth Card. Consider these traits on opposite ends of a continuum with varying degrees of middle ground or moderate behaviors in between.

Note: Some authors that describe the Destiny Card system equate higher and lower personality traits of each Birth Card as positive and negative traits, respectively. I carry a different viewpoint in that I believe not all lower traits are negative. For example, a 10♠ Birth Card has the lower trait of being a workaholic. Yet, if their work led to a cure for cancer, is this a negative thing? Perhaps, part of this person's destiny in life was to find that cure while learning lessons about being a workaholic.

c) Childhood Influence Mercury Cards – If you are familiar with astrology, a person's Birth Chart is a visual representation of the position of planets and other celestial objects at the exact moment of one's birth. A Birth Chart provides insights into one's core purpose, personality, life lessons, and potential in life. In the Destiny Card system, the *Life Spread* associated with any given Birth Chart is like a person's Birth Chart. This section identifies the *Mercury Cards* associated with a specific Birth Card that are part of a child's Life Spread. Mercury Cards are predetermined energies, experiences, and/or people that influence a child from birth through age twelve. Because these cards affect children during their formative years, they represent significant environmental factors that carry the potential to shape the character and personality traits of a child. As these influences can be positive or negative, they can reinforce higher or lower personality traits, respectively.

In some cases, a Mercury Card may be an exact match to the Birth Card of another person who is an influence in this child's early life. In other cases, a Mercury Card may indicate an influential person more generically by using a *Personality Card*. Personality Cards are the Jack, Queen, or King of a Birth Card's suit that are affiliated with gender. For example, if a Q♥ has been identified as a Childhood Influence Mercury Card, it can indicate any female of the Hearts suit as being influential. Alternatively, outside of any specific person associated with a Mercury Card, the basic meaning of a card may describe energies and experiences that are influential during a child's formative years. For instance, if a 4♥ has been identified as a Mercury Card, because the 4♥ is known as the *stability in love* card, this can mean a child will likely experience a stable and harmonious childhood.

d) Potential Callings / Vocations by Zodiac Sign – This section uses knowledge of each Birth Card's personality traits combined with a child's zodiac sign and Planetary Ruling Card(s) to identify potential vocations that align well with a child's birthdate. This list of vocations is naturally limited and not intended to represent all potential vocations.

e) Famous [Birth Card] – This section identifies some famous people associated with each Birth Card. Sharing these people with a child who possesses the same Birth Card may help them to further understand the array of personality traits associated with any given Birth Card.

2. Find the child's Planetary Ruling Card and learn about it.
Use the tables on pages 15 through 18 to look up the Planetary Ruling Card(s) of a child. Remember some birth dates have more than one Planetary Ruling Card. Or, if they are born on the cusp of a zodiac sign, they are assigned two Planetary Ruling Cards and you must decide which best fits this child (as explained in Chapter 2). Next, search through Chapters 4 through 17 to find the applicable pages of the Birth Card description. (Birth Card descriptions are in

order beginning with Aces and ending with the Joker.) Read the related content and make notes particularly about the personality traits that ring true for the child involved.

3. Embrace the personality traits and destiny of this child's Birth and Planetary Ruling Cards!

Using a child's formative years to mold them without considering a child's true nature and potential destiny may be problematic. For example, a child associated with a 6♣ Birth Card often displays the trait of procrastination. As much as someone may or may not want to accept this, a 6♣ child must express itself authentically. Trying to change their nature based upon one's own beliefs will often result in conflict. And such conflict will likely hinder a child in their spiritual growth. No matter a child's Birth or Planetary Ruling Cards, the goal for any child is to achieve spiritual growth by experiencing and learning from God's lessons. And most people find that spiritual growth tends to be less arduous when they become self-aware. Without self-awareness, a child may have difficulty navigating between lower and higher personality traits associated with their Birth and Planetary Ruling Cards. Instead, a child may spend much of their life trapped manifesting their lower traits. A child's formative years offer a critical time when adults can help jumpstart a child's path toward self-awareness. The first step is for an adult working with a child to understand and embrace the true nature of a child's Birth and Planetary Ruling Cards.

4. Use knowledge of a child's higher personality traits (or superpowers) to reinforce them.

Every child possesses superpowers or higher traits inherent to their Birth and Planetary Ruling Cards. Make sure you learn about these gifts, embrace them, and communicate them to the child. Try to focus mostly on a child's higher traits. When a child's behavior reflects a higher trait, praise them for it. Knowing and supporting a child's personality strengths, an adult can boost a child's self-esteem and help them become aware of their purpose in life. Adults should aim to guide a child toward their higher traits by encouraging them to participate in activities and experiences that reinforce these traits. Below are some examples of how an adult can do this:

- Let's say a child's Birth Card is a J♠, a card known for artistic creativity. A teacher equipped with this knowledge can encourage this child to apply their gift in an assignment or project. Likewise, a parent made aware of this knowledge can look for ways to foster this ability through gifts, hobbies, and extra-curricular activities.
- Perhaps a child's Birth Card is an 8♣. 8♣ possess a superpower of being an excellent systems thinker. A systems thinker understands that a system is more than just the sum of its parts. They understand both the individual parts of a system and how all the parts work together in a synergistic manner. Such a skillset is often found in engineers, internal medicine physicians, film producers, and people who work as operations managers. An adult can leverage knowledge of a child's superpowers to help steer a child toward a suitable career choice.
- Imagine a child is a 2♥ Birth Card, a card known for needing emotional connections with others. A parent of a 2♥ can nurture this child by understanding the importance of providing them with a daily routine of cuddling before bedtime. A teacher can be conscious of the fact that this child ideally needs a harmonious partner for collaborative assignments.

- Suppose a child's Birth Card is a 6♦, a card associated with many competitive athletes. An adult can encourage this child to discover a sport that holds passion for them and then support them in pursuing it.

5. Use knowledge of a child's lower personality traits to manage them.

There are so many daily happenings that reveal a child's lower and higher traits, but let's be honest – it's so easy to fixate on the lower ones. If an adult solely communicates to a child about their lower traits, such a focus can manifest a self-fulfilling prophecy. Therefore, refrain from obsessing over a child's lower traits. And keep in mind some children may need to experience lower traits of their cards for a longer time before they can appreciate and apply their higher traits. Such cases may be difficult to witness. In these situations, an adult may feel compelled to come to the child's rescue, even shield them from life's challenges. Unfortunately, this action may at times backfire. People, and especially children, learn best through direct experience. In the Destiny Card system, these challenging experiences represent shorter-term lessons that occur in learning progressions. Remember, as noted in Chapter 2, when a person does not learn from these shorter-term lessons, they repeat the lessons until they do learn from them. These lessons often get harder and more painful each time they are repeated. By jumping in to solve a child's problem or life lesson, adults often rob them of experiencing the lower traits of their Birth and Planetary Ruling Cards. These experiences are necessary for them to become self-aware, improve, and spiritually grow. This is not to say an adult should deal with a child by being laisse-faire, or by letting them deal with painful experiences alone. Instead, adults should consider a child's lower traits as opportunities for spiritual growth.

I suggest cultivating a *growth mindset* when communicating with a child about their lower traits. A growth mindset is a popular concept in the field of education that was developed by psychologist Carol Dweck. According to Dweck, people can possess either a fixed or growth mindset. A fixed mindset is where a person believes intelligence and personality traits are unable to change. People with a fixed mindset tend to fear challenges and regard failures as negative setbacks. On the other hand, a person with a growth mindset believes intelligence and traits are malleable and can change through effort and practice. As a result, people with a growth mindset view challenges as opportunities to learn and grow through persistence. And making mistakes is part of the process. Therefore, try not to be negative or frustrated when your child is manifesting lower traits of their Birth and Planetary Ruling Cards. If this is difficult for you, try to calm yourself down and relax your body language before having a discussion with the child involved. Then, help the child recognize and identify their feelings and behaviors, reflect upon their situation, and then help them plan ways they can grow and improve with practice.

Understanding a child's lower personality traits, an adult can be better prepared to support and manage a child's lower expressing behaviors. Below are some examples of how an adult can do this:

- Let's say a child's Birth Card is a J♥, a card known to be challenged with emotional dysregulation in that they respond to situations with emotions that are considered outside a normal range of behavior. Having this knowledge, a teacher can set up a calming corner in the classroom to help this child when they are struggling with big emotions. Calming corners contain calming furniture and objects, such as a bean bag chair, stuffed animals, soothing music, and relaxation videos. This area can also include a chart that guides a child through deep breathing exercises. A parent who is aware of this same personality challenge can seek out books, videos, and other resources to help their child identify difficult emotions and learn simple strategies to manage them.

- Suppose a child is a 3♦ Birth Card. In general, 3♦ like to break rules or make up their own as they are exploring different values, which is one of their life lessons. Parents and teachers working with a 3♦ would be wise to establish clear expectations, boundaries, and consequences around rules and acceptable behavior.

- Imagine a child is a 7♣ Birth Card, a card known for engaging in negative self-talk. In a school setting, they are their own worst critics. A teacher having this knowledge can benefit from using negative self-talk worksheets with this child as it can help them reframe negativity. At home, a parent of a 7♣ can teach them how to practice *mindfulness.* Mindfulness involves practices that allow one to be fully present. It opens a space for one to connect with their surroundings, situations, and feelings without overreacting negatively to them.

- Perhaps an adult is nurturing a child associated with a 10♠ Birth Card, a card known for workaholic tendencies. As such, 10♠ need to be taught to balance work and health. An adult working with a 10♠ child can help them understand they will benefit from taking mental breaks that allow them to get thoughts of work out of their mind. Encouraging sports activities that require mental attention are great for a 10♠.

6. Use reflection to help a child make informed choices toward their higher personality traits.
Jack Mezirow, a renowned sociologist stated, "A defining condition of being human is that we have to understand the meaning of our experience." This is such a powerful statement. I would add that humans are not born knowing how to accomplish this. Children especially need to be taught how to reflect upon and construct meaning from their experiences. There are, however, certain ages when teaching reflection is not effective. Jean Piaget was a child psychologist famous for his theory on the *four stages of child cognitive development*. Between the ages of two and six, children are in the *preoperational stage*, which is characterized as a time when they are egocentric and have difficulty seeing situations from another's perspective. Because children under the age of six will tend to have difficulty understanding other people's perspectives, reflective processing of experiences is most effective to use with children above the age of six.

a) How to process or solve an issue with a child under the age of six.
If the child involved is six years old or younger, the adult working with this child will need to personally engage in reflection and apply knowledge of the Destiny Card system to process or solve an issue. Let's look at an example of such an issue and how an adult used reflection and knowledge of a child's Birth and Planetary Ruling Cards to work it out.

Born August 9, Bradley recently turned five years old. Having had early exposure to reading through his attentive parents coupled with participation in preschool, Bradley was academically ahead of his peers. As an example, Bradley can identify all upper and lower-case letters and sound them out. He can also spell his name. In the springtime and prior to Bradley starting kindergarten, Bradley's parents decided to sell their home. This sale entailed moving to a different school district. While the plan was to move during the summer, there were delays. Bradley began all-day kindergarten at the elementary school connected to his old home only to be pulled out two weeks later to attend his new elementary school. Three weeks into his new school, Bradley's parents began receiving emails from his teacher. To their surprise, their previously well-mannered child was now misbehaving. He was acting impulsively and emotionally reacting inappropriately to other students. When disciplined, he was whiny and disrespectful to adults. In an email to Bradley's parents, Bradley's teacher suggested a visit to a doctor for a potential diagnosis, implying he needed medication.

To assist with this issue, Bradley's mom decided to reflect upon Bradley's Birth and Planetary Ruling Cards. Born August 9, Bradley is a Leo, which means he has the same Birth and Planetary Ruling Card, 4♦. Hence, he has double the 4♦s' traits. Reading about the 4♦'s description in this book, Bradley's mom realized that a need for security and structure are essential parts of Bradley's personality. In school, 4♦ thrive with routines, structure, and clear expectations of rules and behaviors. They do not do well with change and ambiguity. They are prone to impatience and agitation as lower expressions. 4♦, however, are not innately impulsive. Based upon this and Bradley's behavior at his previous school, Bradley's mom does not feel he needs medication. Having an August 9 birthdate also meant Bradley was a young kindergartener, thus less mature than his peers. Using this information, Bradley's mom scheduled a conference with his teacher. She asked the teacher to explain what events or places seemed to be triggering Bradley's poor behavior. The teacher said Bradley did well in structured activities at his desk, but acted out during recess, transitions, and lunch. Bradley's mom went on to ask about the teaching of routines and expectations, and found they were taught the first two weeks of school when Bradley was at his old school. Finally, Bradley's mom shared with the teacher her theory of how the move and change of school was the root of Bradley's problem. She asked the teacher if she would be willing to re-teach some routines and expectations and set up a behavior plan to reinforce them with Bradley. The teacher agreed this was a good plan. At home, an effort was made to be more consistent with Bradley such as with mealtimes and bedtimes. Although much of the home remained unpacked, Bradley's mom and dad told him they would prioritize unpacking and organizing his bedroom. The objective was to make Bradley's room feel less chaotic. In a month's time, Bradley's behavior was back on track.

b) How to use reflection to process or solve an issue with a child above the age of six.
An adult that understands the traits of a child's Birth and Planetary Ruling Cards can create opportunities for a child to reflect upon their feelings and experiences when processing an issue. If you are a teacher, you can use class or morning meetings to share and reflect upon classroom issues. Or in the event an issue has arisen with an individual child, a teacher can make time to discuss and reflect with the child privately. If you are a parent, dinner is a great time to practice reflection for the whole family by asking each family member to share something that happened during the day and reflect upon it. Encourage the sharing of both

good and challenging issues. If you are dealing with an adolescent who resists sharing, share your own issues and invite them to interpret the meanings and lessons learned. In addition, look for and take advantage of in-the-moment opportunities to reflect upon specific events that occur in a child's daily life. Such events can range from a child being frustrated after a poor sporting performance, being hurt after finding out they were excluded from a friend's party, to feeling awkward after being praised during parent-teacher conferences. During these opportunities, model *effective reflection*. I recommend implementing Gibb's Reflective Cycle because it is simple and translates well into normal conversation with a child or adolescent. The Gibb's Reflective Cycle is illustrated below.

Gibb's Reflective Cycle (1988)

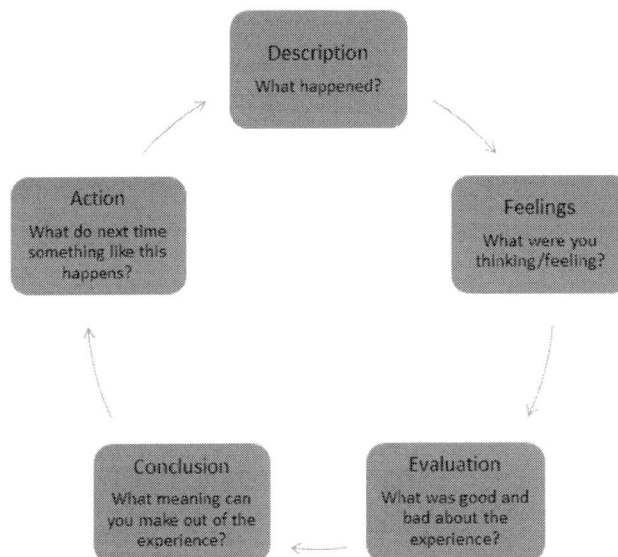

Let's look at an example of how an adult used knowledge of a child's Birth and Planetary Ruling Cards and applied the Gibb's Reflective Cycle in conversation with a child to work through an issue, starting with a *description of the issue* and ending with a *planned action*.

Carter is an eleven-year-old boy currently in the sixth grade. On several occasions Carter's teacher observed Carter aggressively pushing people out of his way to exit the classroom as soon as the bell rang. One day, a student named Jacob stayed after class to complain that Carter elbowed him hard on his way out of class. The teacher tells Jacob she will handle the issue. The teacher examines Carter's Birth and Planetary Ruling Cards prior to having a planned conversation with Carter. The teacher finds Carter was born on March 22, so he is an A♦ Birth Card. Lower personality traits of an A♦ include impulsiveness, low self-esteem, and being easily frustrated. A higher trait of an A♦ the teacher recognizes about Carter is that he is compassionate, particularly about animals. Carter's Planetary Ruling Card is a 3♣, whose lower traits include negative self-expression. Yet, the teacher knows a 3♣ possesses the potential for flexibility which is a higher trait and a wonderful quality to leverage in this situation.

Below is the private, reflective conversation the teacher has with Carter:

Teacher: Carter, I've noticed you pushing people out of your way as you leave my classroom. I'm trying to understand why this is happening. What's going on? [Description]

Carter: It's not me. Randy and Jacob are just so slow. If I'm late for the lunchroom the line gets too long.

Teacher: So, let me see if I understand what's happening. Are you saying that because you sit at the side of the room opposite the door, when the bell rings other students get in front of you and move slower than you'd like?

Carter: Yeah.

Teacher: When Randy and Jacob are in your way and moving slowly, how do you feel? [Feelings]

Carter: I feel frustrated. It's because of that I don't have enough time to eat AND play basketball.

Teacher: You are pushing them because it gets you to the lunchroom faster, so you have time to eat and play basketball?

Carter: Well, ya, but...

Teacher: Is it fair to say that Randy and Jacob might feel you are being impatient and hurtful? [Evaluation]

Carter: I don't know... (A common adolescent response that would suggest they do know but do not want to admit it or their empathy button has been programmed to the off mode.)

Teacher: You understand I could give you a detention for this behavior because pushing is hurtful. [Evaluation]

Carter: No, don't do that...

Teacher: Well, now I understand the situation and I think we all make mistakes. Let's figure out a new plan...one in which we both give something. How about I move your seat closest to the classroom door? If I do that, you agree to apologize to Randy and Jacob for pushing. Does that seem fair? [Conclusion]

Carter: I guess...

Teacher: I will also expect you to make better choices. What choices will you make next time? [Conclusion]

Carter: I guess I can say excuse me and try not to push others.

Teacher: Great. Let's both make this work.

Chapter 4

Descriptions of the Ace Birth Cards

Welcome to the world of the inquisitive A♥!

A♥ = Seeker of affection and self-expression

According to the Destiny Card system, souls chronologically experience God's lessons across 52 life incarnations. (Think of these as the universe's lessons if this aligns more with your beliefs.) The Birth Card each soul is born into determines the order and type of lessons a soul experiences. When you examine a Birth Card, you will notice it displays a suit of either a Heart, Club, Diamond, or Spade. This suit is significant because it represents the gifts a person born into this suit will possess and how they will direct their energies to learn lessons in their current life incarnation. A Heart Birth Card retains gifts and experiences life lessons around love and relationships. A Club Birth Card holds capabilities and experiences life lessons in their ability to communicate and absorb knowledge. A Diamond Birth Card possesses talents and experiences life lessons around money and values. And finally, a Spade Birth Card manifests gifts and experiences life lessons in work and health. Souls progress through incarnations and life lessons beginning as Hearts, moving on to Clubs, then Diamonds, and finally as Spades. Therefore, individuals born as Heart Cards are the youngest souls and individuals born as Spades Cards are the oldest souls.

In addition, the number on a Birth Card is equally meaningful as souls sequentially experience life lessons beginning as an Ace and culminating with lessons as a King. If you have played the card game poker, you know that Aces represent the number one. More broadly speaking, the number one symbolizes new beginnings because other numbers are created when added to the number one. A life incarnation as an Ace represents a soul's initial journey on their path toward spiritual enlightenment as they are singularly focused upon exploring life in the area associated with their suit. **It makes sense, then, that an A♥ child's purpose, gifts, and life lessons revolve around** *exploration* **in life. And due to being a Heart, this child will learn lessons through exploration in** *love* **and** *relationships***.**

How to Nurture the Temperament and Personality of an A♥ Child

From birth onward, A♥ are *highly sensitive* individuals. For instance, an A♥ baby will often cry upon hearing a negative tone of voice. Let's say this baby overhears siblings engaged in an argument. Even if this A♥ cannot comprehend the words expressed, they are able to absorb the negative emotions. This same temperament causes an A♥ to overly seek approval and affection from others. And they are not willing to wait for it. This is the child found crying at recess claiming, "No one will play with me!" Looking more closely at the situation, the impulsiveness of this child may be a contributing factor. Perhaps, this child has good intentions in seeking attention from classmates or approval from a teacher. Yet, when translating this desire into actions, this child is overly aggressive or does not know when to stop. In some cases, and in the short term, it may be appropriate to comfort and reassure this child through approval and praise. Long term, however, there may be a hidden danger when a child constantly seeks validation outside of themselves because they can develop a dependency toward external approval. These children will benefit from learning *self-love* and patience. Remember, they are the youngest souls. They tend to be *naïve* and *immature* when compared to their peers. This is the six-year-old child who believes chocolate milk comes from brown cows because an older siblings told them so.

As mentioned, some A♥ can be impulsive. However, not all emotions an A♥ impulsively displays are negative. For instance, imagine you are a first-grade teacher planning a science lesson around survival behaviors between adult animals and their offspring. An example of such a survival behavior would be that babies cry when they need feeding. You know that your A♥ student loves dogs. You decide to start your lesson by showing videos of adult female dogs interacting with their puppies. After showing the video, you ask your A♥ to share what behaviors they noticed. Your A♥ student is beyond excited! Their love of dogs and enthusiasm toward your lesson is infectious. Thanks to this A♥'s passion, you have hooked the rest of your students into the lesson. Leveraging an A♥'s passion may be replicated by parents in the home. A♥ love to have books read to them from an early age. Read them bedtime stories. Quality relationship time mixed with educational activities is an excellent recipe for an A♥. The experience satisfies their need for cuddling, love, and adventure. Parents can leverage the inquisitive-loving nature of an A♥ to teach them many things. Just be cautious if an A♥ starts to spread their interests out too much. Help them explore interests but then guide them to stick with just a few. In fact, A♥ are most successful when they pick a line and stick with it. This behavior is similar to what motocross racers do. Motocross racers ride motorcycles over harsh terrain. As they lap the course, they establish lines. Frequently picking different lines can be dangerous. In a similar way, a lack of focus for an A♥ can deplete their energy and potential.

A♥ are most impulsive in their expression of emotions. Therefore, a good way to nurture an A♥ is to expose them to *socio-emotional learning lessons* that teach self-expression. Socio-emotional learning is an approach used to help children understand their own emotions, the emotions of others, and how to communicate with kindness and empathy. For an A♥, choose lessons that help them learn how to express and soothe their emotions in healthy ways. As one example, use *emotional visual charts* at home or at school to help these children identify and express their emotions. Plenty of examples can be found on the Internet. Also, search for online programs such as Mind Up for Life that provide free resources to teach children about their emotions. In addition, because A♥ are highly sensitive, they may need a safe space to express and soothe their emotions. In a classroom setting, *safe spaces* or peace corners allow students to calm down and manage their feelings. Safe spaces are designated, less active areas of a classroom that contain calming objects, such as bean bag chairs, soft stuffed animals, breathing balls, and headphones that allow students to listen to music. These spaces can also display posters that assist children by suggesting healthy ways to problem-solve their way through negative emotions. Similar spaces can be established at home. Before using safe spaces, teachers and/or parents should explain their purpose, demonstrate how and when to use them, and praise an A♥ when they choose to use them.

Because the one energy of an A♥ can manifest a tendency toward selfishness, it is imperative to teach them *social awareness* in concert with self-expression. Social awareness is the ability to understand and respond to other people's feelings. Let's consider an example. Imagine you are a teacher of a nine-year-old A♥ boy named Alex. Alex has such an uncontrollable need for affection, he constantly gets up from his desk, meanders to the pencil sharpener all the while running his fingers over a classmate's shoulder or hair. Alex's behavior is distracting to other students. In a case like this, an A♥ child should be taught to consider how their actions make others feel as well as alternative ways to express themself. Again, there are lessons you can access on the Internet that teach social awareness skills. At home, social awareness can be effectively taught using role-play. If you are a parent of an A♥, explain an emotionally challenging scenario with your child. Ask them to describe feelings through the lens of different people and perspectives. Advocate for them to consider the emotions of others before acting. And help an A♥ discover they stand to achieve more affection when they display consideration toward others.

The potential selfish and impulsive lower traits demonstrated by a teenage A♥ can be especially daunting to parents as adolescence is a time when all children are characterized as self-centered. For example, as a parent of an A♥ you may notice impulsive behaviors in dating. They may tax your peace of mind by jumping into unhealthy relationships without thinking. If you perceive your teenager is in an unhealthy relationship, it is not wise to criticize them. Instead, invite them to share specific challenging events in the relationship and ask them how it makes them feel without expressing your own opinion unless they ask for it. If your teen is unwilling to share, tell a story of a similar challenge faced by a person in pop culture or from your own personal experience without making it about them. Ask them to unpack and analyze the situation. Allow safe spaces for an A♥ teen as well by allowing them alone time in their room to reflect. If your A♥ is challenged by selfish behaviors, encourage and model opportunities that promote kindness, such as volunteer work or donating to causes. Foster an A♥'s interests and beautiful openness to exploration. For instance, if your child loves pets, support them by urging them to volunteer at an animal shelter. Expose them to and communicate with them to deconstruct unjust, real-life problems and help support them in acting toward improving the problem. Help your child establish friendships with other teens who are *service-oriented*. In addition, try to get them into the practice of self-reflection before responding to a challenging situation. They can listen to music, journal in a diary, write poetry, write songs, paint, draw, do yoga or another form of physical exercise; and then come back to the situation they are facing.

Summary of Higher and Lower Personality Traits

Higher: Courageous, risk-takers, optimistic, passionate, creative, inventive, sweet-natured.

Lower: Selfish, impulsive, emotionally restless, highly sensitive, immature, lacks patience.

Childhood Influence Mercury Cards
It is common knowledge that a child's personality is most malleable during the formative years – from birth to eight years of age. In the Destiny Card system, the Mercury Cards in a Birth

Card's Life Spread reveal influences a child with this Birth Card will experience between birth through age 12. As such, a child's Mercury Cards must be considered so an adult can nurture a child from a place of awareness and work with them from where a child is at in their development. An A♥ child has the following Mercury Cards: **A♦ and J♠**. The J♠ may mean there is an influential father or brother who is likely a Spade Birth or Planetary Ruling Card. Alternatively, outside of any specific person associated with these two cards, the basic meanings of these cards describe experiences that may be impactful during this child's formative years. These cards suggest an A♥ is naturally impulsive and selfish and may be motivated to make money at a young age. Attaching money to doing chores is an excellent idea for an A♥. Also, be on the lookout for escapist behaviors such as excessive videogame playing with an A♥. There is the possibility of some deception or restriction in the home that may push them toward escapist behaviors.

Potential Callings / Vocations by Zodiac Sign

December 30 - Capricorn: 3♠ Planetary Ruling Card
Only one date, December 30, is associated with an A♥. As many Capricorns prefer to be the boss and not be bossed around, A♥ under this sign are inclined to professions where they have tremendous autonomy. This card may feel called to be a counselor, teacher, sports athlete, writer, business owner, or real estate broker. If an A♥ enjoys being at the center of attention, they may be attracted to being a comedian or TV personality.

Famous A♥
LeBron James, basketball player – 12/30/1984
Kim Tashyung, pop singer – 12/30 1995
Tiger Woods, golfer – 12/30/1975
Laila Ali, boxer – 12/30/1977
Tracey Ullman, comedian – 12/30/1959

Welcome to the world of the inquisitive A♣!

A♣ = Seeker of knowledge

According to the Destiny Card system, souls chronologically experience God's lessons across 52 life incarnations. (Think of these as the universe's lessons if this aligns more with your beliefs.) The Birth Card each soul is born into determines the order and type of lessons a soul experiences. When you examine a Birth Card, you will notice it displays a suit of either a Heart, Club, Diamond, or Spade. This suit is significant because it represents the gifts a person born into this suit will possess and how they will direct their energies to learn lessons in their current life incarnation. A Heart Birth Card retains gifts and experiences life lessons around love and relationships. A Club Birth Card holds capabilities and experiences life lessons in their ability to

communicate and absorb knowledge. A Diamond Birth Card possesses talents and experiences life lessons around money and values. And finally, a Spade Birth Card manifests gifts and experiences life lessons in work and health. Souls progress through incarnations and life lessons beginning as Hearts, moving on to Clubs, then Diamonds, and finally as Spades. Therefore, individuals born as Heart Cards are the youngest souls and individuals born as Spades Cards are the oldest souls.

In addition, the number on a Birth Card is equally meaningful as souls sequentially experience life lessons beginning as an Ace and culminating with lessons as a King. If you have played the card game poker, you know that Aces represent the number 'one.' More broadly speaking, the number one symbolizes new beginnings because other numbers are created when added to the number one. A life incarnation as an Ace represents a soul's initial journey on their path toward spiritual enlightenment as they are singularly focused upon exploring life in the area associated with their suit. **It makes sense, then, that an A♣ child's purpose, gifts, and life lessons revolve around *exploration* in life. And due to being a Club, this child will learn lessons through exploration around *communication* and *knowledge*.**

How to Nurture the Temperament and Personality of an A♣ Child

All A♣ are born with *inquiring minds*. This is the toddler who will wake up a parent at 6:00 am by repeatedly poking them in the face and saying, "You need to act like a robot today!" If you are the parent of an A♣ toddler and take them to the zoo, be prepared for them to refuse to stay by your side or hold your hand. Seeing a new animal will stimulate them so much, they will run to get a closer look. Make sure you wear comfortable shoes to keep up with them! Perhaps drink a lot of coffee, too. An A♣ will ask a bazillion questions about what they are experiencing. They will not be satisfied with, "I don't know" answers. They simply love learning and will likely be lifetime learners. If you are a parent of an A♣, take stock of their interests and passions and guide them to resources that support their related learning efforts. Don't be surprised if your school-aged A♣ becomes obsessed with facts to the extent that they memorize what you may perceive as irrelevant information. Exposure to books and educational experiences easily nurture an A♣ child. Start reading to them at an early age. Fortunately, many A♣ are born to powerful mothers who provide stimulating experiences that support their need to learn new things. If you are such a parent, refrain from being overly rigid with your child in what they learn. Allow some choice. Let them explore.

A good educational foundation is critical for an A♣. Without it, they will become discontent in life. Traditional schooling may not be enough for an A♣ as they might become bored. A school that offers an *inquiry-based learning* approach will often benefit an A♣. Inquiry-based learning represents a student-centered approach to learning that involves students asking and discovering the answers to real-life questions using problem-solving techniques and experiential methods. In addition, an A♣ should participate in *informal educational activities*. Informal educational activities include opportunities to learn outside of school or from a structured curriculum. Examples of such activities include after-school club, summer camps, museum, and zoo visits to name a few. Adolescent A♣ love to use technology and create content with apps such as Tik Tok, Instagram, Snap Chat, etc. The other side to this interest, though, is that some A♣ can become distracted with technology. While times of bingeing is okay for them, just make sure they do not abuse media time.

If you are a teacher of an A♣, recognize them for their action-oriented nature, always eager to start new projects. They are gifted at *brainstorming* and generating creative ideas. However, know that their thirst for new ideas means they may not always exercise good follow-through. Support them by teaching them how to set and accomplish short-term goals. As they grow older, help them break larger projects into smaller goals with different deadlines. A young A♣ may be impulsive, particularly in how they communicate. They may get so excited about a new idea they blurt out comments without raising their hand. Or they are impatient in their desire to communicate what they learned, and they interrupt others. In situations like this, address the issue by explaining expectations to the whole class. Read and discuss the book, *My Mouth is a Volcano*, by Julia Cook which addresses the issue of blurting. If the issue continues, develop individualized classroom management strategies for your A♣. Perhaps, set up a nonverbal and less confrontational signal alerting them they are not following classroom expectations. In some situations, like when they are passionate about something and blurt out comments, let the behavior slide. Otherwise, you may be constantly criticizing their behavior. And always remember their intentions are wonderful. If an A♣'s misbehaviors raise to a level of concern, collaborate with their parents to provide consistency, and reinforce consequences.

An adolescent A♣ may demonstrate a selfish drive for knowledge. For example, let's say your thirteen-year-old A♣ daughter is reading a new book. You have called her to dinner four times without a response. If this happened, she would benefit from agreeing in advance to family expectations and the consequences for not following them. Alternatively, your A♣ may become overly and unfairly demanding in their desire to pursue their own interests. If you are the parent of an A♣ and have other children, you know it is problematic to allow one child to drive all family activities. A♣ tend to feel they are special. Establishing special *choice activities* may help. As one example, designate every Sunday night as family fun night. This involves the entire family eating dinner and participating in some game or movie activity together. Each week a different child gets the privilege of choosing what the family will eat and do. This simple activity will not only help your A♣ feel special, but they may also feel some control over what they want to do. Speaking of what an A♣ may prefer to do, you may notice that your A♣ has moments of being an introvert, wanting to be locked in their room for hours and hours. This worries you because they normally act like an extrovert. Do not worry. A♣ need to recharge their batteries and often do so by reading, listening to music, or watching TV or YouTube videos. An A♣ can also recharge through physical exercise. And exercise may help dispense some of their impulsive energy.

Speaking of impulsive energy, some A♣ may lean into behaviors that cause them to be labeled with *attention deficit hyperactivity disorder* (ADHD). These A♣ might benefit from healing techniques intended to balance the body's *chakras*. Chakras are energy centers that receive and transmit energy throughout the body. There are seven major chakras running along the spine of one's body that are associated with different nerves, organs, joints, and tissues near a chakra's location. A person may experience negative physical and emotional symptoms when their flow of energy becomes unbalanced – either under or overactive – at a specific chakra site. For instance, chronic stress or poor habits can cause a chakra to become imbalanced. Various healing techniques directed at chakra revitalization include yoga, toning sounds, acupuncture, affirmations, aromatherapy, light therapy, breathing practices, crystal healing, and massage (especially reiki, shiatsu, and reflexology). If interested in crystal healing, the Lepidolite crystal is known to benefit individuals diagnosed with ADHD.

Summary of Higher and Lower Personality Traits

Higher: Curious, intellectual, witty, good communicator, initiate ideas, eternally youthful.

Lower: Emotionally restless, impulsive with ideas, poor follow-through, self-indulgent, nosy.

Childhood Influence Mercury Cards

It is common knowledge that a child's personality is most malleable during the formative years – from birth to eight years of age. In the Destiny Card system, the Mercury Cards in a Birth Card's Life Spread reveal influences a child with this Birth Card will experience between birth through age 12. As such, a child's Mercury Cards must be considered so an adult can nurture a child from a place of awareness and work with them from where a child is at in their development. An A♣ child has the following Mercury Cards: **Q♣, 4♦, and 3♥**. The Q♣ may mean there is an influential mother who is likely a Club Birth or Planetary Ruling Card. Alternatively, outside of any specific person associated with these three cards, the basic meanings of these cards describe experiences that may be impactful during this child's formative years. These cards suggest A♣ are excellent students and can process information faster than most other children. They may be prone to mood swings so it would be helpful to help them adopt coping strategies such as listening to music. anxiety which can be redirected into creative expression. Also, they often experience financial protection during their childhood.

Potential Callings / Vocations by Zodiac Sign

May 31 - Gemini: Q♣ Planetary Ruling Card
With a Q♣ Planetary Ruling Card, the need for communication and versatility is strong in these A♣, making them well suited to service and people-oriented vocations such as teacher, school psychologist, or counselor. Other possible careers include being a news commentator, comedian, or writer.

June 29 - Cancer: 3♥ Planetary Ruling Card
The caring aspect of Cancer makes these A♣ attracted to public service jobs. Being extremely creative, they can succeed in careers that do not demand strict organization such as a musician, artist, singer, or actor. Work that includes travel can also be good so long as it is not sales.

July 27 - Leo: A♣ Planetary Ruling Card
Ambition is high in these A♣. The issue with being a double A♣ is that they can lose focus if they do not have structure during childhood. Possessing the power and leadership qualities of a

Leo, they can make a wonderful attorney, teacher, writer, theatrical director, scientist, researcher, or business owner.

August 25 - Virgo: Q♣ Planetary Ruling Card

Intensely curious and analytical, these A♣ find purpose in scientific research and engineering; especially in fields such as conservation, forestry, chemistry, or mathematics. For those who lean toward service, others career options include attorney, teacher, counselor, gardener, x-ray technician, or landscape architect.

September – Libra: Q♣ or 10♠ Planetary Ruling Card

These A♣ are born on the cusp of Libra and Virgo so they can possess characteristics of each sign. They can do well in careers that involve partnerships or working with women. They have strong work ethics. They also hold the potential to make money in music, entertainment, or jobs that require a mechanical inclination.

October 21 – Libra: 10♠ Planetary Ruling Card

Expressing the pure artistic qualities of a Libra, these A♣ can be prosperous in any artistic path, including dancing, singing, music, acting, photography, and graphic design. They can also direct restless energy into sports and make a career of doing so. When the working hard aspect of a 10♠ Planetary Ruling Card is directed toward more mental pursuits, they can be successful at writing or research.

November 19 – Scorpio: 5♣ and 5♠ Planetary Ruling Cards

With the five energies of their Planetary Ruling Cards, these versatile and persuasive A♣ can excel in many careers. They feel satisfaction when their job allows them to make improvements to things, which makes them an excellent mechanic, housekeeper, or construction worker. They can also succeed as a politician, entertainer, or sales associate.

December 17 – Sagittarius: 3♦ Planetary Ruling Card

With the enthusiasm of Sagittarius, these A♣ can be quite successful as a real estate broker or travel agent. More inner-focused personalities can find success as a researcher, inventor, or financial advisor. Those more adventurous types may prefer to work with horses or work outdoors.

Famous A♣

Walt Whitman, writer – 5/31/1819
Doja Cat, rapper – 10/21/1995
Sean Connery, actor – 8/25/1930
Ray Charles, musician – 9/23/1930
Brooke Shields, actress – 5/31/1965
Rachel Ray, cook and author – 8/25/1968

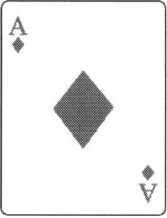

Welcome to the world of the inquisitive A♦!

A♦ = Seeker of worth and money

According to the Destiny Card system, souls chronologically experience God's lessons across 52 life incarnations. (Think of these as the universe's lessons if this aligns more with your beliefs.) The Birth Card each soul is born into determines the order and type of lessons a soul experiences. When you examine a Birth Card, you will notice it displays a suit of either a Heart, Club, Diamond, or Spade. This suit is significant because it represents the gifts a person born into this suit will possess and how they will direct their energies to learn lessons in their current life incarnation. A Heart Birth Card retains gifts and experiences life lessons around love and relationships. A Club Birth Card holds capabilities and experiences life lessons in their ability to communicate and absorb knowledge. A Diamond Birth Card possesses talents and experiences life lessons around money and values. And finally, a Spade Birth Card manifests gifts and experiences life lessons in work and health. Souls progress through incarnations and life lessons beginning as Hearts, moving on to Clubs, then Diamonds, and finally as Spades. Therefore, individuals born as Heart Cards are the youngest souls and individuals born as Spades Cards are the oldest souls.

In addition, the number on a Birth Card is equally meaningful as souls sequentially experience life lessons beginning as an Ace and culminating with lessons as a King. If you have played the card game poker, you know that Aces represent the number one. More broadly speaking, the number one symbolizes new beginnings because other numbers are created when added to the number one. A life incarnation as an Ace represents a soul's initial journey on their path toward spiritual enlightenment as they are singularly focused on exploring life in the area associated with their suit. **It makes sense, then, that an A♦ child's purpose, gifts, and life lessons revolve around *exploration* in life. And due to being a Diamond, this child will learn lessons through exploration around *values* and *money*.**

How to Nurture the Temperament and Personality of an A♦ Child

A♦ tend to be the most difficult Birth Card to teach and parent. In extreme cases, they are difficult to love. During childhood, they are often impulsive and have low self-esteem. Their current life lesson is to learn what values truly matter in life. As such, they experiment with an assortment of values. A young A♦ will likely make a lot of mistakes when they act out negative or unhealthy values. These A♦ receive negative attention which in turn may cause them to get frustrated. When they fail at something or get into trouble, they may be reactive and blame others. Let's consider an example. Imagine a situation in which an A♦ eight-year-old boy is visiting his grandmother in another state. His grandmother decides to take him sledding after a recent snowstorm. He has never been sledding so his grandmother tries to explain the nuances of using a sledding disc. Because he is so focused on the desire to act, he is not listening. As a result, try after try he has trouble staying on the sled. He is frustrated and impulsive. On his next run, he crashes into another child. There are tears and anger. The A♦ blames the other child for getting in his way. He is done and wants to leave. Grandmother is disappointed because her intentions were to make her grandson happy. Fortunately, A♦ tend to quickly move on to new experiences. Two hours later this A♦ is baking cookies with his grandmother.

Out of all the Ace Birth Cards, A♦ are often the most impulsive. Some A♦ can also be hyper. It is common for an A♦ to be labeled with *attention deficit hyperactivity disorder* (ADHD). Some A♦ might benefit from healing techniques intended to balance the body's *chakras*. Chakras are energy centers that receive and transmit energy throughout the body. There are seven major chakras running along the spine of one's body that are associated with different nerves, organs, joints, and tissues near a chakra's location. A person may experience negative physical and emotional symptoms when their flow of energy becomes unbalanced – either under or overactive – at a specific chakra site. For instance, chronic stress or poor habits can cause a chakra to become imbalanced. Various healing techniques directed at chakra revitalization include yoga, meditation, toning sounds, acupuncture, affirmations, aromatherapy, light therapy, breathing practices, crystal healing, and massage (especially reiki, shiatsu, and reflexology). If interested in crystal healing, the Lepidolite crystal is known to benefit individuals diagnosed with ADHD.

Although A♦ are bright and inquisitive, they may not do well in traditional schooling due to their impulsivity. Furthermore, A♦ are primarily motivated by what they value. If they do not perceive 'self-gains' from their education, they will lose interest and put little effort towards it. In a classroom, A♦ love to brainstorm and initiate ideas and projects, but they can easily become bored. These A♦ are notorious for not following through and finishing tasks. This can become a habitual problem for an A♦. Pressuring them to redirect efforts toward their education, particularly an adolescent A♦, may backfire. As a rule, A♦ do not respond well to the slightest amount of criticism. Criticizing an A♦ repeatedly for poor performances in school further lowers their self-esteem. Dare it be said, but it may be better to hold lower expectations for an A♦ when it comes to earning high grades in school. This situation is even more challenging if an A♦'s parent(s) have type-A personalities. If you are a parent of an A♦, I would suggest reading the personality traits of your own card to determine if your traits are oppositional to those of an A♦. Also, check your astrology sign. Are you a Virgo? A Virgo parent may be perfectionistic which may intensify parent-child conflicts.

Another behavior commonly observed in an A♦ is *tattling*. There are two main reasons for this behavior. First and previously mentioned, A♦ tend to be impulsive. Scientists have associated impulsive behavior with poor executive functioning in the brain. Deficits in executive function can mean a child lacks the ability to filter information. This can mean they have difficulty thinking before they act. Secondly, tattling represents a misdirected way of boosting their low self-esteem. Clearly, such behavior can be problematic in a classroom. Group dynamics are impacted when one classmate continuously tattles on others. An A♦ may alienate others and find themselves a loner. Thus, in a situation like this, it is better to start solving this problem by addressing the whole class. I recommend reading and discussing the children's book, *Don't Squeal Unless It's a Big Deal,* by Jeanie Franz and then establish class procedures with regards to tattling. If this behavior continues with an A♦, it may be necessary to implement individualized *behavior management strategies*. Behavior management strategies are techniques used to redirect and improve student behaviors. To manage tattling, it is important to teach a child several steps they should go through before getting an adult involved. Tattle problem-solving worksheets and charts can be found on the Internet. For a short time, establish positive and negative consequences for adhering to the expectations. In addition, try to observe what may be triggering the A♦. If an incident occurs, refrain from calling out wrongdoing until the A♦ has time to calm down and process the situation at hand.

A♦ require training in how to slow down and process information. They can accomplish this by making sure they get enough reflective time, time outs, extracurricular activities (especially sports), listening to relaxing music, and yoga. Studies have shown that when people listen to relaxing music before a stressful medical procedure, their cortisol (stress hormone) levels are lower than people who don't listen to relaxing music before similar events. If you are a teacher of an A♦, know that this child requires daily *brain breaks*. Brain breaks are physical and mental breaks used in school to get students moving or to help them relax. A♦ are often unaware they need time to recharge their batteries, so you may need to look for related signs (i.e., fidgeting, excessive irritability, lack of focus, etc.). A♦ benefit the most from physical outlets. The best physical activities for an A♦ are often individual sports such as biking, fishing, golf, tennis, ice skating, swimming, surfing, and skiing. Without such outlets, these individuals may subconsciously search for unhealthy ways to calm themselves. At an extreme, they may be susceptible to drug use during adolescence.

Often the root of most problems for an A♦ is low self-esteem. Therefore, the best way to nurture them is to help them develop self-worth. Beginning as early as possible, encourage an A♦ to experience the *act of giving* or *small acts of kindness*. Researchers have found that children who give tend to improve their self-esteem. Besides, it is something an A♦ can do and receive well-deserved praise in the process. Adults should model acts of kindness and then involve an A♦ child to conduct their own acts such as giving away their old toys or helping a new student in school make friends. Establish traditions that value family and love and are not materialistic, like decorating a Christmas tree, having family game night, or writing thank you cards. If they show interest in a cause, nudge them toward actions to support it. For an adolescent A♦, encourage volunteer work such as feeding homeless people on Thanksgiving or working at a local pet shelter. Rather than pushing them into any activity, let them choose.

A♦ are gifted with the heart of an *entrepreneur*. As children, these individuals are the ones who initiate and run a lemonade stand business that is attractive and employs a creative way of making money. And because A♦ children are easy to talk to, they will surprise adults by selling a lot of lemonade! Encourage their ideas and praise them for their inventiveness. Tread lightly with any criticism. If they have a remotely good idea, let them try it. Because A♦ are inherently motivated by money, a parent can use this trait to their advantage. Set up an allowance attached to specific chores. However, keep in mind that A♦ hate to be told what to do! Instead, involve them in the process of assigning chores and give them choices. Make sure to modify chores and re-negotiate allowance from time to time. Also, within this arrangement, know that an A♦ needs more praise than the average child. If they are responsible for completing five chores, but only completed four, do not make a bigger deal out of what they did not do. Praise them for the four chores they did do.

A♦ are often skilled at brainstorming ideas. If you are a teacher who wants students to brainstorm creative ideas or solutions, you can count on an A♦ to be forthcoming with lots of suggestions. An A♦ not only has the potential to invent an idea or business that is cutting edge, but they are also not afraid of pitching them to others. Some A♦ can redirect their ability to brainstorm into *improvisation*. Improvisation is a technique in which a person reacts spontaneously to unexpected situations. Actors and comedians are often associated with improvisation. These traits explain why Tina Fey and Ellen DeGeneres who are both A♦ are well known for their improvisational comedy.

Living in the digital age is particularly difficult for an A♦ adolescent. They are easily distracted and can become obsessed with the use of technology. If you are a parent of an A♦, establish rules about time spent with media, especially video game playing time. Do not be swayed when an impulsive A♦ claims you to be the worst parent by having such rules. They will appreciate your boundaries when they are older and have children of their own. It is not a good idea to take away the technology all together. They will rebel and direct their one energy with anger towards you. They will wear you down in the battle. Rather, monitor their use of technology to prevent it from becoming an addiction. It is remarkable how many parents of an A♦ boy diagnosed with ADHD are baffled by the fact that their child maintains a long attention span when it comes to playing video games. If this is the case for your A♦, you might want to check out EndeavorRx, the first prescription video game approved by the Food and Drug Administration for treating ADHD. Above all it is advisable to reduce other forms of extreme stimulation for an A♦ child such as excess candy, sound, or other children running around to name a few. Too much stimulation is a sure ticket to crazy town for an A♦!

Summary of Higher and Lower Personality Traits

Higher: Compassionate, philanthropic, improvisation, youthful, self-starter, versatile, creative.

Lower: Opportunistic, impulsive in values/money, low self-esteem, easily frustrated, angry.

Childhood Influence Mercury Cards
It is common knowledge that a child's personality is most malleable during the formative years – from birth to eight years of age. In the Destiny Card system, the Mercury Cards in a Birth Card's Life Spread reveal influences a child with this Birth Card will experience between birth through age 12. As such, a child's Mercury Cards must be considered so an adult can nurture a child from a place of awareness and work with them from where a child is at in their development. An A♦ child has the following Mercury Cards: **Q♦, 8♣, and 3♦**. The Q♦ may mean there is an influential mother who is likely a Diamond Birth or Planetary Ruling Card. Alternatively, outside of any specific person associated with these three cards, the basic meanings of these cards describe experiences that may be impactful during this child's formative years. These cards suggest A♦ are independent and desire freedom early in life. They desire money but insecure family finances may make them feel restricted. Also, establishing a strong educational foundation for an A♦ will benefit them through challenging times.

Potential Callings / Vocations by Zodiac Sign

January 26 – Aquarius: 7♣ Planetary Ruling Card
Because Aquarians love technology, it is essential to prevent these individuals from becoming addicted to it which in turn, may sabotage their achievement in life. Because they have a powerful need for freedom in their career, they can do well as an airline attendant, tour guide, blogger, web developer, or sports instructor. For those that are motivated to make money, other good career choices are investment counselor or stockbroker.

February 24 – Pisces: 5♦ Planetary Ruling Card
These Pisces born individuals can draw from the empathetic side of this sign and find success in service-oriented careers. They have a propensity toward daydreaming, so they are often late bloomers. Gifted at trying new things and inventing, they can do well as a bartender, perfumier, sommelier, inventor, or pharmacist. Those attracted to the sea and travel can do well as a boat captain, fisherman, or entertainer on a cruise ship.

March 22 – Aries: 3♣ Planetary Ruling Card
With Mars as their ruler, these A♦ are prone to being over-stimulated and indecisive when it comes to a career. Applying the creativity of their 3♣ Planetary Ruling Card, they can find success as an artist, actor, salesperson, or construction worker.

April 20 – Aries: 3♣ or 5♥ Planetary Ruling Card
Born on the cusp, these A♦ can lean Aries or Taurus and therefore are pulled in different directions to the extent that they can have too many fires in the oven. Once focused, they can do well as an actor, artist, writer, mechanic, construction worker, or musician.

May 18 – Taurus: 5♥ Planetary Ruling Card
The influence of Venus in these individuals combined with a 5♥ Planetary Ruling Card makes these individuals sociable, friendly, and affectionate. Therefore, they are well suited to people-oriented careers as an interior designer, hairdresser, architect, or actor.

June 16 – Gemini: Q♦ Planetary Ruling Card
The influence of a Q♦ Planetary Ruling Card makes these A♦ appreciate luxury so they can do well in jobs that provide luxury (e.g., hotel/resort managers and jewelry/fur sales). Their intellect serves them well in leadership within service-oriented jobs. They can also make good secretaries or aides in the health industry.

July 14 – Cancer: A♥ Planetary Ruling Card
With the caring aspect of Cancer, these A♦ do best at jobs in which they can nurture others (e.g., elder care aide, dog walker, home or pet sitter, or personal trainer). More ambitious individuals can find success as a lawyer, singer, or TV personality.

August 12 – Leo: A♦ Planetary Ruling Card

A♦ Leos are extroverts who are magnetic and need creative expression. Above all, they love ostentation and projecting affluence. They can make an excellent actor, writer, advertising agent, or film director/producer.

September 10 – Virgo: Q♦ Planetary Ruling Card

The influence of Virgo makes these A♦ hold a strong sense of integrity and a need for freedom when it comes to vocation. They are well suited to work as a technician or military officer. If inclined toward a sport, they can often make a career out of it.

October 8 – Libra: 5♥ Planetary Ruling Card

With the influence of Libra, many of these A♦ are born with good looks, which can be leveraged into a career such as acting and/or modelling. Blessed with an equally attractive personality due to their 5♥ Planetary Ruling Card, these people can also do well as a counselor, fitness trainer, politician, business manager, or as a business owner.

November 6 – Scorpio: 3♣ and Q♠ Planetary Ruling Cards

Having a 3♣ Planetary Ruling Card means these A♦ excel at self-expression and so they can do well as a musician, writer, theater actor, or artist (particularly with sculpture). If shy, they may prefer more mundane work.

December 4 – Sagittarius: 3♠ Planetary Ruling Card

With an innate sense of money and having the capacity to handle risk, these A♦ can succeed in professions that deal with money (e.g., real estate broker, financial counselor, stockbroker, entrepreneur, or salesperson). Having a 3♠ Planetary Ruling Card means they enjoy diverse interests, so these individuals are also capable of many other professions.

Famous A♦

Steve Jobs, inventor/ entrepreneur – 2/24/1955
Jay-Z, musician – 12/4/1969
Adolf Hitler, politician/ dictator – 4/20/1889
Tyra Banks, model – 12/4/1973
Bruno Mars, singer – 10/8/1985
Kai Lenny, extreme surfer – 10/8/1992

Welcome to the world of the inquisitive A♠!

A♠ = Seeker of wisdom

According to the Destiny Card system, souls chronologically experience God's lessons across 52 life incarnations. (Think of these as the universe's lessons if this aligns more with your beliefs.) The Birth Card each soul is born into determines the order and type of lessons a soul experiences. When you examine a Birth Card, you will notice it displays a suit of either a Heart, Club, Diamond, or Spade. This suit is significant because it represents the gifts a person born into this suit will possess and how they will direct their energies to learn lessons in their current life incarnation. A Heart Birth Card retains gifts and experiences life lessons around love and relationships. A Club Birth Card holds capabilities and experiences life lessons in their ability to communicate and absorb knowledge. A Diamond Birth Card possesses talents and experiences life lessons around money and values. And finally, a Spade Birth Card manifests gifts and experiences life lessons in work and health. Souls progress through incarnations and life lessons beginning as Hearts, moving on to Clubs, then Diamonds, and finally as Spades. Therefore, individuals born as Heart Cards are the youngest souls and individuals born as Spades Cards are the oldest souls.

In addition, the number on a Birth Card is equally meaningful as souls sequentially experience life lessons beginning as an Ace and culminating with lessons as a King. If you have played the card game poker, you know that Aces represent the number one. More broadly speaking, the number one symbolizes new beginnings because other numbers are created when added to the number one. A life incarnation as an Ace represents a soul's initial journey on their path toward spiritual enlightenment as they are singularly focused on exploring life in the area associated with their suit. **It makes sense, then, that an A♠ child's purpose, gifts, and life lessons revolve around *exploration* in life. And due to being a Spade, this child will learn lessons through exploration around *health* and *work*.**

How to Nurture the Temperament and Personality of an A♠ Child
A♠ children tend to absorb spiritual energy and then internally transform it into physical energy. This process in turn, can cause them to be physically impulsive. Let's consider an example. Imagine you are the mother of a five-year-old A♠ boy. One afternoon, you hear a commotion in the garage. The noise sounds like something being pulled across the concrete floor, but then all goes quiet, and you shrug it off. The next thing you hear is your A♠ crying. You follow the cries outside to the garden shed. There you find a ladder leaned sideways against the shed. Several feet from the bottom of the ladder you see your child, Superman cape in place, holding an injured arm. You sum up the situation quickly, knowing your A♠ secretly tried to fulfill a fantastical dream of flying. As this anecdote demonstrates, A♠ children often jump into situations without thinking. What also can be true is that an impulsive A♠ may be prone to desiring instant gratification. Therefore, an A♠ may benefit from being given short-term over long-term goals and rewards. As one example, imagine this same parent of a five-year-old A♠ boy has difficulty getting her son to keep his room clean. Each day he is reminded that he can earn an agreed upon small reward if he picks up his toys at the end of the day. Rewards can include an extra 15 minutes to stay up before bedtime, time to watch a favorite TV show, or a favorite dessert after dinner. For bigger goals, A♠ enjoy spontaneous adventures. Reward them with surprise outings such as a trip to the zoo, a putt-putt golf center, or spending an hour at a local playground. Adolescent A♠ love using new technology. An adult can leverage

this interest to motivate behavior as well. Just be aware that some A♠ teens can be secretive, and this trait can be negatively expressed in their use of technology.

During adolescence, an A♠ physical impulsiveness may cause them to be extreme daredevils. And if an A♠ is anxious they may express their anxiety by engaging in risky behaviors. From time to time, this trait gets them into difficult spots. The reason for this is because they tend to be less reflective than other Birth Cards. Therefore, a good way to nurture an A♠ is to teach them how to *self-reflect*. If you are a parent of an A♠, I recommend using the Gibbs Reflective Cycle (described in Chapter 3) to debrief risky situations with your A♠. Start this practice at the youngest possible age. Also, research the Internet for *problem-solving charts* that can teach the process of considering consequences ahead of actions. Ask them to identify alternative ways to deal with their intense feelings and energy. Make sure they are listening because an A♠ can tune you out. Ask them to repeat back important parts of the discussion if you find this to be an issue.

The notorious *terrible two* stage can be particularly difficult for an A♠ because they are prone to physical outbursts. Fortunately, A♠ often display signs of an impending outburst so adults working with them can try to calm them before this happens. For instance, an A♠ will clench their fists, or their face will turn red. As an A♠ gets older, teach them how to recognize their own physical signs of an approaching outburst and ways to cope. One effective strategy is to teach them how to conduct a *body scan meditation*. A body scan meditation involves lying down, taking deep breaths, and paying attention to how one's body is feeling. If the body is feeling tense, a person systematically attempts to calm parts of the body, thereby restoring a healthy balance of energy. Check the Internet for kid-friendly videos on how to practice body scan meditation.

If you are a teacher, it is important to provide an A♠ student with daily *brain breaks*. Brain breaks are mental and physical breaks used in school to get students moving or help them relax. Again, there are countless ideas and videos for brain breaks on the Internet. I recommend the website www.Gonoodle.com which offers guided dances, sing-a-longs, and calming exercises. One form of brain break that focuses mainly on mental breaks is called *mindfulness exercises*. I highly recommend *Mindful Kids: 50 Mindfulness Activities for Kindness, Focus, and Calm* by Whitney Stewart. This activity pack offers easy-to-follow directions for 50 different mindfulness activities that can be used with all ages of children.

Left to navigate intense spiritual and physical energies on their own, an adolescent A♠ may develop issues with anger management. These individuals may alienate others to the point where loneliness and depression set in. It is imperative for them to develop a *spiritual viewpoint* to find happiness. Without it, life can seem like a constant struggle. Interestingly, these individuals come with so much prior knowledge because they have experienced many past lives. As an A♠, they are initiating whole new lessons – spiritual lessons. Older approaches to solving problems no longer work. Until an A♠ embraces their spiritual side, life may be difficult. If you are a parent of an A♠, prepare them to deal with struggles by communicating how you navigate your own. For example, let's say you are stressed by a difficult interaction with a co-worker. Take your child on a hike with you and explain how you are feeling. Describe how you felt like you wanted to yell at your co-worker. Instead, you decided to schedule a hike, as nature soothes and recharges you. Older A♠ are excellent at *brainstorming*. Ask them to brainstorm personal ways they can redirect their negative energy. For example, an A♠ may learn that physical exercise helps. Burning off their intense energy by running is especially good for an A♠. Some A♠ may even benefit from journaling, writing about their feelings, or playing music.

Some A♠ may exhibit impulsive behaviors that cause adults around them to label them with *attention deficit hyperactivity disorder* (ADHD). These A♠ might benefit from healing techniques intended to balance the body's *chakras*. Chakras are energy centers that receive and transmit energy throughout the body. There are seven major chakras running along the spine of one's body that are associated with different nerves, organs, joints, and tissues near a chakra's location. A person may experience negative physical and emotional symptoms when their flow of energy becomes unbalanced – either under or overactive – at a specific chakra site. For instance, chronic stress or poor habits can cause a chakra to become imbalanced. Various healing techniques directed at chakra revitalization include yoga, meditation, toning sounds, acupuncture, affirmations, aromatherapy, light therapy, breathing practices, crystal healing, and massage (especially reiki, shiatsu, and reflexology). If interested in crystal healing, the Lepidolite crystal is known to benefit individuals diagnosed with ADHD.

Summary of Higher and Lower Personality Traits

Higher: Initiate projects well, spiritually motivated, inventive, compassionate, psychic.

Lower: Anxiety, depression, secretiveness, lack self-discipline, physically impulsive.

Childhood Influence Mercury Cards
It is common knowledge that a child's personality is most malleable during the formative years – from birth to eight years of age. In the Destiny Card system, the Mercury Cards in a Birth Card's Life Spread reveal influences a child with this Birth Card will experience between birth through age 12. As such, a child's Mercury Cards must be considered so an adult can nurture a child from a place of awareness and work with them from a child is at in their development. An A♠ child has the following Mercury Cards: 7♥, Q♥, and 8♥. The Q♥ may mean there is an influential mother who is likely a Heart Birth or Planetary Ruling Card. Alternatively, outside of any specific person associated with these three cards, the basic meanings of these cards describe experiences that may be impactful during this child's formative years. These cards suggest A♠ may be prone to jealousy, possibly of other siblings. They may experience emotional disappointments that involve them feeling obligated to take care of others. Young A♠ are blessed with a charming persona which helps them attract a lot of friends.

Potential Callings / Vocations by Zodiac Sign

January 13 – Capricorn: 9♣ Planetary Ruling Card
These A♠ prefer to work behind the scenes and not be in the limelight. Having the brilliance of a 9♣ Planetary Ruling Card, they can do well in academic research (e.g., scientific fields of

geology, archeology, or geotechnical engineering), or as a nurse or statistician. Some may embrace their spiritual nature and prefer to work within a religious institution.

February 11- Aquarius: 9♠ Planetary Ruling Card

The intellectual aspect of Aquarius when combined with the mystic influence of a 9♠ Planetary Ruling Card causes these A♠ to be drawn to the occult or mysteries of the universe. Science and invention intrigue them so they can excel at any field within these areas. They can also make a great detective or military strategist.

March 9 – Pisces: 2♥ Planetary Ruling Card

Having a 2♥ Planetary Ruling Card causes these A♠ to have a more serious and idealistic nature. Therefore, these individuals may need to support a cause as part of their vocation. They can work well in non-profit jobs, teaching, or in government service.

April 7 – Aries: 5♠ Planetary Ruling Card

The protective nature of these A♠ makes them well suited to careers in which they help others but are not too conventional because they dislike routine (owing to their 5♠ Planetary Ruling Card). They can be religious leaders or activists. They can also do well as a TV personality or actor.

May 5 – Taurus: 7♦ Planetary Ruling Card

Taurus born A♠ tend to be stubborn and hold fixed opinions. They can do well in journalism, philosophy, or politics. Creative leaning individuals can succeed in fashion design or in the entertainment industry.

June 3- Gemini: 7♥ Planetary Ruling Card

These A♠ are restless, get bored easily, and may resist traditional forms of education. Being easy to talk to and pleasant looking, they can do well in sales, persuasive writing (e.g., travel or food critic), or as a musician or actor.

July 1 – Cancer: 3♦ Planetary Ruling Card

Both secretive and sensitive, Cancer A♠ are drawn to careers in scientific research or medicine (e.g., nurse, physician assistant, or physician). Those inclined toward mathematics or economics can do well as a stock analyst due to their analytical 3♦ Planetary Ruling Card.

Famous A♠

Yuri Gargarin, astronaut – 3/9/1934
Thomas Edison, inventor – 2/11/1847
Jennifer Aniston, actress – 2/11/1969
Liam Hemsworth, actor – 1/13/1990
Anderson Cooper, TV personality – 6/3/1967
Nate Silver, statistician – 1/13/1978

Chapter 5

Descriptions of the Two Birth Cards

Welcome to the world of the relational 2♥!

2♥ = Intimate connections

According to the Destiny Card system, souls chronologically experience God's lessons across 52 life incarnations. (Think of these as the universe's lessons if this aligns more with your beliefs.) The Birth Card each soul is born into determines the order and type of lessons a soul experiences. When you examine a Birth Card, you will notice it displays a suit of either a Heart, Club, Diamond, or Spade. This suit is significant because it represents the gifts a person born into this suit will possess and how they will direct their energies to learn lessons in their current life incarnation. A Heart Birth Card retains gifts and experiences life lessons around love and relationships. A Club Birth Card holds capabilities and experiences life lessons in their ability to communicate and absorb knowledge. A Diamond Birth Card possesses talents and experiences life lessons around money and values. And finally, a Spade Birth Card manifests gifts and experiences life lessons in work and health. Souls progress through incarnations and life lessons beginning as Hearts, moving on to Clubs, then Diamonds, and finally as Spades. Therefore, individuals born as Heart Cards are the youngest souls and individuals born as Spades Cards are the oldest souls.

In addition, the number on a Birth Card is equally meaningful as souls sequentially experience life lessons beginning as an Ace and culminating with lessons as a King. In the case of all Two Birth Cards, the number two connotes a pairing. And the word *pair* implies something that has two parts joined for a combined function. For instance, think of a pair of socks. Two socks function well at keeping your feet warm. Yet, what happens when you wash laundry and discover one sock is missing? Having only one sock negates the function of this garment. If you are like most people, you eventually throw out this unpaired sock, finding it useless. This analogy explains the energy behind all Two Birth Cards. You see, they experience life with a driving need to join forces with someone else or risk feeling useless. **It makes sense, then, that a 2♥ child's purpose, gifts, and life lessons revolve around developing *connections* with others. And due to being a Heart, this child will learn lessons through *emotional* and *intimate love* connections.**

How to Nurture the Temperament and Personality of a 2♥ Child

Starting at birth, 2♥ need a harmonious and stable home environment. Because of this, a sudden family divorce can be quite traumatic for a 2♥. If you are a parent of a 2♥, a good way to provide a peaceful setting is to design their bedroom into a cozy haven. Purchase them stuffed animals to put on their bed, cuddly blankets, and paint the walls a soothing color. As they get older, allow them to decorate their room according to their own tastes. 2♥ also thrive in a home that has routines and traditions. This may mean they struggle when routines are changed. A routine that is sure to nurture a young 2♥ is to set up a bedtime ritual that includes snuggling and one-on-one time with a parent. 2♥ children love being read to in bed. Such an activity satisfies both their intellectual curiosity and need for affection. You see, 2♥ crave more affection than most other Birth Cards. This is an extremely clingy toddler and a child who may become attached to sleeping in their parent's bed. And this is a child who may express jealousy toward a new baby in the family. When a new baby is brought home from the hospital, this is the three-year-old who says, "Whose baby is this? Are her parents coming to pick her up?" Jealousy for parental attention may also be an issue for a 2♥ in a family with multiple siblings. Try as much as possible to give a 2♥ some one-on-one quality time, such as a special date activity with a parent. 2♥ need to feel they are receiving enough attention and affection within the family. Are you a parent pressed for time? Co-plan a secret recipe with your 2♥, make dinner together, and then serve it to the whole family. Or set up a family tradition that allows each of your children to take turns feeling special. For instance, you could designate every Sunday night as a family night in which one child gets to decide what to eat and what activity the family does together. Alternatively, support a 2♥ child in getting extra love by purchasing them a pet, especially one that can reciprocate affection.

In an educational setting, 2♥ typically shine. If you are a teacher of a 2♥, you can use their need for relational connections to your advantage. For instance, you can incentivize them to achieve an academic goal by rewarding them with time to work with a friend. Besides, they tend to learn well with a study buddy. If a 2♥ requires reteaching, know that they respond well to one-on-one tutoring. Overall, 2♥ tend to do well in school and make model students. If you are a parent of a 2♥, indulge all their interests in learning because they are capable of success in any field. Older 2♥ enjoy quality time with friends so much that you can motivate them by having time with friends as a reward. A sleepover at a friend's house is a perfect example of this. In addition, encourage sports and activities that involve two players such as chess, canoeing, tennis, badminton, table tennis, or playing cards (yes, playing cards can be for entertainment, too). 2♥ love conversation and can do well at learning foreign languages. Therefore, enroll them in a foreign language class as young as possible. A dual language or international school setting would be ideal for them.

Ever hear a young child, perhaps around the age of five, claim they have a boyfriend or girlfriend? You may laugh at the notion, but this is a serious perception in the mind of many a young 2♥. Refrain from ridiculing a 2♥ for such a comment. This same 2♥ may not like to share any special person with others for fear of not getting enough intimacy. This viewpoint can be problematic when parents try to set up playdates. Let's consider an example. Imagine you are a parent of an eight-year-old 2♥ daughter named Felicia. You have invited two of Felicia's friends over to play, Mara and Kayla. Mara is Felicia's best friend. Because you know Felicia loves arts and crafts activities, you set up a table for the three girls to make jewelry out of beads. Felicia directs her friends to the table and explains they will make necklaces. The girls begin the process by collecting their own beads. Then, Kayla decides to switch the plan and designs a bracelet. She encourages Mara to follow suit. Next thing you know it, Felicia is extremely upset. She no longer wants to participate in this activity or play with these friends. You think your child is making a mountain out of a molehill. Nevertheless, you must understand that 2♥ are *overly sensitive* to the affections of others. They are like porcelain teacups. One upset or fall, and they shatter. In this situation, your child perceives rejection, and perception is reality for a 2♥. Therefore, as a parent of a 2♥ it may be better to only invite one other friend over for a play date until you can better prepare them for playing with multiple friends. Preparation for such playtime should include explaining expectations of receiving attention from friends. Perhaps role play various situations that might trigger them and ask your 2♥ to reflect upon how they can react so that everyone is happy.

As a 2♥ approaches adolescence, they will prefer an emotional connection with friends and romantic partners. As a parent of a 2♥, you may be annoyed with their insistence to have many friends on Facebook, Instagram, TikTok, or Snap Chat and their increasing time spent on social media. You may need to set boundaries or rules in this area of their life. Speaking of friends – it is common for a 2♥ to be attracted to friends with power. You know them – the popular kids in school. Do not be surprised if your fifteen-year-old 2♥ daughter wants to date the eighteen-year-old captain of the football team! Regardless of the type of relationship a 2♥ is trying to establish, be on the lookout for them trying to change themselves to be the perfect match for a friend or romantic partner. An adolescent 2♥ may go to great lengths to secure relationships with popular kids because it makes them feel important. At an extreme, they may lose their own identity in the process. If this is an issue for your 2♥, help them consider and attend to their own needs. They need to learn to love themselves apart from what others want or expect from them. Keep in mind this may be an extremely difficult endeavor for a 2♥ because they fear being alone.

Speaking of romantic partners, initial relationships for a 2♥ are significant because they set the tone for the future. If you are a parent of a 2♥, it would be helpful to prepare them ahead of such experiences. Specifically, they need help achieving balance in matters of the heart and mind. You see, 2♥ tend to act straight from the heart. While this may be precious at times, it can be troublesome when a 2♥ emotionally rushes into relationships. For example, let's say a sixteen-year-old 2♥ boy named Nathan observes his girlfriend flirting with another boy named Alex at school. Noticing this same interaction, Nathan's best friend makes a snide comment about it. Immediately, the 2♥ jumps to conclusions. Nathan approaches his girlfriend and makes unfounded accusations which in turn causes them to break up. Later that afternoon, still feeling heartache, Nathan gets into a physical altercation with Alex and ends up in the principal's office. Clearly, this 2♥ must learn to consult the mind before acting from the heart. An adult can help by processing situations like this with a 2♥. Within such a discussion, an adult should refrain from downplaying the emotions or professions of love from a 2♥. Rather, it would be good to share your own trials and tribulations in love and validate their feelings. Let them know it is okay to date and lose many frogs before they find their prince or princess. Then, help them engage in distracting activities, especially ones that include a connection with a safe friend. If you are dealing with a teen that does not want to discuss such matters with you, encourage them to talk through things with a close friend before making rash decisions.

Navigating expectations in love is often a challenging life lesson for many 2♥. As another example, some 2♥ have the tendency to accelerate the level of seriousness within a romantic relationship before their partner is ready to do so. As such, their emotional expectations may be unrealistic. These 2♥ may scare their partner and precipitate a breakup. If a relationship ends this way, this 2♥ often blames themself and takes it hard. Over time, they may develop dysfunctional relational patterns. At an extreme, a 2♥ may subconsciously be a party to *triangulation*. Psychologists describe triangulation as when one person uses another person to manipulate a third person. Let's consider an example. Fifteen-year-old Sophia is a 2♥ and has a best friend named Isabelle. Isabelle has recently been spending more time with a new boyfriend named Lucas. Isabelle invites Sophia to their high school event to watch Lucas's basketball game. Sophia declines and then invites another friend, Beth, to this same event. Sophia makes sure to give Beth a lot of attention in the hope that Isabelle will see them and become jealous. The underlying motive for Sophia is to manipulate Isabelle to give her more affection and attention. And if these kinds of tactics are successful, a 2♥ will continue to employ them. Without realizing it, a 2♥ may be sabotaging the intimate relationships they so strongly desire if their partner feels they are being manipulated. If you are a parent of a 2♥ and you observe this, it may be necessary to make your child aware of this behavior. Start with subtle messages such as discussing similar behaviors from TV or movie characters. Then, hint at the consequences of such behavior in real-life situations. If these consequences manifest, refrain from saying, "I told you so." In extreme cases, therapy may be needed.

Summary of Higher and Lower Personality Traits

Higher: Physical beauty, brilliant in business, diplomatic, compassionate, magnetic.

Lower: Unrealistic in love, needy, overly sensitive, manipulative triangulation, moody.

Childhood Influence Mercury Cards
It is common knowledge that a child's personality is most malleable during the formative years – from birth to eight years of age. In the Destiny Card system, the Mercury Cards in a Birth Card's Life Spread reveal influences a child with this Birth Card will experience between birth through age 12. As such, a child's Mercury Cards must be considered so an adult can nurture a child from a place of awareness and work with them from where a child is at in their development. A 2♥ child has the following Mercury Cards: **K♥, A♠, and 2♣**. These cards may represent people who are influential during this child's early life. The K♥ may mean there is an influential father who is likely a Heart Birth or Planetary Ruling Card. Alternatively, outside of any specific person associated with these three cards, the basic meanings of these cards describe experiences that may be impactful during this child's formative years. These cards suggest a 2♥ may be shy or introverted as a young child, keeping their secrets close to their heart. They will likely begin talking earlier than their peers and as they grow older, they will love discussing ideas one-on-one with friends and family members.

Potential Callings / Vocations by Zodiac Sign

December 29 – Capricorn: 2♦ Planetary Ruling Card

Like the A♥, only one zodiac sign rules 2♥. When you combine the financially ambitious aspect of a 2♦ Planetary Ruling Card with the 2♥'s brilliance in business and management of people, it is clear there are many vocations in which a 2♥ may excel. They can make an excellent stock or real estate broker, diplomat, human resource officer, civil engineer, or business manager.

Famous 2♥

Jude Law, actor – 12/29/1972
Paris Berelc, gymnast – 12/29/1998
Dylan Minette, actor – 12/29/1996
Christen Press, soccer player – 12/29/1988
Dylan Hartman, Instagram star – 12/29/2004

Welcome to the world of the relational 2♣!

2♣ = Mental connections

According to the Destiny Card system, souls chronologically experience God's lessons across 52 life incarnations. (Think of these as the universe's lessons if this aligns more with your beliefs.) The Birth Card each soul is born into determines the order and type of lessons a soul experiences. When you examine a Birth Card, you will notice it displays a suit of either a Heart, Club, Diamond, or Spade. This suit is significant because it represents the gifts a person born into this suit will possess and how they will direct their energies to learn lessons in their current life incarnation. A Heart Birth Card retains gifts and experiences life lessons around love and relationships. A Club Birth Card holds capabilities and experiences life lessons in their ability to communicate and absorb knowledge. A Diamond Birth Card possesses talents and experiences life lessons around money and values. And finally, a Spade Birth Card manifests gifts and experiences life lessons in work and health. Souls progress through incarnations and life lessons beginning as Hearts, moving on to Clubs, then Diamonds, and finally as Spades. Therefore, individuals born as Heart Cards are the youngest souls and individuals born as Spades Cards are the oldest souls.

In addition, the number on a Birth Card is equally meaningful as souls sequentially experience life lessons beginning as an Ace and culminating with lessons as a King. In the case of all Two Birth Cards, the number two connotes a pairing. And the word *pair* implies something that has two parts joined for a combined function. For instance, think of a pair of socks. Two socks function well at keeping your feet warm. Yet, what happens when you wash laundry and discover one sock is missing? Having only one sock negates the function of this garment. If you are like most people, you eventually throw out this unpaired sock, finding it useless. This analogy explains the energy behind all Two Birth Cards. You see, they experience life with a driving need to join forces with someone else or risk feeling useless. **It makes sense, then, that a 2♣ child's purpose, gifts, and life lessons revolve around creating *connections* with others. And due to being a Club, this child will learn lessons through how they *communicate* and share *knowledge* with others.**

How to Nurture the Temperament and Personality of a 2♣ Child

A 2♣ baby will watch in fascination when others around them are communicating. They simply love language and communication. As a toddler, they will amaze adults with how quickly they learn new words. Be careful of what you say around a young 2♣ as they can soak up new vocabulary like no other Birth Card. This is the toddler that tells strangers in the grocery store that, "Mommy has a bagina!" A 2♣ may be thought to be older than peers of similar age because of their *advanced communication skills*. Adults should nurture this trait by exposing them to reading and new vocabulary. Also, 2♣ tend to be auditory learners who love using unique technologies to learn information. Therefore, a 2♣ is a model candidate to purchase toys for that encourage speech and vocabulary development. These toys include Leap Frog, Touch and Teach Word Book, and Osmo's Little Genius kits. If finances allow, provide a 2♣ with an iPad and download apps that help boost children's language development. 2♣ often have a lot of success with these activities which in turn gives them confidence for when they begin school. If you are a teacher of a 2♣, you may notice they need to *verbally process* new information. Therefore, support them by allowing them to discuss ideas with others through strategies such as *think-pair-share* and *turn and talk*. A 2♣ supported in all these ways will likely go on to academically achieve. For instance, many 2♣ do well on the Scholastic Aptitude Test (SAT) for college admission. And a 2♣ will generally score higher on the Evidence-Based Reading and Writing portions of this test.

Like many things in life, too much of a good thing can be problematic. For a 2♣, strong communication skills can also manifest as a lower expression. Let's consider an example. Imagine you are a parent of an eight-year-old 2♣ girl named Katerina who is the oldest of three children. One morning you notice your children are playing 'school.' You chuckle as you hear Katerina acting like an adult teacher directing her sibling how to behave. Soon, the siblings want out of this game because the teacher is too bossy and opinionated. In response, Katerina becomes verbally aggressive and critical of her siblings. When you intervene, Katerina justifies her behavior with an adult sounding explanation and a little bit of attitude. You laugh and think her behavior is hilarious. Be careful. *Precocious* is a word that comes to mind when describing this 2♣. You may be unintentionally reinforcing willfulness and insubordination. While a parent needs to allow this child to be who they are, they may also need to rein them in a bit. Otherwise, they may be fostering a child into an adolescent who is unafraid of waging a battle in every situation where there is disagreement. An adolescent 2♣ will surprise adults with how well they can talk around an adult and win an argument. They are quite capable of persevering with their point of view and convincing others to give up their alternative view.

Are you currently parenting a 2♣ adolescent who is constantly defensive and argumentative? While there are likely several reasons for this behavior, there are two elements that an adult should consider. The first element is a superficial one – 2♣ tend not to respond well to criticism. Even a comment by a parent such as, "Are you really going to wear that to school?" can set them off. The second element that underlies the superficial one is that 2♣ *struggle with fear*. When they receive criticism from another person, it equates to rejection. Remember the earlier reference to an unpaired sock being useless? Criticism can make a 2♣ feel useless. This feeling may trigger anger and argument. 2♣ tend to respond better when adults use *"I feel" statements.* "I feel" statements allow a person to speak with assertiveness without accusing the other person to blame. In turn, a person receiving the statement is less likely to be defensive. I feel statements have three parts: a description of the behavior ("When you..."), a person's feelings ("I feel..."), and the effect of the behavior ("because..."). Let's consider an example. Imagine you are a parent of a twelve-year-old 2♣ boy who frequently practices soccer with friends after school in your front yard. One day your son nearly gets hit by a car because he was chasing after an errant soccer ball. Applying an "I feel" statement to this scenario, a parent would say, "When you chase after the soccer ball into the street, I feel worried because a person in a car might not see you and then hit you. Can we talk about a way to solve this?" Another strategy to try is to help them channel their love of argument into something constructive, such as being a member of a debate team. Or redirect their anger into physical activity of some kind. Without strategies such as this, a 2♣ may reinforce an argumentative behavior over time, and they can be difficult to parent. If this situation already exists and the quarreling seems extreme, family therapy may be needed.

If you are a parent of a 2♣, be on the lookout for fear being expressed in other ways. For instance, a 2♣ toddler may be afraid of the dark. Even older 2♣ may exhibit fears or phobias. An adolescent 2♣ may hate to swallow large pills or get a shot at the doctor's office. As a parent, take these fears seriously as they are real for your child. Brain research in childhood trauma has shed a lot of light on what happens to children when they experience fear. The body responds to fear by adopting a *fight or flight* reaction and releasing chemicals that cause intense feelings and physical symptoms. For instance, a child may feel sick to their stomach. Their heart may race. Wanting to avoid these feelings, they overreact to the things that trigger them and engage in bad behavior. This explains why some 2♣ respond to fear by acting argumentative. As such, 2♣ benefit when adults help them become aware of and confront their fears. To be effective, adults should help a child start this process with minor fears before dealing with major fears. Success with minor fears holds the potential to internally motivate a 2♣ to face major fears.

Let's look at an example of how an adult might respond to a situation that involves a child experiencing fear. Pretend you are a parent of a four-year-old 2♣ boy named Matthew. Matthew's preschool teacher has contacted you explaining that Matthew refused to complete his lessons during the week. The teacher describes how they are spending the next several weeks learning about animals and shapes using a circus theme. At home, when Matthew is calm, you ask him about the lessons. You learn that his refusal to participate is because he fears clowns. You validate Matthew's fears and try to understand the whole story. In asking questions, you discover Matthew's older brother allowed him to watch a movie in which an evil clown was killing people. Knowing the cause of Matthew's fear, you may be tempted to ask the teacher to excuse your child from these lessons. Instead, provide your child with an opportunity to face their fear with you as their support. Use children's books to help this child discuss their fears. I recommend *You Can Face Your Fears* by Daniel Kenney. The main character, Henry, talks about things that are scary to him and how he overcomes his fears. The book also includes tips for a parent on how to discuss fears with a child. Then, co-create a plan. Explain to Matthew that the purpose of clowns in a circus is to create laughter. Suggest watching a short YouTube video showing real clowns and if he laughs, you will treat him to ice cream. If a 2♣ does not learn how to manage fears when they are young, as an adolescent they may express fears through anxiety, hypochondria, or argumentative behavior. If you are a parent of a 2♣ in this situation, it would be helpful to teach them what fear does to the brain. You can find kid-friendly video explanations of this topic on the Internet. Alternatively, try calming aromatherapy or essential with these 2♣. Certain essential oils, like lavender, have been shown to positively impact the limbic system which controls emotional behaviors such as fear and anxiety.

Summary of Higher and Lower Personality Traits

Higher: Witty, intelligent, physical beauty and grace, great conversationalist, detail oriented.

Lower: Argumentative, sarcastic, fearful, precocious, opinionated, defensive, hypochondriac.

Childhood Influence Mercury Cards
It is common knowledge that a child's personality is most malleable during the formative years – from birth to eight years of age. In the Destiny Card system, the Mercury Cards in a Birth Card's Life Spread reveal influences a child with this Birth Card will experience between birth through age 12. As such, a child's Mercury Cards must be considered so an adult can nurture a child from a place of awareness and work with them from where a child is at in their development. A 2♣ child has the following Mercury Cards: **K♣, 9♥, and 2♠**. These cards may represent people who are influential during this child's early life. The K♣ may mean there is an influential father who is likely a Club Birth or Planetary Ruling Card. Alternatively, outside of any specific person associated with these three cards, the basic meanings of these cards describe experiences that may be impactful during this child's formative years. These cards suggest 2♣ have the mental potential to achieve in school and enjoy collaborating with others. They may experience an early emotional loss or disappointment that has long-lasting impacts. As one example, divorce or separation from a parent may emotionally impact them.

Potential Callings / Vocations by Zodiac Sign

May 20 – Gemini: K♣ Planetary Ruling Card
With the influence of communicative Gemini, these 2♣ possess a double dose of skill in conversation. They can be a successful promotional speaker, speech writer, lecturer, social and digital media manager, public relations specialist, attorney, or politician.

June 28 – Cancer: 7♠ Planetary Ruling Card

Less gifted in gab and self-esteem due to their 7♠ Planetary Ruling Card, these 2♣ prefer occupations in health care, science, music, literature, or art.

July 26 – Leo: 2♣ Planetary Ruling Card

In love with the spotlight, these 2♣ can do well as an actor, director, or film producer. Those that demand a leadership position can be successful leading a business or institution (especially in banking or government).

August 24 – Virgo: K♣ Planetary Ruling Card

Interested in the home, these 2♣ do well at selling home products, from furniture to art to home audio and media systems. More introverted than other 2♣, these individuals may prefer jobs where they take directions from others. They can do well as a system engineer, coder, or information technology technician.

September 22 – Virgo or Libra: K♣ or J♦ Planetary Ruling Card

Having a visionary nature, these 2♣ do well as a musician, artist, inventor, attorney, teacher, or architect. With the power of their King or Jack Planetary Ruling Cards, some desire to improve common welfare and can lead in politics or humanitarian causes.

October 20 – Libra: J♦ Planetary Ruling Card

These Libra ruled 2♣ hold gifts in diplomacy, so they can make a fine ambassador, customer service representative, mediator, or counselor. Those who prefer creative expression due to their J♦ Planetary Ruling Card can succeed in painting, writing, teaching or as a marketing and advertising professional.

November 18 – Scorpio: 4♥ and 6♠ Planetary Ruling Cards

These intense 2♣ can be successful at anything they set their minds to do. They can be a successful attorney, politician, or business leader. Their potential to be famous is high.

December 16 – Sagittarius: 4♦ Planetary Ruling Card

Equally interested in being behind or in the limelight, these 2♣ can be successful as an attorney, financial advisor or broker, writer, researcher, scientist, or politician. Those that love the sea can work with the coast guard.

Famous 2♣

Sandra Bullock, actor – 7/26/1964
Elon Musk, inventor – 6/28/1971
John Cusack, actor – 6/28/1966
John Elway, football player – 6/28/1960
Kamala Harris, vice-president of the United States – 10/20/1964
Jane Austen, writer – 12/16/1775

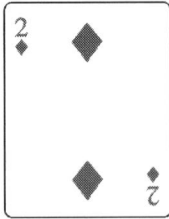

Welcome to the world of the relational 2♦!

2♦ = Connection through values and money

According to the Destiny Card system, souls chronologically experience God's lessons across 52 life incarnations. (Think of these as the universe's lessons if this aligns more with your beliefs.) The Birth Card each soul is born into determines the order and type of lessons a soul experiences. When you examine a Birth Card, you will notice it displays a suit of either a Heart, Club, Diamond, or Spade. This suit is significant because it represents the gifts a person born into this suit will possess and how they will direct their energies to learn lessons in their current life incarnation. A Heart Birth Card retains gifts and experiences life lessons around love and relationships. A Club Birth Card holds capabilities and experiences life lessons in their ability to communicate and absorb knowledge. A Diamond Birth Card possesses talents and experiences life lessons around money and values. And finally, a Spade Birth Card manifests gifts and experiences life lessons in work and health. Souls progress through incarnations and life lessons beginning as Hearts, moving on to Clubs, then Diamonds, and finally as Spades. Therefore, individuals born as Heart Cards are the youngest souls and individuals born as Spades Cards are the oldest souls.

In addition, the number on a Birth Card is equally meaningful as souls sequentially experience life lessons beginning as an Ace and culminating with lessons as a King. In the case of all Two Birth Cards, the number two connotes a pairing. And the word *pair* implies something that has two parts joined for a combined function. For instance, think of a pair of socks. Two socks function well at keeping your feet warm. Yet, what happens when you wash laundry and discover one sock is missing? Having only one sock negates the function of this garment. If you are like most people, you eventually throw out this unpaired sock, finding it useless. This analogy explains the energy behind all Two Birth Cards. You see, they experience life with a driving need to join forces with someone else or risk feeling useless. **It makes sense, then, that a 2♦ child's purpose, gifts, and life lessons revolve around creating *connections* with others. And due to being a Diamond, this child will learn lessons through connections around *values* and *money-making*.**

How to Nurture the Temperament and Personality of a 2♦ Child

From a young age, 2♦ tend to demand attention. And a 2♦ toddler may become rebellious if their demands for attention are not met. Let's consider an example. Let's say you are a parent of a 2♦ toddler named Sam who has told you he is hungry for lunch. While preparing lunch, your cell phone rings. The call is from a friend who you have not spoken to in a while and so you know the call would likely take some time. If you take the call and attention is directed away from Sam, do not be surprised if Sam constantly interrupts you during your call. Some 2♦ may engage in a temper tantrum to control your attention. In this situation, it would be better to let the call go to voicemail and then chat with your friend later. Far better, make a deal with your

2♦ because they respond well to negotiation. Beginning around the age of two, an adult can begin teaching a child about the concept of *taking turns*. There are children's books and videos on the Internet that can assist adults in teaching this concept. I recommend *Llama Llama Time to Share* by Anna Dewdney. This book explores the feelings and consequences that arise when one friend refuses to share toys with a new friend. It may also be helpful for an adult to explain the concept of taking turns within different situations with a 2♦. Going back to the phone call scenario, you would explain to Sam that a friend has called, but it is Sam's turn; his time to get lunch and eat together. Once lunch is over, you intend to call this friend back, and give them a turn with your attention. Therefore, you expect Sam to play without interrupting your phone call. Finally, plan what activities Sam can do while you are talking to your friend.

As a 2♦ gets older, adults should encourage them to enhance their gift of *negotiation*. Let's look at an example. Imagine you are a parent of a ten-year-old 2♦ girl named Zerlina. Zerlina loves to paint. The home refrigerator is completely covered with many of Zerlina's creations. Making new pieces of art, Zerlina decides she wants to sell her artwork. Zerlina's parents offer to help. Dad sets up a table and chairs on the sidewalk in front of the house. Mom helps make signs, display the paintings, and discuss pricing. Zerlina decides each item will be priced at $2.00. While Zerlina's Mom suggests how to communicate with potential buyers, Zerlina is expected to transact business on her own. The first customer is a female neighbor who is walking her dog. The neighbor can't decide between three pieces and takes out a five-dollar bill. Zerlina quickly evaluates the situation and says, "I'll give you a special. All three for $5.00." The deal is made, and Zerlina is well on her way to developing a 2♦'s greatest gift — financial deal-making.

Two additional traits you may notice in a young 2♦ is that they are highly *independent* and *creative*. As such, they will want to develop their own sense of style. For instance, this is the four-year-old child who wants to pick out and wear their own style of clothing. If you are a parent of a 2♦, you may be inviting a battle with your child if you demand they wear clothing you picked out. Even as adolescents, these 2♦ often refuse to wear what everybody else is wearing. They prefer to create their own unique look and they do not care what others think. As a bonus many 2♦ possess physical beauty, which means they make their own style look good! As such, they are often *trendsetters*. Encourage this kind of behavior as a 2♦ can easily apply their creativity into other areas of their life, including hobbies that can lead to a profession. These professions can include being a musician, painter, actor, or writer. Also, sign a 2♦ up for theater and drama classes if they show interest because they can succeed as a performer. Allow them to join many clubs and after school activities. Most 2♦ love socializing and can juggle participation in numerous activities.

The source of all these previously mentioned traits is rooted in the fact that 2♦ possess a *transactional personality*. A transactional personality involves a person who acts only if there is something to gain. Adults working with a 2♦ should leverage this trait. 2♦ are ambitious and will work hard to get what it is that they desire. If you are a parent of a 2♦, this means they often respond well to attaching monetary rewards to bringing home good grades from school. Rewards that combine time with friends, such as pairs of movie or concert tickets can be motivating to a 2♦. In school, a 2♦ will achieve when they perceive value in doing so. A teacher can capitalize on a 2♦'s need for and value towards having a connection with others. Therefore, a wonderful way to nurture a 2♦ is to provide them with *cooperative learning* opportunities. Cooperative learning is a teaching approach in which students are put into small groups to complete an assigned task. Such a task includes socially constructing meaning and learning. And because cooperative learning involves students sharing the workload and the teacher assigns a group grade amongst group members, a 2♦ tends to view such an approach as a fair deal.

When a person has a transactional personality, they expect reciprocation, and this tends to be an area where a 2♦ has lessons to learn. While reciprocation tends to be predictable when it comes to money, that may not be the case with other things of value. Take, for example, relationships. 2♦ value relationships but relationships can be complicated and unpredictable. A 2♦ is most challenged when a relationship does not reciprocate connection. For some 2♦, this challenge may be heightened due to abandonment from a parent during their youth. Because of this experience a 2♦ may act impulsive or selfish. These 2♦ often have difficulty putting themselves in other people's shoes because they are apt to see only their own needs. As an example, if a 2♦ child always wants the first turn on the slide at the playground or the last word in an argument, they may be operating on the lower side of their Birth Card. If this is the case for a 2♦ you are caring for, it may be helpful to read about the A♦ Birth Card because there are uncanny similarities between an A♦ and the 2♦.

Therefore, it is important to nurture a young 2♦ by not triggering abandonment issues. Let's consider an example. Imagine you are a mother of a five-year-old 2♦ named Megan. You are a single parent, having raised Megan on your own after her father left. Megan has been invited to celebrate a friend's birthday at Chuck E. Cheeses. Megan is excited about the party because she loves the novelty of the place and spending time with her friends. After arriving at the party, you tell Megan you both will need to leave in an hour because you have a dental appointment. When it is time to leave, Megan is not happy. The gift opening part of the party has not happened yet. When you insist on leaving, Megan gets argumentative. You say, "Fine. I'm leaving right now" and you start walking toward the exit. Megan immediately breaks down crying and begrudgingly goes with you. That worked. Parenting accomplished. This type of strategy to control your child is the worst thing to do with a 2♦ due to their *fear of abandonment*. While this may work short term, long-term this kind of behavior will likely become a trigger for a 2♦ that can negatively affect their ability to sustain healthy relationships later in life. In this scenario, it would have been far better to have discussed the dentist appointment ahead of time and negotiated a solution with Megan. Perhaps another parent could drive Megan home after the party. While negotiating, if you can convince your 2♦ they got the better end of the bargain, this is parenting accomplished.

Summary of Higher and Lower Personality Traits

Higher: Attractive, independent, wheeler-dealer, discern quality well, strong work ethic.

Lower: Fixed ideals about love, abandonment issues, argumentative, selfish.

Childhood Influence Mercury Cards

It is common knowledge that a child's personality is most malleable during the formative years – from birth to eight years of age. In the Destiny Card system, the Mercury Cards in a Birth Card's Life Spread reveal influences a child with this Birth Card will experience between birth through age 12. As such, a child's Mercury Cards must be considered so an adult can nurture a child from a place of awareness and work with them from where a child is at in their development. The Mercury Cards in a 2♦'s Life Spread reveal influences a child with this Birth Card will experience between birth through age 12. A 2♦ child has the following Mercury Cards: **J♠, 9♣, and 7♣**. These cards may represent people who are influential during this child's early life. The J♠ may mean there is an influential father or brother who is likely a Spade Birth or Planetary Ruling Card. Alternatively, outside of any specific person associated with these three cards, the basic meaning of these cards describes experiences that may be impactful during this child's formative years. These cards suggest a young 2♦ may have to navigate a difficult family situation in which they feel ripped off (possibly abandonment). These feelings may produce a negative mindset that in turn results in depression.

Potential Callings / Vocations by Zodiac Sign

January 25 – Aquarius: 10♦ Planetary Ruling Card

These analytical 2♦ possess gifts in mathematics and understanding mechanisms. They can do well as a real estate broker, appraiser, manufacturer, musician, mechanical engineer, physician, or scientific researcher.

February 23 – Pisces: 8♣ Planetary Ruling Card

These intuitive Pisces are skilled at diagnosis and can make an excellent physician or healer. Loving the freedom of expression, many can succeed in the entertainment industry. Some can become famous due to the power inherent to their 8♠ Planetary Ruling Card.

March 21 – Pisces or Aries: 8♣ or 6♦ Planetary Ruling Card

The influence of Mars in these 2♦ makes them brilliant promoters and so many may enjoy occupations in publishing, writing, marketing, or advertising.

April 19 – Aries: 6♦ Planetary Ruling Card

A more restless and procrastinating Aries due to their 6♦ Planetary Ruling Card, these 2♦ need activity in their work. They can make a good salesperson or appraiser. Those that love travel may prefer to work in the entertainment industry or work as a flight attendant.

May 17 – Taurus: 8♣ Planetary Ruling Card

A more grounded 2♦ due to their 8♣ Planetary Ruling Card, these individuals enjoy traditional occupations such as a teacher, banker, or stockbroker. Some like to share their positive health or spiritual practices as a club or fitness leader, yoga instructor, or Sunday school teacher.

June 15 – Gemini: J♠ Planetary Ruling Card

Having a keen eye for quality, these 2♦ can succeed by selling real estate, jewelry, art, or their keen sense of style or fashion (e.g., interior decorator or personal shopper). Those preferring jobs that utilize their good communication skills may do well as an attorney, writer, or public speaker.

July 13 – Cancer: 4♣ Planetary Ruling Card

Embracing the nurturing aspect of Cancer, these 2♦ can do well as teachers or in careers related to the home (e.g., real estate broker, gardener, landscape architect, decorator, or cook).

August 11 – Leo: 2♦ Planetary Ruling Card

Leos love the limelight, and these 2♦ can literally reach the stars. Many are drawn to and do exceptionally well on the stage as an actor, musician, model, composer, or politician.

September 9 – Virgo: J♠ Planetary Ruling Card

These detail-oriented 2♦ can do well as an attorney (particularly dealing with contract or corporate law), real estate broker, or business leader. With the influence of Virgo, they should take care not to be overly perfectionistic in work.

October 7 – Libra: 8♣ Planetary Ruling Card

With the influence of Libra, these 2♦ love art and beauty, and so they can do well in theater, writing (especially poetry), art, or filmmaking. Those preferring a statelier audience can do well as a politician or pastor.

November 5 – Scorpio: 6♦ and A♥ Planetary Ruling Cards

With the influence of Scorpio, these intensely magnetic 2♦ can succeed as an actor. They love the challenge of getting into character. Some desire a profession that requires deep thinking (e.g., attorney, researcher, or diplomat).

December 3 – Sagittarius: 4♠ Planetary Ruling Card

Artistic and social expression are important to these 2♦, making them an excellent critic, art dealer, writer, or musician.

Famous 2♦

Harrison Ford, actor – 7/13/1942
Julianne Moore, actor – 12/3/1960
Alicia Keys, musician – 1/25/1981
Chris Helmsworth, actor – 8/11/1983
Kevin Jonas, musician – 11/5/1987
Hugh Grant, actor – 9/9/1960

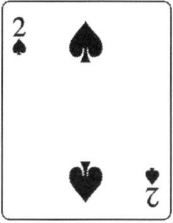

Welcome to the world of the relational 2♠!

2♠ = Connections in work and health

According to the Destiny Card system, souls chronologically experience God's lessons across 52 life incarnations. (Think of these as the universe's lessons if this aligns more with your beliefs.) The Birth Card each soul is born into determines the order and type of lessons a soul experiences. When you examine a Birth Card, you will notice it displays a suit of either a Heart, Club, Diamond, or Spade. This suit is significant because it represents the gifts a person born into this suit will possess and how they will direct their energies to learn lessons in their current life incarnation. A Heart Birth Card retains gifts and experiences life lessons around love and relationships. A Club Birth Card holds capabilities and experiences life lessons in their ability to communicate and absorb knowledge. A Diamond Birth Card possesses talents and experiences life lessons around money and values. And finally, a Spade Birth Card manifests gifts and experiences life lessons in work and health. Souls progress through incarnations and life lessons beginning as Hearts, moving on to Clubs, then Diamonds, and finally as Spades. Therefore, individuals born as Heart Cards are the youngest souls and individuals born as Spades Cards are the oldest souls.

In addition, the number on a Birth Card is equally meaningful as souls sequentially experience life lessons beginning as an Ace and culminating with lessons as a King. In the case of all Two Birth Cards, the number two connotes a pairing. The word *pair* implies something that has two parts joined for a combined function. For instance, think of a pair of socks. Two socks function well at keeping your feet warm. Yet, what happens when you wash laundry and discover one sock is missing? Having only one sock negates the function of this garment. If you are like most people, you eventually throw out this unpaired sock, finding it useless. This analogy explains the energy behind all Two Birth Cards. You see, they experience life with a driving need to join forces with someone else or risk feeling useless. **It makes sense, then, that a 2♠ child's purpose, gifts, and life lessons revolve around creating *connections* with others. And due to being a Spade, this child will learn lessons around *health* and *work* connections.**

How to Nurture the Temperament and Personality of a 2♠ Child

As the 2♠ is also known as the 'friendship' card, school is like a candy shop for them because it presents so many potential friends. As such, 2♠ are excellent candidates for preschool. They easily acclimate to school as they are old souls and mature for their age. If you are a teacher of a 2♠, it will be important to keep them busy or they may become bored and daydream in class. Of course, they will be dreaming about all the fun they could be having with their friends! Assign them roles that allow them to demonstrate their gift of *collaboration*. For instance, you can pair them with an English-language-learner or a student with a learning disability. Praise them when they help others in their learning. This pairing will benefit both students so long as harmony is maintained. You see, a young 2♠ often takes their role of helping very seriously.

And they can hold fixed ideas about how to do things in life. These ideas are usually good. However, a 2♠ may come across as too controlling for certain students. They have wonderful intentions. If these 2♠ are faced with a consistently uncooperative partner and they get fixed in their ideas, they may act *stubborn* and *dogmatic*.

A higher expressing 2♠ will make an excellent role model in a classroom. Assign these 2♠ other roles that highlight their ability to cooperate and care for others. Designate them as a Friendship Ambassador for their grade level; someone who shows new students around. Ask them to lead *cooperative learning* activities. Cooperative learning is a teaching approach in which students are put into small groups to complete an assigned task. In fact, cooperative learning represents an environment in which a 2♠ can thrive for a couple of reasons. 2♠ learn best when they can socially construct meaning in small groups. You see, 2♠ need to share and bounce off their ideas with others. This is easier to do within a small group than within a whole class discussion or when a teacher uses a lecture to teach. Also, 2♠ are *logical thinkers*. As such, they benefit from *problem or project-based learning* approaches which rely on cooperative or group learning. Problem-based learning is a teaching methodology that uses real-life problems to drive student learning of concepts that are related to solving problems. Likewise, project-based learning uses real-life problems, but students are also expected to demonstrate learning through the development of a product or presentation.

Do you have over 500 friends on Facebook? A 2♠ adolescent does. If you are a parent of a 2♠, you may need to talk to them about social media, as they do not always have common sense in this area. Wanting to be friends with everyone, they will accept friend requests from strangers. If they are not into social media, they still have many friends and are popular at school. They have just as many girlfriends as boyfriends, too. Physical and mental activities with friends will be a top priority for an adolescent 2♠. They often love playing video games, listening to music, and attending events – with as many friends as possible. As a parent, assist a 2♠ in coordinating gatherings and activities. Volunteer to be the driver and host events for them. They will love you for it. In addition, this collaboration can position you well when a 2♠ is an adolescent. You see, they love inviting their friends over to play or hang out and you get to eavesdrop about everything going on in their life.

If you need to discipline a 2♠, because they are logical thinkers, it makes sense to implement *logical consequences*. Logical consequences represent a discipline approach that provides respect and focuses on how to learn from mistakes rather than enacting punishment. Let's consider an example. Let's say you are a second-grade teacher, and you have a 2♠ boy named Matthew in your class. During a science lesson, students are simulating the process of pollination using baking soda to represent the pollen. Matthew is so excited to do the activity, he runs across the room to get his lab materials. In doing so, he runs into Katy, who is holding a cup of baking soda. When the baking soda splatters onto Katy's sweater, Katy screams. You walk over and consider telling Matthew to sit in time out because you have told him many times not to run in class. However, that reaction would be punishment. Instead, you address the situation by saying, "Katy, I see you are upset because your sweater got messy but let me talk with Matthew and then we'll figure out how to help you." Then, you privately ask Matthew to explain what happened. You remind Matthew of classroom expectations and ask him to provide ideas on how to help Katy clean her sweater. Matthew cleans off Katy's sweater and apologizes to her. Not only will you likely see a 2♠ respond well to this kind of classroom management, but you may also notice them applying similar techniques when they experience a conflict with another student. They are quick learners when it comes to cooperation.

Because being alone is their greatest fear, many 2♠ tend to hide their true feelings out of fear of rejection. These 2♠ often compensate by adopting passive-aggressive behaviors, expressing their feelings or aggressions indirectly. For a 2♠ sarcasm tends to be the most common form of passive-aggressive behavior. As an example, let's say you are the mother of a 2♠ fourteen-year-old boy named Liam. Liam loves being part of the school basketball team. During the first couple games in the season, you notice Liam is the teammate who encourages and uplifts the whole team. You mention this to your husband, and he decides to join you in attending the games. Weeks later you ask Liam if he is excited about an upcoming game. Liam says, "Yeah. Whatever." You go to the game and are surprised to see a different version of your child playing basketball, that is, a less sure, and more passive version. What is up? Then, you notice your husband is yelling out critical comments toward Liam. You decide to have a talk with Liam. You describe the difference in Liam's attitude, and he says, "Well, I can't be as perfect as everyone else in this family." Ah, sarcasm – a sure sign that you have hit a nerve. 2♠ do not thrive under constant disapproval because they are innately hard on themselves. When Liam's father is acting like Mr. Disapproval and it is hurtful, Liam has difficulty communicating his feelings to his father. Instead, he acts passive and communicates his feelings in covert ways through sarcasm. Therefore, an important way to nurture a 2♠ is to teach them how to express their true feelings in a safe setting. This process should begin when there is conflict between you and them. As a parent it is helpful to start these conversations with, "It's okay if you are feeling upset with me about..." Above all, make sure you are calm if they communicate that they are upset with you over something you did. Verbalize forgiveness and your unconditional love. Model how to express unpleasant feelings with others in front of them and emphasize that the relationship was maintained. Then, encourage a 2♠ to speak their truth with others.

Summary of Higher and Lower Personality Traits

Higher: Popular, logical, cooperative, collaborative, strong will, excellent spouse/parent.

Lower: Dogmatic, prone to illness, controlling, indecisive, passive aggressive.

Childhood Influence Mercury Cards

It is common knowledge that a child's personality is most malleable during the formative years – from birth to eight years of age. In the Destiny Card system, the Mercury Cards in a Birth Card's Life Spread reveal influences a child with this Birth Card will experience between birth through age 12. As such, a child's Mercury Cards must be considered so an adult can nurture a child from a place of awareness and work with them from where a child is at in their development. The Mercury Cards in a 2♦'s Life Spread reveal influences a child with this Birth Card will experience between birth through age 12. The Mercury Card in a 2♠'s Life Spread reveal influences a child with this Birth Card will experience from birth through age 12. A 2♠

child has the following Mercury Cards: **8♥, 9♦, and 7♠**. These cards may represent people who are influential during this child's early life. Alternatively, outside of any specific person associated with these three cards, the basic meanings of these cards describe experiences that may be impactful during this child's formative years. These cards suggest a young 2♠ will be charming and easily attracts friends. They may experience limitations due to family finances or restrictions due to a health issue.

Potential Callings / Vocations by Zodiac Sign

January 12 – Capricorn: 10♠ Planetary Ruling Card

These Capricorn 2♠ are ambitious and hardworking. While most Two Birth Cards prefer to work with others, this individual is an exception to the rule. They may prefer to work for themselves. They can do well as a writer, business owner, politician, or independent contractor.

February 10 – Aquarius: 8♦ Planetary Ruling Card

These 2♠ enjoy working with others in service-oriented work (e.g., pastor, government worker, or counselor). Some prefer making more money for their efforts due to their 8♦ Planetary Ruling Card; so, these individuals may lean toward careers in business or acting.

March 8 – Pisces: K♠ Planetary Ruling Card

Having a disposition toward service, these 2♠ like to serve in the navy, coast guard, or work as a diplomat. They can also do well in business, particularly working with foreigners.

April 6 – Aries: 6♠ Planetary Ruling Card

With the influence of the procrastinating 6♠ Planetary Ruling Card, these 2♠ can get into ruts and refuse to make changes. If they can fight this tendency, they can do well in artistic or inventive occupations (e.g., painter, writer, journalist, or conductor).

May 4 – Taurus: 6♠ Planetary Ruling Card

These grounded 2♠ love nature and the home, and therefore jobs related to these areas (e.g., construction, forestry, or a business with home-related or natural products). Also, they can do well as an actor or entertainer.

June 2 – Gemini: 8♥ Planetary Ruling Card

With communicative Mercury as their ruler, these 2♠ can succeed in banking, writing, accounting, journalism, research, or as a television correspondent.

Famous 2♠
Audrey Hepburn, actor – 5/4/1929
Lance Bass, singer – 5/4/1979
Jeff Bezos, entrepreneur – 1/12/1964
Randy Travis, singer – 5/4/1959
Abby Wambach, soccer player – 6/2/1980

Chapter 6

Descriptions of the Three Birth Cards

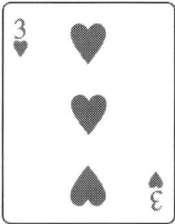

Welcome to the world of the indecisive 3♥!

3♥ = Variety in love

According to the Destiny Card system, souls chronologically experience God's lessons across 52 life incarnations. (Think of these as the universe's lessons if this aligns more with your beliefs.) The Birth Card each soul is born into determines the order and type of lessons a soul experiences. When you examine a Birth Card, you will notice it displays a suit of either a Heart, Club, Diamond, or Spade. This suit is significant because it represents the gifts a person born into this suit will possess and how they will direct their energies to learn lessons in their current life incarnation. A Heart Birth Card retains gifts and experiences life lessons around love and relationships. A Club Birth Card holds capabilities and experiences life lessons in their ability to communicate and absorb knowledge. A Diamond Birth Card possesses talents and experiences life lessons around money and values. And finally, a Spade Birth Card manifests gifts and experiences life lessons in work and health. Souls progress through incarnations and life lessons beginning as Hearts, moving on to Clubs, then Diamonds, and finally as Spades. Therefore, individuals born as Heart Cards are the youngest souls and individuals born as Spades Cards are the oldest souls.

In addition, the number on a Birth Card is equally meaningful as souls sequentially experience life lessons beginning as an Ace and culminating with lessons as a King. A Three Birth Card is one of many odd numbered Birth Cards. And odd numbered cards have more difficulty than even numbered cards in dealing with their energies. Not only do they struggle with balancing their internal energy, but odd numbered cards also have the extra burden of trying to figure out how to direct that energy outward into the world. A person associated with a Three Birth Card struggles the most with managing an imbalance of energy as they are experiencing their first life incarnation in a suit as an odd numbered card. (Ace Birth Cards direct a 'one' energy, so they do not experience imbalance.) **It makes sense, then, that a 3♥ child's purpose, gifts, and life lessons revolve around an *imbalance of energy* in their life. And, due to being a Heart, this child will learn lessons through managing an imbalance of energy around *love* and *relationships*.**

How to Nurture the Temperament and Personality of a 3♥ Child

Because 3♥ possess a heightened acquisition of and response to emotional stimuli, they are like emotional sponges. A household where there is a lot of argument is toxic for a young 3♥. For example, parents of a 3♥ who decide to stay together for the sake of a 3♥ child but are constantly fighting is not a good idea. If being part of a discordant family is unavoidable, a young 3♥ will need support in managing their emotions. You see, not only is it common for a 3♥ to absorb a lot of emotion, but their emotions tend to behave like fluids. Fluids, like water, have no definite shape or volume. As such, they are difficult to manage unless they are contained. This said, having a fluidity of emotions has advantages and disadvantages. A disadvantage is that a 3♥ can have difficulty containing their emotions and can be perceived as being extremely moody. One way an adult can nurture a 3♥ is to help them learn how to channel their emotions into positive expressions. This process ideally should begin at a young age. A 3♥ child needs to express what they are feeling, especially when they are experiencing difficult emotions. Children's books can assist adults in helping a child with this, such as using the book *Listening to My Body*, by Gabi Garcia. This book helps children identify and voice their emotions, especially when they are feeling overwhelmed. Search the Internet for other books that target the specific emotions your child is having difficulty voicing or managing.

Once a 3♥ has learned to manage their emotions, they should learn how to direct their emotions in advantageous ways. Most often a 3♥ will do this by expressing themselves through artistic behaviors. These 3♥ children are often recognized as being *creative* and gifted in *self-expression*. In fact, many 3♥ can make a career out of art, writing, acting, or music. Their ability to tap into a dynamic array of emotions gives them a clear advantage in the dramatic arts. Some of Hollywood's finest actors and actresses are 3♥. Another advantage of being self-expressive is that 3♥ enjoy relating to many different people regardless of their background. You see, they love meeting new people and being exposed to the mosaic of emotions different people emote. If you are a teacher of a 3♥, you can leverage this trait by pairing a 3♥ with an English-language-learner, someone who is from another country and learning to speak English.

In a school setting, 3♥ should be allowed educational experiences that allow social mingling and artistic expression. If you are a teacher of a 3♥, provide them with *alternative assessments*. Alternative assessments allow students to demonstrate what they learned in ways other than traditional testing. Alternative assessment may also be referred to as authentic, performance, or informal assessment. For instance, let's say you are a fifth-grade teacher working with a 3♥ student named Aaron. In science, your students are learning about ways communities are protecting Earth's resources and the environment. To assess this concept, you have assigned students into groups of four and provided them with a choice. They can create either a poem, rap song, or video commercial to present an environmental problem and how one community is solving it. Aaron will benefit from this assignment as it allows him self-expression and the ability to work with others. This is not to say a 3♥ thrives with having choices in all areas of their life. Case in point – too many choices when it comes to relationships can trigger indecision for a 3♥. Going back to the science assignment, perhaps you also decided to allow students to choose who they work with. If so, Aaron may struggle with picking a group. You may need to help him make this decision.

If you are a parent of a 3♥, you may notice they like to interact with an assortment of friends. Help accommodate this by allowing them to participate in a variety of group activities such as summer camp, marching band, choir, a theater group, or a community project. Do not forget to expose your 3♥ to art classes, theater, dance, music, and creative writing to complement and foster their visionary self-expression. Allow them to jump from one kind of activity to another. If they find an activity that resonates with their soul and that they want to stick with, they will let you know. Some enjoy physical activity so encourage team sports. Interestingly, 3♥ regardless of gender prefer female to male coaches and teachers. Perhaps, this is because females can better manage and not reject their emotional sensitivities. Keep this in mind in the event your 3♥ conflicts with an adult overseeing them.

The poet, Robert Frost, have a 3♥ Planetary Ruling Card expressed this card's mindset well when he wrote, "Two roads diverged in a yellow wood, And sorry I could not travel both…" Three Birth Cards are born with a keen awareness of the many exciting choices in life – concerning things, ideas, work, and people. In real life, most of us know it is not always possible or reasonable to experience two things at the same time, like two forks in the road. Sometimes one must choose between different things and be okay with their choice. Three Birth Cards see this differently. They want to keep what they have, while at the same time pursuing what they do not have. For a 3♥, they want to have their cake and eat it too when it comes to love and relationships.

As a parent of an adolescent 3♥, do not be surprised to find them struggling with love and relationships. While experimentation in love is typical during adolescence, a 3♥ may experiment with sex at an earlier age than what their parents would want. This is a child who would benefit from having early conversations about what it means to be sexually responsible. In addition, a 3♥ may act out the 'grass is greener' syndrome when it comes to dating and relationships. This means that even if things are going well in their current relationship, they have a lingering feeling that there is someone better out there. Regrettably, this attitude in love can lead them into sticky and hurtful situations. Some date or forge relationships with multiple people. If acting from their lower traits, they may lie to others to juggle these relationships. Such behavior may cause them to have trouble maintaining long-term relationships as an adult. Another manifestation common to a 3♥ due to their need for diversity is that they may experiment with their sexual identity. As such, they may identify themselves across a spectrum of all genders and sexualities such as lesbian, gay, bisexual, trans, queer, questioning, intersex, asexual, aromantic, pansexual, or polysexual (LGBTQIAA+).

Summary of Higher and Lower Personality Traits

Higher: Artistic, cheerful, charming, creative, risk-taker, flexible.

Lower: Moody, fickle, promiscuous, gossip, liar, resistance to commitment.

Childhood Influence Mercury Cards
It is common knowledge that a child's personality is most malleable during the formative years – from birth to eight years of age. In the Destiny Card system, the Mercury Cards in a Birth Card's Life Spread reveal influences a child with this Birth Card will experience between birth through age 12. As such, a child's Mercury Cards must be considered so an adult can nurture a child from a place of awareness and work with them from where a child is at in their development. A 3♥ child has the following Mercury Cards: **A♣, 4♥, and 2♥.** Alternatively, outside of any specific person associated with these three cards, the basic meanings of these

cards describe experiences that may be impactful during this child's formative years. These cards suggest 3♥ are curious to learn new things and are unafraid of initiating relationships. They are fortunate to have a harmonious home environment and a close relationship with one member of their family.

Potential Callings / Vocations by Zodiac Sign

November 30 – Sagittarius: 5♣ Planetary Ruling Card
Found to be appealing to large audiences, these 3♥ can do well as an artist, entertainer, sports athlete, wedding planner, inspirational speaker, politician, or writer. They need to be careful not to earn and overspend.

December 28 – Capricorn: 3♦ Planetary Ruling Card
Due to having a 3♦ Planetary Ruling Card, these 3♥ are more serious and ambitious. They can succeed as an actor, musician, politician, business manager, or business owner.

Famous 3♥
John Legend, music producer/singer – 12/28/1978
Winston Churchill, politician – 11/30/1874
Denzel Washington, actor – 12/28/1954
Bo Jackson, baseball player – 11/30/1962
Maggie Smith, actress – 12/28/1934
Otto Wood, drummer – 12/28/1990

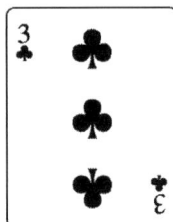

Welcome to the world of the indecisive 3♣!

3♣ = Diversity in communication and ideas

According to the Destiny Card system, souls chronologically experience God's lessons across 52 life incarnations. (Think of these as the universe's lessons if this aligns more with your beliefs.) The Birth Card each soul is born into determines the order and type of lessons a soul experiences. When you examine a Birth Card, you will notice it displays a suit of either a Heart, Club, Diamond, or Spade. This suit is significant because it represents the gifts a person born into this suit will possess and how they will direct their energies to learn lessons in their current life incarnation. A Heart Birth Card retains gifts and experiences life lessons around love and relationships. A Club Birth Card holds capabilities and experiences life lessons in their ability to communicate and absorb knowledge. A Diamond Birth Card possesses talents and experiences life lessons around money and values. And finally, a Spade Birth Card manifests gifts and experiences life lessons in work and health. Souls progress through incarnations and life lessons beginning as Hearts, moving on to Clubs, then Diamonds, and finally as Spades. Therefore, individuals born as Heart Cards are the youngest souls and individuals born as Spades Cards are the oldest souls.

In addition, the number on a Birth Card is equally meaningful as souls sequentially experience life lessons beginning as an Ace and culminating with lessons as a King. A Three Birth Card is one of many odd numbered Birth Cards. And odd numbered cards have more difficulty than even numbered cards in dealing with their energies. Not only do they struggle with balancing their internal energy, but odd numbered cards also have the extra burden of trying to figure out how to direct that energy outward into the world. A person associated with a Three Birth Card struggles the most with managing an imbalance of energy as they are experiencing their first life incarnation in a suit as an odd numbered card. (Ace Birth Cards direct a 'one' energy, so they do not experience imbalance.) **It makes sense, then, that a 3♣ child's purpose, gifts, and life lessons revolve around an *imbalance of energy* in their life. And, due to being a Club, this child will learn lessons through managing an imbalance of energy around *ideas* and *communication*.**

How to Nurture the Temperament and Personality of a 3♣ Child

3♣ possess a mind that is constantly overflowing with ideas and interests. This is the toddler a parent takes to the mall, and they refuse to stay in their stroller. If you don't let them out of the stroller, they try to chew through the harness! And if you allow them out of the stroller, they are hard to manage. They are easily distracted by various stimuli, and they may want to explore everything. Drawn to new interests, they will not take the time to fully explore one interest before moving on to the next one. You see, variety is the spice of life for a 3♣! As 3♣ grow older, this same behavior might be applied to other aspects of their life. If you are a parent of a 3♣, be on the lookout for them seeking variety – in food, clothing, hobbies, sports, friends, romantic partners, and daily activities. In school, they may frustrate you when their attention and efforts toward academics goes up and down like a yo-yo. Without practice in how to sustain focus, a young 3♣ may become a shallow learner who spreads their interests and ideas too far out. In doing so, they may dilute their talent and chances for success. To be clear, 3♣ struggle with an over-flowing mind and not impulsive behavior. Other adults may suggest they have attention deficit hyperactive disorder (ADHD). They do not. However, if they are allowed to jump from activity to activity willy-nilly, a 3♣ can develop impulsive tendencies over time.

From a young age, 3♣ often need help in managing their uncontrolled ideas and interests. For a possible solution, let's consider the actions of a juggler. Close your eyes and picture a juggler who is juggling three balls in the air. The key to this juggler's success is that they have learned to handle one ball at a time and apply short, but equal amounts of energy to each ball. Now imagine the juggler pushes one ball a bit too hard. The rhythm of the balls is upset. No problem. The juggler's muscle memory kicks in and they adjust their body in real time to retain control of the balls. In other words, this juggler has learned the skill of *balance*. In a similar way, a 3♣ can balance their overflowing ideas by focusing on one idea or activity at a time, breaking it into parts, and then applying short, but equal amounts of time and energy toward it. As an example, a single homework assignment should be broken up into smaller parts and a 3♣ should take mental breaks between each part. This way a 3♣ can enjoy some variation but also maintain focus on one activity. This means a great way to nurture a 3♣ is to teach them about *time management*. Purchase a planner for these 3♣ and show them how to use it. As a bonus, 3♣ will love planning because it helps them fit in more fun activities.

Clearly, if you are a parent of a young 3♣, you can see they can benefit from some structure and boundaries when pursuing interests. Set up rules regarding how long they should remain in one activity before moving on to a different one. Have them practice concentrating on small activities and in shorter amounts of time, and then gradually move toward larger activities and over longer amounts of time. Once a 3♣ has practiced managing their mental energy, adults working with them can provide less structure. In addition, it may benefit a 3♣ to engage in activities that teach concentration in fun ways such as karate, tai chi, yoga, dance, reading, origami making, or learning to play a musical instrument. To boost focus, older 3♣ may benefit from *background noise* or sounds a person is not explicitly listening to in the background. Typical background noise can be provided through playing music. Research has shown background noise not only can help some people with concentration, but it can also improve mood, energy levels, and task performance. It may also be prudent to limit activities for a 3♣ that hold the potential to shorten their attention span. This means you may need to monitor and limit a 3♣'s use of technology, as it may be particularly distracting for them. In fact, too much technology can hijack a 3♣'s creativity.

Speaking of creativity – a 3♣'s superpower is *creativity*. They have the heart and soul of an artist. They are truly the most *creative* of all the Birth Cards. Not only can a 3♣ analyze a variety of ideas simultaneously, but they can also combine them in original ways. 3♣ can easily synthesize ideas into new inventions and make a career using their imagination. Some 3♣ may want to take things apart to see how they work. In the field of engineering, this behavior is called *reverse engineering*. These 3♣ may apply their creativity to invent improved designs by doing just that. This same skillset can be applied to writing. In fact, many famous writers are 3♣. As an example, supernatural-fiction writer Stephen King is a 3♣. A 3♣ can imagine a climax or ending of a story. Then they work in reverse, writing it backwards and filling in all the details. You see, it is common for a 3♣ to work in a non-linear manner when completing a task. King claims to write like this and does so every single day. Not all writers can do this. But remember, a 3♣ can do this because of their overflowing ideas. King has described his writing process by saying he "throws up in the morning and cleans up in the afternoon." Clearly, King has learned how to manage his overflowing ideas.

The primary way to nurture a 3♣ is to encourage creative pursuits – such as playing instruments, writing stories or songs, or creating artwork. If this seems expensive to do, there are plenty of low-cost ways to expose your child to creative activities. For instance, take your 3♣ to garage sales. There are plenty of families that host garage sales to sell lightly used kits, games, and creative toys their children have outgrown. And your 3♣ will love to do garage sale hunting with you. They will enjoy meeting new people and the excitement of finding cool, new things to do. You see, with a need to experience diverse ideas, many 3♣ tend to be *social butterflies*. A social butterfly is not only a people person, but they tend to flutter from person to person just as a butterfly does. At an event like a birthday party, these 3♣ are in their happy place. They love to keep a busy social schedule so they may interact with a diverse and large number of people.

A lower expressing 3♣ child has difficulty managing the flow of their ideas. Their ideas tend to behave more like a *hamster wheel*. Their ideas get into an unhealthy cycle of flowing that is difficult to stop. These 3♣ may manifest different difficulties. Some worry about events or communications with others and then replay these ideas repeatedly in their head. These individuals often manifest *stress* and *insomnia*. 3♣ who struggle to develop the ability to manage their minds may manifest *anxiety*. They overthink ideas or decisions to be made and then they fall into a negative thought loop. Some develop *insomnia*. If you are a parent of a 3♣ who appears to be anxious, there are several good strategies and tools that can help. Consider using various energy healing techniques that target and revitalize specific *chakras* in your child's body. Chakras are energy centers that receive and transmit energy throughout the body. There are seven major chakras running along the spine of one's body that are associated with different nerves, organs, joints, and tissues near a chakra's location. A person may experience negative physical and emotional symptoms when their flow of energy becomes unbalanced – either under or overactive – at a specific chakra site. For instance, chronic stress or poor habits can cause a chakra to become imbalanced. Various healing techniques directed at chakra revitalization include yoga, meditation, toning sounds, acupuncture, affirmations, light therapy, breathing practices, crystal healing, and massage (especially reiki, shiatsu, and reflexology).

Also, you may want to try *calming apps*. For younger children, I suggest calming apps like Sesame Street's *Breathe, Think, Do Sesame*, *Think Kids*, or *Breathing* Bubbles. Teens may prefer apps such as *Calm, Smiling Mind*, or *Take a Chill*. If insomnia is an issue, encourage a 3♣ to take aromatherapy baths and refrain from using blue light technology before bedtime. Certain essential oils, like lavender, have been shown to positively impact the limbic system which controls emotional behaviors such as fear and anxiety. Purchase a weighted blanket for your 3♣ as some research has found it helps with anxiety that prevents peaceful sleep. Help them set up *white noise*. White noise is noise that combines sounds across a spectrum of frequencies. Studies have demonstrated this noise allows the brain to relax. Check the Internet for devices that can provide white noise. Another suggestion that helps with both anxiety and insomnia is to get a 3♣ engaged in activities that physically wear them out. This means highly physical tasks, exercises, or sports. And make sure a 3♣ has access to recess at school. These students should not be disciplined by taking away their recess. If anxiety or insomnia continues to be an issue for a 3♣, seek help from a professional.

Additionally, having a mind overflowing with ideas and interests can mean some 3♣ may struggle with *indecision*. Therefore, 3♣ need to learn to manage their minds when making decisions. You see, there are so many choices for a 3♣, they really find themselves overwhelmed! Therefore, it is better to present either/or choices for these children. For example, let's say you are a parent of a nine-year-old 3♣, and it is almost dinnertime. Do not ask your 3♣, "What do you want for dinner tonight?" Instead, give two choices. Ask, "Would you prefer to eat spaghetti and meatballs or barbecued chicken for dinner tonight?" This same technique can be used if you are a teacher working with a 3♣. Perhaps, it is *choice time* in the classroom, a time when students get to select an activity to engage in from an assortment of choices. For instance, students can decide to build a bridge with Legos, explore bubbles, paint with watercolors, care for and pet the class guinea pig, or read about sharks with a friend. A 3♣

may not be able to decide what to do. If this happens, a teacher knowing the interests of this student can say, "I know you love animals so would you rather care for and pet the class guinea pig or read about sharks with a friend." For older 3♣, make sure they practice making decisions when they are not emotional. Perhaps support them in making decisions by encouraging them to use a *Decision Tree*. A Decision Tree is a graphic representation of a problem that identifies possible choices and likely consequences. If you are dealing with a teen and this tool seems childish, verbally take them through the decision-making process.

Summary of Higher and Lower Personality Traits

Higher: Creative, flexible, artistic, versatile, analytical, salesmanship, social butterfly.

Lower: Worrisome, unfaithful, negative self-expression, shallow learner, scatter-brained.

Childhood Influence Mercury Cards

It is common knowledge that a child's personality is most malleable during the formative years – from birth to eight years of age. In the Destiny Card system, the Mercury Cards in a Birth Card's Life Spread reveal influences a child with this Birth Card will experience between birth through age 12. As such, a child's Mercury Cards must be considered so an adult can nurture a child from a place of awareness and work with them from where a child is at in their development. A 3♣ child has the following Mercury Cards: **3♠, 10♥, and 6♦**. Alternatively, outside of any specific person associated with these three cards, the basic meanings of these cards describe experiences that may be impactful during this child's formative years. These cards suggest 3♣ have many friends and prefer socializing with large groups of people. They are highly artistic and must express themselves in a creative way. Due to family circumstances, they tend to experience a static financial situation.

Potential Callings / Vocations by Zodiac Sign

May 29 – Gemini: 3♠ Planetary Ruling Card

With a 3♠ Planetary Ruling Card, these 3♣ have double the energy of a Three card. Therefore, they are more inclined to being antsy and cannot abide desk jobs. They can do well as an artist, composer, salesperson, comedian, freelance journalist, or in a job that includes travel.

June 27 – Cancer: 5♥ Planetary Ruling Card

These more nurturing 3♣ can make an excellent nurse, counselor, or teacher (particularly art, drama, or music). Some are inclined to help the broader public and can do so in the role of a museum director, tutor, activist, or public speaker.

July 25 – Leo: 3♣ Planetary Ruling Card

These 3♣ love fame so they often lean toward leadership careers in the entertainment industry (e.g., director, actor, producer, or film/TV agent). More financially minded 3♣ can do well in business, especially in selling their own artwork.

August 23 – Leo or Virgo: 3♣ or 3♠ Planetary Ruling Card

The Leo affiliated individuals with this birth date can succeed as a performer, whether it be as a singer, actor, dancer, sports athlete, or musician. The Virgo affiliated 3♣ are meticulous, so they tend to do well as a writer, editor, scientist, banker, real estate broker, or physician.

September 21 – Virgo: 3♠ Planetary Ruling Card

More self-critical, these 3♣ tend to get in the way of their own accomplishment. If redirected, they can succeed as a literary or art critic, editor, or writer.

October 19 – Libra: 9♥ Planetary Ruling Card

These highly imaginative 3♣ can make a living as a writer, poet, or musician. The more academic leaning individuals with this birthdate can also do well in politics or law.

November 17 – Scorpio: 7♣ and 7♠ Planetary Ruling Cards

With a flair for making money, these 3♣ can succeed as a politician, actor, or physician. Some can develop athletic talent and make money from it.

December 15 – Sagittarius: 5♦ Planetary Ruling Card

With a 5♦ Planetary Ruling Card, these individuals tend to dislike traditional learning in school. They prefer to learn a trade through mentorship or an apprenticeship. They are gifted salespeople so they may prefer to work as a business owner or other sales-related occupation.

Famous 3♣

Kobe Bryant, basketball player – 8/23/1978
Stephen King, writer – 9/21/1947
Rachel McAdams, actress – 11/17/1978
John F. Kennedy, president – 5/29/1917
Bob Hope, comedian – 5/29/1903

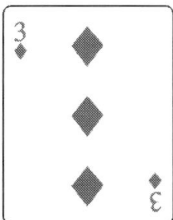

Welcome to the world of the indecisive 3♦!

3♦ = Variety in values and money

According to the Destiny Card system, souls chronologically experience God's lessons across 52 life incarnations. (Think of these as the universe's lessons if this aligns more with your beliefs.) The Birth Card each soul is born into determines the order and type of lessons a soul experiences. When you examine a Birth Card, you will notice it displays a suit of either a Heart, Club, Diamond, or Spade. This suit is significant because it represents the gifts a person born into this suit will possess and how they will direct their energies to learn lessons in their current life incarnation. A Heart Birth Card retains gifts and experiences life lessons around love and relationships. A Club Birth Card holds capabilities and experiences life lessons in their ability to

communicate and absorb knowledge. A Diamond Birth Card possesses talents and experiences life lessons around money and values. And finally, a Spade Birth Card manifests gifts and experiences life lessons in work and health. Souls progress through incarnations and life lessons beginning as Hearts, moving on to Clubs, then Diamonds, and finally as Spades. Therefore, individuals born as Heart Cards are the youngest souls and individuals born as Spades Cards are the oldest souls.

In addition, the number on a Birth Card is equally meaningful as souls sequentially experience life lessons beginning as an Ace and culminating with lessons as a King. A Three Birth Card is one of many odd numbered Birth Cards. And odd numbered cards have more difficulty than even numbered cards in dealing with their energies. Not only do they struggle with balancing their internal energy, but odd numbered cards also have the extra burden of trying to figure out how to direct that energy outward into the world. A person associated with a Three Birth Card struggles the most with managing an imbalance of energy as they are experiencing their first life incarnation in a suit as an odd numbered card. (Ace Birth Cards direct a 'one' energy, so they do not experience imbalance.) **It makes sense, then, that a 3♦ child's purpose, gifts, and life lessons revolve around an *imbalance of energy* in their life. And, due to being a Diamond, this child will learn lessons through managing an imbalance of energies around *values* and *money*.**

How to Nurture the Temperament and Personality of a 3♦ Child

What is often most problematic for a 3♦ is that they tend to manifest an imbalance of energy around values. Personal values are self-developed beliefs of what is right and what is wrong which motivates a person to act one way or another. Because a child is not born with personal values, they will explore a spectrum of values – higher and lower – to discover truths in the world. A 3♦ tends to adopt and act out from extreme high and low values. As such, 3♦ children may act and appear as good or bad characters. What complicates this experience for a 3♦ is that out of all the Birth Cards, 3♦ are known to experience dysfunctional childhoods. Therefore, 3♦ are often developing their values within a toxic environment. And this explains why 3♦ are considered to have the most challenging life path.

Let's consider a real-life example. Born November 4, actor Matthew McConaughey is associated with a 3♦ Birth Card. In his memoir book, *Greenlights*, McConaughey shocked his fans by describing his abusive childhood. Some of this had to do with the dysfunctional relationship between his parents, Kay and Jim, who were married three times and divorced twice to each other. His parents often engaged in violent fights. In one fight, Kay broke Jim's nose. On four different occasions, Jim broke Kay's middle finger after she offensively raised it. McConaughey also described abusive parenting techniques. As an example, Kay violently threw McConaughey to the ground for answering to the name Matt. Kay named him Matthew from the Bible and would not tolerate him answering to any other name, even a shortened one. Thankfully, McConaughey was able to overcome his challenging childhood and go on to manifest higher traits of his Birth Card.

Clearly, it is important for adults working with a 3♦ to help them manifest higher values. This can be accomplished in three different ways. First, adults working with them should try as much as possible to assume the best of them and discover what may be the underlying cause of their poor behavior. For example, imagine a first-grade 3♦ student named Diann is in a classroom that houses two rabbits as class pets. Diann's teacher wants her students to experience both the responsibility and benefits of caring for pets. One Monday morning, Diann is agitated as her family was evicted from their apartment over the weekend. Upon entering the classroom, Diann harshly grabs one of the rabbits out of the hands of another student named Donna. The teacher observes this and reprimands Diann by telling her, "That was not very kind of you. You will lose the privilege of playing with the rabbits this week." Diann replies, "Fine. I don't care!" Yet is she fine? Does she not care? In a case like this, Diann would have benefitted from her teacher taking the time to discover all the facts. Through questioning, perhaps her teacher could understand that Diann is craving security. Diann sub-consciously knows holding a rabbit could give her some comfort. Perhaps the teacher could tell Donna that Diann is having a bad day and ask Donna if it would be okay to make an exception and let Diann have special time with the rabbit. Overall, adults working with a 3♦ need to understand that a part of their life lesson is to navigate a home life that is pulling their values in different directions. Perhaps a parent has unexpectedly died or disappeared. Or they feel oppressed by living in poverty or living with extremely religious parents. No matter their circumstance, these individuals all lack something of great value – security. Young 3♦ often act out from an array of personal values in search of self-esteem. And this means they are bound to select lower values from time to time.

Another way an adult can nurture a 3♦ is to encourage them to engage in *creative expression*. Creative expression represents a healthy way a 3♦ can channel negative energy into something positive. Examples of creative expression include painting, knitting, dance, singing, or playing a musical instrument. In fact, singing or public speaking might be just the ticket for a 3♦ because many have *commanding voices*. Also blessed with a dramatic flair, many 3♦ can find success as a performer – actor, comedian, TV personality, or musician. And because 3♦ explore different values during their childhood, they tend to have amazingly wild stories to tell. When 3♦ shares such stories with a dramatic flair, they are simply hysterical. These individuals can do well as comedians. The third way a 3♦ can manifest higher values is to adopt and stick to a specific spiritual ideology or religion. For instance, they can embrace astrology or become an evangelical Christian. The nature of their spirituality or religious identity does not matter. Adhering to a definitive set of principles will help contain a 3♦'s values. Moreover, developing a spiritual side will offset 3♦ material tendencies and help them express their higher traits.

Speaking of higher traits – a 3♦'s superpowers include being *resourceful* and *financially creative*. Teenage 3♦ tend to be willing to work more than one job at a time when times are tough. In addition, with their own experience in exploring different values, a 3♦ may possess a broad understanding what other people value. Applied to business, these teens can promote and sell products or services to others. Adults should focus on a 3♦'s strengths and provide them with opportunities to experience success when they apply them. Let's consider an example. Imagine you are a fifth-grade teacher who has assigned a persuasive writing assignment to your students using the prompt: Pets should be allowed in schools. One student, Sofia, who is a 3♦ and normally a good writer suddenly appears sullen. Ten minutes into the assignment, Sofia's paper remains blank. You check in with Sofia and ask, "Sofia, what do you think? Should pets be allowed in school?" Sofia replies, "I don't know." You push, "Sure you do." Sofia starts doodling with her pencil and explains, "No, no, I don't. I'm, I guess I'm stupid…" You decide to question Sofia more to find out if the prompt is somehow triggering Sofia. You discover Sofia's dog was recently diagnosed with diabetes. Unable to afford medication, Sofia's parents put the dog down and Sofia was unable to say goodbye. With this understanding, you modify the assignment. You see, another superpower for a 3♦ is *persuasiveness*. Keep in mind a lower expressing 3♦ can sell swampland in Florida! However, this trait can be leveraged to help a 3♦ shine and experience success. Try to encourage a 3♦ to use their persuasive voice to achieve noble objectives. Higher expressing 3♦ hold the potential to persuade others to take up humanitarian causes. And because 3♦ have likely experienced traumatic childhoods, many have learned how to survive under difficult pressure and chaos. As such, they may be much better prepared than others to stay calm and work through the chaos of a problem or situation. There are many careers that suit a 3♦ for having this trait. They can do well as a first responder, a leader within a disaster relief organization, or an entrepreneur who saves failing businesses.

Without a set of higher values to guide them, a 3♦ tends to behave like a Cocklebur plant. Have you ever been hiking in nature, veering off the path into a cluster of plants and grasses for only a few minutes only to find your pants are covered with small, sticky seeds? If so, you have rubbed up against a Cocklebur plant. The Cocklebur plant produces sticky seeds to help with seed dispersal and plant survival. The seeds have burrs or hooks that cause them to attach to an animal's fur, feathers, or clothing so the animal will transport the seed to a new place to take root. In a similar way, this is how a lower expressing 3♦ may act to survive in life. They literally spread their lower values across a broad landscape and then see what germinates. In the process, they tend to use people to get what they want, like a Cocklebur plant relies on other animals. These lower expressing 3♦ often break the rules or make up their rules to gain control of their life. These 3♦ do not take responsibility for their actions and may blame others for their problems. At an extreme, they may engage in the lowest of values by participating in activities that may be described as *reckless* or *crafty*. They continue to act like a Cocklebur plant, spreading their influence to see what will stick and using others in the process. Therefore, it is imperative for 3♦ experiencing dysfunctional childhoods to seek out therapy.

Summary of Higher and Lower Personality Traits

Higher: Financially creative, commanding voices, persuasive, artistic, resourceful.

Lower: Insecurity, worrisome, reckless, bitter, low achiever, self-protective.

Childhood Influence Mercury Cards
It is common knowledge that a child's personality is most malleable during the formative years – from birth to eight years of age. In the Destiny Card system, the Mercury Cards in a Birth Card's Life Spread reveal influences a child with this Birth Card will experience between birth through age 12. As such, a child's Mercury Cards must be considered so an adult can nurture a child from a place of awareness and work with them from where a child is at in their development. A 3♦ child has the following Mercury Cards: **A♠, 6♠, and 7♥**. Alternatively, outside of any specific person associated with these three cards, the basic meanings of these

cards describe experiences that may be impactful during this child's formative years. These cards suggest 3♦ experience heavy karmic relationships and often struggle with unconditional love and insecurity in their early years. These experiences may cause them to keep secrets or adopt scheming behaviors.

Potential Callings / Vocations by Zodiac Sign

January 24 – Aquarius: 9♣ Planetary Ruling Card

More inclined toward humanitarianism, these 3♦ prefer work in politics, teaching, public service, or speaking. Those more apt to internalize stress might be better off working with their hands, through a job as a writer, artist, construction worker, or auto mechanic.

February 22 – Pisces: 9♠ Planetary Ruling Card

These sensitive and idealistic 3♦ fight for causes which can lead to their life's work. They can also make a great actor, politician, diplomat, public service leader, first responder or musician.

March 20 – Pisces or Aries: 9♠ or 7♦ Planetary Ruling Card

Prone to worry, these 3♦ need careers that act as a conduit for self-expression. They can do well as a writer (screenplay or fiction), artist, singer, musician, or actor.

April 18 – Aries: 7♦ Planetary Ruling Card

With a 7♦ Planetary Ruling Card, these 3♦ tend to be erratic with their own money, but they can rise to higher values when handling other people's money. Therefore, they can do well in accounting, banking, running a charity or non-profit organization.

May 16 – Taurus: 7♥ Planetary Ruling Card

More grounded due to stable and methodical Taurus, these 3♦ have great potential to make and keep money. Many do well as a financial advisor, real estate broker, or business owner. More extroverted 3♦ of this birth date can also do well in the entertainment industry.

June 14 – Gemini: A♠ Planetary Ruling Card

These 3♦ dislike the routine of deep study and favor careers that depend on personality over intellect. Due to their A♠ Planetary Ruling Card, these individuals may be more impulsive with money. They can do well in theater, car sales, photography, or as magicians.

July 12 – Cancer: 5♣ Planetary Ruling Card

Having a 5♣ Planetary Ruling Card allows these 3♦ to work well under pressure or within a chaotic setting (e.g., community activist, disaster relief worker, social worker). The most philosophical of the 3♦, these individuals can also find success as a politician or public speaker.

August 10 – Leo: 3♦ Planetary Ruling Card

Being Leos, these 3♦ are born to lead. They can do well running their own business or making a career in the entertainment industry. More academically focused individuals with this birthdate can succeed as an engineer, writer, or inventor.

September 8 – Virgo: A♠ Planetary Ruling Card

The analytical nature of Virgo combined with the mystic A♠ Planetary Ruling Card can make these 3♦ succeed as a writer, scientific researcher, attorney, or engineer. Those desiring some limelight can do well as a public leader, politician, or actor.

October 6 – Libra: 7♥ Planetary Ruling Card

Blessed by Venus, these 3♦ are charming and so they can do well in artistic or literary careers. Some who struggle with anxiety do well pursuing outdoor sports jobs, or a job as a park ranger or geologist as nature calms them.

November 4 – Scorpio: 7♦ and 2♥ Planetary Ruling Cards

These innovative 3♦ can succeed as a scientist, artist, engineer, inventor, or in various medical-related jobs (e.g., pharmacist, physician, or nurse).

December 2 – Sagittarius: 5♠ Planetary Ruling Card

While not always responsible with their own money, these 3♦ can assist others with their money as a banker, accountant, or stockbroker. The more introverted types may prefer to write and can make a career of it. With a 5♠ Planetary Ruling Card, some prefer artistic work that includes travel (musician or actor).

Famous 3♦

Britney Spears, singer/clothes designer – 12/2/1981
Gaten Matarazzo, actor– 9/8/2002
Donald J Trump, president – 6/14/1946
Malala Yousafzia, civil rights leader – 7/12/1997
Tucker Carlson, TV host – 5/16/1969
Pink, singer – 9/8/1979

Welcome to the world of the indecisive 3♠!

3♠ = Variety in work and health

According to the Destiny Card system, souls chronologically experience God's lessons across 52 life incarnations. (Think of these as the universe's lessons if this aligns more with your beliefs.) The Birth Card each soul is born into determines the order and type of lessons a soul experiences. When you examine a Birth Card, you will notice it displays a suit of either a Heart, Club, Diamond, or Spade. This suit is significant because it represents the gifts a person born into this suit will possess and how they will direct their energies to learn lessons in their current life incarnation. A Heart Birth Card retains gifts and experiences life lessons around love and relationships. A Club Birth Card holds capabilities and experiences life lessons in their ability to

communicate and absorb knowledge. A Diamond Birth Card possesses talents and experiences life lessons around money and values. And finally, a Spade Birth Card manifests gifts and experiences life lessons in work and health. Souls progress through incarnations and life lessons beginning as Hearts, moving on to Clubs, then Diamonds, and finally as Spades. Therefore, individuals born as Heart Cards are the youngest souls and individuals born as Spades Cards are the oldest souls.

In addition, the number on a Birth Card is equally meaningful as souls sequentially experience life lessons beginning as an Ace and culminating with lessons as a King. A Three Birth Card is one of many odd numbered Birth Cards. And odd numbered cards have more difficulty than even numbered cards in dealing with their energies. Not only do they struggle with balancing their internal energy, but odd numbered cards also have the extra burden of trying to figure out how to direct that energy outward into the world. A person associated with a Three Birth Card struggles the most with managing an imbalance of energy as they are experiencing their first life incarnation in a suit as an odd numbered card. (Ace Birth Cards direct a 'one' energy, so they do not experience imbalance.) **It makes sense, then, that a 3♠ child's purpose, gifts, and life lessons revolve around an *imbalance of energy* in their life. And, due to being a Spade, this child will learn lessons through managing an imbalance of energy around *work* and *health*.**

How to Nurture the Temperament and Personality of a 3♠ Child
All children born with a Spade Birth Card are old souls who tend to carry heavy burdens in life for the purpose of learning higher wisdom. 3♠ are no exception to this rule. 3♠ experience early physical and mental challenges that are like how one might feel skydiving for the first time. Visualize yourself in such a position. In the plane, just before the jump you start to doubt yourself. You look down at the ground and feel overwhelmed with anxiety. Why did you think this was a good idea? Then you jump and immediately feel the weight of your tandem instructor pushing down on you. The force of gravity is pulling you down. Soon, air resistance increases, pushing up on your body. You feel tremendous adrenaline coursing through you. Next, the parachute opens, and you are jolted upward, gradually slowing down in speed. Finally, you hit the ground hard, stand up, and feel instant relief, thinking you just stared death in the face. Does this sound scary to you? At a young age, 3♠ tend to be tangled in a heavy burden that makes them feel pushed and pulled in many directions, just like a skydiver. Interestingly, they often experience a karmic obligation toward a male in their life. For instance, this can manifest as having an alcoholic father or a brother who has a physical disability. The issue is that a young 3♠ feels disappointment within their home environment because of the added responsibility this situation forces upon them. If a 3♠ learns to accept their fate and not fight against it, they are more likely to experience a successful landing. This is to say they develop resilience that serves them well in adulthood.

Without the ability to counterbalance the hard aspects of a 3♠'s early life with joyful diversions, a 3♠ child will wallow in despair and attract other negative energy into their life. Therefore, guide a young 3♠ to identify and implement *self-care*. For children, self-care can include learning daily tasks to advance their independence such as drinking from a cup on their own, brushing their teeth, or tying their own shoes. As children become older, self-care should also include teaching strategies to care for one's mental and physical health. If you are a parent of a 3♠, model and discuss ways you engage in self-care. Then, assist your child in scheduling self-care breaks on a daily or weekly basis. It may be helpful to create a *self-care box* ahead of time that contains supplies and activities they can independently attend to. Allow them input to what this box contains. Also, make sure a 3♠ has access to music. Studies have shown that when people listen to relaxing music before a stressful medical procedure, their cortisol (stress hormone) levels are lower than people who don't listen to relaxing music before similar events. If you are a teacher of a 3♠, provide self-care by implementing *brain breaks*. Brain breaks are mental and physical breaks used in school to get students moving or help them relax. There are countless ideas and videos for brain breaks on the Internet. I recommend the website www.Gonoodle.com which offers guided dances, sing-a-longs, and calming exercises.

With wisdom from numerous past lives, many 3♠ refuse to conform to principles that go against their common sense. This can mean they may have difficulty adhering to schooling that is strict or primarily uses *teacher-focused instruction*. Teacher-focused instruction involves learning in which the teacher provides the information, leads activities, and uses traditional assignments. You see, most 3♠ dislike routine, busy work, and assignments that are too structured. 3♠ need choice in the learning process and product. If you are a teacher of a 3♠, know that these children need *student-centered learning*. Student-centered learning involves learning in which students lead activities, socially construct learning with peers, and perhaps even choose their own topics to explore. If you are a parent of a 3♠, advocate for this type of learning for your child. In addition, investigate charter or performing arts schools that value and foster creative expression.

Interestingly, 3♠ are often poor test takers which can add to their negative view of school and produce anxiety. If you are a teacher of a 3♠, provide them with *alternative assessments*. Alternative assessments allow students to demonstrate what they learned in ways other than traditional testing. Alternative assessment may also be referred to as authentic, performance, or informal assessment. For instance, let's say you are a fifth-grade teacher working with a 3♠ student named Ariana. You know Ariana to be outgoing and artistic. In social studies lessons, students are learning how early Americans settled and adapted to various places and climates. To demonstrate her learning, you allow Ariana to research this topic and then create drawings of various environments that depict ways people adapted to them. In addition, Ariana is expected to explain these drawings through an oral presentation.

Outside of school, an adolescent 3♠ may need more structured boundaries. They tend to attract a wrong crowd and respond to that crowd's influence. What is hard in parenting a 3♠ is that they tend to be independent problem-solvers. They will not turn to their parents for advice. If you are a parent of a 3♠ who will not listen to your advice, be sure to get some help from teachers, counselors, or coaches at school. Make sure to stick to the rules you express and follow through with consequences if they are broken. But pick your battles as too much discipline may backfire. The uplifting side to a rebellious 3♠ adolescent is that most learn hard lessons and go on to have productive lives. Some may even use their life experience to help others in similar situations. These individuals can become gifted writers, speakers, teachers, psychologists, school counselors, and youth ministers.

Additionally, an adult working with a 3♠ can nurture them by helping them find constructive, rather than destructive ways to express their pain. Many 3♠ can direct their negative energy into a positive expression by creating art. You see, a 3♠'s imbalance of energy makes them physically and mentally sensitive. Their heightened sensitivity accords them with the heart and soul of an *artist.* They possess so much artistic talent they can earn a living from it. Not only are these individuals inventive, but they are also gifted *iterators.* They love to improve and optimize their creative work. Through the process, they can create brilliant products. And because they are also *versatile* when it comes to work, they can do well selling their product or artwork. If you are a parent of a 3♠, nurture their artistic trait above all. Support them in adopting hobbies such as drawing, painting, writing, singing, acting, playing an instrument, or listening to music. If their creativity appears to be blocked, encourage them to escape to a setting that will spark their creativity such as going to an art gallery, a zoo, a concert, or museum. Are finances to fund these activities an issue? If so, urge a 3♠ to take a walk-through nature, have a picnic at a local park, or run around at the school playground for fun. Artistic expression solves two problems for a 3♠. It helps them re-direct stress and develop a skill that can be turned into a career.

Speaking of stress – if a 3♠ is unable to direct their heightened sensitivity into creative expression, then they tend to manifest stress and/or anxiety. If a 3♠ is struggling with anxiety, a weighted blanket or headphones that block out stressful noises may help. A 3♠ may also benefit from healing techniques intended to balance the body's *chakras.* Chakras are energy centers that receive and transmit energy throughout the body. There are seven major chakras running along the spine of one's body that are associated with different nerves, organs, joints, and tissues near a chakra's location. A person may experience negative physical and emotional symptoms when their flow of energy becomes unbalanced – either under or overactive – at a specific chakra site. For instance, chronic stress or poor habits can cause a chakra to become imbalanced. Various healing techniques directed at chakra revitalization include yoga, meditation, toning sounds, acupuncture, affirmations, aromatherapy, light therapy, breathing practices, crystal healing, and massage (especially reiki, shiatsu, and reflexology). To be clear, a 3♠ child must learn ways to manage stress. If they do not, they will adopt unhealthy practices, like biting their nails or smoking. In extreme cases, too much stress can manifest a physical illness or a 3♠ may become preoccupied with their health and act like a hypochondriac. Because 3♠ have similar aspects as a J♠, you may want to read about the traits of this Birth Card.

Summary of Higher and Lower Personality Traits

Higher: Artistic, inventive, multitasker, eccentric, romantic, sociable, business acumen.

Lower: Fear responsibility, lack sympathy, unstable, intolerance, poor health habits.

Childhood Influence Mercury Cards
It is common knowledge that a child's personality is most malleable during the formative years – from birth to eight years of age. In the Destiny Card system, the Mercury Cards in a Birth Card's Life Spread reveal influences a child with this Birth Card will experience between birth through age 12. As such, a child's Mercury Cards must be considered so an adult can nurture a child from a place of awareness and work with them from where a child is at in their development. A 3♠ child has the following Mercury Cards: **9♥, 10♦, and 7♦**. Alternatively, outside of any specific person associated with these three cards, the basic meanings of these

cards describe experiences that may be impactful during this child's formative years. These cards suggest 3♠ experience early disappointments in love that may instill fears and challenges around values. They may be blessed in receiving an inheritance or have access to money.

Potential Callings / Vocations by Zodiac Sign

January 11 – Capricorn: J♣ Planetary Ruling Card
If these 3♠ can cultivate discipline, they can harness their compassionate nature to excel in work in public service as a teacher, counselor, psychologist, or religious leader.

February 9 – Aquarius: 9♦ Planetary Ruling Card
An extremely likeable 3♠, these individuals can do well in theater, acting, teaching, or as a non-profit worker.

March 7 – Pisces: 7♠ Planetary Ruling Card
More imaginative and artistic, these 3♠ most often succeed as an artist (especially painter), writer, singer, or musician. Due to their 7♠ Planetary Ruling Card, some hold inner secrets of healing which can help them do well as a nurse, vet, doctor, or gardener.

April 5 – Aries: 5♦ Planetary Ruling Card
These energetic and hardworking 3♠ like to invent and sell progressive ideas or products. They can do so as a scientist, engineer, politician, artist, salesman, musician, or small business owner. Some have magnetic voices and can succeed as a singer or actor.

May 3 – Taurus: 7♣ Planetary Ruling Card
These methodical 3♠ work hard and can do well as an artist (e.g., musician, actor, writer, painter, interior designer, or graphic designer) or as a scientific researcher.

June 1 – Gemini: 9♥ Planetary Ruling Card
Disliking routine, these 3♠ have a hard time finishing projects they start. They prefer jobs that include travel (e.g., salesman or journalist) or include time in the limelight (e.g., actor, musician, or comedian).

Famous 3♠
Bryan Cranston, actor – 3/7/1956
Pharrell Williams, singer – 4/5/1973
Carole King, singer – 2/9/1942
Colin Powell, secretary of state – 4/5/1937
Amy Schumer, actor/comedian – 6/1/1981
Sterling Brown, actor – 4/5/1976

Chapter 7

Descriptions of the Four Birth Cards

Welcome to the world of the constructive 4♥!

4♥ = Stability in love

According to the Destiny Card system, souls chronologically experience God's lessons within each life incarnation. (Think of these as the universe's lessons if this aligns more with your beliefs.) The Birth Card each soul is born into determines the order and type of lessons a soul experiences. When you examine a Birth Card, you will notice it displays a suit of either a Heart, Club, Diamond, or Spade. This suit is significant because it represents the gifts a person born into this suit will possess and how they will direct their energies to learn lessons in their current life incarnation. A Heart Birth Card retains gifts and experiences life lessons around love and relationships. A Club Birth Card holds capabilities and experiences life lessons in their ability to communicate and absorb knowledge. A Diamond Birth Card possesses talents and experiences life lessons around money and values. And finally, a Spade Birth Card manifests gifts and experiences life lessons in work and health. Souls progress through incarnations and life lessons beginning as Hearts, moving on to Clubs, then Diamonds, and finally as Spades. Therefore, individuals born as Heart Cards are the youngest souls and individuals born as Spades Cards are the oldest souls.

In addition, the number on a Birth Card is equally meaningful as souls sequentially experience life lessons beginning as an Ace and culminating with lessons as a King. Consider representations of the number four in the world around us. Four legs of a chair. Four wheels on a car. Four legs on a dog, cat, and many other animals. Now imagine these same living and nonliving things have their four parts reduced to three – three legs of a chair, three wheels on a car, and three legs on an animal. In each of these cases, balance becomes compromised. The fourth part is critical because it provides strength and stability that helps ground these objects. **It makes sense, then, that a 4♥ child's purpose, gifts, and life lessons revolve around the need to produce security and *stability* in life. And due to being a Heart, this child will learn lessons constructing stability through *love* and *relationships*.**

How to Nurture the Temperament and Personality of a 4♥ Child

Generally, 4♥ have fortunate and easy childhoods. They cooperate well with adults, do well in school, and easily make friends. As an adult interacting with them, keep in mind they are extremely sensitive young souls. For example, imagine your seven-year-old 4♥ daughter spills cereal and milk all over herself right before school. Stressed with the possibility she will miss the school bus, you yell in a harsh voice, "What are you doing? Quick, go change your clothes!" A 4♥ child does not easily shrug off a comment like this. In such a case, it is important to discuss this incident later and apologize. Adults make mistakes. Lucky for you, a 4♥ will forgive you due to their *loving nature*. However, if this type of communication is used repeatedly without an apology, this child may literally take it to heart. This can result in a 4♥ cultivating an inferiority complex. Over time, this way of thinking can morph into an opposite way of thinking. They may manifest a *superiority complex*; an attitude in which they believe they are superior to others. For instance, let's say you are a parent of a ten-year-old 4♥ named Elijah. Elijah does well in school and sports. At parent-teacher conferences you are surprised to learn Elijah has gotten into trouble for being rude to other students during group assignments. The teacher overhears Elijah say, "You people must be exhausted from watching me do everything!" When a child perceives, rightly so or not, that they are inadequate, they may criticize others to boost their egos. The solution here is to help your child with their perception of self. Try to praise them for their higher traits but do not offer false praise. 4♥ love traditions and family time. Set up a weekly movie night and complement them on their choices of movies.

A loving and stable home and school life is fertile ground for a 4♥. Nurture a 4♥ by providing a lot of affection and harmony in relationships. Also, provide them with consistency in schedules and expectations. 4♥ dislike change. For example, it may be normal for them to have *separation anxiety* when dropped off at daycare. While this may be normal for most children the first couple of weeks in a new setting, it may last for months for a 4♥. You might help them adjust by allowing them to bring a favorite stuffed animal from home. Tell them they are safe. Change in the home is especially difficult for a 4♥, such as dual custody situations where they move back and forth between parents. If there is conflict within the family or friendships, keep in mind that 4♥ are likely to feel heartache harder than most other children.

One superpower of a 4♥ is that they have enormous *compassion* for others. Encourage this child to donate their old toys or contribute a toy to a Christmas toy drive. Older children can volunteer at a local soup kitchen to serve the homeless at Thanksgiving or a different holiday. Some 4♥ adolescents feel strongly about global causes. Find out what issues they feel passionate about and encourage them to act. If you are their parent or teacher, help support them in their efforts whether it is sending care packages to serve veterans or proposing an anti-bullying campaign for their school. Being warm and compassionate, a 4♥ may attract emotionally needy individuals. This behavior can get complicated for an adolescent 4♥ if they try to save others. Furthermore, a 4♥ can become addicted to helping others. You may need to help them navigate situations in which others pull them into their drama or unhealthy situations. They tend to be naïve and see the best in others. It is important for an adult to assist a 4♥ to reflect and problem-solve through situations like this. Fortunately, because 4♥ are innately stable individuals, in time they will learn the value of setting up relational boundaries with others.

The highest purpose for a 4♥ is for them to build security for themselves and for others by way of love and relationships. This means a 4♥ feels *protective* over all living things. Let's consider an example. Imagine you are a parent of a ten-year-old 4♥ daughter. One day while getting her bicycle out of the garage she discovers several mice running around. You decide to buy mouse traps to get rid of them. Refrain from buying the mouse traps that kill. Rather, purchase a catch and release mouse trap. Something as simple as killing mice can be traumatic for a 4♥. They adore animals. In fact, a 4♥ is a wonderful child to reward by purchasing them a pet. Such a deep love of all living things is also why it is common for a 4♥ to develop committed love relationships at a young age. And because the 4♥ is also known as one of two marriage cards, do not be surprised if your adolescent 4♥ desires marriage at an age younger than what you might want for them.

Summary of Higher and Lower Personality Traits

Higher: Humanitarian, protective, compassionate, good at marriage, intuitive.

Lower: Codependent, pretentious, insecure, overly sensitive, superiority.

Childhood Influence Mercury Cards

It is common knowledge that a child's personality is most malleable during the formative years – from birth to eight years of age. In the Destiny Card system, the Mercury Cards in a Birth Card's Life Spread reveal influences a child with this Birth Card will experience between birth through age 12. As such, a child's Mercury Cards must be considered so an adult can nurture a child from a place of awareness and work with them from where a child is at in their development. A 4♥ child has the following Mercury Cards: **4♦, Q♠, and 5♠.** The Q♠ may mean there is an influential mother who is likely a Spade Birth or Planetary Ruling Card. Alternatively, outside of any specific person associated with these three cards, the basic meanings of these cards describe experiences that may be impactful during this child's formative years. These cards suggest a 4♥ is born into a family with stable finances and values. And there tends to be numerous changes in the home due to moves and/or family travel.

Potential Callings / Vocations by Zodiac Sign

October 31 – Scorpio, 8♥ and 8♦ Planetary Ruling Cards
These curious Scorpios enjoy solving mysteries and can make excellent physicians, healers, or scientific researchers. All are in search of truth and justice so they can succeed as authors, teachers, counselors.

November 29 – Sagittarius, 6♣ Planetary Ruling Card
Having a 6♣ Planetary Ruling Card instills a peacemaking aspect to these 4♥. They often feel called to make a difference in the world through preaching, educating, counseling, or work as a therapist, politician, actor, or musician.

December 27 – Capricorn, 6♠ Planetary Ruling Card
More practical and ambitious, these 4♥ can persevere in educational pursuits. This allows them access to many different occupations such as scientist, writer, journalist, or actor.

Famous 4♥
Russell Wilson, football player – 11/29/1988

Howie Mandel, TV personality – 11/29/1955
Savannah Guthrie, journalist/TV personality – 12/27/1971
Chadwick Boseman, actor – 11/29/1976
Shay Mooney, singer – 12/27/1991
Dan Rather, journalist – 10/31/1931

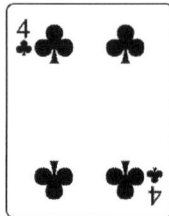

Welcome to the world of the constructive 4♣!

4♣ = Stability through knowledge

According to the Destiny Card system, souls chronologically experience God's lessons within each life incarnation. (Think of these as the universe's lessons if this aligns more with your beliefs.) The Birth Card each soul is born into determines the order and type of lessons a soul experiences. When you examine a Birth Card, you will notice it displays a suit of either a Heart, Club, Diamond, or Spade. This suit is significant because it represents the gifts a person born into this suit will possess and how they will direct their energies to learn lessons in their current life incarnation. A Heart Birth Card retains gifts and experiences life lessons around love and relationships. A Club Birth Card holds capabilities and experiences life lessons in their ability to communicate and absorb knowledge. A Diamond Birth Card possesses talents and experiences life lessons around money and values. And finally, a Spade Birth Card manifests gifts and experiences life lessons in work and health. Souls progress through incarnations and life lessons beginning as Hearts, moving on to Clubs, then Diamonds, and finally as Spades. Therefore, individuals born as Heart Cards are the youngest souls and individuals born as Spades Cards are the oldest souls.

In addition, the number on a Birth Card is equally meaningful as souls sequentially experience life lessons beginning as an Ace and culminating with lessons as a King. Consider representations of the number four in the world around us. Four legs of a chair. Four wheels on a car. Four legs of a dog, cat, and many other animals. Now imagine these same objects have their four parts reduced to three – three legs on a chair, three wheels on a car, and three legs on an animal. In each of these cases, the object becomes unbalanced. The fourth part is critical because it provides strength and stability that helps ground these objects and insure balance. **It makes sense, then, that a 4♣ child's purpose, gifts, and life lessons revolve around their need to produce *stability* in life. And due to being a Club, this child will learn lessons constructing stability in life through *communication* and *knowledge*.**

How to Nurture the Temperament and Personality of a 4♣ Child
Constructing knowledge through traditional schooling works well for a 4♣. And preschool versus a day care environment is important to help propel these builders of knowledge. While all 4♣ are *intelligent* beings who learn quickly, they *need time to process* acquired knowledge. They need to reflect upon new information and ideas, integrate them with preexisting ideas

and opinions, and then construct their own meaning. When given time to process information, they will amaze you with how well they can clearly lay out the facts and make connections between their thoughts and ideas. This explains why school age 4♣ excel at making presentations, debating, and writing persuasive papers. For all that, however, they need proper time to process information. You see, they dislike it when others put them on the spot to provide answers or ask them to make quick decisions. For example, let's say you are a high school social science teacher who is confident that your 4♣ student named Ben has read the homework material. You fire off a higher order thinking question and pick Ben to answer it even though he has not raised his hand. In education, this teacher behavior is called cold calling. This technique is not ideal for a 4♣. Instead, have small groups discuss your questions and tell your 4♣ student you expect him to summarize ideas from the group later in the class period.

4♣ thrive in structured settings and respond well to routines and consistency. This also means breaking routines can be unsettling for a 4♣. This is the six-year-old child who complains when you pick them up from school because they are used to grandma doing so! They are *reliable* students who follow through with assignments. Teach them how to do chores at a young age and they will handle them responsibly. Try to maintain a strict schedule of after school activities for them such as sports, music lessons, and homework study times. In addition, 4♣ can be thrown off balance when consistency is not maintained. For example, imagine you are at a friend's house for dinner with your three-year-old 4♣ son. Your friend praises his good behavior, saying he is an exception to the proverbial 'terrible threes' rule. And generally, this observation is true for your son. This makes you overly confident and you decide to stay at your friend's house well past your son's normal bedtime. Suddenly, your Dr. Jekyll becomes Mr. Hyde. Not familiar with my reference to this famous book or movie? The main character has a dual nature – extremely good at times (Dr. Jekyll) and evil at other times (Mr. Hyde). Your friend is shocked at the change of your child in such a short time. Yet, you should not be surprised. 4♣ are not flexible individuals when their schedules change so you should try to maintain this stability for them.

As 4♣ get older, make sure their need for security does not make them avoid making changes. Encourage some risk taking otherwise they may grow up playing things safe all the time. For instance, an adolescent 4♣ may be hesitant to apply to an Ivy League school, doubting their abilities. Push them to take that risk. If they avoid taking risks, 4♣ are prone to become more opinionated and fixed in their thinking. Over time, any kind of risk feels like a threat to their security. If others engage in the risk, a 4♣ might be quick to speak judgmentally toward them as a way of justifying their own stance in not pursuing the risk. Perhaps, urge your 4♣ to take more risks in hobbies and educational opportunities.

Do not encourage financial risks or risks regarding their judgments of others. Be on the lookout for a 4♣ to attract dishonest people. During adolescence, your 4♣ might be attracted to the so called "bad" boys or girls. While it is parental human nature to forbid relationships with teens of low character, such a declaration may not work. A 4♣ needs to experience each new idea or person and process these things in conjunction to their own philosophies in life, not based upon their parent's point of view. Therefore, it is imperative to begin co-processing core values and making meaning of social situations when a 4♣ is a preteen. It is helpful that many

4♣ tend to grow up close to their father or a father figure who can mentor them in unpacking experiences and discerning higher truths in life.

Using reflection to process situations is highly effective for 4♣ children. I suggest using Gibb's Reflective Cycle that was described in Chapter 3. Is your 4♣ already a teen who is unable to share their feelings about difficult situations? Model reflection using your own situations. For instance, say you are at the local grocery store with your thirteen-year-old daughter and run into a neighbor who asks you about your skin care routines. The neighbor claims to be using the best product and can get you some products for free if you host a party. You suspect the products are part of a pyramid scheme type of business, whereby you receive products by enrolling others to subscribe. After this interaction, ask your teen, "Did that interaction seem strange to you? What is your gut feeling about it? What do you think their intentions were?" 4♣ may hold such a strong desire for stability with others that they dismiss their suspicious gut feelings. They may push aside their intuition and feelings without taking time to process them. Without being processed, these ideas may become compartmentalized and hidden within their subconsciousness. Inadvertently, when these individuals feel deceived by others, the reality is they are often deceiving themself. To overcome this life challenge, they must learn how to think with, trust, and process their gut feelings.

Summary of Higher and Lower Personality Traits

Higher: Organized mind, smart, hardworking, methodical, forward-looking, negotiation.

Lower: Dogmatic, dishonest, judgmental, undemonstrative.

Childhood Influence Mercury Cards
It is common knowledge that a child's personality is most malleable during the formative years – from birth to eight years of age. In the Destiny Card system, the Mercury Cards in a Birth Card's Life Spread reveal influences a child with this Birth Card will experience between birth through age 12. As such, a child's Mercury Cards must be considered so an adult can nurture a child from a place of awareness and work with them from where a child is at in their development. A 4♣ child has the following Mercury Cards: **2♦, J♥, and 5♠**. The J♥ may mean there is an influential father or brother who is likely a Heart Birth or Planetary Ruling Card. Alternatively, outside of any specific person associated with these three cards, the basic meanings of these cards describe experiences that may be impactful during this child's formative years. These cards suggest they may need to make sacrifices for a family member or because the family frequently travels and/or moves. They tend to cultivate values through close relationships with friends.

Potential Callings / Vocations by Zodiac Sign

April 30 – Taurus, J♠ Planetary Ruling Card
The stubborn bull of Taurus can double the judgmental aspect of these 4♣. They would be better served to channel their critical views into a profession that critics music, art, or food.

Those who enjoy a mentally challenging occupation can succeed in accounting, scientific research, or computer coding.

May 28 – Gemini, 2♦ Planetary Ruling Card

The quick-thinking and acting aspect of Gemini adds to the mental capacity of these 4♣, making them suitable to jobs in law, diplomacy, engineering, or science. With the wheeler-dealer aspect of a 2♦ Planetary Ruling Card, these 4♣ can lead in business.

June 26 – Cancer, 6♥ Planetary Ruling Card

These sensitive Cancer 4♣ have the gift of healing and often succeed as a doctor, nurse, medical researcher, or master gardener. Those more inclined to be in the spotlight can do well in acting or sports.

July 24 – Leo, 4♣ Planetary Ruling Card

These 4♣ tend to be more capable of taking and benefiting from risks in their career. Therefore, many become famous as an actor, explorer, business leader or owner, politician, lobbyist, or community activist.

August 22 – Leo or Virgo, 4♣ or 2♦ Planetary Ruling Card

Strong minded, these 4♣ tend to lead behind the scenes as writers, researchers, inventors, producers, and musicians. Conservative women may decide to raise children rather than forging a career, while conservative men may seek a career in the military.

September 20 – Virgo, 2♦ Planetary Ruling Card

The methodical aspect of Virgo allows these 4♣ to excel at jobs that require detail in writing contracts (e.g., real estate broker, mortgage broker) or research (medical or law).

October 18 – Libra, J♠ Planetary Ruling Card

With a J♠ Planetary Ruling Card, these 4♣ may initially shrug off responsibility. Popular within large groups, these 4♣ can succeed as hairdressers, personal shoppers, artists, actors, or sports players. Those who capitalize on an early educational foundation often do well as lawyers or politicians.

November 16 – Scorpio, 8♣ and 8♠ Planetary Ruling Cards

These intense 4♣ are quite inflexible having two Eight-based Planetary Ruling Cards. If their fixed ideas are directed at work or causes, they can go far as scientific researchers or government officials. Many have musical gifts.

December 14 – Sagittarius, 6♦ Planetary Ruling Card

More restless than others of the same card, these 4♣ prefer occupations that can combine travel and money (e.g., sales, acting, or translator). A 6♦ Planetary Ruling Card instills a competitive edge and enjoyment of work related to the outdoors (e.g., professional athlete, outdoor gear salesperson, or guide).

Famous 4♣
Ariana Grande, singer – 6/26/1993
Jennifer Lopez, singer/actor – 7/24/1969
Derek Jeter, baseball player – 6/26/1974
Pete Davidson, comedian – 11/16/1993
James Corden, TV personality – 8/22/1978

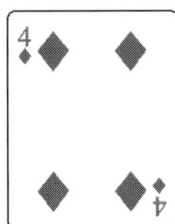

Welcome to the world of the constructive 4♦!

4♦ = Stability in values and money

According to the Destiny Card system, souls chronologically experience God's lessons within each life incarnation. (Think of these as the universe's lessons if this aligns more with your beliefs.) The Birth Card each soul is born into determines the order and type of lessons a soul experiences. When you examine a Birth Card, you will notice it displays a suit of either a Heart, Club, Diamond, or Spade. This suit is significant because it represents the gifts a person born into this suit will possess and how they will direct their energies to learn lessons in their current life incarnation. A Heart Birth Card retains gifts and experiences life lessons around love and relationships. A Club Birth Card holds capabilities and experiences life lessons in their ability to communicate and absorb knowledge. A Diamond Birth Card possesses talents and experiences life lessons around money and values. And finally, a Spade Birth Card manifests gifts and experiences life lessons in work and health. Souls progress through incarnations and life lessons beginning as Hearts, moving on to Clubs, then Diamonds, and finally as Spades. Therefore, individuals born as Heart Cards are the youngest souls and individuals born as Spades Cards are the oldest souls.

In addition, the number on a Birth Card is equally meaningful as souls sequentially experience life lessons beginning as an Ace and culminating with lessons as a King. Consider representations of four in the world. Four legs of a chair. Four wheels on a car. Four legs of a dog, cat, and many other animals. Now imagine these same objects have their four parts reduced to three – three legs on a chair, three wheels on a car, and three legs on an animal. In each of these cases, the fourth part is critical because it provides strength and stability that helps ground these objects and ensure balance. **It makes sense, then, that a 4♦ child's purpose, gifts, and life lessons revolve around their need to construct *stability* in life. And due to being a Diamond, this child will learn lessons constructing stability in life through *values* and *money*.**

How to Nurture the Temperament and Personality of a 4♦ Child

Young 4♦ act like little adults. When given clear directions and expectations, they can accomplish great things. Sometimes it's hard to remember they are children and it's easy to load them up with a lot of responsibility. They appear so calm, dependable, and mature. They like fixing things. Tread carefully here. Even if they ask for more work and responsibility, regulate the amount of work, and explain the importance of balance in life. Expecting too much of these individuals at an early age can cause them to become over or under achievers. Some of this depends upon the zodiac sign they are born under. For example, if pushed to an extreme in workload, Virgos can become perfectionists and develop anxiety and fears around failure. Pisces 4♦ can rebel, under achieve and become directionless in life. Encourage your 4♦ to find joy in their work and pursue careers of their choosing. Most 4♦ are destined to work all their lives and they are happier when they feel called to their work.

When 4♦ experience a process or format that works well for them, they prefer to stick with it and will resist changing the process. Therefore, allow some flexibility for your 4♦ to do things in their own way. For example, imagine you are a teacher, and your school has adopted a new mathematics curriculum. This curriculum requires students to solve the same problem in a multitude of different ways. In turn, you have asked your 4♦ to solve the problem in three different ways. Your 4♦ child looks at you as if you asked them to jump off a bridge. They want to solve the problem in one way and the way they deem most efficient. Solving a problem in a way that takes twice as much time makes absolutely no sense to them. Negotiate with this 4♦. If they can demonstrate that they can solve a specific type of problem in multiple ways and replicate it on a test, you will reduce the times you require them to do busy work. Alternatively, put them into a small group and assign them to solve each problem in one way that makes the most sense to them, while assigning different methods to others in the group. This same personality trait will manifest when a young 4♦ is in search of the best process for accomplishing a goal. Perhaps, you are a parent of a 4♦ who is a girl scout determined to sell the most cookies. Your child has a plan. You see holes in this plan and want to help her be successful. Not so fast. It is better to adopt a more hands-off approach in this situation. Do not micro-manage this child. They are fiercely independent and learn best by experiencing the consequences of their own decisions and actions.

The *independent nature* of a 4♦ goes into high gear during adolescence. If nurtured well, they will soar. As a Diamond Birth Card, they will likely be motivated by money. Give them chores with allowance attached to it. Assign them big organizational projects for extra cash. Rather than micromanaging them, check in to see if they need help. A parent's role should look a bit different when interacting with a 4♦. A parent's role is to set flexible, yet consistent boundaries and expectations. Act more like a coach and sounding board rather than a strict authority figure. Often 4♦ have a karmic relationship with a female, perhaps a mother. If you are a mother of a 4♦, consider the traits of your own card and determine how this may be impacting your relationship. For instance, if you make the habit of jumping in to rescue or interrogate your 4♦, they may become secretive. A 4♦ will go to great lengths to avoid triggering a nosey parent. Often, they learn to express a stoic, 'poker face' which makes it difficult for a parent to know when their child is really struggling. Over time, 4♦ may suppress their true feelings, and then they find it difficult to be open with others. Asking for help will be hard for these individuals. They fear it will come across as being dependent and incompetent – qualities diametrically opposed to their core nature.

4♦ need to communicate vulnerabilities without others overreacting to them. Suppressing vulnerabilities can lead to denial or avoidance of true feelings and circumstances. What happens then? The well-known TED Talk presenter, Brene Brown, spoke eloquently about such a quandary when she stated, "You either walk inside your story and own it or you stand outside your story and hustle for your worthiness." Avoiding issues often means a 4♦ will stick with a bad situation or relationship. They may feel restless and taken advantage of, which can in turn manifest into resentment. However, the truth is that control resides inside of them. They must face their feelings and values and do the hard work of aligning their actions with them.

Summary of Higher and Lower Personality Traits

Higher: Highly organized and efficient, independent, sentimental, practical, dependable.

Lower: Impatient, agitated, resentful toward work, apathetic.

Childhood Influence Mercury Cards
It is common knowledge that a child's personality is most malleable during the formative years – from birth to eight years of age. In the Destiny Card system, the Mercury Cards in a Birth Card's Life Spread reveal influences a child with this Birth Card will experience between birth through age 12. As such, a child's Mercury Cards must be considered so an adult can nurture a child from a place of awareness and work with them from where a child is at in their development. A 4♦ child has the following Mercury Cards: **2♠, J♣, and 6♠**. The J♣ may mean there is an influential father or brother who is likely a Club Birth or Planetary Ruling Card. Alternatively, outside of any specific person associated with these three cards, the basic meanings of these cards describe experiences that may be impactful during this child's formative years. These cards suggest a 4♦ will take on responsibility with work at a young age. They are often extremely creative and do well in school, particularly in creative writing. They are likely blessed with loyal friends. Some may be impacted by a karmic relationship.

Potential Callings / Vocations by Zodiac Sign

January 23 – Aquarius, 10♣ Planetary Ruling Card
Adept at assessing value and human behavior, these individuals can succeed as a psychologist, human resource specialist, teacher, real estate broker, real estate, or an art assessor.

February 21 – Pisces, 8♦ Planetary Ruling Card
With an 8♦ Planetary Ruling Card, these 4♦ can succeed at running their own business (e.g., in real estate, event planning, or as an insurance agent). Some can make a career of writing, acting, art, or musical talent. These individuals require some freedom in work. If pushed into a fixed job, they may rebel by chasing get-rich-quick schemes that seldom pan out.

March 19 – Pisces, 8♦ Planetary Ruling Card

Practical and organized, these 4♦ prefer careers that recognize their innate talents and provide service to others (i.e., working for a non-profit organization or for local government) rather than a job that provides high compensation. They can also succeed in artistic lines of work.

April 17 – Aries, 6♣ Planetary Ruling Card

The competitive aspect of Aries in these individuals expresses a more ambitious 4♦ who can be successful as a lawyer, banker, financial planner, and business leader (especially if dealing with foreign goods or travel).

May 15 – Taurus, 8♥ Planetary Ruling Card

These practical 4♦ prefer working out of their home and being their own boss. Those with a more academic leaning can succeed as lawyers, negotiators, and scientists.

June 13 – Gemini, 2♠ Planetary Ruling Card

Ruled by fast-paced Gemini, these 4♦ enjoy occupations that are exciting and intellectually stimulating, such as a courtroom lawyer, sports or television personality, actor, or comedian. They can also successfully manage others in many different roles.

July 11 – Cancer, 4♥ Planetary Ruling Card

Being a Cancer and having a 4♥ Planetary Ruling Card may compel these 4♦ to own a business connected to women's accessories or products for the home. Some may settle for retail work or stay home raising children. If patience and discipline are developed, these individuals can succeed in any business or career involved with managing money.

August 9 – Leo, 4♦ Planetary Ruling Card

These 4♦ are hardworking, which assists them through the ups and down in life. They can be quite successful in sales, manufacturing jobs, or some form of entertainment.

September 7 – Virgo, 2♠ Planetary Ruling Card

These meticulous 4♦ prefer jobs that utilize their analytical minds, such as scientist, researcher, writer, or professor. They may want to work independently, but they should not because of their collaborative 2♠ Planetary Ruling Card.

October 5 – Libra, 8♥ Planetary Ruling Card

The entertaining traits of Libra are strong in these 4♦. Plus, the 8♥ Planetary Ruling Card makes them charming and popular, so many can succeed in lines of work that place them in the public eye. They can also do well as a writer, artist, actor, politician, ambassador, or public speaker.

November 3 – Scorpio, 6♣ and K♠ Planetary Ruling Cards

These deep thinking 4♦ must be careful not to fall so deep into thoughts that they get stuck in a rut. They can do well in occupations that use their minds such as a poet, writer, editor, or detective.

December 1 – Sagittarius, 6♠ Planetary Ruling Card

Fiercely independent, these 4♦ work hard to make sure they maintain their freedom and anatomy in life. They often become leaders. And they can succeed as a small business owner, especially if their business includes travel.

Famous 4♦

Kate Winslet, actress – 10/5/1975
J. P. Morgan, banker – 4/17/1837
Colin Kaepernick, football player/activist – 11/3/1987
Giorgio Armani, fashion designer – 7/11/1934
Whitney Houston, singer – 8/9/1963
Neil deGrasse Tyson, astrophysicist/ TV personality – 10/5/1958

Welcome to the world of the constructive 4♠!

4♠ = Stability in work and health

According to the Destiny Card system, souls chronologically experience God's lessons within each life incarnation. (Think of these as the universe's lessons if this aligns more with your beliefs.) The Birth Card each soul is born into determines the order and type of lessons a soul experiences. When you examine a Birth Card, you will notice it displays a suit of either a Heart, Club, Diamond, or Spade. This suit is significant because it represents the gifts a person born into this suit will possess and how they will direct their energies to learn lessons in their current life incarnation. A Heart Birth Card retains gifts and experiences life lessons around love and relationships. A Club Birth Card holds capabilities and experiences life lessons in their ability to communicate and absorb knowledge. A Diamond Birth Card possesses talents and experiences life lessons around money and values. And finally, a Spade Birth Card manifests gifts and experiences life lessons in work and health. Souls progress through incarnations and life lessons beginning as Hearts, moving on to Clubs, then Diamonds, and finally as Spades. Therefore, individuals born as Heart Cards are the youngest souls and individuals born as Spades Cards are the oldest souls.

In addition, the number on a Birth Card is equally meaningful as souls sequentially experience life lessons beginning as an Ace and culminating with lessons as a King. Consider representations of four in the world. Four legs of a chair. Four wheels on a car. Four legs of a dog, cat, and many other animals. Now imagine these same objects have their four parts reduced to three – three legs on a chair, three wheels on a car, and three legs on an animal. In each of these cases, the fourth part is critical because it provides strength and stability that helps ground these objects and ensure balance. **It makes sense, then, that a 4♠ child's purpose, gifts, and life lessons revolve around their need to construct *stability* in life. And due** to being a Spade, this child will learn lessons constructing stability in life through *work* and *health*.

How to Nurture the Temperament and Personality of a 4♠ Child

From a young age, 4♠ demonstrate *advanced motor skills* in physical activities such as crawling or walking when compared to peers of the same age. They often amaze family members with their athletic accomplishments. If nurtured to do so, these individuals can make a career in sports or occupations that require fine motor skills, such as a dentist, surgeon, artist, mechanic, or pilot. Enroll your 4♠ in numerous physical activities and let them select which ones to stick with. You see, physical exercise is required for 4♠ to maintain their vitality. Take the time to explain good eating and workout habits to them. They are the Birth Card most likely to incorporate healthy practices into their lifestyle. 4♠ desire security and if their security feels endangered, they are open to finding solutions.

As old souls, 4♠ are born knowing the *value of hard work*. Do not suppress this trait. If you are a parent of a 4♠, it is important not to spoil these children. Yet it is tempting to do so because they are so darn charming and easygoing. While spoiling is not ideal for any child, it is particularly harmful to a 4♠. You see, a 4♠ feels the most satisfied in life when they work. Give these children chores and an allowance. Expect good grades. Count on them to step up and help others even if there is no financial gain. Many 4♠ enjoy raising money for worthy causes so support them in these efforts. When adults do not teach the dignity of work to a 4♠ – or worse, when a parent does the work for them – these children become robbed of their power to find happiness in life. They may not achieve their highest potential. 4♠ must work and perceive achievements as a direct result of their efforts. When nurturing a 4♠ to work hard and take responsibility, make certain they do so in a structured and scheduled environment. They tend to feel unbalanced when dealing with ambiguity or when clarity and expectations are lacking. Set up schedules that model work/life balance. This will help offset the proclivity a 4♠ has toward becoming a *workaholic*.

It is common knowledge that adolescence is a time when people make mistakes. If a 4♠ makes the mistake of failing to work hard, let them suffer the consequences. For example, let's say your 4♠ child decides to take the AP Chemistry exam which allows high school students that score well to earn college credits. You have bought your child the practice materials and as the exam date gets closer, you notice your child has not used them or studied for the exam. You ask your child about their level of readiness, and they tell you to back off claiming you should not worry because they have been acing their Chemistry tests throughout the school year. Most 4♠ are *stubborn* and dislike being micromanaged. This is interesting because they often *micro-manage others*. Nevertheless, you decide to back off. Low and behold, the exam results come back, and your child has not passed. While you may be tempted to give them the "I told you so" speech, refrain from doing so. You see, 4♠ internally criticize and punish themselves when they make mistakes. In addition, because they are also *strong willed*, a 4♠ can truly crash and burn when they make mistakes. When they do, avoid harsh criticism or punishments.

A 4♠ is one of the few Birth Cards that an adult should always explain their reasoning to when making decisions that involve them. Even if they appear not to be listening, they are.

They might not agree with you, but sometimes they will, and in turn take your advice. One topic you should discuss and push with your 4♠ is the importance of being flexible in thinking and considering the perspectives of others. They tend to hang around like-minded individuals in school. While you may consider this a safe space for your 4♠, it can also cause them to become more *fixed in their thinking*. You need to teach them how to "walk in other people's shoes" or how to negotiate with others, rather than expressing "it is their way or the highway." Begin these discussions at preschool age. In authentic situations, point out the emotions of others and ask how their actions may have unintentionally caused these emotions. Read children's books that depict a character that has a problem because they hold a different perspective from others. One of my favorites is *No, David!* by David Shannon, in which the main character's perspective and that of his mother are at odds when it comes to the character's behavior. If you are a teacher, consider using a Circle of Viewpoints activity in the classroom whereby students learn how people can think and feel differently when discussing the same topic. (You can find Circle of Viewpoints graphic organizers on the Internet.) For instance, you notice in situations that involve bullying, your 4♠ acts as a bystander, observing and not intervening. Conduct a read aloud of *The Hundred Dresses* by Eleanor Estes. It is a story of a Polish immigrant teased by classmates for wearing shabby clothing. Engage students in identifying and explaining the feelings, perspectives, and actions of the three characters: Wanda, Maddie, and Peggy. 4♠ need to learn how to consider others' perspectives, or they will limit their own potential by alienating others or burning bridges due to their own fixed opinions.

Summary of Higher and Lower Personality Traits

Higher: Strong work ethic, persistence, organized, physically fit, want to please others.

Lower: Stubborn, opinionated, micromanaging, inflexible, workaholic, narrow-minded.

Childhood Influence Mercury Cards

It is common knowledge that a child's personality is most malleable during the formative years – from birth to eight years of age. In the Destiny Card system, the Mercury Cards in a Birth Card's Life Spread reveal influences a child with this Birth Card will experience between birth through age 12. As such, a child's Mercury Cards must be considered so an adult can nurture a child from a place of awareness and work with them from where a child is at in their development. A 4♠ child has the following Mercury Cards: **10♥, K♦, and J♣**. The K♦ and J♣ may mean there is an influential father or brother who is likely a Diamond or Club Birth or Planetary Ruling Card. Alternatively, outside of any specific person associated with these three cards, the basic meanings of these cards describe experiences that may be impactful during this child's formative years. These cards suggest a 4♠ is born into an affectionate and fun-loving family. They are creative, independent, and enjoy learning new things. They are financially protected in their youth.

Potential Callings / Vocations by Zodiac Sign

January 10 – Capricorn, A♦ Planetary Ruling Card
Double amounts of determination and ambition are inherent to these Capricorn 4♠. They will succeed at anything their hearts desire, which often tends to be as a business executive, sports ♦player, or an entertainer.

February 8 – Aquarius, Q♦ Planetary Ruling Card
These creative 4♠ invent themselves and therefore can do well in any profession. Many prefer leadership positions or jobs that enable them to influence large audiences (e.g., as a military leader or Special Forces soldier, scientific inventor, actor, writer, or director).

March 6 – Pisces, 5♥ Planetary Ruling Card
Highly tuned into the feelings of others and needing self-expression due to their 5♥ Planetary Ruling Card, these 4♠ often prefer work as a musician, actor, artist, dancer, or writer.

April 4 – Aries, 8♠ Planetary Ruling Card
Blessed with Aries competitive nature, these 4♠ have the power to achieve anything they set their minds to. Some love acting or working in the entertainment industry. Having an 8♠ Planetary Ruling Card blesses them with a strong physical body so they can succeed as a sports athlete.

May 2 – Taurus, 10♦ Planetary Ruling Card
These 4♠ are both security (due to Taurus) and luxury driven (due to 10 Planetary Ruling Card), which makes them well suited to occupations that provide products for the home, security, or entertainment to others. This may be achieved through business ownership, or a degree in law or medicine.

Famous 4♠
Dwayne Johnson 'The Rock', wrestler/actor – 5/2/1972
George Foreman, boxer – 1/10/1949
Maya Angelou, poet/writer – 4/4/1928
Shaquille O'Neil, basketball player – 3/6/1972
David Beckham, footballer – 5/2/1975

Chapter 8

Descriptions of the Five Birth Cards

Welcome to the world of the adventurous 5♥!

5♥ = Restless heart

According to the Destiny Card system, souls chronologically experience God's lessons across 52 life incarnations. (Think of these as the universe's lessons if this aligns more with your beliefs.) The Birth Card each soul is born into determines the order and type of lessons a soul experiences. When you examine a Birth Card, you will notice it displays a suit of either a Heart, Club, Diamond, or Spade. This suit is significant because it represents the gifts a person born into this suit will possess and how they will direct their energies to learn lessons in their current life incarnation. A Heart Birth Card retains gifts and experiences life lessons around love and relationships. A Club Birth Card holds capabilities and experiences life lessons in their ability to communicate and absorb knowledge. A Diamond Birth Card possesses talents and experiences life lessons around money and values. And finally, a Spade Birth Card manifests gifts and experiences life lessons in work and health. Souls progress through incarnations and life lessons beginning as Hearts, moving on to Clubs, then Diamonds, and finally as Spades. Therefore, individuals born as Heart Cards are the youngest souls and individuals born as Spades Cards are the oldest souls.

In addition, the number on a Birth Card is equally meaningful as souls sequentially experience life lessons beginning as an Ace and culminating with lessons as a King. The number five succeeds the number four. Given that the Destiny Card system is based upon the concept of reincarnation, a Five Birth Card's previous life incarnation was as a Four. Now, picture yourself in the following scenario. You have two bottles of soda; one has been shaken up and the other one has not. You open each bottle. What do you predict will happen? You got it – when opened, the soda that was shaken up explodes into the air. The soda you did not shake up stays in the bottle. Being a Four Birth Card is like being soda from a bottle not shaken up. Being a Five Birth Card is like being the soda from the bottle that has been shaken up. You see, all Five Birth Cards are born restless and subconsciously wanting to break free from the stable but confining mindset of a Four. **It makes sense, then, that a 5♥ child's purpose, gifts, and life lessons revolve around their gas-like behavior; their need to pursue *change*, expand freely, and explore all that the world has to offer. And due to being a Heart, this child will learn lessons through change and restlessness around *love* and *relationships*.**

How to Nurture the Temperament and Personality of a 5♥ Child

Infant and preschool 5♥ are endearing because often they are sensitive *love bugs*. They love cuddling and experiencing physical displays of affection. 5♥ require a lot of care and emotional attention. You see, many 5♥ experience some form of emotional adversity early in life that is outside of their control. Examples of such circumstances include family divorce, frequent moves, death of a special pet, or having a parent who is either emotionally detached or is required to spend a lot of time away from home (like a parent who is in the military). Therefore, they need more emotional nurturing to help offset the impact of their circumstances. This inclination may be difficult to accommodate for a parent who possesses a less affectionate demeanor. Or perhaps a parent believes their child might become spoiled if they are given too much attention. If a 5♥ is a male, a parent might even worry that accommodating this need might emasculate them. Generally, 5♥ will be better off having extra emotional support and attention. If you are a single, working parent of a 5♥ wondering how to provide lots of attention to your sensitive 5♥, look for outside support. Grandparents, aunts, friends, neighbors, afterschool programs, summer camps, and the Boys and Girls Club of America are all potential sources of assistance to help provide supplementary emotional security. If you are a teacher of a 5♥, perhaps you are familiar with a well-known framework called *The Developmental Assets*. The Developmental Assets is an inventory of 40 ingredients that research has shown helps children grow up to be emotionally healthy adults. If you have never heard of it, look it up on the Internet. Beneficial for all children, these assets are particularly vital as a support to have in place for a 5♥.

5♥ also benefit from an assortment of opportunities to feed their need for adventure and release their emotions. Since 5♥ tend to dislike monotony and restrictive environments, adults should help them choose their extra-curricular activities with intention. First, they need physical activities and regular exercise. Because 5♥ are also sociable, group activities are the best. If you are a parent of a 5♥, take them on road trips or day trips that include physical activity. Special trips are a great incentive or reward for a 5♥. Planning spontaneous adventures with a 5♥ will literally make their day. Secondly, and perhaps most importantly, 5♥ need *creative self-expression*. 5♥ are creatively gifted. Provide a 5♥ with choices – art classes, music lessons, dancing, theater classes, photography, choir, sewing, and baking. Are you short on funds to help a 5♥ stay busy? Explore free community music events or online training; from learning how to code (www.code.org) to teaching oneself how to do magic tricks on YouTube. In school, encourage them to join the debate team as they love observing the emotional reactions they can produce through their gift of gab. When a 5♥ fosters creative expression, they tap into one of their superpowers – *design thinking*. Design thinking is the ability to think in a non-linear manner, apply empathy, and create innovative solutions to problems.

Without a way to express or release their emotions, a young 5♥ may have a hard time removing emotions when making relational decisions. Let's consider an example. Imagine you are a single parent of an eleven-year-old 5♥ boy named Nathan who is excited about spending Spring Break with his dad. The week before the break, Nathan's dad cancels. The next day, Nathan's teacher calls you explaining how Nathan was moody and expressed unkind words with another student. You are surprised because you believe Nathan is kind and caring to others. This is true, but in extremely emotional situations a 5♥ may make impulsive and not thoughtful decisions. Alternatively, a 5♥ may adopt escapist behaviors to run away from their problem. These escapist behaviors can manifest as overeating, promiscuity, drug use, or overuse of technology or video game playing. When a 5♥ is experiencing emotional instability, urge them to put off decision making. Tell them to go outside and play to regroup their emotions. Or go to their room and listen to music. When they are in an emotionally better space, help them talk through the decision-making process. Going back to Nathan, a parent could help Nathan communicate his disappointment to his dad and offer ideas to spend some time together. If your 5♥ tends to feel emotionally vulnerable, some benefit from *aromatherapy*. Aromatherapy uses essential oils like lavender to positively impact the limbic system. The limbic system controls emotional behaviors such as fear and anxiety. If your child's circumstances seem extremely overwhelming, perhaps seek out a counselor or child therapist.

No matter the age of a 5♥, they often desire some sense of freedom. For instance, this is the school-age child who wants to ride their bike to school rather than taking the bus. If you are a parent of a 5♥, offer some freedom. This can be as simple as allowing a preschool 5♥ to pick a nighttime book to be read or select their own outfit to wear for the day. If you feel riding their bike to school is unsafe, offer other opportunities to ride a bike in a safer environment. Perhaps, grandma's neighborhood is safer, and they can ride their bike to the local convenience store. The great part of a 5♥'s hunger for freedom is that you can incentivize them to do chores or homework by bribing them with independent or grown-up activities, such as driving an ATV or engaging in a zip line adventure. Yes, bribery is okay in moderation. If an adolescent 5♥ asks to go on a special class trip or study abroad, try to make that happen for them as they adore travel and adventure.

5♥ are destined to experience changes in the heart from time to time. An adolescent 5♥'s love life can make a parent's head spin! For example, imagine you are a parent of an eleven-year-old 5♥ named Maria. On Monday, Maria is in a new relationship with a boy named Landon. By Tuesday, Landon is so lame, and Maria is now in a relationship with Anthony. This said, what might be hardest for a parent of a 5♥ is allowing them to make mistakes when it comes to relationships. Many life lessons for a 5♥ comes in the form of heartache and disappointment. They are often prone to falling in love quickly and without much introspection. You should not overprotect your child from these experiences, as they are part of their life lessons. For example, let's say you are a parent of a sixteen-year-old 5♥ male named Trevor. Trevor is in a new relationship with a girl named Allison. Through several interactions with Allison, it is completely obvious to you that Allison is not only ill suited for your son, but she is also using him because he has a car. On top of that, you believe Allison is taking advantage of your son – enticing him to buy her gifts and tickets to events. Your loveable son aims to please because the emotional reward is so gratifying. Sadly, it is not wise to intervene. A month later, Trevor discovers Allison has cheated on him. Trevor is devastated and his self-esteem takes a hard hit. In your mind, Allison proved herself unworthy and your son's rosy colored glass's view of this girl is confounding. However, you must remember that a 5♥'s purpose is to gather emotions in life, even painful ones. To be a supportive parent, the most important thing you can do is to validate their feelings. Be prepared if they do not want to talk about their feelings. Give them some time. Provide some distractions in the meantime. When they are ready to discuss the situation, refrain from saying, "I told you so" and focus upon lessons learned.

Summary of Higher and Lower Personality Traits

Higher: Affectionate, romantic, creative, progressive, inspirational, thrive in mental chaos.

Lower: Moody, promiscuous, emotional instability, emotional discontent.

Childhood Influence Mercury Cards

It is common knowledge that a child's personality is most malleable during the formative years – from birth to eight years of age. In the Destiny Card system, the Mercury Cards in a Birth Card's Life Spread reveal influences a child with this Birth Card will experience between birth through age 12. As such, a child's Mercury Cards must be considered so an adult can nurture a child from a place of awareness and work with them from where a child is at in their development. A 5♥ child has the following Mercury Cards: **3♣, 4♠, and K♦**. The K♦ may mean there is an influential father who is likely a Diamond Birth or Planetary Ruling Card. Alternatively, outside of any specific person associated with these three cards, the basic meanings of these cards describe experiences that may be impactful during this child's formative years. These cards suggest a 5♥ may experience anxiety connected to difficulty relating to a parent and/or they demonstrate curiosity and creativity from a young age. They are often exposed to an environment that provides work/life balance.

Potential Callings / Vocations by Zodiac Sign

October 30 – Scorpio: 9♥ and 9♦ Planetary Ruling Cards

Less likely than other 5♥ to make impulsive changes, these individuals can succeed in an assortment of occupations that require staying power and/or higher education. Many are gifted at design so they can do well as a graphic artist, fashion designer, architect, interior designer, animator, or software designer.

November 28 – Sagittarius: 7♣ Planetary Ruling Card

These Sagittarius 5♥ love travel so they often do well in jobs that keep them outdoors or moving from place to place (e.g., salesman, musician or other type of entertainer, park ranger, outdoor adventure guide, landscape architect, or tour guide).

December 26 – Capricorn: 5♦ Planetary Ruling Card

Due to the influence of Capricorn, these individuals are more persistent and ambitious than other 5♥. Having a 5♦ Planetary Ruling Card makes them prefer flexible careers. They can excel in business, real estate, public speaking, or acting.

Famous 5♥

Marcus Mariota, football player – 10/30/1993
Jon Stewart, TV show host – 11/28/1962
Anna Nicole Smith, Reality TV show star – 11/28/1967
Kit Harington, actor – 12/26/1986

Alexander Wang, fashion designer – 12/26/1983
Ivanka Trump, businesswoman – 10/30/1981

 Welcome to the world of the adventurous 5♣!

5♣ = Restless mind

According to the Destiny Card system, souls chronologically experience God's lessons across 52 life incarnations. (Think of these as the universe's lessons if this aligns more with your beliefs.) The Birth Card each soul is born into determines the order and type of lessons a soul experiences. When you examine a Birth Card, you will notice it displays a suit of either a Heart, Club, Diamond, or Spade. This suit is significant because it represents the gifts a person born into this suit will possess and how they will direct their energies to learn lessons in their current life incarnation. A Heart Birth Card retains gifts and experiences life lessons around love and relationships. A Club Birth Card holds capabilities and experiences life lessons in their ability to communicate and absorb knowledge. A Diamond Birth Card possesses talents and experiences life lessons around money and values. And finally, a Spade Birth Card manifests gifts and experiences life lessons in work and health. Souls progress through incarnations and life lessons beginning as Hearts, moving on to Clubs, then Diamonds, and finally as Spades. Therefore, individuals born as Heart Cards are the youngest souls and individuals born as Spades Cards are the oldest souls.

In addition, the number on a Birth Card is equally meaningful as souls sequentially experience life lessons beginning as an Ace and culminating with lessons as a King. The number five succeeds the number four. Given that the Destiny Card system is based upon the concept of reincarnation, a Five Birth Card's previous life incarnation was as a Four. Now, picture yourself in the following scenario. You have two bottles of soda; one has been shaken up and the other one has not. You open each bottle. What do you predict will happen? You got it – when opened, the soda that was shaken up explodes into the air. The soda you did not shake up stays in the bottle. Being a Four Birth Card is like being soda from a bottle not shaken up. Being a Five Birth Card is like being the soda from the bottle that has been shaken up. You see, all Five Birth Cards are born restless and subconsciously wanting to break free from the stable but confining mindset of a Four. **It makes sense, then, that a 5♣ child's purpose, gifts, and life lessons revolve around their gas-like behavior; their need to pursue** *change*, **expand freely, and explore all that the world has to offer. And due to being a Club, this child will learn lessons through change and restlessness around** *ideas* **and** *communication***.**

How to Nurture the Temperament and Personality of a 5♣ Child
Most parents would agree that preschool age is the time when children ask the most questions. A preschool 5♣ takes this behavior to an extreme level. For instance, in the span of 15 minutes, a preschool 5♣ can ask: Why is the sky blue? Where did the dinosaurs go? If I eat Cheeto Puffs will my poop turn orange? If you are a parent of a 5♣, this propensity can make your head spin!

What is amazing about a 5♣ is that they never seem to outgrow asking questions about anything and everything. Throughout their life, 5♣ maintain an *inquisitive nature* and crave explanations to life's mysteries. As a parent of this child, you are asking one question: Can I call 911 on this behavior? If this is not enough, 5♣ are extremely talkative and inclined to process their understanding of ideas aloud. Does raising this kind of child seem mentally exhausting to you? Well, they can be physically and emotionally exhausting, too. This same child may rattle a parent by running off and hiding from them in a department store. When they are confronted by their unsafe actions, they admit they acted without thinking. In general, 5♣ need to be kept mentally busy. Without this need met, a 5♣ may resist routines, which is problematic since routines are foundational to good teaching and parenting.

Keeping a 5♣ mentally busy is easier said than done. You see, 5♣ are mentally wired to explore all aspects of ideas and situations. However, this can mean that making choices may feel traumatizing to them. For example, pretend you are a parent of a five-year-old 5♣ daughter named Cassidy. Although Cassidy is an only child, to you it feels like you have five children because of the weekly stack of laundry. Upon close inspection of the laundry, most pieces of clothing are from Cassidy. Why? Cassidy literally changes her clothes five times a day! If a 5♣ feels overwhelmed with choices, they tend to change their mind numerous times. Ideally, 5♣ benefit from being given both structure and freedom around choices. Adults can accommodate this by playing games with a 5♣ that provides structure and freedom within *decision-making*. Examples of such games include *musical chairs* or *would you rather*. Would you rather is a game where kids are asked to choose between two preferences. As an example, an adult would ask: "Would you rather have a pet cat or dog? Would you rather vacation at the beach or in the mountains?" Older kids might prefer computer games that foster decision-making skills, such as The Oregon Trail, Quandry, Community in Crisis, or Sim City. In addition, provide your 5♣ with games that improve their attention span. I recommend Candy Land, UNO, and The Memory Game. Check the Internet for free videos and other resources that aim to improve children's ability to focus (websites like Play Adventure and S.M.A.R.T. Games). Within the games that include other participants, encourage a 5♣ to listen to others. Some are chatterboxes and need practice in allowing others to have a voice. If by chance your 5♣ has been diagnosed with attention deficit hyperactivity disorder (ADHD), you might want to check out EndeavorRx, the first prescription video game approved by the Food and Drug Administration for treating ADHD.

A good educational foundation is essential for a 5♣. To achieve this, they also need a delicate balance of structure and freedom in their learning environment. Let's consider an example. Imagine you are a fifth-grade teacher with a 5♣ boy in your classroom named Mason. Mason has advanced math skills. Lately, Mason is refusing to finish math assignments, claiming, "It's boring!" You decide to make a deal with Mason. If he can demonstrate competence solving half the problems of his choice, you will continue to modify his assignments. Of course, you will do this so long as he spends the extra time in agreed upon activities. Without accommodations like this, a 5♣ will likely initiate change on their own in the form of inappropriate behavior. They may wander around the room at inappropriate times, refuse to do assigned work, and disrupt other students. Alternatively, a 5♣ can get the right balance of structure and freedom through *differentiated instruction*. Differentiated instruction simply means that a teacher differentiates the content, process, assessments, or learning environment for a student. An example would be when a teacher uses *choice boards*. Choice boards are graphic organizers that display a variety of different ways to learn about or demonstrate learning of a topic. Choice boards can also be fun as an interactive online learning module.

As 5♣ grow into adolescence, they are inclined to spend a lot of time on social media. They must know what everyone else is doing. This behavior may be acerbated by a different 5♣ personality trait. 5♣ are gifted at *improvisation* or winging it. This trait may drive a parent crazy because getting a 5♣ to get off social media to prepare for a school presentation is like pulling teeth. If you are a parent of a 5♣, you may need to make compromises. You might worry that your child may get behind. Do not. 5♣ are intellectually brilliant. They may not need as much time to study or prepare ahead of time as other kids. Providing them with some freedom may pay off academically. Some even do their best when they are allowed to fly by the seat of their pants as the saying goes. Besides, 5♣ tend to learn best from *natural consequences*. Natural consequences are consequences of a child's behavior that happen without parental intervention. If a 5♣ fails to prepare for a school assignment and then does poorly, they tend to naturally learn from their mistake.

Ever watch the TV show, *The Bachelor* or *The Bachelorette*? In these reality shows, an attractive and eligible person dates multiple people. Contestants are vying to capture a proposal of marriage. The diversity of the contestants and elimination-style format of the show is exciting to watch. That type of adventure is the dream or close to the reality of every 5♣. In real life, some adult 5♣ are either having an affair, wishing to have a secretive relationship, or are obsessed with watching these kind of TV shows and living vicariously through them. You see, 5♣ who are unable to rein in their restlessness and make decisions tend to manifest serious problems in personal relationships. Therefore, it may help to watch these types of shows with an adolescent 5♣. Then use the emotions of the contestants to discuss the damage that can result when people are secretive and cheat on others. The underlying issue is that a lower expressing 5♣ may have trouble making and committing to a relationship. Their brilliant minds allow them to see flaws in every choice they make. They need to learn to be satisfied with imperfect decisions. In other words, they need to learn to shake off the negatives they feel. If you have listened to the singer and songwriter Taylor Swift, you probably know of her song, *Shake it Off*. The lyrics are about a person criticized for their inability to stay in a committed relationship. The negative criticism does not help the situation, so the person decides to shake it off. This is particularly interesting advice because Taylor Swift is a 5♣!

Summary of Higher and Lower Personality Traits

Higher: Inquisitive, talkative, improvisation, analytical, versatile, lucky, ability to appraise.

Lower: Unfaithful, skeptical, temperamental, interrogative, dissatisfaction.

Childhood Influence Mercury Cards
It is common knowledge that a child's personality is most malleable during the formative years – from birth to eight years of age. In the Destiny Card system, the Mercury Cards in a Birth

Card's Life Spread reveal influences a child with this Birth Card will experience between birth through age 12. As such, a child's Mercury Cards must be considered so an adult can nurture a child from a place of awareness and work with them from where a child is at in their development. A 5♣ child has the following Mercury Cards: **3♦, K♠, and Q♦**. The K♠ and Q♦ may mean there is an influential father or mother who are likely a Spade or Diamond Birth or Planetary Ruling Card, respectively. Alternatively, outside of any specific person associated with these three cards, the basic meanings of these cards describe experiences that may be impactful during this child's formative years. These cards suggest 5♣ often experiences security around family finances to the extent that they have access to many opportunities. They may struggle with vacillating values due to their difficulty relating to a mother and/or father.

Potential Callings / Vocations by Zodiac Sign

March 31 – Aries: 7♥ Planetary Ruling Card
These headstrong Aries are more inclined toward impulsivity and so careers that require educational staying power are often not within their reach. Many can cultivate careers from their musical or artistic talents. A career in home building, construction, or sales can also bring success.

April 29 – Taurus: A♠ Planetary Ruling Card
Ruled by Taurus, these individuals tend to be slightly more grounded in work than other 5♣ which helps them excel in many occupations. They can do well as an actor, comedian, publisher, music composer, or business entrepreneur.

May 27 – Gemini: 3♦ Planetary Ruling Card
With the influence of conversational Gemini, these individuals can do well in writing, sales, entertainment, journalism, or politics. With the financial creativity of a 3♦ Planetary Ruling Card, they can also succeed as a financial adviser or commercial broker.

June 25 – Cancer: 10♠ Planetary Ruling Card
Caring about social justice issues, these 5♣ prefer jobs that help people or solve real-world problems. Having a 10♠ Planetary Ruling Card affords them the staying power to stay in school longer. Therefore, these individuals can also achieve professional careers as a physician, mental health counselor, attorney, researcher, scientist, or teacher.

July 23 – Cancer or Leo: 10♠ or 5♣ Planetary Ruling Card
The Leo affiliated 5♣ need to cultivate perseverance to experience success. They tend to experience more success as a business leader, stockbroker, or actor. The Cancer affiliated 5♣ are hard workers and can succeed as a teacher, attorney, mathematician, or physician.

August 21 – Leo: 5♣ Planetary Ruling Card
These Leo-ruled 5♣ aspire to be experts in their field. They are original and analytical thinkers and can do well as a mathematician, researcher, professor, publisher, engineer, or teacher.

September 19 – Virgo: 3♦ Planetary Ruling Card

The detail-oriented influence of Virgo makes these individuals excel at many different careers such as a researcher, scientist, accountant, appraiser, translator, or dietician. They should be careful not to self-sabotage their efforts if things are not perfect.

October 17 – Libra: A♠ Planetary Ruling Card

Social and charming, these Venus ruled 5♣ prefer artistic forms of work. Careers can also include real estate broker, art dealer, interior decorator, or entertainer.

November 15 – Scorpio: 7♥ and 9♠ Planetary Ruling Cards

The imaginative aspect of these Scorpio 5♣ makes them well suited to occupations in law, engineering, medicine, journalism, or fashion design. Some tend to learn better through an apprenticeship experience than through traditional education.

December 13 – Sagittarius: 7♦ Planetary Ruling Card

More restless and fearful than other 5♣ due to their 7♦ Planetary Ruling Card, these individuals may have difficulty achieving through traditional schooling. They are better suited to putting effort into their talents (e.g., music, sports, acting, or writing).

Famous 5♣

Taylor Swift, singer – 12/13/1989
Dale Earnhardt, racecar driver – 4/29/1951
Sonia Sotomayor, lawyer/ Supreme Court judge – 6/25/1954
George Michael, singer – 6/25/1963
Jamie Foxx, actor – 12/13/1967
Mae Jemison, astronaut – 10/17/1956

Welcome to the world of the adventurous 5♦!

5♦ = Restless values

According to the Destiny Card system, souls chronologically experience God's lessons across 52 life incarnations. (Think of these as the universe's lessons if this aligns more with your beliefs.) The Birth Card each soul is born into determines the order and type of lessons a soul experiences. When you examine a Birth Card, you will notice it displays a suit of either a Heart, Club, Diamond, or Spade. This suit is significant because it represents the gifts a person born into this suit will possess and how they will direct their energies to learn lessons in their current life incarnation. A Heart Birth Card retains gifts and experiences life lessons around love and relationships. A Club Birth Card holds capabilities and experiences life lessons in their ability to communicate and absorb knowledge. A Diamond Birth Card possesses talents and experiences life lessons around money and values. And finally, a Spade Birth Card manifests gifts and experiences life lessons in work and health. Souls progress through incarnations and life lessons beginning as Hearts, moving on to Clubs, then Diamonds, and finally as Spades. Therefore, individuals born as Heart Cards are the youngest souls and individuals born as Spades Cards are the oldest souls.

In addition, the number on a Birth Card is equally meaningful as souls sequentially experience life lessons beginning as an Ace and culminating with lessons as a King. The number five succeeds the number four. Given that the Destiny Card system is based upon the concept of reincarnation, a Five Birth Card's previous life incarnation was as a Four. Now, picture yourself in the following scenario. You have two bottles of soda; one has been shaken up and the other one has not. You open each bottle. What do you predict will happen? You got it – when opened, the soda that was shaken up explodes into the air. The soda not shaken up stays in the bottle. Being a Four Birth Card is like being soda from a bottle not shaken up. Being a Five Birth Card is like being the soda from the bottle that has been shaken up. You see, all Five Birth Cards are born restless and subconsciously wanting to break free from the stable but confining mindset of a Four. **It makes sense, then, that a 5♦ child's purpose, gifts, and life lessons revolve around their gas-like behavior; their need to pursue *change*, expand freely, and explore all that the world has to offer. And due to being a Heart, this child will learn lessons through change and restlessness around *values* and *money*.**

How to Nurture the Temperament and Personality of a 5♦ Child
Young 5♦ often struggle with restlessness due to some disharmony in the home during their childhood. This disharmony can manifest in various ways – being born into a family that is arguing a lot, or their freedoms are restricted most often through a strict or extremely religious mother. Diarist Anne Frank, a 5♦ born June 12, is a perfect example of this. Anne was a Jew who endured a restricted lifestyle during the Holocaust. As a child, Anne spent several years hiding from the Nazis in a tiny, concealed room with her family. To deal with her restlessness, Anne kept a diary which was later published into a famous book. You see, a 5♦ may be soothed through *creative expression* of their restless values. 5♦ also appreciate learning about different values and perspectives of others. As such, they tend to be curious about different cultures. As a parent or teacher, you can help fulfill their curiosity by providing or reading to them books that expose them to different cultures. I recommend *A Ticket around the World* by Natalia Diaz and Melissa Owens, *Around the World in a Bathtub: Bathing All over the Globe* by Wade Bradford, and *Just Like Me, Climbing a Tree* by Durga Yael Bernhard. Then, you can also expose them to arts and crafts activities such as origami, coffee can drum, maracas, totems, or piñatas that celebrate other cultures. If you are a parent of a 5♦, plan family dinner nights in which your 5♦ helps you prepare traditional foods from a different culture. Enroll your 5♦ in foreign language classes at an early age. In fact, a dual language or international school environment might be ideal for them.

A 5♦'s need for experiencing different values also means they crave adventure and different places to travel. If you are a parent or teacher of a 5♦, support this need by supplying books where the characters engage in outrageous and worldly adventures. Some 5♦ enjoy the *Where's Waldo?* or *Geronimo Stilton* book series. Older 5♦ will love the choose your own adventure book series or video games. In these formats of stories, the reader imagines themselves in the role of the main character. Then in various sections of the book or game, the reader makes choices that influence the character's actions and the outcome of the plot. Additionally, as a parent, get input from a 5♦ when planning a family trip and make sure to let them pick an activity they want to do. Their sense of joy during that experience will make it worth your effort. Plus, these experiences hold the potential of sparking an interest that can lead to a career involving travel, international sales, or foreign affairs. Older 5♦ may be attracted to adventurous activities or organizations that expose them to diverse values. If this is true for a 5♦ child you are working with, urge them to sign up for community programs, such as boy or girl scouts, or volunteer work at school or church. Or encourage them to explore global causes and programs, such as World Vision, Kids Go Global, or summer abroad programs.

It is common for a young 5♦ to resist routines if they do not perceive value in them. Additionally, a 5♦ can thrive in a somewhat chaotic environment. This means your 5♦ may have a high tolerance for clutter and do not see value in cleaning their bedroom. This can be frustrating for a parent, especially if a parent is a tidy Virgo or a highly organized 4♣, 8♣, or Q♣ Birth Card. If you are a parent of a 5♦, you may want to set up a contract with a 5♦ to keep their room clean. These 5♦ often need to be incentivized by attaching rewards to routines. For example, set up a weekly bedroom cleaning checklist that includes removing dirty dishes and clothing. A completed checklist for the week can earn an extra 15 minutes before bedtime on Friday and Saturday night. Perhaps have a behavior contract for your child that rewards them with choices of engaging activities. Because they are a Diamond Birth Card, they value money so offer financial rewards. In some cases, using *natural consequences* may be effective. Natural consequences are accomplished when an adult allows a child to suffer the natural results of their behavior or when they apply a consequence that is related to the misbehavior. Let's consider an example. Imagine you are a parent of a five-year-old 5♦ who consistently refuses to pick up toys in the family room. You can introduce a natural consequence called *toy jail*. Toy jail involves jailing a toy that a parent asked a child to put away, but then they failed to do so. Of course, you can make up your own versions of this – shoe jail, clothes jail, video game jail, cell phone jail, etc. Just make sure jail time is not too long and you provide ways your child can earn back the object in jail.

Interestingly, 5♦ also tend to have a high tolerance for financial chaos. Furthermore, many 5♦ have charitable souls which may contribute to speculative or impulsive spending. Let's consider an example. Your 15-year-old 5♦ daughter named Mia is going on a class trip to a local art museum. Because you both did not have time to make lunch for this day, you gave Mia your credit card. Later you discover Mia spent about $50. on lunch that day. When questioned, Mia explains that her two best friends did not like what was in their lunch bag, so she bought them lunch, too. This is typical behavior for a 5♦. As a parent you are conflicted between wanting to scream at her and wanting to hug her for being so sweet! Talk through situations like this with a 5♦, specifically discussing the difference between wants and needs as well as what it means to give too much. Their idealistic nature makes them susceptible to exploitation by others. In this situation with Mia, as an example, it would be advantageous to help Mia reflect upon her actions. For instance, a parent could say: "Did you sit and eat with other friends? What if another friend was too shy to admit she did not like her lunch? Perhaps, she felt excluded by your actions. The safest way to avoid that is to stick to buying your own lunch." It may also be helpful to *role play* different scenarios or discuss real-life situations around spending with a 5♦ to help them from repeating such behaviors.

In addition, it is helpful to teach 5♦ *money management skills*. If you are a parent of a 5♦, start this process at a young age by gifting them two different piggy banks: one for savings and one for spending. Explain the concept of *delayed gratification* tied to keeping a piggy bank for savings. Then, have them practice delayed gratification. Start with small items, like saving to buy a candy bar. As they grow older, apply this to larger items that require more time to save. As an example, let's say your 12-year-old 5♦ wants a bicycle. Refrain from just buying them the bicycle. Help them set up a plan to earn the bicycle by doing chores over a negotiated period to earn money for their savings piggy bank. Make sure the goal is achievable, even if you need to match each dollar they earn. 5♦ are not opposed to working hard for what they want. Encourage them to do odd jobs for neighbors like babysitting or mowing lawns. Additionally, play board games with your 5♦ that teach them about money management. I recommend the following board games: *Game of Life*, *Cash Flow 101*, and *Charge Large*.

5♦ often establish a strong foundation of values through the influence of a dominating and strict mother or mother figure. All goes well as the young 5♦ mimics the same ideologies of this female. Then, all that changes in adolescence. Seeking autonomy and independence from their parents, adolescents start searching for truths outside of the family. Through this process, they begin to view their parents through a more realistic lens. An adolescent will question and at times may reject their parent's thinking or values, especially if they see flaws in it. While this transition often does not go smoothly for many teens, it may be particularly challenging for a 5♦. Variety is the spice of life for all Five Birth Cards. And 5♦ explore variety in values. As an example, let's say one day your 5♦ decides to no longer keep a clean bedroom. When a teenage 5♦ steps off the path of expected values, a parent may react by restricting the 5♦ even more. This may completely backfire in this situation. You see 5♦ need to explore and choose values based upon their own experiences. You cannot expect them to accept your values without question or to always step up to your expectations. While a 5♦'s capacity to thrive in chaos may be frustrating to a parent, keep in mind it is this same trait that can serve them well in a future career. Many 5♦s do well as investment bankers, financial traders, emergency responders to name a few careers.

Summary of Higher and Lower Personality Traits

Higher: Excellent salesperson, youthful, charitable, inventive, loyal, travel for work.

Lower: Irresponsible, immature, argumentative, dreamer, idealistic.

Childhood Influence Mercury Cards
It is common knowledge that a child's personality is most malleable during the formative years – from birth to eight years of age. In the Destiny Card system, the Mercury Cards in a Birth

Card's Life Spread reveal influences a child with this Birth Card will experience between birth through age 12. As such, a child's Mercury Cards must be considered so an adult can nurture a child from a place of awareness and work with them from where a child is at in their development. A 5♦ child has the following Mercury Cards: **Q♠, A♦, and 10♦**. The Q♠ may mean there is an influential mother who is likely a Spade Birth or Planetary Ruling Card. Alternatively, outside of any specific person associated with these three cards, the basic meanings of these cards describe experiences that may be impactful during this child's formative years. These cards suggest they may act impulsively as a child, but they often outgrow this. Often a strict mother helps them through this. They tend to be born into a financially secure family and therefore have ample funds to explore numerous interests.

Potential Callings / Vocations by Zodiac Sign

January 22 – Aquarius: K♣ Planetary Ruling Card
While these 5♦ are brilliant, they may need to overcome childhood family issues. Once they do, they often do well as a musician, poet, artist, actor, TV personality, or a foreign language translator.

February 20 – Aquarius or Pisces: K♣ or J♦ Planetary Ruling Card
The compassionate aspect of Pisces makes these 5♦ well suited to being a veterinarian, nurse, counselor, massage therapist, or non-profit organizer. Some can make a career out of singing, dancing, photography, or as a musician.

March 18 – Pisces: J♦ Planetary Ruling Card
Due to their J♦ Planetary Ruling Card, these 5♦ make excellent salespeople. They may also be attracted to well-paid professions such as an attorney, politician, or foreign affairs officer.

April 16 – Aries: 9♦ Planetary Ruling Card
With Mars-ruled Aries, these 5♦ are hardworking and can find success as a sports athlete (or working for a sports organization), actor, comedian, security guard, or soldier.

May 14 – Taurus: J♣ Planetary Ruling Card
Stable Taurus when combined with the brilliant J♣ Planetary Ruling Card helps to ground these 5♦. Therefore, they can succeed in occupations that require more staying power (e.g., entrepreneur, scientist, researcher, business leader, or sales executive).

June 12 – Gemini: Q♠ Planetary Ruling Card
Gemini's fast-paced nature combined with the inherent restlessness of 5♦ makes these individuals prone to scattering their talents. An occupation in sales, real estate, or any job that allows them to travel tends to work best for them.

July 10 – Cancer: 7♣ Planetary Ruling Card

More of a homebody than other 5♦, these individuals are better suited to freelance work, running an Internet business, or working a job that involves telecommuting.

August 8 – Leo: 5♦ Planetary Ruling Card

The independent aspect of Leo makes these hard-working 5♦ better suited to leadership positions. They can be a successful business leader, sports athlete, entertainer, director, or producer.

September 6 – Virgo: Q♠ Planetary Ruling Card

With the influence of Virgo, these 5♦ are skilled at critical thinking and can do well as an inventor, scientist, attorney, comedian, psychologist, or critic (e.g., travel, food, wine, or other products).

October 4 – Libra: J♣ Planetary Ruling Card

Many Libras gravitate towards the arts. Having the creativity of a J♣ Planetary Ruling Card makes this a definite possibility. These 5♦ can make a career out of acting, comedy, art, music, or writing. These individuals need strong role models at a young age, otherwise they may underachieve.

November 2 – Scorpio: 9♦ and 4♥ Planetary Ruling Cards

Highly sensitive and ambitious, these 5♦ can do well across a span of occupations: attorney, physician, scientist, engineer, politician, actor, or sports athlete.

Famous 5♦

Shawn Mendes, singer – 8/8/1998
Rhianna, singer – 2/20/1988
Guy Fieri, restauranteur/ TV personality – 1/22/1968
Chance the Rapper, singer – 4/16/1993
Mark Zuckerberg, entrepreneur/business leader – 5/14/1984
Anne Frank, writer – 6/12/1929

Welcome to the world of the adventurous 5♠!

5♠ = Restless in work and health

According to the Destiny Card system, souls chronologically experience God's lessons across 52 life incarnations. (Think of these as the universe's lessons if this aligns more with your beliefs.) The Birth Card each soul is born into determines the order and type of lessons a soul experiences. When you examine a Birth Card, you will notice it displays a suit of either a Heart,

Club, Diamond, or Spade. This suit is significant because it represents the gifts a person born into this suit will possess and how they will direct their energies to learn lessons in their current life incarnation. A Heart Birth Card retains gifts and experiences life lessons around love and relationships. A Club Birth Card holds capabilities and experiences life lessons in their ability to communicate and absorb knowledge. A Diamond Birth Card possesses talents and experiences life lessons around money and values. And finally, a Spade Birth Card manifests gifts and experiences life lessons in work and health. Souls progress through incarnations and life lessons beginning as Hearts, moving on to Clubs, then Diamonds, and finally as Spades. Therefore, individuals born as Heart Cards are the youngest souls and individuals born as Spades Cards are the oldest souls.

In addition, the number on a Birth Card is equally meaningful as souls sequentially experience life lessons beginning as an Ace and culminating with lessons as a King. The number five succeeds the number four. Given that the Destiny Card system is based upon the concept of reincarnation, a Five Birth Card's previous life incarnation was as a Four. Now, picture yourself in the following scenario. You have two bottles of soda; one has been shaken up and the other one has not. You open each bottle. What do you predict will happen? You got it – when opened, the soda that was shaken up explodes into the air. The soda not shaken up stays in the bottle. Being a Four Birth Card is like being soda from a bottle not shaken up. Being a Five Birth Card is like being the soda from the bottle that has been shaken up. You see, all Five Birth Cards are born restless and subconsciously wanting to break free from the stable but confining mindset of a Four. **It makes sense, then, that a 5♠ child's purpose, gifts, and life lessons revolve around their gas-like behavior; their need to pursue *change*, expand freely, and explore all that the world has to offer. And due to being a Heart, this child will learn lessons through change and restlessness around *work* and *health*.**

How to Nurture the Temperament and Personality of a 5♠ Child

Author and activist, Helen Keller, is famous for saying, "Life is either a daring adventure or nothing. To keep our faces toward change and behave like free spirits in the presence of fate is strength undefeatable." 5♠ are born embracing this philosophy of life but struggle to achieve it during their childhood because they often experience some restriction within the home. This restriction tends to be associated with a sacrifice that is forced upon them. This sacrifice can manifest in various ways – a family figure in their life is ill, they themselves are immobilized by a temporary illness, or they are born to extremely religious or poor parents. As a rule, 5♠ are *daring* and *adventurous*. However, adventure is not so easy to manifest when you are thirteen years of age and living as a dependent under the rules of strict parents. These circumstances explain why many young 5♠ feel restless. If a young 5♠ is not provided with opportunities for adventure and freedom, they may impulsively create their own. A 5♠ may seek adventure on a small to large scale and everything in between. On a smaller scale this is the five-year-old boy with a Big Wheel bike who repeatedly tries to ride his bike inside the house. When reprimanded by an adult, he says, "Ugh, I'm so frustrated. My rules are better than yours!" On a larger scale, this is a fourteen-year-old girl who feels oppressed and then runs away from home. Therefore, the best way to nurture a 5♠ is to ensure they experience some freedom and adventure in intentional and structured ways.

If you are a parent of a 5♠, support them in their need for adventure through fun activities such as visiting a community playground, an exploratory science museum, or a haunted house attraction to name a few. Older 5♠ often love amusement parks. This is the child who takes the dare from friends to ride the scariest ride in the park. And they love every minute of it. However, an adolescent 5♠'s need for adventure means they are susceptible to unhealthy *risk-taking*. Sure, you are thinking, all adolescents go through a stage like this. The prefrontal cortex in the brain of an adolescent is not fully developed. This part of the brain is associated with one's ability to make decisions, which is why they are likely to make poor decisions from time to time. This is also why adolescents feel so invincible that they engage in risky behaviors. This stage can look much different for a 5♠. At an extreme, they may fall into an *invincibility complex* on steroids. An invincibility complex is when a person believes they are indestructible no matter what they do, and they will not get caught or hurt in the process. Yes, I know, I am describing every parent's worst nightmare of behaviors – drug and alcohol use, drinking and driving, or unprotected sex to name a few. What is a parent to do?

The good news is, 5♠ can be encouraged to direct their risk-taking into constructive pursuits. Also, 5♠ tend to attract loyal friends who help guide them through difficult times. If you are a parent of a 5♠, urge them to participate in physically hard activity, exercise, or group sports. Let your child pick which activities to pursue. Co-create a list of activities and talk through the tradeoffs of participating in each, such as costs, time commitment, and interest level. Some 5♠ may need several physical activities in which to participate. And some may be attracted to extreme sports and activities such as rock-climbing, parkour, motocross racing, skate boarding, and ice hockey. Begin these activities with a 5♠ when they are young. As your child gets older, they will become more aware of how physical activity represents a healthy outlet for their feelings and they will more likely choose exercise over high-risk behaviors. In fact, if exercise or sports become an important outlet for a 5♠, never punish them by taking it away. Some 5♠ can even make careers out of their athleticism. 5♠ also love watching sports. Any troubles a 5♠ is experiencing are temporarily forgotten as they watch their favorite team play. If financially possible, take your 5♠ to professional sporting events. As a bonus, these events may promote bonding between you and your child.

In school, 5♠ need adventure, too. This can be accomplished best by engaging a young 5♠ in *play-based learning*. Play-based learning is active learning in which students explore, experiment, discover answers, and solve problems in playful ways. For example, a teacher can design questions for a child to answer while playing with blocks. This teacher would pose a question like, "How can you strengthen a building made with blocks to make it taller?" Play-based approaches to learning are often used in Montessori and Waldorf schools. The country of Finland has embraced play-based learning in their schools and believe it is why they maintain higher achievement scores than other developed nations including the United States. For a more comprehensive look at the rationale and ways to give students more play in the classroom, I recommend reading Peter Gray's book, *Free to learn: Why unleashing the instinct to play will make our children happier, more self-reliant, and better students for life*. Additionally, a new form of play-based learning that may benefit a 5♠ is *Forest School*. As it sounds, Forest School delivers education outdoors and uses natural spaces to teach leadership skills, problem-solving, and social skills in addition to grade level content. Because 5♠ love the outdoors, a Forest School may be a wonderful educational setting for them.

If you are a teacher of a 5♠ and play-based learning is not available or a realistic option, a good alternative is *differentiated instruction*. Differentiated instruction involves differentiating the content, process, assessments, or learning environment for a student. An example would be when a teacher uses *choice boards*. Choice boards are graphic organizers that display a variety of different ways to learn about or demonstrate learning of a topic. A teacher may also accommodate a student by allowing them to select objectives, who they work with, or how they will complete an assignment (Google Slides, a poster, or a presentation). Another kind of choice approach teachers are using with great success is *flexible seating*. Flexible seating is a strategy that allows students to sit or do their work using non-traditional objects, such as couches, beanbag chairs, exercise balls, standing desks, wobble chairs, mats, or stools. Flexible seating is a daily way to allow a 5♠ to have control over their environment.

Because a young 5♠ often feels restless by experiences outside of their control, it is also a good idea to give them some control or *freedom* in their life. Is the word freedom too scary a word for you? You may be thinking this is the worst kind of thing to give a child that is prone to risky behavior. However, some degree of freedom is needed for most 5♠. Let's consider a typical scenario. Have you ever heard of the poet, Maya Angelou? In her book, *I Know Why the Caged Bird Sings*, Dr. Angelou writes, "The caged bird sings with fearful trill of the thing unknown but longed for still and his tune is heard on the distant hill for the caged bird sings of freedom." A young person born a 5♠ is a caged bird in search of freedom. First, being in a cage is not so bad. After all, they are prone to restlessness so having some structure early in life is beneficial. Some preschool age 5♠ display this restlessness by being overly sensitive to external stimuli in their environment. Fortunately, many 5♠ tend to be supported through the influence of a dominating or strict mother. All goes well as the young 5♠ mimics the same ideologies of this female. They sing the same songs if you will. Then, all that changes in adolescence. Seeking autonomy, adolescents start searching for truths outside of the family. Through this process, they begin to view their parents through a more realistic lens. An adolescent will question and at times may reject their parent's thinking or values, especially if they see flaws in it. While this transition often does not go smoothly for many teens, it may be particularly challenging for a 5♠. As an example, imagine you are a parent of a seventeen-year-old 5♠ named Roxie. You and Roxie have visited numerous colleges over the past year and Roxie has received acceptances from most of them. One day Roxie announces she no longer wants to go to college. Because college has always been an expectation of your children, you refuse to accept this. This may completely backfire. Your 5♠ may feel like a caged bird who can no longer sing. If you are a parent of a 5♠ reading this, please understand you cannot expect them to accept your values without question or to always step up to your expectations.

To consider a resolution to Roxie's situation, let's replace the word freedom with another word – *flexibility*. A flexible solution might be a better solution for Roxie. One way to inject flexibility would be to allow Roxie to take a *gap year* with the understanding that she will attend college afterwards. A gap year is when a student takes a planned break from schooling to discover themselves through experiential learning. Such a break typically happens between high school and before college enrollment. A 5♠ will likely want to travel. Examples of gap learning abroad include mission work, service-learning, foreign internships, or global leadership programs. In general, if you are a parent of a 5♠, try to provide them with flexibility and small periods of freedom throughout their childhood. Perhaps allow your 5♠ to occasionally stretch the rules, whether this means extra time playing video games, staying overnight at a friend's house, or staying up late. Giving some flexibility in these ways helps to reduce the overall amount of rebellion your 5♠ will want to create. You see, rigid parenting often pushes a 5♠ toward risky behaviors. Finally, it may be helpful to know that most 5♠ outgrow the restlessness of their youth. Many 5♠ go on to establish a stable and fortunate life.

Summary of Higher and Lower Personality Traits

Higher: Versatile, organized, popular, compassionate, loyal, nonjudgmental.

Lower: Nomadic, discouraged, impatient, risk-taker, rebellious.

Childhood Influence Mercury Cards
It is common knowledge that a child's personality is most malleable during the formative years – from birth to eight years of age. In the Destiny Card system, the Mercury Cards in a Birth Card's Life Spread reveal influences a child with this Birth Card will experience between birth through age 12. As such, a child's Mercury Cards must be considered so an adult can nurture a child from a place of awareness and work with them from where a child is at in their development. A 5♠ child has the following Mercury Cards: **J♥ and Q♣**. The J♥ and Q♣ may mean there is an influential father, brother, or mother who are likely a Heart or Club Birth or Planetary Ruling Card, respectively. Alternatively, outside of any specific person associated with these two cards, the basic meanings of these cards describe experiences that may be impactful during this child's formative years. These cards suggest a 5♠ may need to make sacrifices or their freedom is restricted due to a family issue or domineering parent. They are likely gifted with a powerful mind but may exhibit impatience with others because of it.

Potential Callings / Vocations by Zodiac Sign

January 9 – Capricorn: K♥ Planetary Ruling Card
The influence of Capricorn on these individuals provides them with much needed persistence that can help them reach great heights, including positions of leadership. They can do well in politics, sports, entertainment, sales, or financial planning.

February 7 – Aquarius: K♦ Planetary Ruling Card
More avant-garde than other 5♠, these individuals are well suited to a career in music, sports, writing, or acting. With the financial power of a K♦ Planetary Ruling Cared, they can also do well as a real estate investor or commercial broker.

March 5 – Pisces: 6♥ Planetary Ruling Card

Well-liked by others, these 5♣ excel in business and sales. The creative aspect of Pisces also compels many to pursue careers where they can improve things (e.g., working in construction, education, or art).

April 3 – Aries: 9♠ Planetary Ruling Card

The competitive aspect of Aries makes these individuals thrive in commission-based jobs, especially if they believe in their product or service. Dramatic by nature, they can also do well in acting or promotional speaking.

May 1 – Taurus: 9♣ Planetary Ruling Card

Known for having strong voices, these 5♣ can do well as an actor, sports announcer, public speaker, or singer. Some make careers out of literary or artistic talent due to the mental brilliance of their 9♣ Planetary Ruling Card.

Famous 5♣

Garth Brooks, singer – 2/7/1962
Jane Goodall, English anthropologist – 4/3/1934
Eva Mendes, actress – 3/5/1974
Yasuko Namba, mountaineer – 2/7/1949
Kate Middleton, Duchess of Cambridge – 1/9/1982

Chapter 9

Descriptions of the Six Birth Cards

Welcome to the world of the harmonious 6♥!

6♥ = Laws of karma around love

According to the Destiny Card system, souls chronologically experience God's lessons across 52 life incarnations. (Think of these as the universe's lessons if this aligns more with your beliefs.) The Birth Card each soul is born into determines the order and type of lessons a soul experiences. When you examine a Birth Card, you will notice it displays a suit of either a Heart, Club, Diamond, or Spade. This suit is significant because it represents the gifts a person born into this suit will possess and how they will direct their energies to learn lessons in their current life incarnation. A Heart Birth Card retains gifts and experiences life lessons around love and relationships. A Club Birth Card holds capabilities and experiences life lessons in their ability to communicate and absorb knowledge. A Diamond Birth Card possesses talents and experiences life lessons around money and values. And finally, a Spade Birth Card manifests gifts and experiences life lessons in work and health. Souls progress through incarnations and life lessons beginning as Hearts, moving on to Clubs, then Diamonds, and finally as Spades. Therefore, individuals born as Heart Cards are the youngest souls and individuals born as Spades Cards are the oldest souls.

In addition, the number on a Birth Card is equally meaningful as souls sequentially experience life lessons beginning as an Ace and culminating with lessons as a King. Because souls reincarnate, a Six Birth Card's previous life incarnation was as a Five. Five Birth Cards explore and comprehend the world through the five senses: sight, smell, hearing, taste, and touch. People born into a Six Birth Card are continuing their soul's growth by experiencing the world through an extra sense: a *sixth sense* or *extrasensory perception*. They use this sixth sense to experience the laws of cause and effect or *karma*. Karma is the spiritual belief that whatever intentions and actions you put out into the universe, similar actions will come back to you either in a current or another life. To understand how this works, let's say you read a news article about a convicted investment advisor who lost all his money upon jail sentencing. The article explains the conviction had to do with fraud as the advisor stole money from his clients. This is an example of karma in current life. If that same investment advisor is financially victimized in his next life incarnation, this is an example of karma from a past life. Keep in mind, karma can be positive or negative. **It makes sense, then, that a 6♥ child's purpose, gifts, and life lessons revolve around managing the *laws of karma*. And due to being a Heart, this child will learn lessons through experiencing the laws of karma around *love* and *relationships*.**

How to Nurture the Temperament and Personality of a 6♥ Child

From an early age, 6♥ experience karmic lessons by being born into an extreme emotional environment. For many 6♥ this involves being part of an environment where there is disharmony in love and relationships. As an example, a 6♥ may be born into a family in which the parents, siblings, or other relatives are constantly arguing. 6♥ are gentle-hearted, so this kind of environment is especially challenging for them. If you are a parent of a 6♥ and this describes the environment, try to minimize their exposure to disagreeable situations that do not directly involve them. You may also notice your 6♥ becomes despondent when there is discord with friends. If a 6♥ child feels distressed by any relationship, encourage them to switch to a more harmonious environment. They can go for a nature walk, garden, listen to music, color, or try *aromatherapy*. Aromatherapy uses essential oils like lavender to positively impact the limbic system. The limbic system controls emotional behaviors such as fear and anxiety. In addition, 6♥ are excellent candidates to take up a competitive sport. They will often forget their worries when they are deeply involved in a sports activity. They easily "get in the zone" and can obtain victory over their competitors. Many professional athletes are 6♥.

Young 6♥ are typically affectionate and caring toward others. This is the five-year-old child you tuck into bed at night who says, "Who needs a warm bed when I have a warm mommy!" 6♥ are easy-going people that have an uncanny ability to put others at ease. They have many friends. If you are a friend of a 6♥, you know them to be affectionate and caring. They are *dependable*. Perhaps you are studying for a test and have put together a study group. You ask friends to help and while several say they will, you are not convinced of their sincerity. One thing for sure is that your 6♥ friend will show up. They may even bring several bottles of soda to help caffeinate everyone through the process. You see, 6♥ tend to be *people pleasers*. However, the central reason they please others is because they have learned to be passive in response to a disharmonious home environment. These 6♥ tend to be overly agreeable and *conflict avoidant*. This may be problematic if reinforced over time. Let's consider an example. Imagine a first-grade classroom where student desks are set up together in learning groups of five. Each group earns or loses behavior points based upon their cooperative ability to follow classroom rules. The yellow group, made up of all boys, just lost behavior points because one member of the team named Jason refused to clean up after an art activity. When the teacher deducted points from the yellow team, others in the group got upset and said hurtful things to their messy teammate. That is, everyone, but the 6♥ member of the team named Andrew. The next time the team had an art activity, what do you suppose Andrew did? You got it. Andrew cleaned up after Jason. On the one hand, Andrew has creatively solved a problem and established peace among the group. On the other hand, Andrew took on the personal responsibility of Jason. Imagine weeks go by with Andrew continuing to clean up after Jason. Other team members begin to bully Andrew, saying, "What? Are you Jason's mommy?" More weeks go by with continued bullying. In a situation like this, it may be helpful to teach a 6♥ how to be more assertive. A great children's book to start this conversation is *Shubert's Big Voice* by Dr. Becky Bailey and Leigh Burdick. In this book, a lightning bug named Shubert is bullied but then discovers assertive words that help him effectively stand up to the bullies. Overall, a 6♥

needs to learn about balance in asserting their own needs while accommodating the needs of others.

6♥ also need to learn about balance around *personal boundaries*. Let's go back to the scenario with Andrew and imagine that you are his teacher. One day you notice Andrew is cleaning up after Jason. Privately you ask Andrew about it. Uncovering the background story, you ask Andrew to consider what Jason is learning from this behavior and what others may be thinking about it. You explain that while Andrew's intentions are good, his action holds Jason back from the opportunity to take responsibility. You ask Andrew to consider other solutions such as reminding Jason, perhaps teaching Jason how to clean, or negotiating a tradeoff within the group whereby Jason is expected to put away supplies while the others clean the left-over stuff. By taking the time to dialogue through situations like this with a 6♥, you will nurture their inner peacemaker skills.

You see, a 6♥'s superpower is that they are *peacemakers*. Whether you are a parent or teacher, train your 6♥ to lead and model peacemaking during times of conflict. I recommend using a strategy designed by Dr. Becky Bailey called Conflict Resolution Time Machine. In her book, *Conscious Discipline: Building Resilient Classrooms*, Bailey uses a time machine mat and theme to resolve interpersonal conflicts. An adult will need to teach and facilitate the process with the goal that children will independently use it later. Let's consider the following example from a second-grade classroom. During a science experiment, Robert keeps grabbing materials away from his partner Erin. Erin complains Robert is not allowing her to participate, but he ignores her. Erin gets angry, grabs a piece of equipment, and a tug-of-war ensues. Soon their loud voices and actions disrupt others. The teacher intervenes, telling them they need to use the Conflict Resolution Time Machine. Robert and Erin step on the mat across from each other and are asked to imagine themselves transported back in time to the conflict. Classmates surround them with hands on their hearts proclaiming, "You can do it!" The perceived victim, Erin, speaks first using "I feel" and "next time" statements. Erin says, "I feel mad when you do all the fun parts of the science experiment. Next time, we should plan who does what part and take turns." Robert responds by agreeing to the "next time" statement or sharing a different, but fair solution. Once the conflict is resolved, Robert and Erin are asked to demonstrate there are no hard feelings by choosing to hug, fist bump, shake hands, high five, or use some other form of positive connection. An older 6♥ who develops peacemaking skills should be encouraged to apply for peer mediator positions at school that use conflict resolution strategies. 6♥ who hone their communicative and peacemaking skills often are attracted into careers as a mediator, counselor, therapist, or financial planner.

So, what is a parent to do when a 6♥ misbehaves and creates their own disharmony? When this happens, refrain from doling out a punishment or using verbally abusive language when you are angry with a 6♥. Instead, wait until you are calmer. If possible, implement *natural consequences* for a 6♥. Natural consequences are accomplished when an adult allows a child to suffer the natural results of their behavior or when they apply a consequence that is related to the misbehavior. Let's consider an example. Imagine you are a parent of an eleven-year-old 6♥ son named Lincoln. For months Lincoln is driving you crazy because he keeps leaving out empty or partially used soda cans all over the house. Even when you remind him to clean up after himself, this behavior continues. Finally, you decide to implement a natural consequence. You explain to Lincoln if this behavior happens again, you will stop buying soda. The next time Lincoln leaves out empty soda cans in the family room, you follow through with this consequence. Later, you offer Lincoln to earn back soda cans and you will likely see that Lincoln learns a lesson.

Summary of Higher and Lower Personality Traits

Higher: Affectionate, sincere, creative, peacemaker, empathetic, fixed principles.

Lower: Lazy, co-dependent, conflict avoidant, passive aggressive, lack of humility.

Childhood Influence Mercury Cards
It is common knowledge that a child's personality is most malleable during the formative years – from birth to eight years of age. In the Destiny Card system, the Mercury Cards in a Birth Card's Life Spread reveal influences a child with this Birth Card will experience between birth through age 12. As such, a child's Mercury Cards must be considered so an adult can nurture a child from a place of awareness and work with them from where a child is at in their development. A 6♥ has the following Mercury Cards: **4♣, 5♦, and 5♣**. Alternatively, outside of any specific person associated with these three cards, the basic meanings of these cards describe experiences that may be impactful during this child's formative years. These cards suggest a 6♥ may experience frequent moves and/or discontent during their childhood. They are active, adventurous, and eager to learn in school. In fact, it is often school where a 6♥ tends to feel the most stability.

Potential Callings / Vocations by Zodiac Sign

October 29 – Scorpio: J♠ and 10♦ Planetary Ruling Cards
The investigative aspect of Scorpio when combined with the caring 6♥ allow these individuals to excel as a nurse, physician, financial planner, physical therapist, or scientific researcher.

November 27 – Sagittarius: 8♣ Planetary Ruling Card
Due to their 8♣ Planetary Ruling Card, these 6♥ tend to be introverted and academically driven. As such, these individuals can do well as a writer, artist, musician, publisher, or producer.

December 25 – Capricorn: 6♦ Planetary Ruling Card
Sensitive and caring toward life's underdogs, these 6♥ can do well as a religious leader, charity or non-profit organizer, attorney (public defender), nurse, physician, counselor, or public servant.

Famous 6♥
Ricky Carmichael, motocross champion racer – 11/27/1979
Robin Givens, actress – 11/27/1964
Bill Nye (the science guy), TV host – 11/27/1955

Jimi Hendrix, musician – 11/27/1942
Winona Ryder – 10/29/1971

6♣

Welcome to the world of the harmonious 6♣!

6♣ = Laws of karma around knowledge

According to the Destiny Card system, souls chronologically experience God's lessons across 52 life incarnations. (Think of these as the universe's lessons if this aligns more with your beliefs.) The Birth Card each soul is born into determines the order and type of lessons a soul experiences. When you examine a Birth Card, you will notice it displays a suit of either a Heart, Club, Diamond, or Spade. This suit is significant because it represents the gifts a person born into this suit will possess and how they will direct their energies to learn lessons in their current life incarnation. A Heart Birth Card retains gifts and experiences life lessons around love and relationships. A Club Birth Card holds capabilities and experiences life lessons in their ability to communicate and absorb knowledge. A Diamond Birth Card possesses talents and experiences life lessons around money and values. And finally, a Spade Birth Card manifests gifts and experiences life lessons in work and health. Souls progress through incarnations and life lessons beginning as Hearts, moving on to Clubs, then Diamonds, and finally as Spades. Therefore, individuals born as Heart Cards are the youngest souls and individuals born as Spades Cards are the oldest souls.

In addition, the number on a Birth Card is equally meaningful as souls sequentially experience life lessons beginning as an Ace and culminating with lessons as a King. Because souls reincarnate a Six Birth Card's previous life incarnation was as a Five. Five Birth Cards explore and comprehend the world through the five senses: sight, smell, hearing, taste, and touch. People born into a Six Birth Card are continuing their soul's growth by experiencing the world through an extra sense: a *sixth sense* or *extrasensory perception*. They use this sixth sense to experience the laws of cause and effect or *karma*. Karma is the spiritual belief that whatever intentions and actions you put out into the universe, similar actions will come back to you either in a current or another life. To understand how this works, let's say you read a news article about a convicted investment advisor who lost all his money upon jail sentencing. The article explains the conviction had to do with fraud as the advisor stole money from his clients. This is an example of karma in current life. If that same investment advisor is financially victimized in his next life incarnation, that is an example of karma from a past life. Keep in mind, karma can be positive or negative. **It makes sense, then, that a 6♣ child's purpose, gifts, and life lessons revolve around managing the *laws of karma*. And due to being a Club, this child will learn lessons through experiencing the laws of karma around *communication* and *knowledge*.**

How to Nurture the Temperament and Personality of a 6♣ Child

From an early age, 6♣ tend to experience karmic lessons by manifesting one of two extreme behaviors: not speaking their truth (communication lesson) or procrastination in learning (knowledge lesson). Let's consider what each of these two behaviors might look like in a child beginning with *not speaking one's truth*. Many parents enroll their child into some sort of day care or preschool program ahead of K-12 schooling. One reason for this arrangement is to help socialize their child. During such a time, if you are a parent of a 6♣ you may notice they are becoming a loner. Why is this? Children at this age are developmentally experiencing an egocentric stage of their life which means conflict with others is inevitable. Because a young 6♣ may have difficulty speaking their truth, they dislike conflict. Some learn that they can minimize conflict by avoiding others. You may be inclined to shrug this behavior off by thinking this child is an introvert or shy. Trust me. Their behavior is more about *conflict avoidance*. You may need to intervene, so your 6♣ does not make this their 'go to' behavior when times get rough. If possible, provide a safe space for your 6♣. You can accomplish this by enrolling your child in a preschool that has fewer students or a smaller class size. Choose nurturing caretakers who prioritize socio-emotional learning over academic rigor. Talk to your child's teacher about setting up one-on-one friend experiences with an easy-going partner. At home, do the same with play dates. When a conflict arises, help facilitate, not solve the conflict.

Another behavior a young 6♣ may manifest to experience the laws of karma around knowledge is to engage in *procrastination*. Let's consider an example. Imagine it is eight o'clock at night and you are looking forward to some down time as you had a stressful day at work. Your twelve-year-old 6♣ daughter Charlotte announces she needs you to take her to the store so she can buy a poster board for her science project. You tell Charlotte you are tired, and it will have to wait until tomorrow. Charlotte explains that will not do because the project is due tomorrow. You throw up your hands into the air, frustrated that once again your daughter has procrastinated! And if you are a type-A personality, you may find it difficult to keep from nagging a procrastinator. You may find yourself nagging – all the time! You see, many 6♣ often start, but do not finish things. You may find yourself having power struggles with your 6♣. They may win. They may win because the root of the issue is control. They take control by being passive and digging in their heels. As such, some 6♣ may underachieve in life. While it can be hard to do, you may need to accept a 6♣ for how they are wired rather than trying to align them with your expectations. Particularly during adolescence, it may be far better to meet them halfway with expectations. As an example, you expect straight As from your child in school. This is unrealistic for most 6♣. You may need to accept straight Bs as their personal best. 6♣ need to learn about the effects of procrastination through their own life experience. If a parent intervenes too much and delays this experience for them, a 6♣ will likely continue this behavior into adulthood.

When a 6♣ procrastinates, one might think they do not care. Yet, this is not the case. They do care. It may be that they are dealing with an intuition that academics is not where their destiny lies. You see, young 6♣ often feel a strong intuition that they have a special purpose in life. Although most people grapple with the big questions of "who am I?" and "what is my purpose in life?" a 6♣ particularly struggles in this area when they sense their destiny is outside of careers obtained through higher education. This intuition can amplify a 6♣'s procrastination. If you are a parent of a 6♣, encourage their dreams outside of school. Perhaps your child wants to be a professional football player. For you, this goal seems unreachable and unrealistic. However, such dreams often can come true for a 6♣. Many 6♣ are professional athletes. And some 6♣ can become a successful musician, actor, or artist. Keep in mind that 6♣ also tend to be late bloomers. They may procrastinate and underachieve until they find their purpose in life. When they find it, they will devote themselves to it and succeed. Be patient with your 6♣.

This said, it is not easy to raise a child who is prone to procrastination. However, there are strategies a parent can implement to help. Of course, the earlier in age you begin these strategies, the better the outcome. As one example, 6♣ need a lot of *structure* in their daily life. They need to be on a strict nap, eating, and bedtime schedule. As they grow older, help them implement schedules for homework, extra-curricular activities, and social media use time. 6♣ often need adult assistance with *time management*, particularly with large projects. Purchase them a planner and teach them how to use it. Help them break down a project into smaller parts or create shorter goals that include separate due dates. Refrain from doing the work for them, even if the quality of their work is poor. Leverage their interests as rewards. 6♣ inherently struggle with pace and get into a rut; so, make sure to even reward partially completed projects. An all or nothing reward may be unrealistic for a 6♣. Tie the amount of a reward directly to the amount completed. For instance, let's say your ten-year-old 6♣ son is required to read for pleasure for 60 minutes per week as homework. Every week this expectation results in an argument between you and your son. One rule in the house is that there is no video game playing on school nights. You decide to reward each minute of reading with equal minutes of video game playing during the school week. If your 6♣ only reads for 30 minutes, he would earn 30 minutes of video game playing.

Finally, it may be helpful to understand there is purpose to a 6♣'s slower pace in life. A 6♣'s superpower is that they are born with a sixth sense, otherwise known as a *gut feeling* or *intuition*. This means they can quickly perceive an insight or instinct about a person or situation. The mechanism through which they tap into this ability is by walking through life as a *flaneur*. What is a flaneur? you ask. During the 1900's, the term flaneur appeared in French literature to describe a person who strolls slowly through life to appreciate its smallest details. In fact, flaneurs were depicted as walking turtles to indicate how slow they were moving. A flaneur embraced such a lifestyle in response to their critical view of modern life. They believed the hustle and bustle associated with modern life hijacked one's ability to connect with the subconscious mind. In other words, to connect with one's sixth sense. 6♣ connect to their sixth sense by living life at a slower pace. As such, 6♣ tend to experience life events that force this tempo upon them. With the time to receive knowledge from a higher source, 6♣ learn the laws of karma around *communication* and *knowledge*. Then they go on to share that knowledge with others through a career. Many 6♣ find success as a teacher, counselor, therapist, or mediator.

If a 6♣ misbehaves, whether at home or at school, refrain from using *punitive discipline*. Punitive discipline involves using punishment and fear as a means of controlling misbehavior. In school, punitive discipline techniques include detention, losing recess time, or in-school suspension. Such techniques tend to shut down a 6♣. If you are a teacher of a 6♣, please know that keeping a 6♣ child from recess to finish classwork is not a good solution. At an extreme, punitive techniques may manifest a 6♣'s traits such as procrastination and passive-aggressive behavior. A better approach for a 6♣, as well as for many other Birth Cards, is to implement *conscious discipline*. Conscious discipline integrates brain research, socio-emotional learning, and behavior management strategies to effectively teach children how to manage their own behavior. I suggest reading the book, *Conscious Discipline*, by Dr. Becky Bailey, who developed this methodology. At home, punitive discipline techniques also tends to fail with a 6♣. Punitive techniques include yelling, criticism, threatening, and restricting activities.

Summary of Higher and Lower Personality Traits

Higher: Integrity, patient, intuitive, good listener, romantic, balanced values.

Lower: Dishonesty, worrisome, self-criticism, procrastinator, low self-esteem.

Childhood Influence Mercury Cards
It is common knowledge that a child's personality is most malleable during the formative years – from birth to eight years of age. In the Destiny Card system, the Mercury Cards in a Birth Card's Life Spread reveal influences a child with this Birth Card will experience between birth through age 12. As such, a child's Mercury Cards must be considered so an adult can nurture a child from a place of awareness and work with them from where a child is at in their development. A 6♣ child has the following Mercury Cards: **6♠, 2♣, and 9♠**. Alternatively, outside of any specific person associated with these three cards, the basic meanings of these cards describe experiences that may be impactful during this child's formative years. These cards suggest a 6♣ may be tested early with karmic health or lifestyle losses that really frustrate or limit them, perhaps even the death of a family member. They may be argumentative and/or have excellent communication skills.

Potential Callings / Vocations by Zodiac Sign

March 30 – Aries: 10♣ Planetary Ruling Card
The energetic influence of Aries allows these individuals to be more motivated than other 6♣. With a structured education, they can succeed as a teacher, professor, or writer. Those less grounded in education may prefer a career as an actor, singer, musician, or artist.

April 28 – Taurus: Q♥ Planetary Ruling Card
These 6♣ possess strong voices that can be leveraged into a career (e.g., singing, comedy, acting, public speaking, or sports announcer). Those inclined toward laziness due to their Q♥ Planetary Ruling Card can limit their career options and they find themselves directed into subordinate jobs. Some prefer a job that is associated with beautification (e.g., interior designer, flower arranger, and hairdresser).

May 26 – Gemini: 6♠ Planetary Ruling Card

Creative and artsy, these 6♣ can make an excellent teacher, actor, writer, or artist. Some enjoy sports and can make a career as a professional athlete.

June 24 – Cancer: 8♥ Planetary Ruling Card

The nurturing aspect of Cancer suggests many of these 6♣ may prefer to serve others as a teacher, preacher, or counselor. Some decide to be stay-at-home Moms or Dads. And some decide to serve their country by joining the military.

July 22 – Cancer: 8♥ Planetary Ruling Card

These 6♣ hold amazing potential for success through their talents in music, acting, or athleticism. Some choose to work for or support charities or non-profit organizations.

August 20 – Leo: 6♣ Planetary Ruling Card

A Leo's need to be in the spotlight often conflicts with a 6♣ desire to serve others. Occupations where they can achieve both may be best accomplished as a charity organizer, attorney, preacher, or business leader (with a philanthropic leaning).

September 18 – Virgo: 6♠ Planetary Ruling Card

The critical aspect of Virgo may cause these 6♣ to doubt themselves and under achieve. They may find more happiness in independent and/or menial labor jobs such as chauffer, handy man, hairdresser, or electrician. Some may excel as a researcher or statistician.

October 16 – Libra: Q♥ Planetary Ruling Card

The balance-loving energy of Libra when combined with harmony seeking 6♣ causes these individuals to be passive early in life and therefore some find themselves in monotonous jobs. Some may capitalize on their charm and find success as an actor or religious leader.

November 14 – Scorpio: 10♣ and Q♣ Planetary Ruling Cards

Due to having the mental achievement influence of a 10♣ Planetary Ruling Card, these 6♣ can be successful in many different careers such as acting, teaching, art, invention, writing, singing, or a professional athlete.

December 12 – Sagittarius: 8♦ Planetary Ruling Card

These outgoing and magnetic 6♣ may excel in show business due to their 8♦ Planetary Ruling Card. Those that prefer mental occupations can do well as an attorney, politician, writer, or teacher.

Famous 6♣

Mindy Kaling, actress – 6/24/1979
Lionel Messi, soccer player – 6/24/1987
Eli Tomac, champion motocross racer – 11/14/1992
Nora Jones, singer – 3/30/1979

Jay Leno, comedian – 4/28/1950
Selena Gomez, actress – 7/22/1992

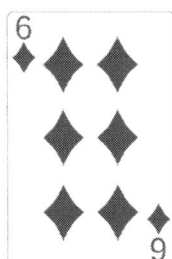

Welcome to the world of the harmonious 6♦!

6♦ = Laws of karma around values and money

According to the Destiny Card system, souls chronologically experience God's lessons across 52 life incarnations. (Think of these as the universe's lessons if this aligns more with your beliefs.) The Birth Card each soul is born into determines the order and type of lessons a soul experiences. When you examine a Birth Card, you will notice it displays a suit of either a Heart, Club, Diamond, or Spade. This suit is significant because it represents the gifts a person born into this suit will possess and how they will direct their energies to learn lessons in their current life incarnation. A Heart Birth Card retains gifts and experiences life lessons around love and relationships. A Club Birth Card holds capabilities and experiences life lessons in their ability to communicate and absorb knowledge. A Diamond Birth Card possesses talents and experiences life lessons around money and values. And finally, a Spade Birth Card manifests gifts and experiences life lessons in work and health. Souls progress through incarnations and life lessons beginning as Hearts, moving on to Clubs, then Diamonds, and finally as Spades. Therefore, individuals born as Heart Cards are the youngest souls and individuals born as Spades Cards are the oldest souls.

In addition, the number on a Birth Card is equally meaningful as souls sequentially experience life lessons beginning as an Ace and culminating with lessons as a King. Because souls reincarnate a Six Birth Card's previous life incarnation was as a Five. Five Birth Cards explore and comprehend the world through the five senses: sight, smell, hearing, taste, and touch. People born into a Six Birth Card are continuing their soul's growth by experiencing the world through an extra sense: a *sixth sense* or *extrasensory perception*. They use this sixth sense to experience the laws of cause and effect or *karma*. Karma is the spiritual belief that whatever intentions and actions you put out into the universe, similar actions will come back to you either in a current or another life. To understand how this works, let's say you read a news article about a convicted investment advisor who lost all his money upon jail sentencing. The article explains the conviction had to do with fraud as the advisor stole money from his clients. This is an example of karma in current life. If that same investment advisor is financially victimized in his next life incarnation, this is an example of karma from a past life. Keep in mind, karma can be positive or negative. **It makes sense, then, that a 6♦ child's purpose, gifts, and life lessons revolve around managing the *laws of karma*. And due to being a Diamond, this child will learn lessons through experiencing the laws of karma around *values* and *money*.**

How to Nurture the Temperament and Personality of a 6♦ Child

Being a Diamond Birth Card, 6♦ tend to experience karmic lessons around values, money, or both. And 6♦ tend to manifest karmic experiences in extremes. Let's unpack each of these karmic experiences beginning with values. Imagine a young 6♦ named Paul is raised in an extremely religious household. The views of this family include a fixed and negative belief toward homosexuality. Growing up, Paul becomes an adult who has adopted similar views as his family. Later, Paul is voted into a political position in his local government running on these and other conservative views. Then karma strikes. Paul's fourteen-year-old child comes out as a homosexual. This is one example of a karmic experience a 6♦ may manifest around values.

A far greater majority of 6♦ manifest karmic lessons around money. Again, they manifest a karmic experience in an extreme manner. At one extreme, some 6♦ children may experience karma by being born into a family with money and then they are irresponsible with it. These lower expressing individuals may pay their bills late and accumulate debt. It is common for these 6♦ to declare bankruptcy at least once in their lifetime. Some shirk financial responsibility by marrying for money. These individuals may become entitled, lazy, and assume others should take care of them. Then there are some 6♦ who gamble by playing the lottery, betting on sports games, or hitting casinos. While a few may strike it rich through luck or with little effort, they can easily go on to lose the money they gained. At the other extreme, some 6♦ experience karma by being born into a family without much money and then they become overly responsible with it. These higher expressing individuals save money and rarely pay their bills late. Some go on to accumulate a lot of wealth. These 6♦ understand the value of money and its connection to power and opportunity.

Because there is a spectrum of values that can manifest, it is difficult to pinpoint all the challenges a 6♦ child may have to manage. What may be helpful is for an adult to look for patterns of behavior and then try to help a 6♦ achieve a more balanced view of this value. Let's consider an example. Imagine you are a kindergarten teacher with a 6♦ in your classroom named Amelia. Amelia is your most well-mannered student. During parent-teacher conferences you were not surprised to find Amelia's parents to be extremely strict. This said, you have noticed a pattern of behavior. Amelia is tattling on other students. While you appreciated her behavior at first, it now seems over the top. You believe Amelia's home values and expected behaviors conflict with other students who are a product of other values and expectations. In such a situation, I recommend reading and discussing the children's book, *Don't Squeal Unless It's a Big Deal,* by Jeanie Franz with Amelia and then establish class procedures with regards to tattling. If this behavior continues with Amelia, it may be necessary to implement individualized *behavior management strategies*. Behavior management strategies are techniques used to redirect and improve student behaviors. To manage tattling, it is important to teach a child several steps they should go through before involving an adult. Tattle problem-solving worksheets and charts can be found on the Internet. No matter what extreme value a child is manifesting, the objective should be to help this child develop a more balanced viewpoint to keep harmony.

When confronted with different values, some 6♦ may learn to manage these situations by becoming *conflict avoidant*. Let's consider an example. Imagine you are a first-grade teacher with a student in your classroom named Tyler. During playtime, you notice Tyler loves creating towers and buildings out of magnetic tiles. In Tyler's future, you see a career in architecture! One day you notice Tyler has stopped playing with the magnetic tiles. You ask him why and he claims they are not fun anymore. Thinking back, you recall a couple of times in the past few weeks where another student named Dominic knocked down Tyler's tile designs and then laughed about it. You found out about this from another student. You wonder why Tyler did not say anything about this to you and suspect this may be related to Tyler's new attitude. Well, Tyler did not tell you because he is a 6♦! They tend to fear any negative response or emotional reaction that results from conflict. Rather than confronting the conflict, they may suppress their true feelings or avoid the situation that led to conflict, like playing with tiles.

6♦ are nurtured when they are taught how to express their feelings during times of conflict. If you are a parent of a 6♦, look for real time opportunities of conflict as teachable moments and start with conflicts between you and them. You can often recognize these moments through a 6♦'s body language – fist tightening, pursing of lips, or when their face turns red. For instance, imagine that you are a parent of an eleven-year-old 6♦ named Emily. You are shopping for new school clothes for Emily who is starting middle school. Emily is being unusually picky about what she wants to purchase. Frustrated, you make the decisions about the clothing and Emily starts to cry. You ask what is wrong and know she is angry with you, but she refuses to say anything. Once home, Emily locks herself in her room and refuses to join the family for dinner. Later, you have a talk with Emily. This process should begin by explaining that no matter what your child says or feels, their relationship with you is strong. You love them unconditionally. Then help them identify emotions and put them into *I Feel statements*. I Feel statements are a non-aggressive way to communicate during conflict. There are three parts to an I Feel statement: "I feel _____ (the feeling), when you _____ (the conflicting behavior). Next time, _____ (suggest what to do)." A good I feel statement for Emily to express might be: "I feel mad when you dismiss my ideas about what clothing to buy. Next time, please listen to my ideas and why they are important to me." Teaching this form of communication during conflicts ideally should start from a young age and continue into adolescence. Without this skillset, a 6♦ may become passive and refuse to speak up. These individuals may learn to repress emotions. 6♦ need to realize they can express disagreement with others and keep a relationship intact. A 6♦ who learns to speak their truth often select careers where they can practice doing it. Such careers are: counselor, teacher, health care mediator, or divorce custody mediator.

It is remarkable how many 6♦ go on to become professional athletes. Sure, the odds are low for a young person to turn a sports interest into a career. For instance, it is a fact that the NFL will draft only 0.08% of senior high school football players. Yet, the odds are higher for a 6♦. Why is this so? 6♦ utilize their *sixth sense* to implement the right things to eat and exercises to do to stay healthy. As such, they retain a strong *physical constitution*. Add to this, many 6♦ value winning and then they manifest experiencing it at an extreme. These 6♦ are highly competitive. And higher expressing 6♦ have learned the right balance of give and take. When a competitor is getting the best of them, a 6♦ instinctually pushes back to take things back into balance. By exposing oneself to more highly skilled competitors, this push and pull kind of training accelerates the growth of their own skillset. Furthermore, many 6♦ have a stoic demeanor. This trait makes it difficult for a competitor to read them and their intentions. For these reasons, it is imperative to expose a 6♦ to physical activity and sports. 6♦ tend to prefer individual sports like tennis, wrestling, or swimming, or sports where their single efforts are recognized due to their competitive nature. Without physical outlets, a 6♦ may become high-strung. Too much stress may cause a 6♦ to embrace lower traits like being conflict resistant, getting stuck in a rut, or underachieving.

Summary of Higher and Lower Personality Traits

Higher: Athletic, competitive, honorable, responsible, perceptive, good listener.

Lower: Lazy, irresponsible, materialistic, emotionally repression, conflict avoidant.

Childhood Influence Mercury Cards

It is common knowledge that a child's personality is most malleable during the formative years – from birth to eight years of age. In the Destiny Card system, the Mercury Cards in a Birth Card's Life Spread reveal influences a child with this Birth Card will experience between birth through age 12. As such, a child's Mercury Cards must be considered so an adult can nurture a child from a place of awareness and work with them from where a child is at in their development. A 6♦ child has the following Mercury Cards: **4♠, K♥, and 10♣**. The K♥ may mean there is an influential father who is likely a Heart Birth or Planetary Ruling Card. Alternatively, outside of any specific person associated with these three cards, the basic meanings of these cards describe experiences that may be impactful during this child's formative years. These cards suggest a 6♦ is born with above average motor skills, and they do well in early education. They also tend to get along well with others.

Potential Callings / Vocations by Zodiac Sign

January 21 – Capricorn or Aquarius: A♥ or A♦ Planetary Ruling Card

The unconventional aspect of Aquarius makes these 6♦ prefer offbeat careers as an engineer, military leader, singer, or artist. Due to the impulsiveness of having two Ace Planetary Ruling Cards, they need to be careful about feeling entitled or erratically searching for the perfect job.

February 19 – Pisces: A♦ Planetary Ruling Card

These 6♦ may be late bloomers due to being parented by a dominating person who has unrealistic expectations of them. When they do find themselves, they can succeed as an actor, artist, or musician.

March 17 – Pisces: Q♦ Planetary Ruling Card

The empathetic aspect of Pisces makes these 6♦ well suited to jobs that serve others (e.g., counselor, teacher, financial planner, attorney, or judge). Those who appreciate the finer things in life due to their Q♦ Planetary Ruling Card may be motivated to pursue a career in sports, dance, or acting.

April 15 – Aries: 10♦ Planetary Ruling Card

The energy of Mars combined with the financial achievement influence of a 10♦ Planetary Ruling Card instills a lot of drive in these 6♦. They can do well in banking, teaching, preaching, or law. Artistic leaning individuals can make a career of their art or writing.

May 13 – Taurus: 10♥ Planetary Ruling Card

Sensitive and dependable, these 6♦ can succeed in sports, manufacturing jobs, construction work, singing, writing, gardening, or working with nature. They can do well in business if there is a cause attached to it that aligns well with their values.

June 11 – Gemini: 4♠ Planetary Ruling Card

These clever 6♦ can do well in sales, acting, politics, or public speaking. Artistic leaning individuals can make a career of their art, music, or writing.

July 9 – Cancer: 8♣ Planetary Ruling Card

The protective and caring aspect of Cancer make these 6♦ prefer jobs where they can implement their values in solving real-world problems. They can succeed as a teacher, writer, elder caregiver, social worker, or engineer.

August 7 – Leo: 6♦ Planetary Ruling Card

Leos love the spotlight, and these 6♦ Leos are no different. They can excel as an actor, director, producer, or sports athlete.

September 5 – Virgo: 4♠ Planetary Ruling Card

These analytical 6♦ enjoy exploring the details of things valued so they can do well as a critic, property appraiser, or real estate broker. Some can excel in acting, business, or as a composer.

October 3 – Libra: 10♥ Planetary Ruling Card

Libra's influence blesses these 6♦ with good looks and expressive voices. Having a 10♥ Planetary Ruling Card ensures they can find success as an entertainer. Many do well in acting, writing, singing, or as a sports athlete.

November 1 – Scorpio: 10♦ and 5♥ Planetary Ruling Cards

Intensely curious, these 6♦ prefer jobs that allow them to search for solutions to problems as a scientist, engineer, physician, attorney, or business leader.

Famous 6♦

Tom Hanks, actor/director – 7/9/1956
Charlize Theron, actress – 8/7/1975
Peter Dinklage, actor – 6/11/1969
Gwen Stefani, singer – 10/3/1969
Clive Owen, actor – 10/3/1964

Tim Cook, Apple CEO – 11/1/1960

Welcome to the world of the harmonious 6♠!

6♠ = Laws of karma in health and work

According to the Destiny Card system, souls chronologically experience God's lessons across 52 life incarnations. (Think of these as the universe's lessons if this aligns more with your beliefs.) The Birth Card each soul is born into determines the order and type of lessons a soul experiences. When you examine a Birth Card, you will notice it displays a suit of either a Heart, Club, Diamond, or Spade. This suit is significant because it represents the gifts a person born into this suit will possess and how they will direct their energies to learn lessons in their current life incarnation. A Heart Birth Card retains gifts and experiences life lessons around love and relationships. A Club Birth Card holds capabilities and experiences life lessons in their ability to communicate and absorb knowledge. A Diamond Birth Card possesses talents and experiences life lessons around money and values. And finally, a Spade Birth Card manifests gifts and experiences life lessons in work and health. Souls progress through incarnations and life lessons beginning as Hearts, moving on to Clubs, then Diamonds, and finally as Spades. Therefore, individuals born as Heart Cards are the youngest souls and individuals born as Spades Cards are the oldest souls.

In addition, the number on a Birth Card is equally meaningful as souls sequentially experience life lessons beginning as an Ace and culminating with lessons as a King. Because souls reincarnate a Six Birth Card's previous life incarnation was as a Five. Five Birth Cards explore and comprehend the world through the five senses: sight, smell, hearing, taste, and touch. People born into a Six Birth Card are continuing their soul's growth by experiencing the world through an extra sense: a *sixth sense* or *extrasensory perception*. They use this sixth sense to experience the laws of cause and effect or *karma*. Karma is the spiritual belief that whatever intentions and actions you put out into the universe, similar actions will come back to you either in your current or next life. To understand how this works, let's say you read a news article about a convicted investment advisor who has lost all their money upon jail sentencing. The article explains the conviction had to do with fraud as the advisor stole money from clients. This is an example of karma in current life. If this same investment advisor is financially victimized in their next life incarnation, this is an example of karma in another life. While karma can be good or bad, 6♠ tend to experience some heavy karma from a past life. **It makes sense, then, that a 6♠ child's purpose, gifts, and life lessons revolve around managing the *laws of karma*. And due to being a Spade, this child will learn lessons through experiencing the laws of karma around *health* and *work*.**

How to Nurture the Temperament and Personality of a 6♠ Child

Every person associated with a Spade Birth Card experiences life lessons to obtain wisdom. 6♠s search for an elusive kind of wisdom – the nature of duality. Most people view dualities or polarities as opposing forces. Light and dark. War and peace. Love and hate. Good and evil. The misconception associated with dualities is that one force can only exist in the absence of its opposing force. For instance, one might believe an evil person is purely evil, absent of any good. Yet this is not true. Most of us would agree Adolph Hitler personified an evil person, yet his biographies reveal he adored his mother and treated her well. 6♠ are destined to learn the spiritual truth concerning duality: that opposing forces co-exist and complement each other. You cannot have a positive without a negative. The Greek philosopher, Plato, explained the true nature of duality well in his cave allegory. Plato described a cave that held a group of prisoners. Kept in chains since birth, the prisoners never lived outside the cave. Their arrangement of chains only afforded them the view of the back wall of the cave. When other people walked in front of the light near the cave's entrance, the prisoners observed shadows on the wall. They believed the outside world consisted of shadows or dark images. One day, a prisoner escaped and discovered the concept of light as well as other realities in the outside world. He returned to the cave and explained his new realities to the other prisoners. The prisoners did not believe him and threatened him until he left the cave. Plato is telling us that there is no darkness (shadow) without light. Again, seemingly opposing forces are complementary forces.

6♠ children learn about duality by being born into a life with some extreme circumstance. For instance, they are born into a rich or poor family. Or, they are neglected or adored by their parents. In response to their environment, they enact opposing behaviors. These experiences are to teach a 6♠ about duality as their behaviors often manifest immediate karma. Let's consider an example. Imagine you are a parent of a fifteen-year-old 6♠ named Levi. In Levi's grade at school, a handful of boys have an established reputation for sneaking off campus during lunch and smoking. While Levi is not part of this group, he does hang around one of its members. One day, after a lot of peer pressure, Levi joins the group and engages in his first cigarette. Minutes later, the vice-principal busts the whole group and Levi gets in the most trouble because he was the one caught holding the cigarette. Experiences like this are common for a 6♠. Any misstep has immediate consequences or karma. Such experiences teach a 6♠ that good and bad behaviors can co-exist in people. This said, a young 6♠ may feel discouraged by life's adversities when bad choices repeatedly come back to bite them. They may feel like they have bad luck and never get a break. At an extreme, these individuals may feel hopeless and struggle with mental health issues. Some may give in to escapist behaviors such as dependence on drugs and alcohol.

Keep in mind, immediate karma can also happen with good karma. It may be helpful to remind and reinforce this happening with a 6♠. With an older 6♠, help them make connections between good actions that result in good outcomes. And when bad things happen, help them search for higher meanings or hidden good things that may result. This is the proverbial 'silver lining' thinking that can help a 6♠. When something bad happens, encourage a 6♠ to ask themselves two things, "What am I supposed to learn from this experience?" and "Are there any good consequences that have or might result from this experience?" Let's consider an example. Imagine a ten-year-old male 6♠ loses his father due to a heart attack. Forced to move into the slums with his mother, life is hard as there is no disposal income to provide entertainment or extracurricular activities for this boy. His mother pushes him to go to church with her and sing in the choir. With nothing else to do, this boy spends a lot of time singing in church and learns to escape his challenging life through his activities. This boy goes on to establish a career in singing and music. By the way, this example is a true story. The ten-year-old boy was Bob Marley who, as you might guess, is a 6♠.

Let's face it, though, children make a lot of mistakes growing up. When a child experiences negative karma for every poor decision, life can be overwhelming. Yet this is exactly what can happen to a young 6♠. How a 6♠ reacts to events like this defines their future. If a young 6♠ becomes a miniature rebel without a cause, continually fighting back without an understanding of why, they may generate *chronic stress*. Recent studies involving traumatized children have shed a lot of light on what happens to children who experience chronic stress. Neuroscientists claim chronic stress chemically triggers a *fight-or-flight* reaction. Let's consider a six-year-old 6♠ named Chloe and how chronic stress may create a fight-or-flight reaction, starting with *fight*. Picture yourself as Chloe's teacher. One day you ask students to draw pictures of animals you would find at a zoo to begin preparing for an upcoming field trip. A classmate's idea to draw a tiger reminds Chloe of her pet cat who recently died. Chloe decides to draw her cat. Seeing Chloe's drawing, you redirect her saying, "Domestic cats do not live in the zoo. Draw an animal you see at the zoo." Suddenly, Chloe gets angry, tears up her picture, and then starts a new drawing. The new drawing is, of course, of her cat. No matter what you say to Chloe, she is defiant. This is an example of a fight response. Now let's consider a *flight* response. Chloe, upon hearing her teacher's comments, does not become defiant. Rather, she becomes passive. She stops drawing and begins daydreaming about her cat and the possibility of getting another cat. This is an example of a flight response as Chloe has checked out.

6♠ need grace and to be given some latitude from the adults who work with them. When a 6♠ has a fight-or-flight reaction, allow them some time for quiet and stillness. All Six Birth Cards benefit when they tap into their 'sixth sense' and this requires solitude. If you are a teacher, implement calming *brain breaks*. Brain breaks are mental breaks used in school to help students relax, such as sitting in a rocking chair with a stuffed animal, listening to calm music, or watching a calming video. Some schools even have calming rooms for students. If you are a parent, you can easily find calming brain breaks on the Internet to implement at home. Or provide time for unstructured play such as playing with dolls, coloring, building with Legos or blocks, silent reading, or dress up games. For older 6♠, *music therapy* may help. Music therapy is administered by a trained professional and is not the same as listening to recreational music. Music therapy can help a child relax, reduce physical pain, and open a child to expressing themselves and their feelings.

Higher expressing 6♠ accept the dualities of life. They understand that people are not one dimensional and they accept others for their lightness and darkness. Their ability to be *non-judgmental* of others is their superpower. They also take responsibility for using their free will to seek balance between dual forces for themselves and how they view others. These 6♠ tend to make better choices over time and go on to share this knowledge with others in very profound ways. Many help others with this knowledge as a counselor, minister, teacher, or writer. Moreover, 6♠ often adopt unconventional ways of sharing their wisdom. You see, another 6♠ superpower is that they are *visionaries*. Their progressive views have the potential to improve and transform structures, processes, or institutions.

They hold the potential to be transformational leaders, implementing their vision by breaking rules. Some 6♠ may even become famous when they become a messenger to the world representing or sharing transformative wisdom. For example, Elvis Presley was a 6♠. He transformed the music industry, earning him the title of The King of Rock and Roll. Stephen Hawking was a 6♠. His knowledge of black holes, scientific writings, and achievements made him a household name despite having physical disabilities.

Summary of Higher and Lower Personality Traits

Higher: Responsible, visionary, old soul, leader, honest, kind, fair, non-judgmental.

Lower: Irresponsible, lazy, stubborn, rebellious, escapist, stressed out.

Childhood Influence Mercury Cards

It is common knowledge that a child's personality is most malleable during the formative years – from birth to eight years of age. In the Destiny Card system, the Mercury Cards in a Birth Card's Life Spread reveal influences a child with this Birth Card will experience between birth through age 12. As such, a child's Mercury Cards must be considered so an adult can nurture a child from a place of awareness and work with them from where a child is at in their development. A 6♠ child has the following Mercury Cards: **Q♥, K♣, and 10♠**. The Q♥ and K♣ may mean there is an influential mother or father who is likely a Heart or Club Birth or Planetary Ruling Card, respectively. Alternatively, outside of any specific person associated with these three cards, the basic meanings of these cards describe experiences that may be impactful during this child's formative years. These cards suggest a 6♠ is born into a warm and traditional home. They enjoy working hard and can master any knowledge they deem worthy of learning.

Potential Callings / Vocations by Zodiac Sign

January 8 – Capricorn: 3♥ Planetary Ruling Card

The persistent personality of Capricorn helps develop talents in these 6♠. They can succeed as a singer, writer, politician, business leader, or scientist.

February 6 – Aquarius: A♣ Planetary Ruling Card

These 6♠ embody the spirit of Aquarius by exploring avant-garde ideas. Because of their A♣ Planetary Ruling Card, their inventive ideas can propel them as an artist, musician, actor, or politician. Religious individuals can succeed as an evangelical leader.

March 4 – Pisces: Q♣ Planetary Ruling Card

More introverted and service oriented than other 6♠ due to their Q♣ Planetary Ruling Card, these individuals can do well as a psychologist, counselor, teacher, minister, or writer.

April 2 – Aries: 8♦ Planetary Ruling Card

Even though these 6♠ are ruled by Mars, they dislike jobs that require long hours. They prefer semi-skilled jobs (e.g., homemaker, truck driver, clerk, construction worker, or auto mechanic). Some can monetize inspiring ideas due to their 8♦ Planetary Ruling Card through writing, singing, acting, or teaching.

Famous 6♠

Stephen Hawking, physicist/ cosmologist – 1/8/1942
Bob Marley, singer – 2/6/1945
Natalie Cole, singer – 2/6/1950
Amy Robach, journalist/ TV anchor – 2/6/1973
David Bowie, singer – 1/8/1947

Chapter 10

Descriptions of the Seven Birth Cards

Welcome to the world of the spiritual 7♥!

7♥ = Faith in love

According to the Destiny Card system, souls chronologically experience God's lessons across 52 life incarnations. (Think of these as the universe's lessons if this aligns more with your beliefs.) The Birth Card each soul is born into determines the order and type of lessons a soul experiences. When you examine a Birth Card, you will notice it displays a suit of either a Heart, Club, Diamond, or Spade. This suit is significant because it represents the gifts a person born into this suit will possess and how they will direct their energies to learn lessons in their current life incarnation. A Heart Birth Card retains gifts and experiences life lessons around love and relationships. A Club Birth Card holds capabilities and experiences life lessons in their ability to communicate and absorb knowledge. A Diamond Birth Card possesses talents and experiences life lessons around money and values. And finally, a Spade Birth Card manifests gifts and experiences life lessons in work and health. Souls progress through incarnations and life lessons beginning as Hearts, moving on to Clubs, then Diamonds, and finally as Spades. Therefore, individuals born as Heart Cards are the youngest souls and individuals born as Spades Cards are the oldest souls.

In addition, the number on a Birth Card is equally meaningful as souls sequentially experience life lessons beginning as an Ace and culminating with lessons as a King. If you were to spread out all Heart Birth Cards in numerical order from Aces to Kings, you would notice the 7♥ is the card in the middle. Seven Birth Cards are spiritual cards because they are at the center of God's lessons. As such, a person associated with a Seven Birth Card sits between and has access to both the physical and spiritual world. Imagine it being like how a person sits on top of a fence with one leg dangling on one side and the other leg dangling on the opposite side. One advantage to this locality is that Seven Birth Cards are conduits to the spiritual world. A disadvantage is that Seven Birth Cards can experience life feeling a bit off balance due to the pull between the spiritual and physical world. Often, physical needs and wants can distract them. The reason for this positionality is that all Seven Birth Cards are here to learn about faith. Faith is having the trust and confidence that God is operative in one's life and will guide one despite stressful life events. **It makes sense, then, that a 7♥ child's purpose, gifts, and life lessons revolve around how they navigate events that test their *faith*. And due to being a Heart, this child learns lessons through experiencing issues around faith in *love* and *relationships*.**

How to Nurture the Temperament and Personality of a 7♥ Child

Have you ever watched a newly born fawn practice using their legs? It is truly a beautiful sight to behold as they bounce up and down with an elated sense of joy. This kind of enthusiasm is like a young 7♥ situated within a large social gathering. For example, picture a five-year-old 7♥ boy during recess on his first day of school. He is playfully chasing around anyone willing to respond to his game. He is not afraid of initiating new friendships. He is not missing his parents. He is in his element. Why? 7♥ simply love being around and relating with others in a positive way. Therefore, if you are a parent of a 7♥ enroll them in preschool as early as possible. Arrange extracurricular activities that allow them to socialize with others such as through group sports, swimming lessons, summer camp, dance classes, and art classes. Encourage play dates. Make sure your 7♥ feels the love by hosting large birthday events and other celebrations.

A 7♥ will capture other people's attention when they smile or laugh as their whole face lights up and others cannot help but smile or laugh back. They are charming, talkative, and friendly. They are someone who can be counted upon if you need some sympathy. One superpower of a 7♥ is that they have a keen eye toward what is beautiful, and they can use this gift to decorate their house, select just the right clothing to wear, or design aesthetically pleasing products for the public. Another superpower of a 7♥ is that they are skilled in finance, which is why many can do well in business. The secret behind all Seven Birth Cards is that they are capable of *channeling*. According to physician and channeler, Helane Wahbeh, channeling is the "process of revealing information and energy not limited by our conventional notions of space and time that can appear receptive or expressive." Channeling can happen across the spectrum, from gut hunches to out-of-body experiences. In the case of a 7♥, they tend to channel financial insights. As your 7♥ grows older, help nurture their *entrepreneurial spirit* as this is one of their greatest gifts. This is the thirteen-year-old who wants to start their own business. Listen to their ideas and take them seriously. If possible, help facilitate and support their goals. Know that your 7♥ could be the next Bill Gates. You see, Gates who was born October 28, is a 7♥.

Going back to the same 7♥ boy described above on his first day of school, imagine this child participating in his first teacher-led nature walk. He observes an intricate spider web along the way. Does he use it to scare the girls? Nope. It is not that a 7♥ lacks a mischievous nature. On the contrary, they will test the limits of relationships through teasing and inappropriate behaviors. What is truly going on in this scenario is that the beauty of the web's construction distracts him. Soon this boy gathers others around him to observe what he has discovered. 7♥ adore being exposed to illustrations of beauty, especially from nature. Moreover, being in nature helps a 7♥ tap into spiritual knowledge. If a 7♥ feels disharmony or anxiety, spending time in nature or a beautiful surrounding can help them recharge their batteries. 7♥ often need time to literally smell the roses. If you are a parent of a 7♥, make sure to introduce them to this practice. Take them for a quiet walk outside and ask them to listen, smell, feel, and observe their surroundings, and then report a noticing or wondering. Notice or wondering is a formative assessment tool used by science and mathematics teachers to foster inquiry thinking. Teachers ask students to notice patterns or relationships and wonder about why something is that they observe. For example, during a nature walk during the Fall a child might say, "I wonder why some tree leaves are green and other tree leaves are changing to yellow and orange." In addition to these types of questions, ask a 7♥ how nature makes them feel and what specific aspects of it brings them joy. The main idea is that you equip your 7♥ with a go-to activity that may help them when they are feeling overwhelmed or anxious.

7♥ are *people pleasers*. In the classroom, they are agreeable and kind. If you are a teacher of a 7♥, you can count on them to show a new kid around school or to sit next to and mentor a classmate who is struggling academically. Pairing a 7♥ up with another student is good so long as the other student is behaviorally stable. 7♥ are emotionally sensitive and so they tend to respond poorly when there is disharmony with others. Because of their sensitivity, you may need to check in with them more frequently than with other students to make sure they are emotionally okay. The Internet has a wonderful assortment of *emotional check-in charts* and worksheets you can use effectively with a 7♥. They may not always come to you if they are suffering emotionally. Body language and less talkative interactions are good indicators of how a 7♥ is feeling. One common issue for a 7♥ is that they may not tell an adult when peers are bothering or bullying them. If a conflict between students occurs and a 7♥ is involved, it is better to separate the 7♥ from the group to discuss the situation. They will rarely tell you how they truly feel in front of their peers if the feeling is not positive.

It is common knowledge that when a child transitions into adolescence they want to spend more time with their friends. Because 7♥ aim to please others, they are more susceptible to peer pressure. They often care for and have naïve faith in their friends. When friends lead them astray by pressuring them to do risky behaviors and bad consequences result, a 7♥ may feel betrayed. For instance, let's say your sixteen-year-old 7♥ named Thomas has just earned his driver's license. You have set up the rule that Thomas can drive your car if he does not pick up friends without your permission. A while later a couple of your son's friends pressure him to sneak out late at night and drive them to a party. During the drive, Thomas is distracted, loses control of the vehicle, and hits a tree. Fortunately, no one was hurt, but your car has sustained damage. When you arrive at the scene, the friends insist sneaking out was Thomas's idea and Thomas does not contradict them. Subsequently, the friends receive no punishment, and the cost of repairs falls squarely on Thomas. Repeated experiences such as this can push a 7♥ toward a *victim complex*. A victim complex is when a person literally feels victimized when anything goes wrong in their life. In adulthood, a lower expressing 7♥ can feel victimized by the smallest of problems, such as missing a sporting event because of traffic. Others that observe them in situations like this find them to be emotionally overreacting. While it may be difficult, try not to minimize a 7♥'s feelings during these situations. Furthermore, guide your 7♥ in how to communicate with peers when they are exerting pressure. Help them learn to say no. Use role-play and various scenarios with your 7♥ to learn how to stand up against peer pressure.

Likewise, consider family dynamics that may cause a people pleaser 7♥ to go too far in making sacrifices for others. Let's consider an example. Imagine you are a mother who expects a clean house. You have two children; an eight-year-old daughter named Melinda and a twelve-year-old son named Michael. Melinda is a 7♥. Melinda always makes sure her room is clean and other household chores are completed. Michael is the complete opposite. His room is constantly messy, and he often skips his weekly chores. Melinda often finds it unsettling to witness her mother and brother fight over Michael's lack of responsibility. To achieve a more loving environment, Melinda secretly starts to complete Michael's chores. Michael notices this and starts to take advantage of it. He uses guilt to get his sister to do more and more, including cleaning his room. Melinda fears upsetting her mother, so she allows this conduct to continue for months. It is likely this 7♥ may adopt this mindset in adulthood and remain sacrificing for others. In doing so they may adopt another complex, a *martyr complex*. In psychology, a martyr complex occurs when a person is in fear of displeasing others, so they repeatedly make sacrifices to make others happy. These sacrifices often mean a person learns to suppress their own needs and wants and go on to believe that love from others is conditional; that is, conditional upon them making sacrifices. To help a 7♥ from developing a victim or martyr complex, provide them with unconditional love. This may mean refraining from tying your affection or love to their behaviors. For instance, imagine a sixteen-year-old boy forgets to get his mother a card or gift on Mother's Day. If this boy were a 7♥, it would be wise to not tease or accuse them of not loving their mother. Another great way to furnish and teach a 7♥ about unconditional love is to purchase them a pet. A faithful dog would make an excellent pet. These children will take on much of the responsibility in caring for their pet and experience the joy of unconditional love.

Summary of Higher and Lower Personality Traits

Higher: Charming, humanitarian, organized, aesthetically gifted, entrepreneurial.

Lower: Dramatic, emotionally unstable, controlling, insecure, jealous.

Childhood Influence Mercury Cards

It is common knowledge that a child's personality is most malleable during the formative years – from birth to eight years of age. In the Destiny Card system, the Mercury Cards in a Birth Card's Life Spread reveal influences a child with this Birth Card will experience between birth through age 12. As such, a child's Mercury Cards must be considered so an adult can nurture a child from a place of awareness and work with them from where a child is are at in their development. A 7♥ child has the following Mercury Cards: **7♦, 3♥, and 9♥**. Alternatively, outside of any specific person associated with these three cards, the basic meanings of these cards describe experiences that may be impactful during this child's formative years. These cards suggest a 7♥ may feel limited due to family financial issues. They may experience indecision, disappointment, and/or loss related to a family member.

Potential Callings / Vocations by Zodiac Sign

September 30 – Libra: 5♠ Planetary Ruling Card

The influence of Libra provides these 7♥ with double the charm and an eye for beauty. They excel at promoting or marketing products (e.g., advertising or business), people (e.g., attorney or publisher), or things (e.g., merchandising jobs), especially if these careers include travel.

October 28 – Scorpio: J♥ & K♦ Planetary Ruling Card

The emotional intensity of Scorpio makes these 7♥ feel compelled to express themselves either in artistic ways (e.g., acting, music, or writing) or through commitment to humanitarian causes (e.g., teacher, counselor, psychologist, or non-profit work).

November 26 – Sagittarius: 9♣ Planetary Ruling Card

The universal knowledge aspect of a 9♣ Planetary Ruling Card translates into a 7♥ who can do well as a counselor, teacher, consultant, or writer. Those inclined toward the arts can make a career of their creations. They can also excel in business as they have masterful communication skills.

December 24 – Capricorn: 9♠ Planetary Ruling Card

The ambitious energy of Capricorn pushes these 7♥ toward success, although they should take care in becoming too perfectionistic. They can do well in business, government work, banking, or as a TV personality or writer.

Famous 7♥

Brad Paisley, singer/songwriter – 10/28/1972
Julia Roberts, actress – 10/28/1967
DJ Khaled, music producer – 11/26/1975
Tina Turner, singer – 11/26/1939
Kate Spade, fashion designer – 12/24/1962
Howard Hughes, entrepreneur – 12 24/1905

Welcome to the world of the spiritual 7♣!

7♣ = Faith in knowledge

According to the Destiny Card system, souls chronologically experience God's lessons across 52 life incarnations. (Think of these as the universe's lessons if this aligns more with your beliefs.) The Birth Card each soul is born into determines the order and type of lessons a soul experiences. When you examine a Birth Card, you will notice it displays a suit of either a Heart, Club, Diamond, or Spade. This suit is significant because it represents the gifts a person born into this suit will possess and how they will direct their energies to learn lessons in their current life incarnation. A Heart Birth Card retains gifts and experiences life lessons around love and relationships. A Club Birth Card holds capabilities and experiences life lessons in their ability to communicate and absorb knowledge. A Diamond Birth Card possesses talents and experiences life lessons around money and values. And finally, a Spade Birth Card manifests gifts and experiences life lessons in work and health. Souls progress through incarnations and life lessons beginning as Hearts, moving on to Clubs, then Diamonds, and finally as Spades. Therefore, individuals born as Heart Cards are the youngest souls and individuals born as Spades Cards are the oldest souls.

In addition, the number on a Birth Card is equally meaningful as souls sequentially experience life lessons beginning as an Ace and culminating with lessons as a King. If you were to spread out all Club Birth Cards in numerical order from Aces to Kings, you would notice the 7♣ is the card in the middle. Seven Birth Cards are spiritual cards because they are at the center of God's lessons. As such, a person associated with a Seven Birth Card sits between and has access to both the physical and spiritual world. Imagine it being like how a person sits on top of a fence with one leg dangling on one side and the other leg dangling on the opposite side. One advantage to this situation is that Sevens Birth Cards are conduits to the spiritual world. A disadvantage is that Seven Birth Cards can experience life feeling a bit off balance due to the pull between the spiritual and physical world. Often, physical needs and wants can distract them. The reason for this positionality is that all Seven Birth Cards are here to learn about faith. Faith is having the trust and confidence that God is operative in one's life and will guide one despite stressful life events. **It makes sense, then, that a 7♣ child's purpose, gifts, and life lessons revolve around how they navigate events that test their _faith_. And due to being a Club, this child will learn lessons through experiencing issues around faith in _communication_ and _knowledge_.**

How to Nurture the Temperament and Personality of a 7♣ Child

7♣ begin to experience lessons around faith in communication and knowledge by navigating unsettling childhood events. These events may include moving frequently, living in poverty, being in a financially fluctuating situation, being an only child, or feeling neglected by an absent parent (most often a father). Feeling unsettled, a 7♣'s attitude can go from happy-go-lucky to pessimistic and spiteful in a nanosecond. If you are a parent of a 7♣, you may notice an elevated amount of whining from this child. This is the toddler who whines and whines to have spaghetti for dinner. You make spaghetti for dinner and then this child whines because they do not want spaghetti for dinner! While it may be difficult, try to stay calm in situations like this. Refrain from using negative body language or comments as 7♣ tend to absorb negative energy and this will likely make the situation worse. Being personally critical of a 7♣ is a sure way to trigger a negative reaction. What is ironic about this reaction is that a 7♣ is sometimes guilty of dishing out criticism and negativity toward others. They can be stubborn and demand things should proceed the way they want – my way or the highway approach. When they do not get their way, they criticize others and whine some more. If your child is engaging in whining, try to offer distractions. Perhaps, allow them to cry to get their negative feelings out of their system. Validate their feelings, but do not give in to the whining. Praise them when they do not whine. Say, "Thank you for asking using a calm voice."

In a school setting, a young 7♣ may come across as an introverted loner or impulsive tattletale. Please remember these children may be acting this way because of challenging issues at home. Be careful not to be reactive in classroom situations in which a 7♣ is tattling. Find out all the facts before disciplining another child. If not, you may be rewarding the tattler. If the tattling becomes problematic, you may need to teach 7♣ strategies to mitigate their impulses. I suggest reading and discussing the children's book titled, *Don't Squeal Unless It's a Big Deal,* by Jeanie Franz and then establish rules and procedures with regards to tattling. Also, it may help to teach this child several steps they should go through before involving an adult. Tattle problem-solving worksheets and charts can be found on the Internet.

7♣ are happier when they establish a stable educational foundation early on in their life. 7♣ are miniature philosophers and respond best to a *Socratic teaching methodology*. You may think this is a teaching method strictly used on college campuses. Not true. Elementary students can engage in this kind of learning, too. Socratic methodology involves teachers asking open-ended and probing questions to stimulate critical thinking. Socratic teaching at the elementary level can be as simple as having children practice *deductive* and *inductive reasoning*. Deductive reasoning is thinking of situations and ideas from whole-to-part, taking a general statement and reducing it to a specific example. Then, the reasoning is up for debate. For example, consider the following statements: 1) Every human being has rights, 2) Travis is a human being, 3) Therefore, Travis has rights. Debate can result by changing these statements up a bit: 1) Every human being has rights, 2) Stewart is a dog, 3) Therefore, Stewart has no rights. 7♣ are geniuses when it comes to thinking deductively. And then there is inductive reasoning, thinking part-to-whole, taking specific data or information, and then making conclusions. In scientific inquiry, when students use data to draw conclusions or explanations, they are thinking inductively. With little training, 7♣ can excel at inductive reasoning, too. Possessing these superpowers, it would be a great idea to encourage an older 7♣ to join the debate team at school. Watch out, though. These skills may be used against you!

7♣ are highly intelligent and yet insecure about their current fund of knowledge. As such, many young 7♣ engage in *negative self-talk*. You see, their connection to the spiritual world makes them aware of the vast amount of knowledge in the universe. Even if they learn and accomplish more than most, they may perceive it as not knowing or achieving enough. If you are a parent of a 7♣ with high academic expectations of them, you may want to dial down the pressure you may be putting on them. They are academically their own worst critics. Criticizing a 7♣ in an academic setting is a sure way to bring about instability. Outside criticism creates a piling-on effect, pushing a 7♣ toward *pessimism*. As a result, some may try to become invisible in a classroom setting, even shut down and refuse to work. If you are a teacher of a 7♣, know they may benefit from using negative self-talk worksheets. These worksheets allow students to refrain negative into positive thoughts. Examples of such worksheets can be found on the Internet. Additionally, know that a 7♣ absorbed with negative self-talk may resort to cheating. Ever watch the movie, *Catch Me If You Can,* starring Leonardo DiCaprio? It is a true story of Frank Abagnale, who worked at jobs such as an airline pilot and physician even though he had no prior training or education to do so. He was a notorious cheater who forged checks. And, yes, he was a 7♣, manifesting the lower traits of his Birth Card. For these 7♣, cheating is a self-defense mechanism. Again, I recommend using children's books to address this issue. For preschool age, I suggest reading *Fox and the Jumping Contest* by Corey Tabor. Determined to win a jumping contest, Fox plans a scheme to cheat. When the scheme backfires, Fox learns a lesson. For older elementary students, the book, *Junie B., First Grader: Cheater Pants* also focuses on what can happen to those who cheat.

A 7♣'s superpower is that they are capable of *channeling*. According to physician and channeler, Helane Wahbeh, channeling is the "process of revealing information and energy not limited by our conventional notions of space and time that can appear receptive or expressive." Channeling can happen across the spectrum, from gut hunches to out-of-body experiences. Such a gift can be both a curse and a blessing. You see, 7♣ are like high frequency towers; highly sensitive to absorbing negativity from those closest to them. While other children may be able to shake off negativity, a 7♣ may not. For instance, if you express two negative and two positive comments to a 7♣, they will selectively hear only the negative. Perhaps, use this book to read about the lower traits of your own Birth Card to determine if you are inclined to be bossy, negative, or fearful. You may need to ask yourself if your own negative attitudes or fears are being projected onto your 7♣ and therefore contributing to the problems at hand. The flip side of this ability is that 7♣ are born with the ability to channel knowledge in the spoken or written word from the spiritual world. Comedian Robin Williams is a great example of a 7♣ with this gift. The first time I ever saw Robin was when I watched him on The Tonight Show with Johnny Carson. I was amazed at how he could transform in and out of numerous personalities in a short time span. He was an improvisational genius. Improvisation is a technique in which actors react spontaneously to unexpected situations. No one else in comedy has done this as well as Robin. However, Robin was not only improvising. He was channeling. He was tapping into the multiple personalities and ideas from spirits on the other side.

Helping a 7♣ child develop a spiritual consciousness is a must-do strategy to nurture them. Perhaps you are wondering how can such a lofty objective be accomplished? While an adult or teen can read spiritual self-help books to attain such consciousness, what about a child? The answers to these questions are quite simple. A 7♣ can develop a spiritual consciousness by learning how to practice *mindfulness.* Mindfulness involves practices that allow one to be fully present. It opens a space for one to connect with their surroundings, situations, and feelings without overreacting to them. 7♣ are best served when they engage in mindfulness activities that foster calmness. Although mindfulness practices are not a magic bullet, the earlier in life they are started, the better overall effectiveness they will have on a 7♣. I recommend the book, *Calm: Mindfulness for Kids* by Wynne Kinder. As its title suggests, the book provides numerous tips and activities to train a child in mindful practices. Do you recall reading *The Very Hungry Caterpillar* by Eric Carle as a kid? Eric Carle has a new version of this classic book titled, *Calm with the Very Hungry Caterpillar.* It is simply adorable. There are also mindfulness apps for young children, such as *Breathe, Think, Do Sesame* developed by Sesame Street for children ages two to five. If your 7♣ child is a teen, there are age-appropriate resources you can find on the Internet. Check YouTube for videos. Show them apps they can access on their phones, such as "Breathr", "Stop Breath, and Think", and "Mindshift."

If you are the parent of a 7♣, ask your child's teacher about incorporating mindfulness practices in the classroom. If they are not using them, ask if they are open to trying them. Help support a teacher's use of these techniques by providing resources through the gifting of books and videos. Finally, if your 7♣ is already displaying signs of pessimism or depression, please take these behaviors seriously. Perhaps try a technique called *tapping* or psychological acupuncture. Tapping involves a person using their own fingers to tap on certain parts of their body to disrupt negative emotions and restore a proper flow of energy. There are several good videos on the Internet that demonstrate this technique and explain how to use it with children. I also recommend reading the book *Tapping Your Way to a Great Big Smile: Emotional Freedom Technique (EFT) Tapping for Little Fingers* by Ana Cybela. This book offers step-by-step instructions to explain other strategies to help a child who is struggling with negativity.

Given that a 7♣ may experience difficulties related to negative thought patterns, they might benefit from healing techniques intended to balance the body's *chakras*. Chakras are energy centers that receive and transmit energy throughout the body. There are seven major chakras running along the spine of one's body that are associated with different nerves, organs, joints, and tissues near a chakra's location. A person may experience negative physical and emotional symptoms when their flow of energy becomes unbalanced – either under or overactive – at a specific chakra site. For instance, chronic stress or poor habits can cause a chakra to become imbalanced. Various healing techniques directed at chakra revitalization include yoga, meditation, toning sounds, acupuncture, affirmations, aromatherapy, light therapy, breathing practices, crystal healing, and massage (especially reiki, shiatsu, and reflexology). As an example, the crystal Charoite is known for purging negativity. For extreme cases in which a 7♣ is struggling with negativity and depression, they stand to benefit from professional counseling and therapy.

Summary of Higher and Lower Personality Traits

Higher: Creative genius, philosophical, deductive thinker, ambitious, giving.

Lower: Whiny, negativity, crafty, judgmental, pessimistic, depressed.

Childhood Influence Mercury Cards
It is common knowledge that a child's personality is most malleable during the formative years – from birth to eight years of age. In the Destiny Card system, the Mercury Cards in a Birth Card's Life Spread reveal influences a child with this Birth Card will experience between birth through age 12. As such, a child's Mercury Cards must be considered so an adult can nurture a child from a place of awareness and work with them from where a child is at in their development. A 7♣ child has the following Mercury Cards: **5♦, A♥, and 9♦.** Alternatively, outside of any specific person associated with these three cards, the basic meanings of these cards describe experiences that may be impactful during this child's formative years. These cards suggest a 7♣ may experience a lack of finances or unsettling changes such as moving a lot. They may experience a lack of affection or low self-esteem.

Potential Callings / Vocations by Zodiac Sign

March 29 – Aries: J♣ Planetary Ruling Card
The Martian energy of Aries can push these individuals into negative attitudes. Parenting with less pressure can bring out the genius in these 7♣. They can excel as a trial attorney, engineer, architect, mechanic, or lab technician.

April 27 – Taurus: Q♠ Planetary Ruling Card

The energy of Taurus helps to ground these individuals, which often provides them with a solid educational foundation. This stability allows them to excel at writing, government jobs, teaching, research jobs, or as an artist. Some may be satisfied with a mundane job.

May 25 – Gemini: 5♦ Planetary Ruling Card

If the mental aspect of these Gemini individuals can be directed toward a positive attitude, these 7♣ can succeed as an attorney, actor, comedian, writer, salesperson, psychologist, or scientist.

June 23 – Cancer: 9♥ Planetary Ruling Card

The sensitivity of Cancer tends to produce a more introverted 7♣ who prefers careers that nurture others (e.g., teacher, scientist, social worker, counselor, or general manager in a business).

July 21 – Cancer: 9♥ Planetary Ruling Card

Creativity is particularly strong in these 7♣ which is why they can excel as an actor, comedian, writer, singer, musician, or any other profession that puts them at the center of attention. Some make good designers or decorators.

August 19 – Leo: 7♣ Planetary Ruling Card

The optimistic aspect of Leo helps to alleviate the negativity of these 7♣ - allowing them to succeed as a business owner, actor, director, police officer, politician, or government official.

September 17 – Virgo: 5♦ Planetary Ruling Card

The discerning aspect of Virgo allows these 7♣ to excel at accounting, scientific research, legal research, tax, or real estate assessing. Individuals with physical talents can succeed as sports athletes.

October 15 – Libra: Q♠ Planetary Ruling Card

Having a Q♠ Planetary Ruling Card instills strong convictions and ideologies in these 7♣. As such, many feel compelled to be a writer, artist, inventor, philosopher, religious leader, or politician.

November 13 – Scorpio: J♣ & J♦

If not managed, the intensity of Scorpio can magnify the negativity within these 7♣. Those able to make fun of and monetize their creative eccentricities will inspire others toward their philosophies as an actor, comedian, philosopher, writer, healer (unorthodox kind), or teacher.

December 11 – Sagittarius: 9♦ Planetary Ruling Card

Having the 9♦ Planetary Ruling Card instills an analytical mind in these 7♣. They are skilled at assessing the value of products or people so they can do well in sales. Acting from their values rather than material side, they can also succeed as a writer, attorney, politician, scientist, or government worker.

Famous 7♣
Aly Raisman, Olympic gymnast – 5/25/1994
Ralph Waldo Emerson, philosopher/writer – 5/25/1803
Amy Klobuchar, politician – 5/25/1960
Cory Booker, politician – 4/27/1969
Rita Moreno, actress/ dancer – 12/11/1931

Welcome to the world of the spiritual 7♦!

7♦ = Faith in values and money

According to the Destiny Card system, souls chronologically experience God's lessons across 52 life incarnations. (Think of these as the universe's lessons if this aligns more with your beliefs.) The Birth Card each soul is born into determines the order and type of lessons a soul experiences. When you examine a Birth Card, you will notice it displays a suit of either a Heart, Club, Diamond, or Spade. This suit is significant because it represents the gifts a person born into this suit will possess and how they will direct their energies to learn lessons in their current life incarnation. A Heart Birth Card retains gifts and experiences life lessons around love and relationships. A Club Birth Card holds capabilities and experiences life lessons in their ability to communicate and absorb knowledge. A Diamond Birth Card possesses talents and experiences life lessons around money and values. And finally, a Spade Birth Card manifests gifts and experiences life lessons in work and health. Souls progress through incarnations and life lessons beginning as Hearts, moving on to Clubs, then Diamonds, and finally as Spades. Therefore, individuals born as Heart Cards are the youngest souls and individuals born as Spades Cards are the oldest souls.

In addition, the number on a Birth Card is equally meaningful as souls sequentially experience life lessons beginning as an Ace and culminating with lessons as a King. If you were to spread out all Diamond Birth Cards in numerical order from Aces to Kings, you would notice the 7♦ is the card in the middle. Seven Birth Cards are spiritual cards because they are at the center of God's lessons. As such, a person associated with a Seven Birth Card sits between and has access to both the physical and spiritual world. Imagine it being like how a person sits on a fence with one leg dangling on one side and the other leg dangling on the opposite side. One advantage to this situation is that Seven Birth Cards are conduits to the spiritual world. A disadvantage is that Seven Birth Cards can experience life feeling a bit off balance due to the pull between the spiritual and physical world. Often, physical needs and wants can distract them. The reason for this positionality is that all Seven Birth Cards are here to learn about faith.

Faith is having the trust and confidence that God is operative in one's life and will guide one despite stressful life events. **It makes sense, then, that a 7♦ child's purpose, gifts, and life lessons revolve around how they navigate events that test their *faith*. And due to being a Diamond, this child will learn lessons through experiencing issues around faith related to *values* and *money*.**

How to Nurture the Temperament and Personality of a 7♦ Child

Early life experiences tend to produce an independent spirit in many 7♦. These experiences may include being born into a large family, poverty, or a rich family with parents who spend very little time with them. Some are part of a family that moves a lot. As a result, many 7♦ experience a freedom to explore and hone great imaginations. At times, their imagination or sense of humor may seem odd to others. This trait may attract teasing from peers. Do not fret too much for them. 7♦ have access to higher truths and know their own value. Deep down they do not care what others think. In fact, their crazy ideas can likely get traction and lead to a lucrative business. The 7♦ is that person at a high school reunion who surprises their peers as they have transformed from a quirky dork into an eccentric and successful entrepreneur. As a parent of a 7♦, encourage their creativity no matter how odd their interests appear to you. For instance, perhaps your eight-year-old 7♦ boy wants to learn how to sew. Allow him to do so. The need to invent is strong in a 7♦ and they do not want to create what everyone else is producing. Open-ended STEM (Science, Technology, Engineering, and Mathematics) or craft kits make an excellent gift for a 7♦.

7♦ are generally *hard workers* and *ambitious*. While not opposed to paying their dues, 7♦ can accelerate achievement by leveraging a superpower. You see, many 7♦ excel at auditory learning. If you are a parent of a 7♦, read books to them as early and as often as you can. They easily learn to read using a *phonetic approach*. A phonetic approach involves learning to read by sounding out words based on the letters used in the words. These children also thrive when adults support learning by using rhyming books and songs, interactive read-alouds, and choral response techniques. To perform an interactive read-aloud, a reader selectively pauses to make comments and ask questions rather than reading a children's picture book from beginning to end without stopping. Choral response is when a teacher uses cues that prompt students to verbally repeat responses in unison. In a school setting, 7♦ also benefit from class discussions, study groups, audio books, and teacher lecture. Older 7♦ love podcasts and music. Support an adolescent 7♦ in their auditory studying preferences, whether it be to have complete silence or white noise in the background.

Young 7♦ are serious little humans. This is because they are born knowing right from wrong. Do not be surprised when your 7♦ child observes unfairness, injustice, or people exhibiting bad behavior, and then feels compelled to act or speak out to address a wrong. 7♦ children hold the potential to grow up to be lightworkers in the world. Lightworkers feel obligated to help others. While such actions are commendable, 7♦ are susceptible to giving too much and tend to put the welfare of others in front of their own needs. Over time, a 7♦ may be programed to feel responsible for everyone and everything. This can be emotionally and physically draining for them. As a 7♦ gets older, teach them to pick their battles or causes carefully. If you are a parent of a 7♦, help direct your child toward constructive ways of promoting truth and fairness. Encourage your child to make a list of causes, such as local people who are homeless, kids living in poverty, or veterans serving away during the holidays. Talk through their ideas and discuss related logistics. Help your 7♦ execute their plan while maintaining boundaries for themself and your family. If your 7♦ is inclined to 'fix' their friends' behavior, they may need to understand they might be doing more harm than good. While they do mean well, sometimes they need to let go of a situation or allow a person to make and learn from their own mistakes. Trying to fix another person's behavior may be construed as manipulation.

It is also important for adults to treat a 7♦ fairly. As an example, imagine that your five-year-old 7♦ has been invited to join a group of friends to play at a local playground. You sit with other parents at a distance away for some adult conversation. Out of the corner of your eye you see a commotion within the group of friends. Several minutes later you observe your child in the middle of the group exhibiting confrontational body language. You go over to the group and hear your child's harsh voice telling another child what to do. Be careful not to jump to conclusions. Do not question the integrity of a 7♦ unless you have strong evidence. While it may seem that your child is acting aggressive, assume the best. Ask questions and get the facts of the situation. Why? Perhaps the real aggressor was not your child and your 7♦ intervened to protect another child. Refrain from suppressing this type of protective behavior. You see, some 7♦ are destined to become social-justice warriors wherein they are aware of and strive to protect the rights of marginalized people. Instead, teach your 7♦ how to be diplomatic. You see 7♦ tend to be blunt when they observe unsound behaviors. This is the six-year-old child who returns home from a play date and says, "Playing at Tommy's was not as fun today. Tommy's mom was drunk." What tends to help a 7♦ is to teach them, "it's not what you say, but how you say it." This lesson can go a long way in equipping them to be successful in life.

Have you ever read or heard about the law of attraction? According to Michael Losier, author of *Law of Attraction: The Science of Attracting More of What You Want and Less of What You Don't*, "You attract to your life whatever you give your attention, energy, and focus to whether wanted or not." Being highly tuned into the spiritual realm, a 7♦ may subconsciously manifest this law. For instance, imagine you are a parent of a fourteen-year-old 7♦ named Keziah. Keziah hates group projects because her teacher often pairs her with students who do not pull their weight. Keziah's social science teacher has announced a group project with plans to assign groups the following day. If Keziah expresses negativity toward her assigned group in her words and thoughts, she may attract her worst scenario. If Keziah expresses gratitude toward sharing the workload and visualizes a group working equally, she may attract that scenario. A lower expressing 7♦ has the tendency to view situations through a more negative lens. As such, they often attract negativity. It is vital to teach a 7♦ about the law of attraction and how to practice positive thoughts, verbal expressions, and gratitude. There are several books to help you introduce this topic to your child. For early elementary children, I suggest *The Magic is Inside You* by Cathy Domoney. For upper elementary children, *The Law of Attraction for Kids* by Jennifer Quaggin, is a great resource. For teens, I recommend Paul Harrington's book titled, *The Secret to Teen Power*. The key for a 7♦ is to make sure their negative experiences do not define them. They can choose their attitude. Moreover, happiness for a 7♦ is more likely attained by appreciating the smaller things in life, that is, things that are typically taken for granted.

Summary of Higher and Lower Personality Traits

Higher: Independent, generous, integrity, responsible, ambitious, social justice perspective.

Lower: Stubborn, materialistic, blunt, quirky, impatient, fear of scarcity.

Childhood Influence Mercury Cards

It is common knowledge that a child's personality is most malleable during the formative years – from birth to eight years of age. In the Destiny Card system, the Mercury Cards in a Birth Card's Life Spread reveal influences a child with this Birth Card will experience between birth through age 12. As such, a child's Mercury Cards must be considered so an adult can nurture a child from a place of awareness and work with them from where a child is at in their development. A 7♦ child has the following Mercury Cards: **5♠, A♣, and 10♥.** Alternatively, outside of any specific person associated with these three cards, the basic meanings of these cards describe experiences that may be impactful during this child's formative years. These cards suggest a 7♦ may experience some chaos in the home due to family moves or difficulties with their own health. They are typically born into a family that values time together and holds large family gatherings. In addition, many 7♦ are talkative and curious from a young age.

Potential Callings / Vocations by Zodiac Sign

January 20 – Capricorn: 2♥ Planetary Ruling Card

The influence of ambitious Capricorn provides a double dose of drive for these 7♦. This is good because these individuals often must work to accumulate wealth. They care for the well-being of others which allows them to succeed as a diplomat, politician, comedian, physician, or business manager.

February 18 – Aquarius: K♥ Planetary Ruling Card

The influence of Aquarius tends to curtail the materialism in these 7♦. They can succeed in just about anything, but their great mind for finance makes them well suited for business. Some do well in the music industry or any other form of entertainment.

March 16 – Pisces: K♦ Planetary Ruling Card

With a K♦ Planetary Ruling Card, these 7♦ are highly motivated to earn money. They can pursue and succeed in any career, from sports athlete to business leader. They often possess a 'my way or the highway' attitude, which means they may be better suited to work independently.

April 14 – Aries: 9♣ Planetary Ruling Card

The competitive aspect of Mars may push these 7♦ to scatter themselves too much. With discipline, they can handle other people's money well by way of being a financial planner or broker. More imaginative individuals can do well in a career as a writer, actor, promoter, or public relations director.

May 12 – Taurus: J♥ Planetary Ruling Card

The stability of Taurus combined with the sacrificing aspect of a J♥ Planetary Ruling Card propels these 7♦ into service-oriented careers (e.g., nursing, teaching, or stay-at-home parent).

June 10 – Gemini: 5♠ Planetary Ruling Card

Changeable Gemini and the adventurous 5♠ Planetary Ruling Card in these 7♦ makes them prefer careers that provide money, variety, and travel. They can do well as a journalist, traveling performer, attorney, or flight attendant.

July 8 – Cancer: 7♥ Planetary Ruling Card

Sensitive Cancer in these 7♦ make these individuals desire money to protect people or projects they care about. They like to spend money. If inclined toward business, they can do well selling artwork, home furnishings, or designer clothing.

August 6 – Leo: 7♦ Planetary Ruling Card

The power of Jupiter in these Leo 7♦ often means these individuals are born into money, marry for money, or receive a large inheritance. They can be successful on their own by fearlessly marketing unconventional ideas.

September 4 – Virgo: 5♠ Planetary Ruling Card

The perfectionistic nature of Virgo can manifest into worry and negativity for these 7♦ unless they can direct their detail-oriented natures into their career. They can do well as a scientific researcher, inventor, engineer, or technician.

October 2 – Libra: J♥ Planetary Ruling Card

The diplomatic aspect of Libra blends well with the higher value mindset of these 7♦, such that they can drive humanitarian causes. They can make an excellent church leader, diplomat, or public defender. Art-loving individuals can excel in painting, composing, or acting.

Famous 7♦

Beyonce Knowles, singer – 9/4/1981
Drew Pinsky, psychologist / TV personality – 9/4/1958
Nikki Haley, politician – 1/20/1972
Jerry Lewis, actor / MDA telethon host – 3/16/1926
Florence Nightingale, founder of modern nursing – 5/12/1820

Welcome to the world of the spiritual 7♠!

7♠ = Faith in work and health

According to the Destiny Card system, souls chronologically experience God's lessons across 52 life incarnations. (Think of these as the universe's lessons if this aligns more with your beliefs.) The Birth Card each soul is born into determines the order and type of lessons a soul experiences. When you examine a Birth Card, you will notice it displays a suit of either a Heart, Club, Diamond, or Spade. This suit is significant because it represents the gifts a person born into this suit will possess and how they will direct their energies to learn lessons in their current life incarnation. A Heart Birth Card retains gifts and experiences life lessons around love and relationships. A Club Birth Card holds capabilities and experiences life lessons in their ability to communicate and absorb knowledge. A Diamond Birth Card possesses talents and experiences life lessons around money and values. And finally, a Spade Birth Card manifests gifts and experiences life lessons in work and health. Souls progress through incarnations and life lessons beginning as Hearts, moving on to Clubs, then Diamonds, and finally as Spades. Therefore, individuals born as Heart Cards are the youngest souls and individuals born as Spades Cards are the oldest souls.

In addition, the number on a Birth Card is equally meaningful as souls sequentially experience life lessons beginning as an Ace and culminating with lessons as a King. If you were to spread out all Spade Birth Cards in numerical order from Aces to Kings, you would notice the 7♠ is the card in the middle. Seven Birth Cards are spiritual cards because they are at the center of God's lessons. As such, a person associated with a Seven Birth Card sits between and has access to both the physical and spiritual world. Imagine it being like how a person sits on a fence with one leg dangling on one side and the other leg dangling on the opposite side. One advantage to this situation is that Sevens Birth Cards are conduits to the spiritual world. A disadvantage is that Seven Birth Cards can experience life feeling a bit off balance due to the pull between the spiritual and physical world. Often, physical needs and wants can distract them. The reason for this positionality is that all Seven Birth Cards are here to learn about faith. Faith is having the trust and confidence that God is operative in one's life and will guide one despite stressful life events. **It makes sense, then, that a 7♠ child's purpose, gifts, and life lessons revolve around how they navigate events that test their *faith*. And due to being a Spade, this child will learn lessons through experiencing issues around faith related to *work* and *health*.**

How to Nurture the Temperament and Personality of a 7♠ Child

7♠ tend to begin talking earlier than other children of a similar age. This accelerated language development will enable them to learn quickly and communicate well with adults. They may be favored by their early educators, easily becoming a teacher's pet. This may cause a young 7♠ to connect better with adults than with children their own age. For instance, a 7♠ often displays an older sense of humor. This is the eight-year-old child who asks friends, "What yes or no question can never be answered with a yes?" When explaining the answer is, "Are you dead?" their friends do not see the humor. And because they are old souls, they may get along better with adults than their immature peers. Be careful not to criticize a 7♠ at this age for being odd because such comments can push them toward isolation. Isolation can also be the case if a 7♠ is born an only child. Those inclined to be introverts may be loners who struggle to create and maintain friendships as they get older. If you are a parent of a 7♠, encourage them to play with children their own age even if you must do so by convincing them they are needed as a role model or leader. Make sure they do not boss others around. Reason with them if they do, rather than taking away a leadership privilege and telling them they cannot handle the responsibility. Even though they are a child, many 7♠ do not like to be treated as such. As an old soul, they *feel older*. Treating them like a baby can be a trigger for some and they may become argumentative. Those inclined to be introverts may be loners who struggle to create and maintain friendships as they get older.

The best way to nurture a 7♠ is to teach them at the earliest possible age about their superpower – *emotional intelligence*. A person with high emotional intelligence can understand and manage both their own emotions and the emotions of people around them. Strengthening this character trait will set them upon an emotionally healthy path to deal with the health and work challenges that are certain to be part of their life. First, teach your 7♠ how to identify and label various emotions. I suggest reading *Listening to My Body* by Gabi Garcia because it tells children how to recognize their emotions by being aware of their bodies. Then, read *How Do You Feel?* by Lizzy Rockwell to learn how to name their emotions. Explain to them that it is okay to feel all kinds of emotions, including negative ones. Finally, and most importantly, teach your 7♠ that they have the power to self-regulate their emotions. They can use techniques to calm down, such as hugging a stuffed animal or cuddling with a pet. Find children's books that focus on specific emotions that your 7♠ may be struggling with such as anger, sadness, worry, or frustration. Urge a 7♠ to practice mindfulness activities. Mindfulness exercises can teach your child how to stand still, calm the mind, and be present in the moment. Once that state is achieved, a child is better able to manage their emotions or deal with problems. In education, mindfulness exercises have become popular to give kids a break from academic activities. If you are the parent of a 7♠, ask your child's teacher about the incorporation of mindfulness exercises in the classroom. Better yet, gift your child's teacher with books and other resources to teach mindfulness. I recommend purchasing a pack of cards titled, *Mindful Kids: 50 Mindfulness Activities for Kindness, Focus, and Calm* by Whitney Stewart. Overall, encourage your 7♠ to practice techniques from various sources and create a list of what works for them.

Many 7♠ are challenged by being empaths, someone who is extremely sensitive to other people's emotions. This trait can be problematic if a 7♠ is primarily exposed to negative emotions of those close to them. When your 7♠ develops an awareness of time, typically after age 5, you can begin to talk to them about the temporary nature of negative emotions – how in time those emotions will go away. Help them navigate these times. For instance, when you notice a 7♠ has been triggered, ask them to close their eyes and pay attention to their physical body. How do they feel? Can they name the feeling? Tell them to imagine a calming light outside of their body and guide them to bring it into each body part. Tell them to relax. Tell them that right now they are safe. Once they feel calmer, they will be in a better place to problem-solve and re-evaluate the situation that caused the emotion. Encourage them to practice this technique in small scale situations so they can experience success. This will empower them to apply similar strategies in other challenging life situations. As your 7♠ enters adolescence, they develop the ability to see the bigger picture in life. Help them discern a broader perspective with any life experience and cultivate an attitude of gratitude. For example, let's say your thirteen-year-old 7♠ has long struggled with scoliosis or a curvature of their spine. The doctor has recommended surgery. This means your 7♠ will go through a long recovery time in which their physical activities will be limited. Discuss the perspective of time. Sure, the next six months to a year will be difficult for them, but the gains of mobility for the rest of their life will outweigh the sacrifices needed now. Also, the time that would normally be spent doing physical activities or sports could be redirected into a new hobby. Perhaps, they can learn to play a musical instrument.

Additionally, 7♠ tend to be sensitive to the vulnerabilities of the physical body. Some hate getting shots or swallowing large pills. If you are a parent of a 7♠, help them leverage this trait in a positive way by teaching them how to connect with and manage the energy in their body. Introduce a 7♠ to the concept of *chakras* or energy centers in the body. I recommend the children's book, *The Rainbow Inside: A Journey through the Chakras* by Caitlynn Wakeman. Chakra exercises can help them get in tune with different energies within and clear them when imbalanced. Additionally, teach them ways they can have some control over their physical health through diet and exercise. 7♠ often experience more than their fair share of challenges in life to teach them spiritual wisdom. When a 7♠ resists learning their lessons, they block the energy flow in their body which in turn may invite illness. In his book, *The Power of Now*, Eckhart Tolle stated, "many types of illnesses are caused by the ego's continuous resistance, which creates restrictions and blockages in the flow of energy through the body." A blocked 7♠ must adopt techniques to improve the flow of energy in their bodies. An alternative medicine strategy that may offer benefits is *dry brushing*. Dry brushing involves using a dry, stiff brush to conduct a skin body massage. Studies have shown dry brushing improves lymphatic flow. One function of the lymphatic system is to remove abnormal cells and toxic fluids from the body.

A 7♠ can also feel imbalanced when certain people plug into them and drain them of energy. Have you ever heard about or watched the movie, *Bruce Almighty*? Jim Carey plays the main character, Bruce, who temporarily receives the powers and responsibilities of God. In one scene, Bruce is overwhelmed because he can literally hear all the prayers from people around the world. This is how a 7♠ can feel at times. They are highly sensitive to the pain and suffering of the world or their own life circumstances. They feel like they are an electrical socket, draining energy with every pain they absorb. Keep in mind, a 7♠ who does not find ways to constructively direct this energy will inadvertently direct it inward in a destructive way. This explains why 7♠ are prone to anxiety and depression. Take these symptoms seriously and help them seek counseling and therapy. As a parent, if you observe this happening in your child, teach them strategies to reduce stress. Recharging oneself is a must for a 7♠. And it is best achieved in a solitary manner. Urge a 7♠ to engage in single person activities, such as fishing, kayaking, yoga, journaling, gardening, photography, biking, knitting, playing video games, or completing crossword puzzles. Music therapy may also benefit a 7♠. Music therapy is administered by a trained professional and is not the same as listening to recreational music. Music therapy can help a child relax, reduce physical pain, and open a child to expressing themselves and their feelings. Some 7♠ can even direct their emotions into song and music writing and make a career doing so. And interestingly, some 7♠ possess the heart of an activist. Some find relief when they direct their awareness of injustices into supporting change.

Summary of Higher and Lower Personality Traits

Higher: Psychic, generous, emotionally intelligent, humble, reliable, honest, care for others.

Lower: Moody, argumentative, pessimistic, accident-prone, stubborn.

Childhood Influence Mercury Cards
It is common knowledge that a child's personality is most malleable during the formative years – from birth to eight years of age. In the Destiny Card system, the Mercury Cards in a Birth Card's Life Spread reveal influences a child with this Birth Card will experience between birth through age 12. As such, a child's Mercury Cards must be considered so an adult can nurture a child from a place of awareness and work with them from where a child is at in their development. A 7♠ child has the following Mercury Cards: **2♣, 3♠, and A♠**. Alternatively, outside of any specific person associated with these three cards, the basic meanings of these cards describe experiences that may be impactful during this child's formative years. These cards suggest a young 7♠ is often talkative and prone to argumentation. They may demonstrate artistic leanings and/or be born into an artistic family. They tend to be private and often keep their own secrets close to their heart.

Potential Callings / Vocations by Zodiac Sign

January 7 – Capricorn: 4♦ Planetary Ruling Card

The responsible nature of Capricorn inspires these 7♠ to lead others. They can be successful in any occupation so long as their idealism does not short circuit their goals. They must work in life. They can make a fine business leader, psychologist, song writer, actor, or singer.

February 5 – Aquarius: 2♠ Planetary Ruling Card

These 7♠ are inclined toward careers that support their spiritual beliefs and allow them to work one-on-one with clients (e.g., clergyman, family therapist, social worker, or non-profit worker). Some that cling to a belief or routine in how to improve their physical body can succeed as a sports athlete.

March 3 – Pisces: 8♥ Planetary Ruling Card
Due to their 8♥ Planetary Ruling Card, these 7♠ can do well in careers that deal with the broader public. They can attract others like a magnet, which means they can sell their ideas and products to others as an artist, decorator, designer, actor, or business owner.

April 1 – Aries: J♦ Planetary Ruling Card

The aspect of passionate Aries in these 7♠ makes them well suited for careers in which they can promote their beliefs and convictions. These individuals can do well as an attorney, political activist, politician, business owner, soldier, or salesman (so long as they believe in their products).

Famous 7♠

Katie Couric, TV host – 1/7/1957
Nicolas Cage, actor – 1/7/1964
Cristiano Ronaldo, Soccer player – 2/5/1985
Rachel Maddow, TV host – 4/1/1973
Laura Linney, actress – 2/6/1964
Alexander Graham Bell, inventor – 3/3/1847

Chapter 11

Descriptions of the Eight Birth Cards

Welcome to the world of the powerful 8♥!

8♥ = Power in love and relationships

According to the Destiny Card system, souls chronologically experience God's lessons across 52 life incarnations. (Think of these as the universe's lessons if this aligns more with your beliefs.) The Birth Card each soul is born into determines the order and type of lessons a soul experiences. When you examine a Birth Card, you will notice it displays a suit of either a Heart, Club, Diamond, or Spade. This suit is significant because it represents the gifts a person born into this suit will possess and how they will direct their energies to learn lessons in their current life incarnation. A Heart Birth Card retains gifts and experiences life lessons around love and relationships. A Club Birth Card holds capabilities and experiences life lessons in their ability to communicate and absorb knowledge. A Diamond Birth Card possesses talents and experiences life lessons around money and values. And finally, a Spade Birth Card manifests gifts and experiences life lessons in work and health. Souls progress through incarnations and life lessons beginning as Hearts, moving on to Clubs, then Diamonds, and finally as Spades. Therefore, individuals born as Heart Cards are the youngest souls and individuals born as Spades Cards are the oldest souls.

In addition, the number on a Birth Card is equally meaningful as souls sequentially experience life lessons beginning as an Ace and culminating with lessons as a King. Because souls reincarnate, an Eight Birth Card's previous life incarnation was as a Seven. All Seven Birth Cards are spiritual cards and those associated with them suffer to some extent to gain spiritual consciousness. The reward for graduating from the challenging life of a Seven is to experience the power of an Eight in the next life. Have you ever heard about or used the toy called the Magic 8-Ball? It looks like an enlarged eight-ball from a pool game and has a window at the bottom from which a triangular shaped block appears with answers to yes-no questions. It is touted as magical because it holds the power of telling one's fortune. But why is it an 8-Ball? Why is it not called the Magic 7-Ball? After all, seven is considered the most spiritual number. What is it about the number eight? The answer is quite simple. If you turn the number eight horizontally on its side, it resembles the infinity symbol. This is not a coincidence. Infinity, also known as the Lemniscate symbol, represents the concept of limitlessness. Infinity is an attribute associated with God. Therefore, the number eight symbolizes the power to accomplish infinite achievements. **It makes sense, then, that an 8♥ child's purpose, gifts, and life lessons revolve around how they manage their unlimited *power*. And due to being a Heart, this child will learn lessons by experiencing power in *love* and *relationships*.**

How to Nurture the Temperament and Personality of an 8♥ Child

The early life of an 8♥ is usually uneventful. During such years, 8♥ are easy and a pleasure to be around. They are quiet, good-natured, and kind. Early educators find them to be low maintenance because they tend to get along with everyone. Young 8♥ see and deeply feel beauty in the world. If you are a teacher and you show a video of baby animals to your classroom, the 8♥ in class will likely be the most delighted. You may hear them express "aww" and "so cute" and see their face glowing with joy. Students around them will be drawn to the 8♥ and in the process be pulled into the moment. This same trait may mean an 8♥ will remain naïve longer than most children. For example, this is the child that continues to believe in Santa well past the normal age of discovery. Try not to crush their beliefs because their beliefs are tied to strong emotions.

8♥ children are loving, sweet, and generous. They do not fear giving too much love because they subconsciously know love is limitless; there is plenty to go around. They see and appreciate the best in others. As an 8♥ grows older, they often become popular in school. The love, care, and attention an 8♥ bestows upon others is like a drug. During pre-adolescence, an 8♥'s reputation of being low maintenance may begin to change. This happens when they begin to develop an understanding of their powerful hold over others. They will explore this power in positive and negative ways. For example, let's say an eleven-year-old 8♥ girl named Allison has a crush on a boy in her class. She asks her close friend, KayLani, to talk to the boy and find out if he likes her. KayLani is shy and does not want to do this. Later that same day, Allison is hanging out with KayLani and another friend, Rebecca. Allison intentionally devotes all her positive energy and praise to Rebecca. She ignores KayLani. KayLani feels so bad she agrees to talk to the boy. The 8♥ in this scenario has discovered the power of how to manipulate others with her affection. It may take a while for a parent or educator to notice this behavior. When you do, it is wise to intervene. Rather than attempting to suppress their persuasive power, help an 8♥ redirect it in positive ways. If you are a teacher of an 8♥ and have a new classmate who has trouble making friends, challenge your 8♥ to bring that child into their inner circle of friends. 8♥ are highly persuasive. Tell an 8♥ about their superpower and hold high expectations for their persuasive skills or in their ability to lead others in maintaining a harmonious classroom.

If you are a parent of an 8♥, expect them to be a loving role model to their siblings. If they show interest in a worthy cause, encourage them to write an email to a decision-maker or collect donations to support it. Some 8♥ have emotional power that can be expressed through acting or persuading others to buy their products or ideas. If you think your 8♥ teen is spending too much time on Instagram, think again. They have what it takes to be an influencer on such platforms and as such, build a following that can be monetized into a business. Dare these 8♥ to try out for the school play, talent show, or start their own YouTube subscription business. You may have noticed the words 'challenge' and 'dare' being used in this paragraph. This is intentional, as some 8♥ do not like to be told what to do. Instead, they enjoy the challenge of applying their emotional power to prove their power to others.

To nurture an 8♥, it is important to consider that they are emotionally energized individuals. Popping their bubble can lead to power struggles and it is never a good idea to get into a power struggle with any Eight Birth Card. With a teenage 8♥, avoid telling them how to feel or be dismissive of their strong feelings. For example, let us continue the story of Allison who has a boy crush. Imagine Allison's dream comes true, and her crush asks her out. They are officially girlfriend and boyfriend. Then, two days later, they broke up. Allison is devastated. She was madly in love. As an adult listening to Allison cry about her situation, you may feel her response is overly dramatic. Keep those feelings to yourself. Refrain from telling this 8♥ that her feelings of love were not real. They were real for an 8♥ and telling them otherwise will only bring about a negative reaction. You will lose that battle because an 8♥ is likely more emotionally powerful than you. Instead, validate her feelings. Console her. An 8♥ is so magnetic, she will attract a new admirer in no time. Just sit back and wait. The sadness will be gone soon enough.

Although 8♥ have access to limitless power, this does not mean their emotional tanks are constantly full. They need time and proper settings to recharge. A day at a spa does wonders for an 8♥. Younger 8♥ prefer to re-energize through their own beautiful surroundings. Therefore, it is important to allow an 8♥ to decorate their own room. You will find they are truly good at it. If you are the parent of an 8♥, and if it is financially possible, make an exception to let them spend a bit more money on items they want for their room. Or allow them enough money to buy clothing as many 8♥ enjoy wearing the latest fashions. You may find this is money well spent for an 8♥ teenager. Their room will act like a calming sanctuary, allowing them to rebalance their emotions. And your 8♥'s peace of mind will likely pay off in furthering your own peace of mind.

Because Heart Birth Cards are younger souls, 8♥ are inclined to share their gifts with young people. This explains why many 8♥ have the potential to become teachers or school counselors. When an individual feels bad or lost, an interaction with an 8♥ can be quite healing. Spiritual writer Eckhart Tolle wrote: "The pain that you create now is always some form of non-acceptance, some form of unconscious resistance to what is." Tolle claims that it is not an easy process for a person to accept what one has long resisted. However, an 8♥ is well suited to help others navigate such a process because they understand the power emotions hold over the mind like no other Birth Card. 8♥ hold the emotional power to see pain for what it is, and they can help others see the silver linings of life's challenges. In addition, 8♥ have the power to receive emotions from the spiritual world and share them with others through artistic expression by way of songs, music, writing, and artwork. When their work is shared, it elicits deep, authentic emotions in others. They can capture large audiences because they help others feel and release their own emotions. As such, many 8♥ can make a successful career out of their creative art or ability to communicate with others.

Summary of Higher and Lower Personality Traits

Higher: Charming, generous, popular, attentive, persuasive, loving, teacher.

Lower: Self-indulgent, idealistic expectation of others, demanding, manipulative.

Childhood Influence Mercury Cards

It is common knowledge that a child's personality is most malleable during the formative years – from birth to eight years of age. In the Destiny Card system, the Mercury Cards in a Birth Card's Life Spread reveal influences a child with this Birth Card will experience between birth through age 12. As such, a child's Mercury Cards must be considered so an adult can nurture a child from a place of awareness and work with them from where a child is at in their development. An 8♥ child has the following Mercury Cards: **6♣, 7♣, and 8♠**. Alternatively, outside of any specific person associated with these three cards, the basic meanings of these cards describe experiences that may be impactful during this child's formative years. These cards suggest an 8♥ is born into an ordinary home environment. Although they may experience an illness or contend with an illness of a family member, they often persevere through their challenges.

Potential Callings / Vocations by Zodiac Sign

August 31 – Virgo: 6♣ Planetary Ruling Card

These meticulous 8♥ are hard-working and like to take their time getting things right which is why they can excel as an accountant, manager, teacher, or healer (spiritual or medical).

September 29 – Libra: 6♠ Planetary Ruling Card

The artsy and fair-minded side of Libra integrates well with these 8♥ which helps them succeed as an artist, actor, writer, or counselor. They tend to dislike manual labor or work that requires a lot of physical movement.

October 27 – Scorpio: Q♥ and A♣ Planetary Ruling Cards

With a Q♥ Planetary Ruling Card, these 8♥ are big-hearted individuals who want to share their gifts with large groups or organizations. They can do well as a counselor, teacher, life coach, writer, song writer, musician, or scientist.

November 25 – Sagittarius: 10♣ Planetary Ruling Card

These brilliant 8♥ blend the power of charm and intellect such that they should follow a professional career (e.g., attorney, politician, physician, teacher, or psychologist).

December 23 – Capricorn: 8♦ Planetary Ruling Card

With an 8♦ Planetary Ruling Card, these 8♥ are destined for recognition and fame. They can lead large organizations. They can harness emotional power through art as a musician, song writer, singer, composer, dancer, writer, or film producer.

Famous 8♥

Richard Gere, actor – 8/31/1949
Van Morrison, singer – 8/31/1945
Maria Montessori, educator – 8/31/1870
Lonzo Ball, basketball player – 10/27/1997

Chrissy Metz, actress– 9/27/1980
Eddie Vedder, musician – 12/23/1964

8♣ = Power of the mind

Welcome to the world of the powerful 8♣!

According to the Destiny Card system, souls chronologically experience God's lessons across 52 life incarnations. (Think of these as the universe's lessons if this aligns more with your beliefs.) The Birth Card each soul is born into determines the order and type of lessons a soul experiences. When you examine a Birth Card, you will notice it displays a suit of either a Heart, Club, Diamond, or Spade. This suit is significant because it represents the gifts a person born into this suit will possess and how they will direct their energies to learn lessons in their current life incarnation. A Heart Birth Card retains gifts and experiences life lessons around love and relationships. A Club Birth Card holds capabilities and experiences life lessons in their ability to communicate and absorb knowledge. A Diamond Birth Card possesses talents and experiences life lessons around money and values. And finally, a Spade Birth Card manifests gifts and experiences life lessons in work and health. Souls progress through incarnations and life lessons beginning as Hearts, moving on to Clubs, then Diamonds, and finally as Spades. Therefore, individuals born as Heart Cards are the youngest souls and individuals born as Spades Cards are the oldest souls.

In addition, the number on a Birth Card is equally meaningful as souls sequentially experience life lessons beginning as an Ace and culminating with lessons as a King. Because souls reincarnate, an Eight Birth Card's previous life incarnation was as a Seven. All Seven Birth Cards are spiritual cards and those associated with them suffer to some extent to gain spiritual consciousness. The reward for graduating from the challenging life of a Seven is to experience the power of an Eight in the next life. Have you ever heard about or used the toy called the Magic 8-Ball? It looks like an enlarged eight-ball from a pool game and has a window at the bottom from which a triangular shaped block appears with answers to yes-no questions. It is touted as magical because it holds the power of telling one's fortune. But why is it an 8-Ball? Why is it not called the Magic 7-Ball? After all, seven is considered the most spiritual number. What is it about the number eight? The answer is quite simple. If you turn the number eight horizontally on its side, it resembles the infinity symbol. This is not a coincidence. Infinity, also known as the Lemniscate symbol, represents the concept of limitlessness. Infinity is an attribute associated with God. Therefore, the number eight symbolizes the power to accomplish infinite achievements. **It makes sense, then, that an 8♣ child's purpose, gifts, and life lessons revolve around how they manage *power*. And due to being a Club, this child will learn lessons by experiencing power through *communication* and *knowledge*.**

How to Nurture the Temperament and Personality of an 8♣ Child

In the late 1990's, the book *Who Moved My Cheese* by Spencer Johnson and Kenneth Blanchard became an overnight sensation. The book used a metaphor of four mice navigating through a maze every day to find and eat their beloved cheese to explain how some people respond to change. The story begins with four mice discovering their cheese is missing. Two of the mice are not fazed by this and go off to find the cheese. The other two mice have difficulty accepting their situation. They complain. They waste lots of energy working the maze the same way, resisting the notion that the cheese moved, and that they need to change their ways. The core message from the book is that change is inevitable in everyone's life path. When it occurs, one must be flexible and adapt to it. However, such behavior tends to be difficult for an 8♣. You see, 8♣ are born with mentally fixed minds. This personality trait has higher and lower expressions. Let's look at a specific example. Imagine you are a parent of an 8♣ daughter named Mathilda. From birth, Mathilda has loved water. Baths are pure joy to her and a routine that allows for a seamless transition to bedtime. Knowing this, you enrolled Mathilda in swimming lessons at age four. Mathilda loves her lessons and does not complain about going to them even on the colder days. Focusing on her skills, Mathilda gets promoted to lessons with older children. Other parents at these swimming lessons view her as easy-going, well-mannered, and mature for her age. This 8♣ is manifesting a higher expression. Several weeks go by and one day you arrive at swimming lessons only to find lessons have been cancelled due to an overuse of chemicals in the pool. Mathilda has a meltdown. A serious meltdown! You try to reason with Mathilda, but it does no good. Yes, this mentally fixed 8♣ is now manifesting a lower expression of their Birth Card – an *inability to accept change*.

Clearly, you may be thinking that an 8♣ would benefit from learning how to be more flexible. The reality is, just as a leopard does not change its spot, an 8♣ is not going to change into a flexible person. Instead, it would be far better to teach them how to react when faced with change that is outside of their control. This should also include teaching them how to communicate with others when there is conflict over their fixed beliefs. Start by explaining the advantages and disadvantages of having a fixed nature. Fortunately, author Spencer Johnson wrote a kid's version of his book titled, *Who Moved My Cheese? For Kids* that would provide a great introduction to this topic. Then, consider various scenarios that could trigger an 8♣ and offer solutions. For instance, let's say you are a second-grade teacher of an 8♣ named Robert. Robert gets angry with last minute changes in the daily schedule. In such times, Robert refuses to transition from one activity to the next. In talking to Robert about this situation, you validate his frustration when there is change. You offer to accommodate this by adopting the routine of talking through the daily schedule first thing in the morning. When there is a change in the schedule you explain it to Robert ahead of transition time, so he is better prepared for it. Robert agrees to this plan and goes on to transition more quickly.

8♣ make the process of goal setting and achievement look easy. This is because they can mentally focus like no other card. For this reason, an 8♣ can be successful at anything that involves developing the mind; from comprehending quantum mechanics, learning new languages, applying statistics, to understanding the complexities of astrology. To boot, they process information more quickly than others. Probably, in any teamwork situation, they are mentally miles ahead of others. This can make them impatient and act bossy. Others may find them opinionated. The bright side of working with an 8♣ is that the work will get completed exceptionally well with every detail covered. All 8♣ are high achievers.

8♣ subconsciously understand the power of knowledge and appreciate its acquisition. As such, most 8♣ enjoy school and the mental stimulation it can offer. In fact, an 8♣ can be the ideal student. If you are a parent or teacher of an 8♣, this is the child that can handle being pushed toward achievement. In fact, they love competition, whether it is academic, or sports related. You can be assured they are well suited for higher education or any career that requires sustained focus. They can practice, practice, practice, and therefore master anything that requires practice. Now, are you reading this and thinking this is the opposite of what your 8♣ is doing? Is your 8♣ battling you and your high expectations of them? Perhaps they make Bs in school with no effort at all. You know they are capable of so much more. If this is the case, then there is likely one ingredient missing for your 8♣. While capable of excelling at anything, 8♣ often resist what others want them to do. This is to say, the missing ingredient is that an 8♣ must be interested in and invested in what they are learning. If they perceive no purpose or rationale for learning a particular topic, they can dig in their heels and refuse to put effort into it. Singer and song writer Bob Dylan argued that "a man is a success if he gets up in the morning and gets to bed at night, and in between he does what he wants to do." Most people would agree Dylan did things his way with great success. This is not surprising because Dylan is an 8♣! Therefore, talk to your 8♣. Assess their buy-in rather than projecting your own expectations upon them. Negotiate with them. Be okay to a point with them underachieving in topics they do not deem worthy so long as they put more effort into areas that interest them. You need not worry they will not be successful in life. They will accomplish much in life, but it must be on their own terms.

Does your 8♣ love to play complex, strategic video games? For instance, do they enjoy games like Aegis Defenders, The Sims, Minecraft, or The Legend of Zelda? If so, there are two reasons for this. An 8♣'s is gifted with two mental superpowers: *logical* and *systems thinking*. A logical thinker is a person who can analyze a situation objectively by getting all the information, allowing input from others, and then coming to a rational conclusion or solution. This is the eight-year-old child who says, "Why do we call them waiters when we do all the waiting?" A systems thinker understands that a system is more than just the sum of its parts. They recognize a system to entail a synergistic interaction between its parts. Let's consider an example of a system. Do you remember learning about food webs in elementary school? A food web is a visual representation showing who eats what in a system, that is, an ecosystem. Picture rabbits eating grass. Then, the foxes and hawks eat the rabbits. Understanding the parts and connections within a system is essential when something goes wrong within a system and efforts need to be made to fix it. Perhaps a disease kills a large portion of the rabbit population. This problem impacts other parts of the ecosystem. There is not enough food for the fox and hawks. Some may die of starvation or be forced to relocate. Food webs are a simple system to grasp. Other systems, like astrology, human economics, software engineering, city planning to name a few, are more complex and difficult for the average person to understand. Yet an 8♣ can easily figure them out. Many 8♣ pursue higher education because they enjoy the challenge of professions that utilize systems thinking. These professions include engineering, scientific research, computer science, and coding. Therefore, encourage an 8♣ to pursue activities and opportunities that can lead to these types of careers. Suggest STEM activities, robotics clubs, and coding classes.

If your 8♣ leans toward more musical or artistic interests, they can apply their systems thinking by way of composing music, creating a comic book, or designing décor for a home. In fact, there are many other professions where a person benefits from being a systems thinker – sports coaching, forensic accounting, mechanic, or architect. Some 8♣ enjoy storytelling and writing novels as they like the challenge of piecing together details of a story. Even an attorney may use systems thinking when building arguments for a case. Ah, speaking of winning an argument, if you are a parent of an 8♣, avoid mental power struggles with your child or adolescent. They will have a good rationale for every belief they hold or action they take. If they are particularly fixed on an opposing belief, you will likely not change their mind to your way of thinking. You may need to make compromises with this 8♣ or agree to disagree. If you demand they act or see things your way every time, they will resist and parenting this child may be emotionally draining. Just remember this same trait can be a blessing. This child has the potential to become a doctor who fights to save a life even though the odds are against them.

Summary of Higher and Lower Personality Traits

Higher: Dependable, mentally focused, logical, systems thinker, achiever, good provider.

Lower: Obstinate, mentally fixed, impatient, opinionated, bossy.

Childhood Influence Mercury Cards
It is common knowledge that a child's personality is most malleable during the formative years – from birth to eight years of age. In the Destiny Card system, the Mercury Cards in a Birth Card's Life Spread reveal influences a child with this Birth Card will experience between birth through age 12. As such, a child's Mercury Cards must be considered so an adult can nurture a child from a place of awareness and work with them from where a child is at in their development. An 8♣ child has the following Mercury Cards: **6♦, 2♥, and 9♣**. Alternatively, outside of any specific person associated with these three cards, the basic meanings of these cards describe experiences that may be impactful during this child's formative years. These cards suggest an 8♣ is born into a financially static situation (good or bad). This situation does not seem to hold them back though because they soak up knowledge on their own to achieve in life, especially if they start a sport or playing an instrument at a young age. They may experience a disappointment in their home life and prefer to spend time with friends.

Potential Callings / Vocations by Zodiac Sign

March 28 – Aries: 10♥ Planetary Ruling Card
Mars energy in these 8♣ tend to make them argumentative and sarcastic. Therefore, they are better suited to careers where they share their knowledge with others from a distance. They can do well acting, singing, playing sports, or working in an online business.

April 26 – Taurus: 4♠ Planetary Ruling Card

The influence of stability-loving Taurus combined with the security driven 4♠ Planetary Ruling Card may motivate these individuals to marry for money. Otherwise, these 8♣ can make a career in teaching, sports, banking, merchandizing, or acting.

May 24 – Gemini: 6♦ Planetary Ruling Card

The communicative gifts of Gemini blend well with these 8♣, making them intellectually curious and brilliant. This curiosity can cause them to resist settling into a specific career early on. When they do settle down, they can do well as a teacher, salesperson, preacher, journalist, speech writer, or song writer.

June 22 – Gemini or Cancer: 6♦ or J♠ Planetary Ruling Card

The Gemini affiliated 8♣ tend to be late bloomers. In time they can do well in creative work (e.g., writing, acting, or composing music, song, or dance). The Cancer affiliated individuals prefer jobs that care for others (e.g., social justice work, teaching, or medical healing as a physician, nurse, dietician, or physical therapist).

July 20 – Cancer: J♠ Planetary Ruling Card

Sensitive and caring Cancer in these 8♣ steers many into humanitarian causes and careers (e.g., teaching, counseling, judge, or social work). Having the J♠ Planetary Ruling Card may reveal musical or dramatic talent in these individuals that may be nurtured into a career.

August 18 – Leo: 8♣ Planetary Ruling Card

With an 8♣ Planetary Ruling card, these 8♣ have a double dose of power and drive. As a rule, they prefer to be leaders. They can lead in business or work as an independent contractor.

September 16 – Virgo: 6♦ Planetary Ruling Card

Detail-oriented Virgo in these 8♣ make them well suited to mental professions (e.g., teacher, writer, researcher, investigator, or scientist).

October 14 – Libra: 4♣ Planetary Ruling Card

Having the arts-loving aspect of Libra, many of these 8♣ thrive in dramatic art careers (e.g., acting, film making, screen writing, or directing). They can also do well in politics or in the world of fashion.

November 12 – Scorpio: 10♥ and Q♦ Planetary Ruling Cards

Imbued with a strong physical constitution, many of these 8♣ prefer occupations that require physical activity (e.g., contractor, stunt actor, sports athlete, park ranger, police officer, or secret service officer). The more studious types can succeed as a physician, researcher, or scientist.

December 10 – Sagittarius: 10♦ Planetary Ruling Card

The excellent decision-making qualities of Sagittarius help these 8♣ to become an attorney, judge, teacher, or business leader. Some are extremely psychic and can make a career out of their abilities. Some are amazing storytellers.

Famous 8♣

Bob Dylan, singer/song writer – 5/24/1941
Lady Gaga, singer/song writer – 3/28/1986
David Copperfield, magician – 9/16/1956
Meryl Streep, actress – 6/22/1949
Andy Samberg, actor/ comedian – 8/18/1978
Reba McEntire, singer – 3/28/1955

Welcome to the world of the powerful 8♦!

8♦ = Power with money and values

According to the Destiny Card system, souls chronologically experience God's lessons across 52 life incarnations. (Think of these as the universe's lessons if this aligns more with your beliefs.) The Birth Card each soul is born into determines the order and type of lessons a soul experiences. When you examine a Birth Card, you will notice it displays a suit of either a Heart, Club, Diamond, or Spade. This suit is significant because it represents the gifts a person born into this suit will possess and how they will direct their energies to learn lessons in their current life incarnation. A Heart Birth Card retains gifts and experiences life lessons around love and relationships. A Club Birth Card holds capabilities and experiences life lessons in their ability to communicate and absorb knowledge. A Diamond Birth Card possesses talents and experiences life lessons around money and values. And finally, a Spade Birth Card manifests gifts and experiences life lessons in work and health. Souls progress through incarnations and life lessons beginning as Hearts, moving on to Clubs, then Diamonds, and finally as Spades. Therefore, individuals born as Heart Cards are the youngest souls and individuals born as Spades Cards are the oldest souls.

In addition, the number on a Birth Card is equally meaningful as souls sequentially experience life lessons beginning as an Ace and culminating with lessons as a King. Because souls reincarnate, an Eight Birth Card's previous life incarnation was as a Seven. All Seven Birth Cards are spiritual cards and those associated with them suffer to some extent to gain spiritual consciousness. The reward for graduating from the challenging life of a Seven is to experience the power of an Eight in the next life. Have you ever heard about or used the toy called the Magic 8-Ball? It looks like an enlarged eight-ball from a pool game and has a window at the bottom from which a triangular shaped block appears with answers to yes-no questions. It is touted as magical because it holds the power of telling one's fortune. But why is it an 8-Ball?

Why is it not called the Magic 7-Ball? After all, seven is considered the most spiritual number. What is it about the number eight? The answer is quite simple. If you turn the number eight horizontally on its side, it resembles the infinity symbol. This is not a coincidence. Infinity, also known as the Lemniscate symbol, represents the concept of limitlessness. Infinity is an attribute associated with God. Therefore, the number eight symbolizes the power to accomplish infinite achievements. **It makes sense, then, that an 8♦ child's purpose, gifts, and life lessons revolve around how they manage *power*. And due to being a Diamond, this child will learn lessons by experiencing power in things of *value*, including *money*.**

How to Nurture the Temperament and Personality of an 8♦ Child

8♦ are born with a lifetime supply of pixie-dust in their pockets. Whatever they value, focus their energy upon, or work toward, it is as if they sprinkle pixie-dust upon it because their efforts turn to gold. They literally manifest gold because most often there is financial gain associated with their endeavors. In fact, many of the rich and famous are 8♦. This is not to say an 8♦ is lazy. On the contrary, from an early age they are programmed to associate hard work and effort with immediate success. This dynamic motivates them to work harder. They are also programmed this way because of the influence of a powerful father or father figure in their life during their early years. This figure held high expectations of them. Or they may have been born into a family situation where they were asked to take on adult responsibilities at an unusually young age. Regardless of their circumstances, 8♦ rise to the occasion. These initial experiences leave imprints upon them that have long lasting impacts. By the time an 8♦ enters school, they are independent. As such, they are ideal candidates for boarding school or attending a camp for the entire summer.

How best to apply their power is a lesson 8♦ learn throughout their life. When an 8♦ is leaning into the lower traits of their Birth Card, they are not using their gifts to help humanity. These individuals may focus their power on acquiring material possessions for themselves. It is not uncommon for an 8♦ teen to become addicted to shopping and spend large amounts of money doing so. These individuals often feel *entitled*. When a certain amount of disharmony is produced from these behaviors, there tends to be negative consequences. Let's consider an extreme example in real life. In and around 2011, do you remember the catchphrase "Winning!" that was coined by actor, Charlie Sheen? At the time, Sheen was facing allegations of domestic and drug abuse. He went on radio and talk shows criticizing his popular sitcom, *Two and a Half Men*. His rants were akin to psychotic meltdowns. When he stated, "The only thing I'm addicted to right now is winning," the "winning" catchphrase took on new life. It was perceived by the public in the opposite way – to mean losing. As you might have guessed, Sheen is an 8♦. This is an example of what can happen when an 8♦ lacks appreciation for their gifts and uses them to hurt others. It would be wise to teach an 8♦ that they need to use their power to equally serve themselves and others. Only when all win, do they truly win.

In the book, *Diary of a Wimpy Kid*, by Jeff Kinney, the main character Greg says, "I'll be famous one day, but for now I'm stuck in middle school with a bunch of morons." This is precisely the attitude of many young 8♦! These individuals learn at a young age that they can direct their power over others to get what they want or value. Let's consider an example. Imagine you have a six-year-old 8♦ daughter named Rachel who just spent the week with her grandparents while you were on vacation. Upon your return home, you go to the store to restock the house with groceries. While shopping, Rachel demands a special treat. You say no. The whole time you are in the store your daughter is whining to get a treat. She claims grandma bought her a treat each time visiting the grocery store. As you are in line to check out, Rachel asks repeatedly for a special treat. You say no – again. Rachel has a meltdown. At this moment, others around you are watching and you feel pressured to give in to stop the noise. Because this child is an 8♦, giving in sets up a terrible precedence. An 8♦ will file this incidence into their brain as a winning formula. Or perhaps I should say whining formula! Over time, they may use this power to wear you down, making it harder and harder for you to tell them no. Instead, you may want to try a method called *gray rocking*. As its name implies, you respond like a rock during your child's meltdown, acting as neutral and unresponsive as possible to deflect their behavior. This method involves keeping your face calm, avoiding eye contact, and acting like nothing out of the ordinary is going on while your child has a meltdown. While some psychologists have found this method to be effective when dealing with manipulative behavior, it may not work with some children. Try it a few times and prepare for the manipulation to get worse before it gets better. If the behavior escalates over time, then stop using it.

Having and maintaining boundaries with an 8♦ is clearly important. If you are a parent of an 8♦, it may help to explain expectations and consequences related to future actions, based upon prior behaviors. Allow them some power by having input to disciplinary consequences. Above all, make sure to follow through with the consequences. Do not let your 8♦ talk you out of the consequences or wear you down by whining or bullying. If needed, have predetermined consequences for such behavior. Determine what privileges are important to your 8♦ and then incorporate them as a consequence for unacceptable behavior. Be prepared that things may get much worse before they get better. Try to use positive comments such as, "I know you are capable of making better decisions,' rather than comments that may invite a power struggle. If they resist the consequence, remind them they had input in the decision-making process. The truth about entitlement is that it gets more difficult to reverse this behavior as a child gets older. If you are dealing with an older 8♦ with this behavior, family therapy may be necessary. Intervention is well worth it. Once an 8♦ constructs and reinforces an entitled personality, they will struggle to maintain healthy relationships throughout their life. They will often manipulate others to get what they want. They tend to put their own needs ahead of others. And later in life, even if they appear to have everything, they may be miserable.

In an educational setting, 8♦ children are what I call 'high profile' students. This is to say they are *influencers*. If you are a teacher of an 8♦, do not underestimate the power they have in your classroom. It does not matter if you are in a position of authority. You cannot assume an 8♦ will view you as such. Have you ever watched the movie *Gladiator*, with actors Russell Crowe and Joaquin Phoenix? Phoenix plays a character who murders his father to seize power as emperor. The movie was set in Roman times when emperors promoted gladiator games as a form of entertainment. Emperors watched the games and held the ultimate power of life or death over a gladiator by signaling with an up or down thumb as to their fate. Such is the power of an 8♦ in a classroom, albeit not quite so dramatic. Their thumbs up or down view of you as the teacher will sway the crowd. If they respect you, the rest of the class will follow. Win them over and your classroom management tends to be easier. It is important to build rapport with these individuals as soon as possible. Some may demand power or recognition in the classroom. Find ways to accommodate this. Give them important classroom jobs. Encourage them to take on leadership roles at school. Suggest activities that provide them with some control or choices to make and watch them shine. You see, an 8♦ acting from the higher side of their Birth Card can influence others in magical ways. These 8♦ can lead and persuade others toward adopting humanitarian principles.

The power dynamics within a family may be likewise impacted when one of the children is an 8♦. You see, 8♦ wish to be the center of attention. Additionally, they keep score of how others are treated and may call out a parent if they feel they are not treated equally. Some even expect to be treated better than their siblings. They need to learn that when it comes to privileges or discipline, it's more important for parents to be fair and not equal because children have different personality traits. Remind them of instances where they were given opportunities due to their individual strengths. Perhaps they were given more freedom at a younger age because of their independent nature. If you have other children and there is constant conflict between one of them and the 8♦, you may want to check the traits of the other child's Birth Card. A child with lower self-esteem or tendency toward negativity may be an easy target for bullying by the 8♦. If you suspect bullying is happening, make sure to intervene. Be prepared that an 8♦ may resist believing they need to change. They may blame the sibling and claim the sibling needs to change. A parent may be swayed by the reasoning of the 8♦ due to their power. As in many cases in life, the truth is likely somewhere in the middle – both children may need to change for the relationship to thrive. Most importantly, when there is a conflict, listen to each child's version of the conflict separately. If put together, the 8♦ will roll over the sibling no matter their age. If discipline is needed, make sure you allow the 8♦ some control in the decision-making or input on consequences.

8♦ are bright children and with little effort can do well in school. However, be on the lookout for them becoming bored. They need a lot of stimulation to get them invested in how they spend their time. As a parent of an 8♦, learn when and when not to hold high expectations. For instance, let's say your thirteen-year-old 8♦ son brings home a report card with all A's and one C. The C is in social studies and your son claims to hate the class. Keep in mind that this grade does not represent what your son has learned. Rather it represents how he felt about that class. Do not see this as a deficit in his learning that will hold him back. It is completely possible for this same child to take an elective class in social studies during high school that propels him into a career in politics or law. An 8♦ will succeed in life, but they need to be in some control over the process. If school is not providing enough challenge for your 8♦, offer alternative after school activities. Support them when they want to pursue self-directed activities, such as starting their own lawn mowing business, or launching their own YouTube channel. Encourage music, singing, or acting classes as many have talents in this area. You see, a superpower of some 8♦ is that they possess a beautiful voice. It is remarkable how many 8♦s attain fame through their singing. 8♦ singers include Dolly Pardon, Janis Joplin, Robert Palmer, Ed Sheeran, Bret Michaels, and will.i.am.

Summary of Higher and Lower Personality Traits

Higher: Ambitious, independent, philanthropic, leadership, free-spirited, quick-minded.

Lower: Domineering, judgmental, vanity, shopaholic, rebel against authority, entitlement.

Childhood Influence Mercury Cards
It is common knowledge that a child's personality is most malleable during the formative years – from birth to eight years of age. In the Destiny Card system, the Mercury Cards in a Birth Card's Life Spread reveal influences a child with this Birth Card will experience between birth through age 12. As such, a child's Mercury Cards must be considered so an adult can nurture a child from a place of awareness and work with them from where a child is at in their development. An 8♦ child has the following Mercury Cards: **K♠ and 8♥**. The K♠ may mean there is an influential father who is likely a Spade Birth or Planetary Ruling Card. Alternatively, outside of any specific person associated with these two cards, the basic meanings of these cards describe experiences that may be impactful during this child's formative years. These cards suggest from their earliest age an 8♦ can master any goals they set their minds to. They tend to be popular and have many friends.

Potential Callings / Vocations by Zodiac Sign

January 19 – Capricorn: 10♠ Planetary Ruling Card
With the hard-working aspect of a 10♠ Planetary Ruling Card, these 8♦ can accomplish anything. Many are athletic and artistic and can achieve fame through writing, singing, or playing professional sports.

February 17 – Aquarius: 5♣ Planetary Ruling Card
The progressive influence of Aquarius makes these 8♦ excel in business. For example, some take avant-garde ideas and create a famous brand out of it. Also, they can do well in occupations that require invention (e.g., writing, engineering, film directing, or song writing).

March 15 – Pisces: 3♦ Planetary Ruling Card
The selfless aspect of Pisces is strong in these 8♦. Their work must provide benefits to the broader community. Many prefer working in government institutions or in service to others. They can make a good diplomat, scientist, researcher, public leader, coach, or hospital administrator.

April 13 – Aries: A♣ Planetary Ruling Card
The authoritative aspect of Aries in these 8♦ cultivates leadership qualities. They hold strong opinions and can succeed as a politician, publisher, public health physician, or public relations director.

May 11 – Taurus: 3♥ Planetary Ruling Card

The grounded and methodical qualities inherent to Taurus allow many of these 8♦ to achieve success as a sports athlete. Those exhibiting artistic talent can propel themself in a career in acting, dance, music, or art.

June 9 – Gemini: K♠ Planetary Ruling Card

The K♠ Planetary Ruling Card imparts a double impact of power in these 8♦. This power may be so intimidating for a young individual that they avoid embracing their power which in turn causes them to become late bloomers. Sooner or later, these individuals must lead others. They can make an excellent attorney, government leader, journalist, or business leader.

July 7 – Cancer: 10♣ Planetary Ruling Card

The caring aspect of Cancer and inherent teacher qualities implied by having the 10♣ Planetary Ruling Card pushes these 8♦ to careers in which they can spread their messages. Many can do well as a film director, religious leader, comedian, or song writer.

August 5 – Leo: 8♦ Planetary Ruling Card

The influence of Leo in these 8♦ instills a strong need for being in the limelight. This goal may be best achieved through a career in acting, politics, entertainment, or sports.

September 3 – Virgo: K♠ Planetary Ruling Card

Critical Virgo can push these 8♦ toward the lower expressions of their card. They are better suited to behind-the-scenes occupations (e.g., scientist, technician, engineer, architect, accountant, producer, or financial analyst).

October 1 – Libra: 3♥ Planetary Ruling Card

Strong aspects of Venus provide these 8♦ with a great deal of charm. They can lead or entertain large groups or audiences as an actor, musician, diplomat, or ambassador.

Famous 8♦
Ed Sheeran, singer/music producer – 2/17/1991
Dolly Pardon, singer – 1/19/1946
Michael Jordan, basketball player – 2/17/1963
Ruth Bader Ginsburg, Supreme Court justice / activist – 3/15/1933
Pete Buttigieg, politician – 1/19/1982
Johnny Depp, actor – 6/9/1963

Welcome to the world of the powerful 8♠!

8♠ = Power in work and health

According to the Destiny Card system, souls chronologically experience God's lessons across 52 life incarnations. (Think of these as the universe's lessons if this aligns more with your beliefs.) The Birth Card each soul is born into determines the order and type of lessons a soul experiences. When you examine a Birth Card, you will notice it displays a suit of either a Heart, Club, Diamond, or Spade. This suit is significant because it represents the gifts a person born into this suit will possess and how they will direct their energies to learn lessons in their current life incarnation. A Heart Birth Card retains gifts and experiences life lessons around love and relationships. A Club Birth Card holds capabilities and experiences life lessons in their ability to communicate and absorb knowledge. A Diamond Birth Card possesses talents and experiences life lessons around money and values. And finally, a Spade Birth Card manifests gifts and experiences life lessons in work and health. Souls progress through incarnations and life lessons beginning as Hearts, moving on to Clubs, then Diamonds, and finally as Spades. Therefore, individuals born as Heart Cards are the youngest souls and individuals born as Spades Cards are the oldest souls.

In addition, the number on a Birth Card is equally meaningful as souls sequentially experience life lessons beginning as an Ace and culminating with lessons as a King. Because souls reincarnate, an Eight Birth Card's previous life incarnation was as a Seven. All Seven Birth Cards are spiritual cards and those associated with them suffer to some extent to gain spiritual consciousness. The reward for graduating from the challenging life of a Seven is to experience the power of an Eight in the next life. Have you ever heard about or used the toy called the Magic 8-Ball? It looks like an enlarged eight-ball from a pool game and has a window at the bottom from which a triangular shaped block appears with answers to yes-no questions. It is touted as magical because it holds the power of telling one's fortune. But why is it an 8-Ball? Why is it not called the Magic 7-Ball? After all, seven is considered the most spiritual number. What is it about the number eight? The answer is quite simple. If you turn the number eight horizontally on its side, it resembles the infinity symbol. This is not a coincidence. Infinity, also known as the Lemniscate symbol, represents the concept of limitlessness. Infinity is an attribute associated with God. Therefore, the number eight symbolizes the power to accomplish infinite achievements. **It makes sense, then, that an 8♠ child's purpose, gifts, and life lessons revolve around how they manage *power*. And due to being a Spade, this child will learn lessons by experiencing power around *work* and *health*.**

How to Nurture the Temperament and Personality of an 8♠ Child
Have you ever played the game in which you stand face-to-face with another person and compete to see who will blink first? Winning at that game requires staying power. An 8♠ can easily win that game because they possess *will power* like no other Birth Card. As you can probably imagine this trait can be applied in positive and negative ways. For example, let's say you are a parent of a five-year-old 8♠ named Ryan. During a family dinner, Ryan announces he has finished eating even though all the vegetables remain on his plate. You tell Ryan he must finish his vegetables before he can leave the table. Ryan claims he hates this vegetable. You explain he must eat some of it and if he chooses not to, he will go to bed early. With this rule in place, Ryan will likely never eat his vegetables. He will choose to go to bed early. Every. Single. Time. He may drive you mad because the consequence will not rattle or sway him. You may

even give up trying to enforce this rule and Ryan will win the battle. Now, consider another scenario with Ryan. For the first time, Ryan is learning to ride his bike without training wheels. You attempt to give him a jump start and inadvertently push the bike too hard, and Ryan falls off the bike. Does Ryan cry? No way. Ryan gets right back on the bike. You encourage Ryan to try riding without your help. Again and again, Ryan fails. You praise Ryan for trying. After a few more attempts, Ryan masters the technique. Practice wins the day, right? In reality willpower won the day because Ryan is an 8♠. Not only is willpower an 8♠'s superpower, but they are also gifted in maintaining *strong convictions*. They are the least wishy-washy card in the deck. Imagine them as having deep roots like a white oak tree. No matter the strength of winds that come their way, they remain fixed in place.

Clearly, the best way adults can nurture an 8♠ is to help them direct their willpower into positive rather than negative ways. Power is their birth right. For an 8♠, power is often perceived by recognition of their hard work. Older 8♠ feel good when they are productive. Encourage them to make to-do lists and use a planner. They tend to get a lot of satisfaction simply by crossing out completed items on their list. Therefore, if you are a parent of an 8♠, it is important to praise your 8♠ for their positive actions and work. Praise will often be powerful in reinforcing good behavior. Make sure your praise is authentic. Be on the lookout for an 8♠ to take on too many projects. Otherwise, they can grow up to be workaholics. Early in life, 8♠ need to learn about work/life balance. Teach your 8♠ about the importance of taking a break when they feel full of energy. Physically active breaks work best. Encourage them to participate in competitive sports. Because 8♠ experience power around health, many are blessed with physically strong bodies. This explains why some 8♠ are professional athletes. Interestingly, 8♠ tend to prefer sports that draw adoring crowds such as football, basketball, soccer, and hockey to name a few. Balance should also be encouraged for an 8♠'s diet, too. 8♠ can be stubborn, though. Early bad eating habits combined with hardheadedness can lead to unhealthy eating habits later in life.

8♠ are born with the subconscious belief that experience is the best teacher. As such, they may resist traditional education. The key to nurturing a young 8♠ is to provide them with *experiential learning*. Experiential learning is a hands-on approach to learning in which students 'learn by doing' and then reflect upon their experiences. If you are the parent of an 8♠, explore local preschools with experiential philosophies, such as Montessori, Waldorf, or Reggio Emelia. As your child gets older, they may thrive in a school that offers project or problem-based learning, where students solve authentic and open-ended, complex problems or challenges. Online learning may be too passive for an 8♠ and should be avoided. In high school, an 8♠ should be encouraged to participate in real-life learning – work-study programs, field experiences, apprenticeships, and after school clubs (i.e., Robotics, STEM, and sports-related clubs). You may notice 8♠ dislike topics in school that hold no practical application. They often lack patience in reading about theories. If you are a teacher of an 8♠, know that these students need a purpose or rationale for learning specific material. Such explanations may help motivate an 8♠.

If you are an educator, you may appreciate 8♠ children for how well *grounded* they are in the classroom. You see, *self-regulation* is another superpower for an 8♠. Self-regulation is the ability of a child to manage their own emotions and behaviors. As an example, after an engaging activity in the classroom, you can count on an 8♠ to settle down and get back to their studies. If an 8♠ enjoys school, you can really push them academically. Applying their power in learning can produce amazing academic results. In the classroom, one issue to look for may be related to social skills. You see, many 8♠ march to the beat of a different drum. They tend to resist conformity. Let's consider an example. Imagine it is recess at school and an eight-year-old 8♠ boy named William announces to his friends he wants to play catch. Shortly after William's declaration, a more popular student yells out to classmates he wants to play basketball and needs players. Many classmates decide to play basketball, including William's friends. Does William join the basketball game? Nope. Does William go to the corner of the school yard and sulk? Nope. William will often react in one of two ways. If William is expressing the higher side of his Birth Card, he will play wall ball catch by himself and be perfectly happy. If William is expressing the lower side of his Birth Card, he may try to impose his will on others to play catch with him. He may even be mean to his friends in the process. He may act like a bully. If you are a teacher witnessing bullying, you know this is unacceptable behavior and requires intervention. Engage this child in a private discussion about their behavior. Listen to their side of the story. Then explain the other side to the story in terms of how others feel when they are bullied. If more incidents arise, discuss bullying as a whole class without calling out William for his behavior. Show the movie, *Wonder*, to the class to prompt discussion. This movie tells the story of fifth grader, Auggie Pullman, who experiences bullying due to facial differences. Use role play around specific situations that include bullying. Look on the Internet for resources on bullying and teach them to the class. Seek the help of support staff, counselors, and administration. An 8♠ who manifests a bully personality will likely generate bad karma that tends to be settled in their next incarnation as a 9♠.

If you are the parent of an 8♠ and have other children, you may notice similar bullying behaviors at home. Use this book to read about the Birth Cards of your other children. A child with lower self-esteem or tendency toward negativity may be an easy target for bullying by an 8♠. Be on the lookout for your 8♠ to steam roll over them in every conflict. Such dynamics require intervention. What is often difficult about this is that an 8♠ may resist believing they need to change. They may blame the sibling and claim they need to change. Explain to them that having a strong willpower is their superpower. They may not be aware of how intimidating they can be to someone with less power. If discipline is needed, make sure you allow your 8♠ some control in the decision-making or input on consequences.

An 8♠ who bullies others to get their own way will often find it harder and harder to work with others as they get older. This is problematic today as many jobs require teamwork. Let's consider an example. Suppose you are a middle school social science teacher. You have assembled students in groups of four to collaboratively work on a Bill of Rights scrapbook. The Bill of Rights is the first ten amendments of the Constitution. You have gathered current newspapers, magazines, photographs, and websites with the expectation that the students will find examples of current events related to these constitutional rights. You tell each group they should review the amendments before analyzing current events. Five minutes into working on this assignment, a student approaches you complaining another student named Steven has left the group. The rogue student is examining the current events and, yes, the rogue student is an

8♠. When you question Steven, he says he already knows the amendments and thinks it is a waste of time to review each one of them, particularly when two members of the group are gossiping about something else. This 8♠ wants to get the work completed right away. In this situation, how can you accommodate Steven? Allow flexibility for all students. Before students need to work in their group, tell them they can choose to work with a partner to review the amendments or start reviewing materials independently. Now, imagine a slight alteration to this scenario. Minutes into the assignment, Steven approaches you and demands to work independently. You are tempted to allow this because you know Steven can do the work of four people. But this is not a good idea. Steven needs to learn to work with others. Additionally, you may need to work with this group to develop a plan of action so that Steven is not able to bully others into doing everything his way.

Summary of Higher and Lower Personality Traits

Higher: Brilliant, grounded, perseverant, strong backbone, sociable, healer, loyal to family.

Lower: Arrogant, judgmental, workaholic, stubborn, rebellious, bully, prideful.

Childhood Influence Mercury Cards
It is common knowledge that a child's personality is most malleable during the formative years – from birth to eight years of age. In the Destiny Card system, the Mercury Cards in a Birth Card's Life Spread reveal influences a child with this Birth Card will experience between birth through age 12. As such, a child's Mercury Cards must be considered so an adult can nurture a child from a place of awareness and work with them from where a child is at in their development. An 8♠ child has the following Mercury Cards: **A♥, 2♦, and A♦.** Alternatively, outside of any specific person associated with these three cards, the basic meanings of these cards describe experiences that may be impactful during this child's formative years. These cards suggest an 8♠ often show early signs of intense ambition and a skill at bargaining with others. They may be impacted by selfish motivations from a family member.

Potential Callings / Vocations by Zodiac Sign

January 6 – Capricorn: 3♣ Planetary Ruling Card
Due to having a 3♣ Planetary Ruling Card, these 8♠ are highly creative. They may prefer expression in work that can also provide an adoring fan base. Thus, these individuals are drawn to work as an actor, comedian, politician, writer, public speaker, entertainer, or sports athlete.

February 4 – Aquarius: 3♠ planetary Ruling Card
Assertive Aquarius combined with the willpower of 8♠ packs a powerful punch in these individuals. While they can accomplish anything, they may prefer a career in medicine, science, engineering, or technology.

March 2 – Pisces: 9♥ Planetary Ruling Card

The compassionate aspect of Pisces makes these 8♠ feel they are called to serve humanity. They can make an excellent healer, religious leader, or soldier.

Famous 8♠

Eddie Redmayne, actor – 1/6/1982
Kate McKinnon, comedian – 1/6/1984
Oscar De La Hoya, boxer – 2/4/1973
Rosa Parks, civil rights activist – 2/4/1913
Chris Martin, singer/songwriter – 3/2/1977
Rebel Wilson, actress – 3/2/1980

Chapter 12

Descriptions of the Nine Birth Cards

Welcome to the world of the transformative 9♥!

9♥ = Global giver of love

According to the Destiny Card system, souls chronologically experience God's lessons within each life incarnation. (Think of these as the universe's lessons if this more aligns with your beliefs.) The Birth Card each soul is born into determines the order and type of lessons a soul experiences. When you examine a Birth Card, you will notice it displays a suit of either a Heart, Club, Diamond, or Spade. This suit is significant because it represents the gifts a person born into this suit will possess and how they will direct their energies to learn lessons in their current life incarnation. A Heart Birth Card retains gifts and experiences life lessons around love and relationships. A Club Birth Card holds capabilities and experiences life lessons in their ability to communicate and absorb knowledge. A Diamond Birth Card possesses talents and experiences life lessons around money and values. And finally, a Spade Birth Card manifests gifts and experiences life lessons in work and health. Souls progress through incarnations and life lessons beginning as Hearts, moving on to Clubs, then Diamonds, and finally as Spades. Therefore, individuals born as Heart Cards are the youngest souls and individuals born as Spades Cards are the oldest souls.

In addition, the number on a Birth Card is equally meaningful as souls sequentially experience life lessons beginning as an Ace and culminating with lessons as a King. In the case of the number nine, nine represents endings as it is the end of the single digit numbers. **It makes sense, then, that a 9♥ child's purpose, gifts, and life lessons revolve around how they deal with the experience of *endings* in their life. And due to being a Heart, this child will learn lessons through experiences of endings in *love* and *relationships*.**

How to Nurture the Temperament and Personality of a 9♥ Child

Academics tends not to be the number one priority for a 9♥. In school, a young 9♥ is often more interested in building relationships than making straight A's. They may feel unappreciated by their teachers because they are criticized for socializing too much. These behaviors can be frustrating for a type-A parent with high academic expectations for their child. If you are a parent of a 9♥ child, please remember the primary way to nurture them is to accept them for who they are. This said, you claim your 9♥ is smart and if they are not achieving high marks, they are underachieving. On the contrary, they are accomplishing a great deal because they are advancing their *interpersonal skills* which is their superpower. From a young age, 9♥ subconsciously understand they must learn lessons around relationships. Once a foundation of interpersonal skills develops, a 9♥ can pursue and succeed in any profession that draws from these skills. Be patient with your 9♥. Model unconditional love. Refrain from putting a lot of academic pressure on them. Encourage them to engage in less academic activities that will foster creativity such as classes in choir, band, art, theater, or dance. If your 9♥ shows interest in the arts, encourage artistic activities because some can create art and then sell it quite successfully. These 9♥ may be better served by attending an arts magnet or charter school.

During the COVID-19 pandemic, there were countless examples of small and large acts of kindness across the world. Perhaps you heard about individuals helping to shop for their elderly neighbors. On the news, maybe you saw groups of individuals clapping and cheering for front line health care workers. Or you may have heard about customers leaving large tips for service workers in the restaurant industry. *Acts of kindness* like these are commonplace behavior for a 9♥ Birth Card. You see, they have huge hearts and are extremely sensitive to the needs of others. Many 9♥ are cherished by their friends because they show care by giving counsel or advice when others need it. This explains why many 9♥ are well suited to careers that include taking care of other people such as a counselor, therapist, nurse, teacher, in-home caregiver, or assisted living caregiver. 9♥ can also do well in positions where they manage others or are part of a human resources department for a business or other organization. And because they care about the needs of others, they can also do well in sales. Typically, Birth Cards of the Diamond suit possess traits that allow them to excel in sales. Interestingly, 9♥ have similar personality traits as a 7♦ Birth Card (You may want to read about the traits of a 7♦ Birth Card.). There is just one catch to a career choice in sales, though. A 9♥ must deeply believe in the product they sell – they must believe the product can help others.

Some 9♥ struggle academically because their emotional needs get in the way of their learning. Most often this happens because 9♥ experience disappointments and endings in love well before the typical age of having crushes or feeling the first physical stirrings of love. These experiences can manifest in different ways; from frequently moving away from loved ones, to having an absent parent (through divorce, substance abuse, or an unexpected death), to losing a close friend or sibling to illness. Such circumstances may be the root of why many 9♥ are highly emotional. Because of this trait, they may need a safe space to redirect their emotions. *Sensory bins* or *calming corners* are great tools to help a child calm down and self-regulate their emotions. Sensory bins are typically large containers filled with materials that stimulate the senses to distract or calm negative emotions. Bins can contain kinetic sand, various types of pasta, water with ice cubes and various sizes of funnels, or soil with plastic snakes and insects. Calming corners are areas in a classroom or home bedroom designated with calming furniture and objects, such as a bean bag chair, soft stuffed animals, a breathing ball, and headphones with soothing music. Also, keep in mind that 9♥ are sensitive to the emotions of others around them. Hence an adult would not be serving their needs well by sitting them next to another emotional or overly negative child. Instead, sit them next to a calm and easy-going child. Using tools and techniques like this in a classroom can be beneficial for a 9♥ because once a 9♥ feels emotionally centered, they are much more likely to increase efforts towards academics.

An adult can nurture a 9♥ by recognizing and appreciating them for their *big hearts*. For example, let's say you are an elementary teacher planning a unit on friendship. Invite your 9♥ to lead specific activities. For instance, assign them to role play ways to act like a good friend in front of the whole class. A 9♥ would make an excellent *friendship ambassador* for their grade level; someone who shows new students around. When developing classroom jobs, try putting your 9♥ in charge of the whole process. They are quite capable of organizing jobs and training others. Some love to plan. These 9♥ enjoy making to-do lists and derive a lot of satisfaction when they check items off their list. Make sure to purchase academic planners for these 9♥. If your 9♥ loves to read, have them read to a peer who struggles to read or is new to learning English. Older 9♥ make excellent *peer counselors*. Facilitated by an adult school counselor, peer counselors help in the process of mediating problems between peers.

In some situations, a 9♥ child may engage in an *emotional outburst* because of their big feelings. If emotional outbursts arise, respect and do not dismiss the feelings of a 9♥ even if they seem over reactionary. Avoid harsh criticism. An adult working with a 9♥ should watch for *triggers*. Triggers are behaviors that precede an emotional outburst. For example, a 9♥ might be triggered by a last-minute change of visitation plans with a separated parent. If you observe a trigger, direct this child to recognize and label their feelings. Help them express their feelings using social and emotional visual charts. Plenty of examples of these charts can be found on the Internet. Teach your 9♥ strategies to manage their disappointment. I also suggest reading to them the book, *Fantastic You*, by Danielle Dufayet. This book provides kids with practical ways to foster self-care when they deal with challenging emotions. The book also includes additional tips for parents and caregivers to help a child implement self-care. When an emotional outburst happens in school, it is common for the child to be separated from other students (such as being sent to the office, the hallway, or told to sit in another teacher's room). Exclusionary disciplinary tactics like this create learning gaps because the child involved is missing academic instruction. When a child repeatedly experiences this kind of discipline, they can develop self-doubt around their own capacity to learn. They may not see themselves as smart. When faced with learning something difficult, they may claim they can't learn it. Such tactics are wrong to use with a 9♥. Therefore, a 9♥ may respond better to *restorative disciplinary practices*. Restorative disciplinary practices adopt a relational approach to managing student misbehavior. For example, students are taught to use affective or "I feel" statements to appropriately communicate their feelings when they are impacted by someone else's behavior.

Be on the lookout for a 9♥'s feelings to be hurt. When things go wrong, they often blame themselves. They feel guilty. For example, imagine an eight-year-old 9♥ girl sneaks a bag of M&Ms into her pocket and decides to share them with friends during recess at school. She doles out twice as many pieces to a popular girl named Ella because she really wants to be Ella's friend. The next day, Ella asks for some candy, but the 9♥ did not bring any. Over the next few days, the 9♥ makes sure to bring candy to school for Ella. The following week, Ella brings her American doll to school for a show and tell activity. During some free time, Ella allows three other girls to play with her doll. When the 9♥ asks to play with the doll, Ella ignores her request. The 9♥ girl is devastated. She takes the rejection personally. She blames herself. What did she do wrong? Instead of letting go of her efforts to befriend Ella, the 9♥ doubles down. She finds out what Ella's favorite candy is and then spends her allowance buying that candy for Ella. The 9♥ continues giving even though her actions are not reciprocated. In this example, this 9♥ is demonstrating early signs of *co-dependency*, a common tendency in many 9♥. In a co-dependent relationship, there is a *taker* and a *giver*. Obviously, the 9♥ is the giver. While there are different types of co-dependent relationships, all involve imbalances in giving and taking. The giver gives so much to the taker that their own feelings or needs become ignored. In time, the giver becomes attached to the taker. The taker makes the giver feel needed and have a sense of purpose in life. This kind of dynamic can become unhealthy for a 9♥. They can lose themselves by pouring all their energies into another person. Then, if the other person ends the relationship, the 9♥ can feel lost and worthless.

Fred Rogers, well-known for the TV Show *Mister Rogers' Neighborhood*, had an intuitive understanding of children's emotional needs. Rogers stated, "How we deal with the big disappointments in life depends a great deal on how the people who loved us helped us deal with smaller disappointments when we were little." This statement is spot on true for a 9♥. If a 9♥ child is exhibiting early signs of co-dependent behaviors, adults involved with this child need to try to peel back the proverbial onion layers to understand the root of the issue. As an example, co-dependent children may be part of a home environment that lacks routines or rules, or the routines and rules are inconsistent or harsh. Or a child may be expected to act like an adult at a younger than normal age due to family trauma. Consequentially, their own emotions are ignored. Or when they do display their emotions, they are shamed or punished for doing so. Such happenings reinforce a belief in them that they must ignore their own feelings and needs and put the needs of others ahead of their own. Without intervention, a co-dependent 9♥ may fall into the co-dependency cycle in which co-dependent behaviors are passed along from generation to generation. Children who are showing signs of co-dependent behaviors require parents and teachers to be highly consistent at implementing routines, rules, and consequences. These children often need therapy and counseling.

Summary of Higher and Lower Personality Traits

Higher: Interpersonal skills, compassionate, charitable, creative, promoter in business.

Lower: Highly emotional, co-dependent, idealistic in love, victim mentality.

Childhood Influence Mercury Cards
It is common knowledge that a child's personality is most malleable during the formative years – from birth to eight years of age. In the Destiny Card system, the Mercury Cards in a Birth Card's Life Spread reveal influences a child with this Birth Card will experience between birth through age 12. As such, a child's Mercury Cards must be considered so an adult can nurture a child from a place of awareness and work with them from where a child is at in their development. A 9♥ child has the following Mercury Cards: **7♣, 8♠, and 8♦**. Alternatively, outside of any specific person associated with these three cards, the basic meanings of these cards describe experiences that may be impactful during this child's formative years. These cards suggest a 9♥ may experience feeling misunderstood by their family, which causes them to want to leave the family nest early. In turn, this feeling motivates them to earn money so they can actualize this move. They also experience having an inner willpower that allows them to persevere through hard work.

Potential Callings / Vocations by Zodiac Sign

August 30 – Virgo: 7♣ Planetary Ruling Card

Having a 7♣ Planetary Ruling Card makes these 9♥ prone to negativity. Self-expression in a career is crucial. They can do well as an actor or writer. Those who lean into the detail-oriented aspect of Virgo can do well as journalists, nurses, scientists, or engineers.

September 28 – Libra: 5♦ Planetary Ruling Card

The diplomatic aspect of Libra in these 9♥ steers many of these individuals into politics or government jobs. Gifted in public speaking, they can also do well as an actor, preacher, or political activist.

October 26 – Scorpio: Q♠ and K♣ Planetary Ruling Cards

Having both Queen and King Planetary Ruling Cards provides these 9♥ with lots of leadership qualities. They have the power to lead in their field as a doctor, businessperson, or politician

November 24 – Sagittarius: J♣ Planetary Ruling Card

The philosophical aspect of Sagittarius shines in these 9♥, making them well suited to a career as a writer, minister, coach, counselor, or artist.

December 22 – Sagittarius or Capricorn: J♣ or 9♦ Planetary Ruling Card

Having another Nine as a Planetary Ruling Card increases the likelihood of childhood trauma for these 9♥. Their charm when combined with the creative aspect of their J♣ Planetary Ruling Card can help them in business or a career in the arts.

Famous 9♥

Cameron Diaz, actress – 8/30/1972
Warren Buffett, investor – 8/30/1930
Hillary Clinton, politician – 10/26/1947
Steve Schmidt, political analyst – 9/28/1970
Katy Tur, journalist – 10/26/1983
Keith Urban, musician – 10/26/1967

Welcome to the world of the transformative 9♣!

9♣ = Global giver of knowledge

According to the Destiny Card system, souls chronologically experience God's lessons within each life incarnation. (Think of these as the universe's lessons if this more aligns with your beliefs.) The Birth Card each soul is born into determines the order and type of lessons a soul experiences. When you examine a Birth Card, you will notice it displays a suit of either a Heart, Club, Diamond, or Spade. This suit is significant because it represents the gifts a person born into this suit will possess and how they will direct their energies to learn lessons in their current life incarnation. A Heart Birth Card retains gifts and experiences life lessons around love and relationships. A Club Birth Card holds capabilities and experiences life lessons in their ability to communicate and absorb knowledge. A Diamond Birth Card possesses talents and experiences life lessons around money and values. And finally, a Spade Birth Card manifests gifts and experiences life lessons in work and health. Souls progress through incarnations and life lessons beginning as Hearts, moving on to Clubs, then Diamonds, and finally as Spades. Therefore, individuals born as Heart Cards are the youngest souls and individuals born as Spades Cards are the oldest souls.

In addition, the number on a Birth Card is equally meaningful as souls sequentially experience life lessons beginning as an Ace and culminating with lessons as a King. In the case of the number nine, nine represents endings as it is the end of the single digit numbers. **It makes sense, then, that a 9♣ child's purpose, gifts, and life lessons revolve around how they deal with the experience of *endings* in their life. And due to being a Club, this child will learn lessons by experiencing endings in *mental ideas* or related to *how they communicate*.**

How to Nurture the Temperament and Personality of a 9♣ Child

Throughout their lifetime, 9♣ tend to mentally consume more information than the average person. From a young age, these individuals know deep down that they have mental gifts. Yet, they grapple with barriers that slow or impede their ability to develop these gifts. During childhood, a 9♣ often experiences challenges outside of their control that have a negative impact on their beliefs or plans. Such experiences come in many different forms. They may be confronted with a death of someone close to them. They may deal with the repercussions of parents who divorce. Perhaps, they are confronted with limitations to their plans due to their own illness. They may be born into a family that does not support their ambitions, or there are no financial resources available to them to follow their dreams. The true test for all 9♣ is how they deal with the mental endings and disappointments that are sure to come in life.

9♣ are one of the most intelligent cards of all. They have exceptionally great short and long-term memory. They think fast. Some even talk fast. They love to talk with others, especially those who are intellectually stimulating. They are also fun to be around due to their quick *wit*. They hunger for knowledge. Growing up do you recall the slogan *a mind is a terrible thing to waste*? Perhaps you heard it on television. This slogan is especially true for a 9♣. You see, many 9♣ have superior *critical thinking* skills. Critical thinking refers to one's ability to understand logical connections between ideas. 9♣ enjoy connecting and weaving diverse ideas together in wondrous ways. This is the eleven-year-old child who investigates how well water-soaked fruit roll-ups can stick to a bedroom ceiling! This explains why many 9♣ are brilliant at constructing claims and making arguments and can do well as a writer, scientist, or attorney.

9♣ also excel in *systems thinking*. Think of a system as a set of interconnected elements and procedures that function together. A systems thinker is skilled at understanding the detailed relationships among these parts. This skill set allows a person to diagnose and solve problems when something goes wrong within a complex system. Once they understand or diagnose the problem within any system or process, they also enjoy trying to find ways to improve it. Because of these combined traits, many 9♣ enjoy studying science, technology, engineering, and mathematics (STEM). They make excellent detectives, doctors, engineers, inventors, mechanics, and technicians. If you are a parent of a 9♣, provide them with enrichment activities such as after school programs in STEM, robotics, coding, or sports. Make sure they have plenty of books to read. Take them to the library. 9♣ have a flair for invention. Engage them with Legos, magnetic building tiles, STEM activity kits, and craft kits. Encourage them to take honors and advanced placement (AP) classes in high school.

An early and strong foundation in education is essential for a 9♣. However, this is easier said than done. Recall that all 9♣ have excellent short and long-term memory. For them, this trait can be a double-edged sword. This skill helps them ace a test, but it also makes them remember painful details of their past. And many 9♣ tend to experience the majority of their challenging or frustrating events during childhood. Therefore, young 9♣ are highly *sensitive* souls. They can become so overwhelmed with current or past problems that they develop *negativity*. For example, imagine a three-year-old 9♣ boy named Doug was born into a military family. The emotional life of this 9♣ has been hard because his dad has been absent much of his short life due to deployment. Recently, Doug has grown close to the family dog, a golden retriever named Cooper. One day while the dad is home on leave, Cooper is diagnosed with cancer and the family makes the difficult decision to put the dog down. Doug is devastated by the news and gives in to fits of crying. Days later Doug is still experiencing bursts of crying. The dad is frustrated by his son's behavior and tells him to "man up" and "crying is for babies." Because Doug desperately wants his dad's approval, he stuffs his emotions inside. Years later Doug's parents decide to divorce. Does Doug respond to this news by crying? Nope. This 9♣ once again internalizes his emotions. Now a new emotion emerges – negativity. When future disappointments surface, this 9♣ is consumed with negativity and blames others. Reinforced over time, these 9♣ cultivate a negative mindset. They feel trapped in situations they believe are outside of their control. At an extreme, they adopt a mindset termed *future tripping*, where they make negative inferences about future outcomes based upon negative experiences from their past. Sadly, such a mindset can generate a negative pattern and a self-fulfilling prophecy.

From the age of three to five, it is developmentally appropriate for children to start to understand their emotions and how to regulate them. When a 9♣ is not taught to express their feelings or is shamed for expressing them, they learn to repress their emotions. And chronic *emotional repression* in turn can manifest health problems. Research has shown a correlation between emotional repression and a decreased functioning of the immune system. An emotionally repressed 9♣ can literally make themselves sick. Therefore, young 9♣ are best nurtured when they are taught strategies to help them identify and regulate their emotions. Specifically, they should be shown how to check in with their bodies for signs of negative emotions. If such signs are found, they need to implement coping strategies. A wonderful book that teaches children how to regulate negative emotions is *How to Get Unstuck from the Negative Muck: A Kid's Guide to Getting Rid of Negative Thinking* by Dr. Lake Sullivan. You can also search the Internet for socio-emotional strategies for children dealing with negativity.

When life gets them down, it is common for an older 9♣ to turn to music. They respond well to listening to or playing music so allow them the time and space to do this. A 9♣ who finds solace in a musical hobby may display some promising related talent.

If your 9♣ shows interest, sign them up to participate in arts, crafts, or theater activities where emotional expression can be supported. Does your 9♣ prefer sports? Negative emotions can be effectively redirected into sports, particularly those that involve physical contact such as football, ice hockey, lacrosse, etc. Without appropriate strategies in hand, a 9♣ adolescent may rebel and engage in self-indulgent behaviors. Because they are more sensual than most cards, some become *sexually promiscuous*. In a situation like this, encourage a 9♣ to participate in physical sports to help redirect their physical energy. School may no longer be a priority and these 9♣ may academically underachieve. If you are a teacher of a struggling 9♣, suggest that they seek out mentors and other individuals for various support needs. Bring in counselors or coaches. As an example, suggest mentoring programs such as the Boys and Girls Club of America or 4H Club. Without emotional support, a 9♣ may also develop anger management issues and become difficult to parent. If you are a parent of an adolescent 9♣ and you are noticing these behaviors, you may need to seek out therapy-based resources. Know that this 9♣ likely holds anger towards themselves. They are smart and know they have made bad choices. They do not need to be told this. In fact, they may need to learn to forgive themselves as part of their healing process. If they are allowed to wallow in their negativity, they can dilute their own power. Not only is this sad for the individual, but it is also sad for humanity. 9♣ possess mental gifts that have potential to change the world for the better.

It is well known that Agatha Christie is one of the most prolific writers of all time. Most people have read her books or watched movies based upon her books, such as the detective stories of Miss Marple and Hercule Poirot. From accounts of her own childhood, Christie experienced mental limitations and disappointments. Her father died when she was eleven, which created financial hardship on the family. While her two older sisters were allowed to attend school, Christie was homeschooled. Her mother refused to teach her to read and so Christie ended up teaching herself. With much older sisters and no children of similar age in her neighborhood to play with, Christie was bored most of her childhood. Christie claimed she made up stories and imaginary friends to cope with her situation. Did Christie go on to write stories about romance and love? No. Did she write stories about inspiring historical figures? No. The bulk of Christie's work was writing about endings. She wrote about the most horrific of all endings – murder. In her stories, Christie unraveled the depth of emotions, motivations, and sophisticated ways in which humans can respond to negative life events. After all, people do not murder when they are happy or satisfied with life. Through her writing about murders, Christie creatively shared the concept of endings with the broader community. In doing so, Christie was modeling a 9♣'s purpose in life – global sharing of knowledge. And, yes, Christie was a 9♣.

A higher expressing 9♣ has learned to process, accept, and let go of ideas or plans that are no longer serving them well. They welcome the idea that their beliefs and plans may need to change for the betterment of all. They learn to make compromises. Some learn to let go of their ego. When they let go of a belief or situation, they trust their gift of ingenuity and reinvent themselves. They gain spiritual truths when they adopt and implement new philosophies toward life. When a 9♣ learns to let go and mentally accept endings, they progress toward spiritual growth. Spiritual growth for a 9♣ also entails them realizing that true happiness does not come when they accumulate knowledge for personal gain. On the contrary, 9♣ are here to gain knowledge for the purpose of sharing it with humanity. Many 9♣ achieve spiritual growth mid-life and spend their remaining years sharing their truths with others.

Summary of Higher and Lower Personality Traits

Higher: Ingenuity, critical thinker, sensuous, scientific mind, witty, excellent memory.

Lower: Selfish, mentally selfish, emotional repression, heightened negativity, dishonesty.

Childhood Influence Mercury Cards

It is common knowledge that a child's personality is most malleable during the formative years – from birth to eight years of age. In the Destiny Card system, the Mercury Cards in a Birth Card's Life Spread reveal influences a child with this Birth Card will experience between birth through age 12. As such, a child's Mercury Cards must be considered so an adult can nurture a child from a place of awareness and work with them from where a child is at in their development. A 9♣ child has the following Mercury Cards: **9♠, 5♣, and K♥**. The K♥ may mean there is an influential father who is likely a Heart Birth or Planetary Ruling Card. Alternatively, outside of any specific person associated with these three cards, the basic meanings of these cards describe experiences that may be impactful during this child's formative years. These cards suggest a 9♣ may experience frustrations, discontent, and/or health issues during these years. Such experiences often produce big feelings for them, and they are forced to learn various ways to manage them.

Potential Callings / Vocations by Zodiac Sign

January 31 – Aquarius: 4♣ Planetary Ruling Card
Progressive and intellectual Aquarius in these 9♣ encourages them to pursue unconventional jobs. They are well suited to computer science work, acting, writing (journalism), and scientific research.

February 29 – Pisces: 2♦ Planetary Ruling Card
Idealism can be strong in these 9♣, making them rebel against conventional education. They may do better by developing talents and careers in arts, theater, music, or sports.

March 27 – Aries: K♥ Planetary Ruling Card
With the charming K♥ Planetary Ruling Card combined with the sexy 9♣, these children are inclined to put themselves first and pave their own way toward success. They can do well as a lawyer, politician, actor, or other type of entertainer.

April 25 – Taurus: 2♥ Planetary Ruling Card

Due to the 2♥ Planetary Ruling Card, these 9♣ may waste some of their time pursuing personal interests versus academics. They can do well in artistic work: acting, painting, singing, and composing. Some have a creative flair for design.

May 23 – Gemini: 9♠ Planetary Ruling Card

Having a 9♠ Planetary Ruling Card means these individuals have double the energy associated with a Nine. This may cause heightened negativity. Developing artistic and physical gifts are beneficial for them and can lead to careers in these fields (e.g., acting, singing, construction work, mechanic, electrician, or sports playing).

June 21 – Gemini: 9♠ Planetary Ruling Card

With the energy of Gemini, these 9♣ prefer jobs that include travel (e.g., journalism, travel writer, tour guide) or put them in the limelight (e.g., film director, actor, or other type of entertainer).

July 19 – Cancer: J♥ Planetary Ruling Card

Having a J♥ Planetary Ruling Card can cause these 9♣ to behave on one side of an opposite spectrum of immaturely indulging in laziness or creatively expressing themselves in work. Work may be associated with sales, writing, medicine, or politics.

August 17 – Leo: 9♣ Planetary Ruling Card

The aspect of Leo in these 9♣ makes them love to be in the spotlight. Many excel in theater, and amaze others with how well they can memorize their lines. They can also find much success as a writer, publisher, politician, lawyer, or business leader.

September 15 – Virgo: 9♠ Planetary Ruling Card

With a 9♠ Planetary Ruling Card, these 9♣ often have more than a fair share of burdens while young. By tapping into their inner strength, they can do well as a technician, scientist, architect, writer, appraiser, or critic.

October 13 – Libra: 2♥ Planetary Ruling Card

Due to their 2♥ Planetary Ruling Card, these 9♣ do better in partnership work or for the betterment of others – be it through business, scientific research, or politics. Some can do well in acting, writing, or as a musician.

November 11 – Scorpio: K♥ and J♠ Planetary Ruling Card

Having both a King and Jack Planetary Ruling Card packs a lot of power into these 9♣. They can make excellent diagnosticians and inventors, so they can do well in medicine, science, or engineering. Some can weave amazing stories as a writer.

December 9 – Sagittarius: K♦ Planetary Ruling Card

With a K♦ Planetary Ruling Card, these 9♣ can do well in any type of financial enterprise, especially if it involves traveling or provides freedom of action. They can also excel in writing, scientific research, acting, and preaching.

Famous 9♣

Benedict Cumberbatch, actor – 7/19/1976
Jon Batiste, singer – 11/11/1986
Alexandria Ocasio-Cortez, politician – 10/13/1989
Leonardo DiCaprio, actor – 11/11/1974
Stacey Abrams, politician – 12/9/1973
Prince Harry, Duke of Sussex in the British royal family – 9/15/1984

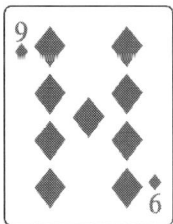

Welcome to the world of the transformative 9♦!

9♦ = Global giver of values and money

According to the Destiny Card system, souls chronologically experience God's lessons within each life incarnation. (Think of these as the universe's lessons if this more aligns with your beliefs.) The Birth Card each soul is born into determines the order and type of lessons a soul experiences. When you examine a Birth Card, you will notice it displays a suit of either a Heart, Club, Diamond, or Spade. This suit is significant because it represents the gifts a person born into this suit will possess and how they will direct their energies to learn lessons in their current life incarnation. A Heart Birth Card retains gifts and experiences life lessons around love and relationships. A Club Birth Card holds capabilities and experiences life lessons in their ability to communicate and absorb knowledge. A Diamond Birth Card possesses talents and experiences life lessons around money and values. And finally, a Spade Birth Card manifests gifts and experiences life lessons in work and health. Souls progress through incarnations and life lessons beginning as Hearts, moving on to Clubs, then Diamonds, and finally as Spades. Therefore, individuals born as Heart Cards are the youngest souls and individuals born as Spades Cards are the oldest souls.

In addition, the number on a Birth Card is equally meaningful as souls sequentially experience life lessons beginning as an Ace and culminating with lessons as a King. In the case of the number nine, nine represents endings as it is the end of the single digit numbers. **It makes sense, then, that a 9♦ child's purpose, gifts, and life lessons revolve around how they deal with the experience of *endings* in their life. And due to being a Diamond, this child will learn lessons by experiencing endings around *money* and what they *value*.**

How to Nurture the Temperament and Personality of a 9♦ Child

9♦ experience endings throughout their life to achieve spiritual transformation. In elementary school, do you remember learning about the four seasons – spring, summer, autumn, and winter? You learned that the seasons occurred in a particular sequence with similar patterns each year. Perhaps, you drew pictures of each season. Your drawings probably showed how a change in sunlight and weather affected plant life. In the spring, plants emerge from the ground, leaves bud from the trees, and flowers bloom. By the summer, growth is accelerated, and plants grow to their fullest potential. When autumn sets in, leaves begin to change color and fall from trees, and flowers begin to die. By winter, many trees have lost all their leaves and plants have gone dormant. Does the death and endings part of a plant's life cycle sound scary to you? Of course not. Life experience has shown you endings are a necessary part of transformation in nature. Endings clear the way for new beginnings. In a similar manner, 9♦ spiritually transform throughout their life span by repeatedly experiencing a series of cycles, of endings and new beginnings. The spiritual teacher and writer, Eckhart Tolle, explained this cycle well when he wrote, "There are cycles of success, when things come to you and thrive, and cycles of failure, when they wither or disintegrate and you have to let them go in order to make room for new things to arise, or for transformation to happen." Tolle understood this process well because he is a 9♦.

A 9♦ will manifest endings and be tested to let go beginning at an early age. There are numerous ways these tests may manifest. They might experience illness or be limited through a physical accident. Perhaps, a domineering or emotionally abusive adult might cause a young 9♦ to struggle with self-worth. Or they might develop abandonment issues due to an absent parent. Therefore, young 9♦ are often *highly sensitive* and feel the need to earn self-worth by giving to others. Being programmed to give, they are generous and difficult to spoil. If you are a parent of a 9♦, you probably do not need to worry they will become entitled. Instead, be on the lookout for your 9♦ to take the act of giving too far. They may need to develop boundaries around giving. Point out and model examples of healthy relationships that involve mutual giving and taking. Teach them how to recognize unhealthy relationships when someone is taking advantage of their giving. If needed, teach assertiveness when they need to say "no" to others. Then, use role play to help them practice saying no. Left unchecked, a giving 9♦ can appear as a pushover, and they can attract others who will use them. Over time, a 9♦ may obsess over their losses and feel victimized. They may associate giving with losing, adopt a negative attitude toward giving, and stop doing it out of fear. Most significantly, a 9♦ may struggle with *low self-worth.*

Low self-worth can be problematic for a 9♦ in two ways. First, an older 9♦ may try to compensate for low self-worth by spending money. These individuals develop *poor money management* skills. Another issue that can manifest for a 9♦ is that they may wrestle with cognitive dissonance. If a young 9♦ is not taught how to manage this issue, they can develop a defeatist attitude that lasts a lifetime. Let's consider an example. A seventeen-year-old male 9♦ has saved money working a part time job to buy a used car. He decides to buy a particular brand and model of car because he is convinced it will be a so-called chick magnet. Arriving to high school for the first time in his new car, he immediately shows the car to a female friend. He values her opinion. The friend makes a negative comment about the car's appeal to her. The

9♦ experiences cognitive dissonance in that the female friend's comment contradicts his own perception of the car. Now, the car is a disappointment. This new perception conflicts with his older perception. The 9♦ feels buyer's remorse and dissatisfaction with the car. What is remarkable about this example, is that this kind of experience for a 9♦ can impact their attitude toward future car or other large item purchases for the rest of their life! Some will automatically assume their next car purchase will be a disappointment. This, in turn, may cause them to feel immobilized in the decision-making process and struggle to even make an intended purchase due to fear from their previous experience.

To prevent difficulties with cognitive dissonance, young 9♦ must be taught to manage their attitude when they give too much, deal with loss, or experience disappointment. One strategy an adult can use to manage a 9♦'s attitude is to help them reflect upon and find solutions to a disappointing situation. Let's consider an example. Ari is an eight-year-old 9♦ who enjoys having an afterschool snack. He prefers peanut-butter pretzels because he can eat them while doing homework. Arriving home one day, Ari discovers his older brother has eaten the entire container of peanut butter pretzels. Ari is disappointed. He is angry. He immediately directs inappropriate language toward his brother. And knowing his brother covets his cell phone, Ari grabs it yelling, "How does it feel when I take something of yours?" Pushing and shoving ensues, and this is where you as a parent come into the situation. Asking a few questions, you get to the bottom of the situation. Knowing both boys are upset, you ask them each to choose an activity that will calm them down and then you will discuss the matter. Ari goes to his room and plays a video game. Thirty minutes later you have a reflective conversation with Ari. (I suggest using the Gibb's Reflective Cycle described in Chapter 3.) In your conversation with Ari, it is important to empathize with his situation. Explain that while it is okay for him to voice his negativity, it is not okay for him to retaliate against his brother by taking his cell phone. Afterall, how did that go for him? He didn't get peanut butter pretzels. Instead, he got into trouble. Then prompt Ari to identify a better way he could have dealt with his situation. Perhaps he could have checked the pantry and settled on finding a different snack.

If 9♦ choose a negative attitude when they are disappointed, they will attract more negativity into their life. When life presents a 9♦ with losses or endings of something valued, they must look for a silver lining. Let's look at an extreme example of this by considering the life of the Mexican painter, Frida Kahlo. At age six, Kahlo contracted polio. The disease left her crippled in the right leg. Unable to be as active as other children, Kahlo developed an interest in art. Then, in her late teens, Kahlo was hit by a bus. She broke her spine, collarbone, pelvis, and had numerous fractures in her already disabled right leg. Kahlo had to face the loss of some mobility and endure physical pain for the remainder of her short life. And, obviously, her medical problems caused a loss of money. While recovering from the accident, she rediscovered her love of art and made the decision to take up painting as a career. Kahlo became well known for her self-portraits that captured the raw feelings of both her physical and emotional pain. By redirecting and expressing her pain through painting, Kahlo found some relief. She also acquired success and praise, including international fame. Moreover, Kahlo gave to humanity. She spread awareness of the feelings people experience when they struggle with mental and physical health. In doing so, Kahlo was modeling what spiritual transformation looks like for a 9♦. And, yes, Kahlo was a 9♦. Hearing Kahlo's story you might be alarmed in thinking a 9♦ is destined for such a difficult life. Keep in mind most 9♦ do not suffer as much as Kahlo. Most 9♦ experience a loss or endings on a smaller scale. But at any degree of endings, a higher expressing 9♦ will persevere through their disappointments and spiritually transform to the extent that they tend to manifest success and happiness. Some even achieve great wealth and go on to use their assets to help others in profound ways.

Have you ever heard of someone being described as a *networker*? A networker is a person skilled at using informal social events to cultivate business contacts. Attending a social event, they will literally work the room; easily striking up conversations with just about everybody. They make an impression on others with their indisputable intellect and humorous banter. If you were to ask these individuals about their birthday, do not be surprised to find that many of them are 9♦. A 9♦'s superpower is that they are gifted networkers. They will not only seek out many friends, but also an eclectic range of them. If they are engaging in an intellectually stimulating conversation, a 9♦ tends to feel energized. Therefore, a good way to nurture a 9♦ is to engage them in a lot of social and mental stimulation. After school enrichment or sports activities can be of great value. Do not fret if a 9♦ wants to experience many different activities rather than sticking with one thing. Let their interests guide the way. Besides, participating in different activities will expose a 9♦ to a variety of people with different points of view. This will enhance their ability to network as they grow older. It will also help them learn that different people have different needs. When a 9♦ learns what others really need, they can hone their networking efforts. Some 9♦ who advance their capacity to understand the needs of others can do well in a career of public service and/or speaking.

When listening to a 9♦, you may notice they possess exceptional *vocal cadence*. Vocal cadence is the flow or rhythm in which a person speaks. A person skilled in vocal cadence intuitively knows the right words and pitch to use when speaking to a specific audience. Do you remember an important figure from the 1980's in gangsta rap named Ice-T? His debut album was *Rhyme Pays*. Literally, the gift of rhyme does pay well as Ice-T has made millions of dollars through his career. And by the way, Ice-T is a 9♦. There are many other 9♦ who are famous in rap or hip-hop music because of this gift, such as MadeinTYO, A-Plus, Kanye West, and 50 Cent. Additionally, a 9♦ can thrive when they combine their *gift of gab* with a sales-related job that requires strong communication skills. They value input from others and find pleasure in bringing people together to achieve common goals. For these reasons, 9♦ can excel in a career as a salesperson or a leader in business. But let us not forget that Diamond Birth Cards possess gifts around both money and *values*. Some 9♦ have an uncanny ability to accurately sum up the value of a product or idea. As such, 9♦ are skilled at *assessment* or the assigning of value to things or people. This explains why 9♦ make excellent appraisers, real estate brokers, life insurance agents, marketing analysts, and quality control inspectors. Then there are some 9♦ who want to spread higher values through their work. These individuals make effective community organizers, recruiters, headhunters, counselors, lawyers, poets, or activists. In fact, some higher expressing 9♦ have a heightened awareness of social justice issues and desire to work toward solutions for the common good.

Summary of Higher and Lower Personality Traits

Higher: Great communicator, smart, philanthropic, networker, compassionate, salesperson.

Lower: Poor money management, low self-worth, fault-finding, financially dissatisfied.

Childhood Influence Mercury Cards

It is common knowledge that a child's personality is most malleable during the formative years – from birth to eight years of age. In the Destiny Card system, the Mercury Cards in a Birth Card's Life Spread reveal influences a child with this Birth Card will experience between birth through age 12. As such, a child's Mercury Cards must be considered so an adult can nurture a child from a place of awareness and work with them from where a child is at in their development. A 9♦ child has the following Mercury Cards: **7♣, 3♣, and K♦**. The K♦ may mean there is an influential father who is likely a Diamond Birth or Planetary Ruling Card. Alternatively, outside of any specific person associated with these three cards, the basic meanings of these cards describe experiences that may be impactful during this child's formative years. These cards suggest 9♦ may experience a struggle with an illness connected to themselves or another family member. This struggle often forces them to learn how to master their values. They may be born into a highly creative family or demonstrate artistic gifts of their own.

Potential Callings / Vocations by Zodiac Sign

January 18 – Capricorn: 4♥ Planetary Ruling Card

The ambitious aspect of Capricorn helps these 9♦ persist through life's difficulties. Such perseverance can launch them successfully into a career as an actor, athlete, writer, or business leader.

February 16 – Aquarius: 4♦ Planetary Ruling Card

The non-conformist trait of Aquarius is prevalent in these 9♦. Funneling this energy in a positive direction can help them succeed as a business owner, politician, rapper, news correspondent, or entertainer.

March 14 – Pisces: 2♠ Planetary Ruling Card

As a Pisces, these 9♦ are deeply intuitive and scientifically minded. They can succeed in numerous careers if they do not get bogged down in exploring too many interests. They can excel as an artist, musician, actor, comedian, athlete, explorer, or business manager.

April 12 – Aries: K♣ Planetary Ruling Card

With a K♣ Planetary Ruling Card, these 9♦ often love to talk, write, and be in positions of leadership. They can succeed as a writer, singer, politician, military leader, public speaker, or salesperson.

May 10 – Taurus: 2♣ Planetary Ruling Card

With a 2♣ Planetary Ruling Card, these 9♦ are well suited to careers that allow them to work with a partner or talk with others. They can direct others well and sell numerous home-related products. Potential careers include politician, actor, food critic, and business owner.

June 8 – Gemini: 7♠ Planetary Ruling Card

The 7♠ Planetary Ruling Card can manifest accidents and health issues in these 9♦, so managing a positive attitude is crucial for them to reach their potential. They possess inventive energy so they can excel as an engineer, writer, composer, TV producer, artist, or architect.

July 6 – Cancer: J♣ Planetary Ruling Card

As Cancers, these 9♦ are highly sensitive and imaginative. They may need to overcome early obstacles, which has the potential to transform them into spiritual leaders. They can do well as an artist, politician, clothing designer, or home designer.

August 4 – Leo: 9♦ Planetary Ruling Card

As Leos, while these 9♦ prefer to be in the limelight, they like to lead in humanitarian causes. They can make an excellent entertainer (e.g., poet, rapper, comedian, or singer), politician, director, or business leader.

September 2 – Virgo: 7♠ Planetary Ruling Card

With a 7♠ Planetary Ruling Card, these 9♦ intuitively know they will experience obstacles in life. They are often big dreamers but can succumb to fears and worry. Redirecting fear into physical activity can help them while also establishing talents that can be turned into a career (e.g., athlete). They can also do well in a career in which they apply their intuition (e.g., writer, or researcher).

Famous 9♦

Barack Obama, president of the U.S. – 8/4/1961
Simone Biles, gymnast – 3/14/1997
The Weeknd, singer – 2/16/1990
Stephan Curry, basketball player – 3/14/1988
Dalai Lama, spiritual leader of Tibet – 7/6/1935
Eckhart Tolle, spiritual writer – 2/16/1948

Welcome to the world of the transformative 9♠!

9♠ = Global giver of spiritual truths

According to the Destiny Card system, souls chronologically experience God's lessons within each life incarnation. (Think of these as the universe's lessons if this more aligns with your beliefs.) The Birth Card each soul is born into determines the order and type of lessons a soul experiences. When you examine a Birth Card, you will notice it displays a suit of either a Heart, Club, Diamond, or Spade. This suit is significant because it represents the gifts a person born into this suit will possess and how they will direct their energies to learn lessons in their current life incarnation. A Heart Birth Card retains gifts and experiences life lessons around love and relationships. A Club Birth Card holds capabilities and experiences life lessons in their ability to communicate and absorb knowledge. A Diamond Birth Card possesses talents and experiences life lessons around money and values. And finally, a Spade Birth Card manifests gifts and experiences life lessons in work and health. Souls progress through incarnations and life lessons beginning as Hearts, moving on to Clubs, then Diamonds, and finally as Spades. Therefore, individuals born as Heart Cards are the youngest souls and individuals born as Spades Cards are the oldest souls.

In addition, the number on a Birth Card is equally meaningful as souls sequentially experience life lessons beginning as an Ace and culminating with lessons as a King. In the case of the number nine, nine represents endings as it is the end of the single digit numbers. **It makes sense, then, that a 9♠ child's purpose, gifts, and life lessons revolve around how they deal with the experience of *endings* in their life. And due to being a Spade, this child will learn lessons by experiencing endings related to *work* and *health*.**

How to Nurture the Temperament and Personality of a 9♠ Child

9♠ tend to experience more difficult endings than other Nine Birth Cards. In the Destiny Card system, the 9♠ is also known as the *death* card. For a person associated with a 9♠ Birth Card, death most often means the ending of a lifestyle which typically manifests through a change in health and/or work. Sadly, 9♠ begin to experience endings during their childhood. Perhaps they are born into a family situation where they must act like a responsible parent because a parent is unhealthy or has died. Perhaps they have a physical ailment that keeps them from engaging in cherished activities. In some extreme cases, a 9♠ may experience an ending to their innocence through emotional, physical, or sexual abuse. After any such event, a 9♠ may struggle with a feeling of heaviness in their heart. The purpose behind these endings is to force a 9♠ to *reinvent* themselves and learn about spiritual transformation. A higher expressing 9♠ does not resist endings and they throw their energy and creative minds into making new beginnings. Some must deconstruct their lifestyle or beliefs in the process. Then they rebuild themselves from scratch. What it takes to become a higher expressing 9♠ is like what happens to a seed. As author Cynthia Occelli stated, "For a seed to achieve its greatest expression, it must come to completely undone. The shell cracks, its insides come out and everything changes. To someone who doesn't understand growth, it would look like complete destruction." This process of transformation is often the path for a 9♠. While reconstructing themselves, they can discover new ways of doing things or they may develop products or processes that are progressive for their time. As a rule, 9♠ are a bit unconventional. Higher expressing 9♠ are often leaders in their field due to their wisdom, quirky personality, and *forward-looking ideas*.

Despite the nature of their experience of an ending, a young 9♠ must learn the *art of surrender*. Have you ever heard of big-wave surfing in Nazare, Portugal? In 2017, Rodrigo Koxa made history and a spot in the Guinness World Records when he surfed an 80-foot wave in Nazare. An 80-foot wave is the height of an eight-story building! No doubt any surfer who rides such monstrous waves must possess nerves of steel. They also have a lot of practice riding *with* versus against the waves. This is to say, these surfers have perfected *duck diving*. As surfers paddle out to their lineup, they initially come against powerful waves. Duck diving is a technique in which a surfer observes an oncoming wave and dives under it so not to be pushed backwards by the wave thus allowing the surfer to continue further out into the water. As such, the surfer finds the path of least resistance. The worst thing a surfer can do is face the wave directly and try to resist its force. Duck diving is like what a 9♠ should be taught to do when they face powerful and challenging life events that can take them down like a monstrous wave.

Most importantly, when life events bring endings, a 9♠ should not stand defiant. In such times they should accept the ending and direct their focus and energy toward a new beginning. Let's consider a real-life example. While working in Texas, I taught a student who I will call Dion. Dion was an extremely talented football player who dreamed of a career in the National Football League (NFL). Even though Dion was not as big as other players, he was scrappy. He was fearless. Dion and I established a good relationship after I started to attend his games. And for many years after, I followed his accomplishments. Dion was honored as an All-American player in high school and then went on to play college football at a Big 12 conference school. And even though only less than 1% of high school football players make it to the NFL, Dion achieved his dream. His first year playing in the NFL was challenging as he struggled through various injuries. In his second year, Dion suffered a life-changing injury that forced him to leave the NFL. Several years after that, I heard that Dion went back to school and reinvented himself. His own experience with physical injury motivated him to earn a degree in physical therapy. He went on to work again for the NFL, but in the role as a physical therapist helping other players manage physical difficulties.

Accepting an ending and embracing a new beginning is easier said than done. A young 9♠ may feel defeated by certain life events and fail to see a better future. 9♠ who choose a defeatist viewpoint as a response to their challenges may fall into a state of *learned helplessness*. Learned helplessness is when a person quits trying to change their circumstances even though they can because they have repeatedly faced negative situations outside of their control. As an example, perhaps a 9♠ child experiences trauma or neglect that is prolonged and outside of their control. Or they repeatedly fail at something no matter their effort or approach taken. They feel powerless. They may start to think there is no reason why they should try anymore when the outcome never changes. In other words, they learn to be helpless. In a school setting, this behavior manifests as a child who refuses to try. When an adult pushes them to try, these children can get defiant. Psychologists assert that when a child adopts learned helplessness, this in turn can lead to them developing anxiety and depression. Therapy may be needed for such a child. Children who develop learned helplessness must learn to build resilience. *Cognitive behavioral therapy* has been shown to help children and young adults break the cycle of learned helplessness and anxiety. Cognitive behavioral therapy involves teaching strategies to a person to change their negative thinking patterns.

If a 9♠ child is experiencing a mild form of generalized anxiety, there are numerous strategies an adult can implement to help them. To start, position them to be around or spend more time with others who are supportive and friendly, whether that be grandparents, school support staff, or calm peers. When they are feeling anxious, try to keep them away from people or situations that are not harmonious. Encourage them to limit time with overly dramatic friends. Try introducing them to a technique called *tapping* or psychological acupuncture. Tapping involves a person using their own fingers to tap on certain parts of their body to disrupt negative emotions and restore a proper flow of energy. There are several good videos on the Internet that demonstrate this technique and explain how to use it with children. I also recommend reading the book *Tapping Your Way to a Great Big Smile: Emotional Freedom Technique (EFT) Tapping for Little Fingers* by Ana Cybela. This book offers step-by-step instructions to explain tapping as well as other strategies to help a child who is feeling anxious. In addition, encourage a 9♠ to release negative emotions in a productive way. Physical activities that cause them to sweat often work best. Above all, avoid punishment that takes away physical activity. These children must participate in recess and physical education. If not, they will express their feelings in more inappropriate ways. Many 9♠ possess *artistic* and *musical* superpowers. And these gifts offer healthy ways for a 9♠ to redirect their emotions. Urge them to draw, paint, or engage in some other artistic activity to express their feelings. Perhaps get them a drum set, art supplies, computer, or perhaps sign them up for a music or dance class, etc.

Another good way to nurture a 9♠ is to engage them in daily mindfulness activities. Mindfulness activities in a classroom involve taking a break from academics and slowing down to pay attention to something. These activities can include breathing exercises, muscle relaxation, and expressing positive affirmations. There are countless mindfulness activities you can find on the Internet. Outside of school, a parent can implement similar activities. 9♠ often feel connected to nature and nature-related activities. Urge them to spend time in and be recharged by nature. This setting also provides a safe space for reflection. Often 9♠ need time for reflection to grapple with big ideas. These big ideas may be related to a 9♠'s tendency to be sensitive to situations involving *injustices* and *unfairness*. To an adult, this trait might seem annoying initially because a 9♠ might come across as insubordinate. If they perceive unfairness directed at them, they can become quite rebellious. They may push against authority and ask hard questions. Please see this behavior for what it is – a 9♠'s superpower. A 9♠ is an old soul who possesses a lot of wisdom. If their accounting reveals injustices, they are probably right in their point of view. Accommodate them by listening to their beliefs. If they are making their point of view known by using inappropriate or negative approaches, help them recognize their approaches are not likely to support their intentions. Learning positive approaches to enact change can empower a 9♠ toward sharing their spiritual truths with others.

An adolescent 9♠ will benefit from having conversations that prepare them to manage challenging endings. If you are a teacher of a 9♠, expose them to books that provoke these kinds of conversations. As an example, encourage them to read the novel, *Holes*, by Louis Sachar. This book tells the story of a teen who is sentenced to a juvenile work-camp having been wrongly convicted of stealing. Even though the teen feels deeply wronged by life events, he perseveres and changes his circumstances for the better. If you are a parent of a 9♠, use current events to initiate conversations. For instance, after the school shooting at Stoneman Douglas high school in Parkland, Florida several survivors such as David Hoag and Emma Gonzalez took action to advocate for gun control. While discussing a topic like this, perhaps explain the concept of *synchronicity* in the universe. Synchronicity is the belief that two or more unrelated events are linked in some way. Synchronicity applied to this topic would involve examining the deeper meanings behind a challenging event. Then, introduce the strategy of *positive reframing*. Positive reframing involves exploring a possible benefit or positive side to a negative situation. For instance, while the school shooting was traumatic for Hoag and Gonzalez, it also motivated them to voice their perspective on gun control which in turn, lead to a national movement. By the way, you may find it interesting to know that both Hoag and Gonzalez are Nine Birth Cards. Conversations like this serve the purpose of planting a seed for a 9♠. At some time in their life a 9♠ may face a traumatic ending and it will help them to see possibilities around creating something good out of something bad.

Having navigated endings, older 9♠ are *compassionate* individuals. As such, friends may come to them with their personal problems. This is because they can relate to other people's problems in life since they have been through difficulties of their own. This explains why 9♠ make effective teachers and counselors. As the spiritual teacher and writer Gary Zukav pointed out, "Only by feeling compassion for yourself can you feel compassion for others." A 9♠'s compassion is often accompanied by sympathy or an ability to share emotions with others. When a 9♠ communicates their emotions and experiences in life through art, singing, or songwriting, they come across as particularly authentic. People are drawn to them. As such, their talents can be monetized. Although 9♠ are exposed to challenges throughout their life, they can find happiness, especially if they accept change and commit to higher truths.

Summary of Higher and Lower Personality Traits

Higher: Old soul, compassionate, counselor, artistic, unconventional thinker, independent.

Lower: Anxious, tyrannical, defiant, erratic, hopelessness, narrow-mindedness, rigid will.

Childhood Influence Mercury Cards

It is common knowledge that a child's personality is most malleable during the formative years – from birth to eight years of age. In the Destiny Card system, the Mercury Cards in a Birth Card's Life Spread reveal influences a child with this Birth Card will experience between birth through age 12. As such, a child's Mercury Cards must be considered so an adult can nurture a child from a place of awareness and work with them from where a child is at in their development. A 9♠ child has the following Mercury Cards: **2♥, 3♦, and A♣**. Alternatively, outside of any specific person associated with these three cards, the basic meanings of these cards describe experiences that may be impactful during this child's formative years. These cards suggest a 9♠ may experience limitations due to their family's poor finances or from inconsistent values. A 9♠ is wired to search for self-improvement and will likely be supported by one close relationship in the family.

Potential Callings / Vocations by Zodiac Sign

January 5 – Capricorn: 4♣ Planetary Ruling Card
With a 4♣ Planetary Ruling Card adding some stability of the mind, these 9♠ can be great leaders so long as they do not force their willpower on others. Ambition and personal magnetism help these individuals in people-related careers such as politics, public speaking, writing, or the entertainment business.

February 3 – Aquarius: 2♦ Planetary Ruling Card
The intellectual and unorthodox aspect of Aquarius suits these 9♠, making them likely to stand out from the crowd as a journalist, artist, musician, composer, athlete, writer, attorney, or inventor. Those preferring finance-based careers can succeed as a business manager or real estate broker.

March 1 – Pisces: J♠ Planetary Ruling Card
With a J♠ Planetary Ruling Card, these 9♠ are creative and emotional, thereby making them well suited to a career as a writer, actor, musician, or artist.

Famous 9♠
Bradley Cooper, actor – 1/5/1975
Justin Bieber, singer/songwriter – 3/1/1994
Amal Clooney, lawyer/activist – 2/3/1978
Marilyn Manson, singer/songwriter – 1/5/1969
Lupita Nyong'o, actress – 3/1/1983

Chapter 13

Descriptions of the Ten Birth Cards

Welcome to the world of the achieving Ten of Hearts!

Ten of Hearts = Group accomplishment

According to the Destiny Card system, souls chronologically experience God's lessons across 52 life incarnations. (Think of these as the universe's lessons if this aligns more with your beliefs.) The Birth Card each soul is born into determines the order and type of lessons a soul experiences. When you examine a Birth Card, you will notice it displays a suit of either a Heart, Club, Diamond, or Spade. This suit is significant because it represents the gifts a person born into this suit will possess and how they will direct their energies to learn lessons in their current life incarnation. A Heart Birth Card retains gifts and experiences life lessons around love and relationships. A Club Birth Card holds capabilities and experiences life lessons in their ability to communicate and absorb knowledge. A Diamond Birth Card possesses talents and experiences life lessons around money and values. And finally, a Spade Birth Card manifests gifts and experiences life lessons in work and health. Souls progress through incarnations and life lessons beginning as Hearts, moving on to Clubs, then Diamonds, and finally as Spades. Therefore, individuals born as Heart Cards are the youngest souls and individuals born as Spades Cards are the oldest souls.

In addition, the number on a Birth Card is equally meaningful as souls sequentially experience life lessons beginning as an Ace and culminating with lessons as a King. Because souls reincarnate, a Ten Birth Card's previous life incarnation was as a Nine. Ten Birth Cards have reached a milestone. They are no longer a single digit number. They have cultivated the knowledge and experiences of past lives as an Ace through a Nine. Think of it as like being a climber who has reached the mountaintop. Dr. Martin Luther King, Jr, gave his famous mountaintop speech on April 3, 1968, the day before being assassinated. In his speech, Martin proclaimed, "I've been to the mountaintop. And I don't mind. Like anybody, I would like to live — a long life; longevity has its place. But I'm not concerned about that now. I just want to do God's will. And, he's allowed me to go up to the mountaintop. And I've looked over. And I've seen the Promised Land." Martin appreciated that being at the mountaintop gives a person a unique perspective. They can see where they have been and what is ahead. Such positionality is power, which is why Ten Birth Cards manifest accomplishment in their current life. **It makes sense, then, that a 10♥ child's purpose, gifts, and life lessons revolve around how they navigate *accomplishment* in their life. And due to being a Heart, this child will learn lessons by experiencing accomplishment from large groups and related to *love* and *relationships*.**

How to Nurture the Temperament and Personality of a 10♥ Child

Did you know that elephants have incredible memories? In 1999, at The Elephant Sanctuary in Tennessee, for instance, a new elephant named Shirley was introduced to a longtime resident elephant named Jenny. Their oddly euphoric behavior toward each other suggested they already knew one another. Doing some research, the staff found out both elephants had worked together for a few months in a circus back in 1976. They had not seen each other in 23 years, yet they recognized each other after all that time! Like elephants, 10♥ have an incredible *memory*. The explanation for this gift can be understood through neuroscience. Neuroscientists have confirmed that emotions play a key role in learning and memory. Simply put, scientists discovered that positive emotions heighten attention to learning, which then causes a person to exhibit increased memory retention and recall. In the case of a 10♥, their early years are somewhat protected and often filled with love. Experiencing mostly positive emotions programs their brains to retain memory well. Once a 10♥ enters the educational system, whether it be preschool or kindergarten, they exhibit good comprehension and an optimistic disposition. Such traits tend to bring forth favorable attention from their teachers which reinforces their positive emotions and in turn, sustains their ability to recall and retain information well across their lifetime. Even though they possess agreeable dispositions, a 10♥ should not be seated next to or partnered with an emotionally disturbed student. Being exposed to negative emotions of others could negatively impact their attention to learning.

Enjoying their early years in education, young 10♥ appear happy to others. As such, they attract others to them like a moth to a flame. This contributes to why 10♥ are often popular and capable of charming large and diverse groups of people. Due to a 10♥'s ability to get along with others, you may think group learning is optimal for them. Yet this is not always the case. Picture yourself as a fifth-grade teacher who is facilitating a group project. Students are creating skits that depict early colonial life. Ten minutes into planning, one group seems to be louder than the other groups. There is a lot of laughter. Upon closer inspection, you find the cause of the noise is due to one student. He is animated and funny. An outsider might label this student as the class clown. Another likely label for this student is that he is a 10♥. You see, 10♥ love to entertain. They may love group work, but it may be too distracting for them as a learner. Therefore, sometimes it may be better for a 10♥ to acquire information through *independent learning.* Independent learning, as its name implies, is when a student takes initiative, directs, regulates, and assesses their own learning. Independent learners take responsibility for their acquisition of knowledge. They set their own goals and timelines. At first, a 10♥ will need to be taught how to self-regulate their learning. Then, they will be on autopilot for independent learning. Certain schools tend to promote this kind of learning. For instance, a Montessori preschool with its philosophy of self-directed play would be a great learning environment for a 10♥. As they get older, direct instruction or lecture format of learning is not ideal for a 10♥. If you are a teacher of a 10♥, accommodate them by offering them learning through independent modalities – from listening to podcasts, watching videos on YouTube, to reading books. Some 10♥ may even do well in an online learning environment or with home schooling. Also, keep in mind that 10♥ prefer a depth over breadth process to learning. Allow their interests to steer their learning. Provide them with research projects. When they need to work in a group – and they should experience this too – give them a specific focus or role to play in the group. For instance, teachers assign roles such as facilitator, recorder, presenter, timekeeper, and artist. Allow them some choice in their role and know they will prefer the artist role. Then, watch in amazement in what a 10♥ can accomplish.

In fact, many 10♥ possess the heart of an artist. If you are a parent of a 10♥ and see this potential in your child, make sure to nurture it. Sign this child up for art, dance, music, or singing classes. As this child grows older it is possible for them to leverage their artistic talents into a career. One of the reasons for this is that they inherently can attract fans. If you think your 10♥ teen is spending too much time on Instagram, think again. They have what it takes to be an influencer on such platforms and as such build a following that can be monetized into a business. If you feel your child is not spending enough time on their schoolwork, negotiate with your 10♥. Perhaps reward acceptable grades with expensive art supplies, musical instruments, or tickets to museums and concerts.

Have you ever heard of or watched the movie, *Miss Congeniality*, starring Sandra Bullock? In the movie, Bullock plays an FBI agent. When the Miss America beauty pageant is spooked by a bomb threat, Bullock goes undercover as a contestant to solve the case. Her quirky, awkward, and non-cutthroat personality wins over the hearts of the other contestants. Bullock's character becomes popular within a large group of competing women, thus earning her the title of Miss Congeniality. No matter the gender, 10♥ are blessed with a *congenial* personality. Moreover, as the card known for group accomplishment, 10♥ tend to be *popular* and can attract fans like no other Birth Card. These 10♥'s qualities explain why many become successful entertainers. They can make a career out of or associated with entertainment, whether it be as an event planner, musician, dancer, writer, TV host, sports athlete, teacher, or artist. If a 10♥ is not entertaining as part of their job, you can bet they are entertaining their friends and family. These 10♥ pull off the most outstanding parties. If you are a parent of a 10♥, be on the lookout for your adolescent 10♥ hosting parties without your permission. And they may be so focused on pleasing their friends that these parties can get out of hand quickly.

From time to time, a 10♥ may need *interpersonal calibration*. The term calibration is often associated with measuring instruments, like a scale that you stand upon to weigh yourself. When this scale is calibrated, the dial indicating weight is adjusted to point directly at zero. If the dial is off by five pounds, it could add or subtract five pounds to one's actual weight. A young 10♥ may need calibration around love and relationships due to their *idealism*. Let's consider an example. Jessica is the most popular girl in the sixth grade. Erika, a 10♥, is also well liked and is friends with Jessica. Recently and ever since her parents divorced, Jessica has become mean toward other girls, including Erika. One day on the bus to school, Jessica and Erika notice they are wearing the same new outfit. While Erika thinks it's great, Jessica is horrified. Jessica wants Erika to change her clothes. Once at school, Jessica demands Erika visit the donations closet and change her clothes. When Erika pushes back at that idea, Jessica tells Erika, "I hate you. I wish you were dead." With that comment, Erika quickly changes into some donated clothes. Later that day, Erika's mom picks her up from school and asks what happened to her new outfit. Erika explains the situation and makes excuses for Jessica's behavior. This would be an instance where advice needs to be offered to a 10♥ in learning how to maintain boundaries in relationships. Without this type of interpersonal calibration, a 10♥ may become a *pushover*. These lower expressing individuals tend to adopt rose-colored views toward their relationships with others and often sustain unhealthy relationships. If an older 10♥ needs this type of calibration, they may not take advice from an adult. Instead, encourage them to bounce ideas off a practical friend. Overall, you do not want to eliminate a 10♥'s idealism. It is part of the reason why they are creative and visionary souls. Just teach them how to calibrate.

Summary of Higher and Lower Personality Traits

Higher: Artistic, entertainer, deep learner, popular, congenial, independent, ambitious.

Lower: Super sensitive, selfish, idealistic, self-deluding in love, pushover, secretive, obstinate.

Childhood Influence Mercury Cards
It is common knowledge that a child's personality is most malleable during the formative years – from birth to eight years of age. In the Destiny Card system, the Mercury Cards in a Birth Card's Life Spread reveal influences a child with this Birth Card will experience between birth through age 12. As such, a child's Mercury Cards must be considered so an adult can nurture a child from a place of awareness and work with them from where a child is at in their development. A 10♥ child has the following Mercury Cards: **10♦, 6♥, and Q♣**. The Q♣ may mean there is an influential mother who is likely a Club Birth or Planetary Ruling Card. Alternatively, outside of any specific person associated with these three cards, the basic meanings of these cards describe experiences that may be impactful during this child's formative years. These cards suggest a 10♥ is born into a financially stable environment perhaps due to an inheritance. They tend to experience a harmonious family environment and parent(s) who support a strong educational foundation.

Potential Callings / Vocations by Zodiac Sign

July 31 – Leo: 10♥ Planetary Ruling Card
Having a 10♥ Planetary Ruling Card doubles these individuals' ability to effectively entertain groups. Many do well as a business leader or manager. The aspect of Leo can drive them to speak out for human rights through a career as an attorney, writer, film director, or politician.

August 29 – Virgo: 10♦ Planetary Ruling Card
The detail-oriented aspect of Virgo allows these 10♥ to succeed in numerous occupations (e.g., scientist, engineer, artist, musician, actor, politician, writer, or professor). Having a 10♦ Planetary Ruling Card often indicates money and/or fame will accompany their success.

September 27 – Libra: 8♠ Planetary Ruling Card
The influence of Libra in these 10♥ makes them attracted to artistic and creative jobs. Many actors, singers, and performers share this birthday. Having an 8♠ Planetary Ruling Card often indicates success in whatever goals they make.

October 25 – Scorpio: A♥ and 3♠ Planetary Ruling Cards

With an A♥ and 3♠ Planetary Ruling Cards, self-expression is key to success for these 10♥. They need to be careful not to scatter their energies. They can do well as an artist, actor, writer, scientist, architect, or singer.

November 23 – Sagittarius: A♦ Planetary Ruling Card

With an A♦ Planetary Ruling Card, these 10♥ prefer occupations that do not stifle their freedom. Many have talents in music, and they can make a career of it. Those seeking an intellectually stimulating career can do well as a physician or scientist.

December 21 – Sagittarius or Capricorn: A♦ or Q♦ Planetary Ruling Card

10♥ affiliated with Sagittarius tend to be fair-minded. Therefore, they prefer careers where they can provide a service for their community (e.g., retail owner, social worker, government worker, or politician). The Capricorn affiliated 10♥ tend to be more materialistic and prefer careers that can bring them a lot of money (e.g., business leader, financial planner, or real estate broker).

Famous 10♥

Lil Wayne, hip-hop artist – 9/27/1982
Katy Perry, singer – 10/25/1984
Mark Cuban, businessman/ entrepreneur – 7/31/ 1958
J. K. Rowlings, author – 7/31/1965
Michael Jackson, singer – 8/29/1958
Miley Cyrus, singer/songwriter- 11/23/1992

Welcome to the world of the achieving Ten of Clubs!

Ten of Clubs = Educational accomplishment

According to the Destiny Card system, souls chronologically experience God's lessons across 52 life incarnations. (Think of these as the universe's lessons if this aligns more with your beliefs.) The Birth Card each soul is born into determines the order and type of lessons a soul experiences. When you examine a Birth Card, you will notice it displays a suit of either a Heart, Club, Diamond, or Spade. This suit is significant because it represents the gifts a person born into this suit will possess and how they will direct their energies to learn lessons in their current life incarnation. A Heart Birth Card retains gifts and experiences life lessons around love and relationships. A Club Birth Card holds capabilities and experiences life lessons in their ability to communicate and absorb knowledge. A Diamond Birth Card possesses talents and experiences life lessons around money and values. And finally, a Spade Birth Card manifests gifts and experiences life lessons in work and health. Souls progress through incarnations and life lessons beginning as Hearts, moving on to Clubs, then Diamonds, and finally as Spades. Therefore, individuals born as Heart Cards are the youngest souls and individuals born as Spades Cards are the oldest souls.

In addition, the number on a Birth Card is equally meaningful as souls sequentially experience life lessons beginning as an Ace and culminating with lessons as a King. Because souls reincarnate, a Ten Birth Card's previous life incarnation was as a Nine. Ten Birth Cards have reached a milestone. No longer are they a single digit number. They have cultivated the knowledge and experiences of past lives as an Ace up through a Nine. Think of it as like a climber who has reached the mountain top. Dr. Martin Luther King, Jr, gave his famous mountaintop speech on April 3, 1968, the day before being assassinated. In his speech, Martin proclaimed, "I've been to the mountaintop. And I don't mind. Like anybody, I would like to live — a long life; longevity has its place. But I'm not concerned about that now. I just want to do God's will. And, he's allowed me to go up to the mountaintop. And I've looked over. And I've seen the Promised Land." Martin appreciated that being at the mountaintop gives a person a unique perspective. They can see where they have been and what is ahead. Such positionality is power, which is why Ten Birth Cards represent accomplishment. **It makes sense, then, that a 10♣ child's purpose, gifts, and life lessons revolve around how they navigate *accomplishment* in their life. And due to being a Club, this child will learn lessons through experiencing accomplishment with large groups and related to *communication* and acquisition of *knowledge*.**

How to Nurture the Temperament and Personality of a 10♣ Child
Imagine you are a guest speaker in a fifth-grade classroom. Arriving early, you sit in the back of the classroom just observing. You immediately notice a boy who is bobbing up and down like a parakeet. You realize he can move that way because he is sitting on a ball chair. When the bobbing stops, another motion begins. He grabs a pencil and begins tapping it on his desk. As the teacher transitions the class to your speaking, this boy gets out of his seat for a quick visit with his neighbor. Five minutes into your speech, this same boy gets up to throw something in the waste basket. You are exhausted by just watching this child's perpetual motion. You conclude this child has a serious case of attention deficit hypertension disorder. You may be right. Or it may be that this child is a 10♣ who has yet to learn how to control their powerfully active mind. Even though 10♣ love to learn, the structure of formal education may not always suit them. Sitting in a hard chair and listening to a long lecture is difficult for some 10♣, particularly the males. To cope in these situations, they may increase their physical movements, create social distractions, or daydream. Clearly, 10♣ need to be taught more healthy ways to settle down and focus their active minds. If you are a teacher of a 10♣, allow them some physical movement during their learning. For example, provide alternative seating such as a ball chair or a chair with a *fidget band.* A fidget band is a strap of stretchy material that is attached around the legs of a chair. A child can move the band with their feet to release physical energy without making noises that distract others. Give them fidget toys — cubes, poppers, spinners, or squeeze toys. You should avoid long lectures and integrate *brain breaks* into the daily schedule. Brain breaks are mental or physical breaks used in schools to get students moving or to help them relax. If you are the parent of a 10♣, make sure to push both physical and mental

activities — yoga, music, calming apps, and sports. Sports that require constant focus are the best such as mountain biking, motocross racing, skiing, tennis, gymnastics, and competitive swimming. The objective of any of these activities to get a 10♣ to disconnect from their active mind. In other words, to give their mind a rest.

Higher expressing 10♣, however, have developed self-discipline when it comes to the mental gymnasts that are going on in their mind. They tend to direct their mental energies in intentional ways. They implement time management strategies when acquiring knowledge. These individuals represent the card of *educational accomplishment*. However, this does not mean they pursue higher education and obtain formal degrees. Although, some do. For every 10♣ that succeeds through formal education, there are just as many that prefer the 'University of Life' and attain self-made success. Richard Branson, the founder of Virgin Records, is a prime example of this type of path and accomplishment for a 10♣. The label of educational accomplishment has more to do with the fact that 10♣ have a strong passion for learning and educating others. This is the reason a 10♣ is also called the teacher card. Many 10♣ can feel called to the teaching profession. For those who choose other careers, there tends to be some element in their job where they are learning and teaching others.

10♣ know they can learn anything and tend to be independent learners. This is the child in school who does not have to work hard to get good grades. Even if a teacher or parent tells them they must learn something as a foundation or they will get behind, a 10♣ does not take them seriously. They know they can miss out on some learning and figure it out later when there is a need for it. Because of this attitude, some 10♣ do not develop traditional study habits. They do things their own way. They may push back when a teacher demands too much structure. They may ask to work alone on a project rather than working within a larger group. It may be helpful to periodically allow a 10♣ some freedom in their learning. Mind you, not complete freedom, just some independent learning. A 10♣ with too much freedom may scatter their energies and fail to follow through with responsibilities. Negotiate with your 10♣. Try to balance freedom and structure. Perhaps accommodate them with *alternative assessments*. Alternative assessments allow students to demonstrate what they learned in ways other than traditional testing. Alternative assessments may also be referred to as authentic, performance, or informal assessment. For instance, because a 10♣ is the teacher card, have them learn something with the goal of presenting it to others. Assess them on this presentation in lieu of a test. Besides, 10♣ have great instincts toward how to explain things to others. This is because 10♣ possess the superpower of having superior *pedagogical content knowledge*. A concept well known to educators, pedagogical content knowledge is the ability to comprehend information, transform it, and teach it in such a way that it makes sense to specific audiences. Sure, a 10♣ might stray off course from time to time. The good news is that 10♣ are self-sufficient learners. They are always learning even if that fact is not reflected in their grades.

As previously mentioned, Ten Birth Cards experience the position of being at the mountaintop. As a Club, 10♣ are at the top of the mountain of knowledge. Such positionality is not always a blessing for a 10♣. Sure, 10♣ can draw and benefit from the subconscious knowledge they have accrued over past lives. Their extensive background knowledge allows them to *process information quickly*. They are not intimidated by intellectual challenges. They readily grasp problems and solve them in innovative ways. Such qualities often propel 10♣ to leadership positions in their field. However, there is also a problematic aspect to this positionality. 10♣ are simultaneously receptive to past and new knowledge. New knowledge calls out to them. This is an overwhelming situation for a person to be in. It is like they are standing on a mountaintop, spinning around in circles, distracted by all the possibilities. This explains why some 10♣ come across as being hyperactive or restless. These 10♣ often have difficulty controlling their active mind. They cannot easily turn off their mind. Some develop insomnia. And some scatter their intellectual energy. The most common way a 10♣ may scatter their energy is by changing their mind a lot about their calling in life. This indecision can continue into young adulthood. For instance, while in college, a 10♣ may change their major several times. Such behavior can be frustrating for a parent of a 10♣. These individuals may be perceived as not being able to settle down or wandering aimlessly. However, recall what was stated earlier about Ten Birth Cards being at the mountain top. 10♣ are aware of all the jobs available to them, and they have the intellectual ability to pursue any one of them.

Therefore, a 10♣ may need some help in discovering their purpose in life. The first step is awareness. If you are a parent of a 10♣, discuss this tendency. Let them know it is okay if they do not readily understand their calling. Start this discussion as young as possible. Have them watch the movie, *A Dog's Purpose*, and then discuss how people experience similar feelings in searching for a career that gives them purpose. Teach them to make pros and cons lists before initiating any change in their life. Assist them in identifying their strengths and work needs. Encourage older 10♣ to take *career aptitude or strength tests*. Career aptitude tests not only help students identify their top aptitudes and soft skills, but they also suggest what employment and career opportunities best match them. I recommend the Myers-Briggs Type Indicator (MBTI), Gallup, Motivational Appraisal of Personal Potential (MAPP), MyMajors, or Career Explorer tests. While a 10♣ should not remain stagnant and resist change, they need to develop a more focused experimentation toward making changing. Most importantly, be patient with a 10♣. They tend to be late bloomers, but they have the potential to accomplish much in life and become leaders in their field.

Summary of Higher and Lower Personality Traits

Higher: Curious, leader, independent, creative, process information well, hard worker.

Lower: Impatient, headstrong, restless, insomniac, uncommitted, indecision in calling.

Childhood Influence Mercury Cards

It is common knowledge that a child's personality is most malleable during the formative years – from birth to eight years of age. In the Destiny Card system, the Mercury Cards in a Birth Card's Life Spread reveal influences a child with this Birth Card will experience between birth through age 12. As such, a child's Mercury Cards must be considered so an adult can nurture a child from a place of awareness and work with them from where a child is at in their development. A 10♣ child has the following Mercury Cards: **8♦, 2♠, and Q♠**. The Q♠ may mean there is an influential mother who is likely a Spade Birth or Planetary Ruling Card. Alternatively, outside of any specific person associated with these three cards, the basic meanings of these cards describe experiences that may be impactful during this child's formative years. These cards suggest a 10♣ experiences ample finances and friends to support them. It is possible that they are impacted by an agreement such as adoption or joint custody between divorced parents. There tends to be times when a 10♣ will struggle with decision-making and so they feel a sense of drudgery.

Potential Callings / Vocations by Zodiac Sign

January 30 – Aquarius: 10♠ Planetary Ruling Card
Having the workaholic 10♠ Planetary Ruling Card means these 10♣ are ambitious and will work hard. These individuals tend to dislike being told what to do so they may do better if they work for themselves as a business owner, writer, artist, politician, or government leader.

February 20 – Pisces: 5♣ Planetary Ruling Card
With a 5♣ Planetary Ruling Card, these 10♣ are more restless and therefore susceptible to desiring changes in work. Some are daydreamers. They need freedom in their work which may be accomplished as an actor, musician, film producer, singer, dancer, business owner, travel photographer, or salesperson.

March 26 – Aries: 3♥ Planetary Ruling Card
With a 3♥ Planetary Ruling Card, these 10♣ tend to experience emotional indecision. Therefore, they may adopt an on-again-off-again approach to projects and work. They are better suited to finding an ideology, product, or hobby they enjoy and leveraging it into work (e.g., salesperson, politician, musician, actor, singer, sports player, promotional marketer, or advertiser).

April 24 – Taurus: K♠ Planetary Ruling Card
Having a K♠ Planetary Ruling Card Due and the stability of Taurus, these 10♣ are meant to be leaders. They can do well as a government or military leader, business owner, entrepreneur, actor, teacher, or administrator.

May 22 – Taurus or Gemini: K♠ or 8♦ Planetary Ruling Card
The Taurus affiliated 10♣ have tremendous power having a K Planetary Ruling Card. This can be a mixed blessing as they may be super achievers who work so hard, they burn out and then under achieve. These individuals tend to engage in careers as a teacher, writer, athlete, or coach. The Gemini affiliated individuals often cultivate artistic talents that are commercialized into a career.

June 20 – Gemini: 8♦ Planetary Ruling Card
With an 8♦ Planetary Ruling Card, these 10♣ can expect success as a writer, politician, actor, or military leader. If business is preferred, they can do well if the business allows them some freedom, travel, or a lot of contact with people.

July 18 – Cancer: Q♥ Planetary Ruling Card
Early home life difficulties may produce low self-esteem in these 10♣. Self-discipline is key, which can lead them to success as a writer, actor, artist, film maker, entrepreneur, or computer coder.

August 16 – Leo: 10♣ Planetary Ruling Card
With a 10♣ Planetary Ruling Card, these individuals possess double the restlessness. By pursuing spiritual lines and humanitarian causes, they can achieve success as a counselor, teacher, community activist, or TV personality. More physically inclined individuals can make a successful professional athlete or entertainer.

September 14 – Virgo: 8♦ Planetary Ruling Card
When the perfectionistic aspect of Virgo is combined with the monetary power of an 8♦ Planetary Ruling Card, financial success is assured for these individuals. They can do well as a researcher, accountant, teacher, engineer, business investor, professional athlete, or counselor/advisor (especially a financial advisor).

October 12 – Libra: K♠ Planetary Ruling Card
With attractiveness and charm inherent to Libra, these 10♣ can do well as an artist, actor, business executive, or politician. The more physically inclined individuals may prefer architecture or construction work.

November 10 – Scorpio: 3♥ and 3♦ Planetary Ruling Cards
Having two Planetary Ruling Cards associated with the number Three embeds a strong need for self-expression in these 10♣. They can do well in writing, acting, scientific research, or engineering.

December 8 – Sagittarius: A♣ Planetary Ruling Card
While having an A♣ Planetary Ruling Card intensifies the ambition in these 10♣, it may also increase the scattering of their energies. They can do well as a teacher, inventor, business owner, or flight attendant.

Famous 10♣
Carson Daly, TV personality – 6/22/1973
Nancy Pelosi, politician – 3/26/1940
Novak Djokovic, tennis player – 5/22/1987
Kelly Clarkson, singer/ TV personality – 4/24/1982
Nas, rapper – 9/14/1973
Nicole Kidman, actress – 6/20/1967

Ten of Diamonds = Accomplishment in values and money

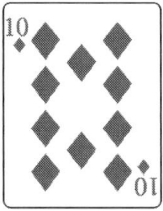

Welcome to the world of the achieving Ten of Diamonds!

According to the Destiny Card system, souls chronologically experience God's lessons across 52 life incarnations. (Think of these as the universe's lessons if this aligns more with your beliefs.) The Birth Card each soul is born into determines the order and type of lessons a soul experiences. When you examine a Birth Card, you will notice it displays a suit of either a Heart, Club, Diamond, or Spade. This suit is significant because it represents the gifts a person born into this suit will possess and how they will direct their energies to learn lessons in their current life incarnation. A Heart Birth Card retains gifts and experiences life lessons around love and relationships. A Club Birth Card holds capabilities and experiences life lessons in their ability to communicate and absorb knowledge. A Diamond Birth Card possesses talents and experiences life lessons around money and values. And finally, a Spade Birth Card manifests gifts and experiences life lessons in work and health. Souls progress through incarnations and life lessons beginning as Hearts, moving on to Clubs, then Diamonds, and finally as Spades. Therefore, individuals born as Heart Cards are the youngest souls and individuals born as Spades Cards are the oldest souls.

In addition, the number on a Birth Card is equally meaningful as souls sequentially experience life lessons beginning as an Ace and culminating with lessons as a King. Because souls reincarnate, a Ten Birth Card's previous life incarnation was as a Nine. Ten Birth Cards have reached a milestone. No longer are they a single digit number. They have cultivated the knowledge and experiences of past lives as an Ace up through a Nine. Think of it as like a climber who has reached the mountain top. Dr. Martin Luther King, Jr, gave his famous mountaintop speech on April 3, 1968, the day before being assassinated. In his speech, Martin proclaimed, "I've been to the mountaintop. And I don't mind. Like anybody, I would like to live — a long life; longevity has its place. But I'm not concerned about that now. I just want to do God's will. And, he's allowed me to go up to the mountaintop. And I've looked over. And I've seen the Promised Land." Martin appreciated that being at the mountaintop gives a person a unique perspective. They can see where they have been and what is ahead. Such positionality is power, which is why Ten Birth Cards represent accomplishment. **It makes sense, then, that a 10♦ child's purpose, gifts, and life lessons revolve around how they navigate** *accomplishment* **in their life. And due to being a Diamond, this child will learn lessons by experiencing accomplishment with large groups and related to** *values* **and** *money.*

How to Nurture the Temperament and Personality of a 10♦ Child

If you are familiar with astrology, you may be acquainted with the concept of a *birth chart*. A birth chart is a visual representation of the planetary positions for a person based upon the location, date, and exact time of their birth. Energetically, it represents a person's individual life plan. The Destiny Card system, likewise, has a chart known as the Life Spread that depicts God's lessons for each Birth Card. In this Life Spread, the 10♦ card is positioned at the very center of this chart. Out of all the Birth Cards, 10♦ are born feeling they are the center of the universe.

As such, 10♦ are often *privileged* individuals and therefore are considered the most blessed card in the deck. Let's consider an example from history. In 1710, Louis XV of France, was born on February 15, designating him as a 10♦. He was born inside the Palace of Versailles, the most opulent residence of its time. Although he was a second born son, destiny had other plans. After the death of his grandfather, parents, and brother, Louis XV became King of France and reined from 1715 until 1774. Yes, he became King of France at age five. Privileged indeed. As you can probably imagine, he was extremely spoiled. Having no siblings or other children around him, he was never forced to share or cooperate. He got used to having anything he wanted and however he wanted it. It is no wonder historians have described Louis XV as an ineffective leader. He did what he wanted and took no advice from others. When a 10♦ child is spoiled, they are destined to manifest the lower traits of their Birth Card. Prolonged spoiling makes it difficult for them to change their trajectory and priorities from materialistic to humanitarian.

Clearly, the most important way to nurture a 10♦ is to refrain from spoiling them and this should begin from an early age. This is no easy feat as young 10♦ are highly *ambitious*. And some 10♦ children can be quite vocal in their demand to have things. For example, imagine you are a parent of a five-year-old 10♦ daughter named Arlena. After picking Arlena up from afterschool care, you need to drop off some paperwork at a colleague's house. Upon arrival, your colleague's family has just finished dinner and is enjoying an ice cream dessert. Having seen this, Arlena demands ice cream on the way home. You respond by saying you need to get home and make dinner and that eating ice cream right before dinner is not a good idea. Arlena has a meltdown, saying how unfair it is that your colleague's kids get to eat ice cream and she can't. Even when you use reason, such as explaining how your colleague's family already had eaten dinner, your daughter refuses to change her mind. Arlena's whining will not stop. You are getting a headache. And an ice cream store is on the way home. What do you do? Careful. If you give in to this type of demand from a 10♦, your actions will set a precedence. A 10♦ child is a child who, if you give an inch, will take a mile. This child will always claim life is not fair when they do not get what they want. The problem is that they will never be satisfied and the bar of what they want will only move higher and higher. If you are a parent of a 10♦, it would be helpful to check your own Birth Card. Are you a Birth Card who is prone to overly nurturing? If so, you may need to ask a close friend or family member for a reality check. Sure, you have wonderful intentions. But are you enabling the spoiling? An honest look at the relational dynamics between you and your child may be needed.

All of this is not to say 10♦ are bad children. It is not their fault that they are born this way. Remember that they are on a mountaintop, seeing all the possibilities life has to offer. A young 10♦ is like a kid in a candy store. They are bright and excited about the possibilities in front of them. They also experience good health, which blesses them with a lot of energy to explore life. If you are a parent of a 10♦, you may need to encourage them to adopt gratitude and share their blessings with others. Let's go back to the anecdote about Arlena. Imagine Arlena's sixth birthday is approaching, and she expects many new toys. Before her birthday, ask Arlena to take stock of her toys and select several she no longer uses. If applicable, ask her to reflect upon memories of enjoying her toys. The idea here is to get her in the practice of voicing appreciation and gratitude. 10♦ need reminders to do this otherwise they will take things for granted. Then, ask how she could help other children benefit from the toys. If a toy is unused, perhaps she could re-gift the toy to someone else. Or she could donate toys to a specific neighbor, Goodwill, or a local preschool program. Make sure Arlena has a say in what happens to the toys and participates in the action of giving. Repeat this kind of gratitude and giving process with your 10♦ as much as possible. In addition, urge a 10♦ to engage in acts of kindness. On the Internet, there are plenty of acts of kindness charts and calendars. Challenge them to implement a specific amount within a certain time frame as a form of a game. You see, 10♦ love competition. As they grow older, encourage them to volunteer at an animal shelter, homeless shelter, or elderly community. The key to these exercises is that you want a 10♦ to associate personal giving with feeling good inside. In doing so, you will help them make the shift later in life from making money to giving money.

Why is the act of giving so important for a 10♦? Let's go back to the example of Louis XV of France. Historians agree that one of the main reasons Louis XV was a poor leader was because he lacked self-confidence. *Self-doubt* can be an issue with many 10♦. In psychology, the concept of *attribution theory* explains why this can be true. Attribution theory explains that there are two different ways a person perceives the causes of events or behaviors: as either internally or externally within their control. For instance, imagine a high school senior named Eric has failed a math test. Does Eric attribute the failure to the teacher's poor instruction or simply because he is not smart in math? Such attributions are external. Or does Eric attribute the failure to the fact that he did not pay attention in class during instruction or study for the test? Such attributions are internal. This is relevant to a 10♦ because it matters how they attribute the successes they are sure to experience in life. Under which viewpoint do they attribute their success? When a 10♦ is reminded every day that they have everything they materially need and want, their achievements in life can feel as if they are attributed outside of themselves. Now let's imagine Eric goes off to college. Four years later and after graduating, Eric lands an outstanding job at a top financial firm. Because his family is well connected to the owner of said firm, Eric experiences self-doubt. Was the job earned through his efforts and skills or through his connection? Psychologists claim that individuals who attribute success outside of themselves tend to develop low self-esteem. To ensure your 10♦ develops high self-esteem, from an early age, teach them to recognize and appreciate their personal gifts. Push them to work hard. When they succeed, praise them for putting in the effort.

10♦ are often blessed with *sound judgement*. Make sure they have opportunities to use and understand this gift. For instance, if you want your 10♦ to attend summer camp, include them in the research of various camp programs. Tell them to trust their gut instincts to pick a camp. Praise their judgement. 10♦ are particularly gifted in applying their sound judgement in business. If you are a parent of a 10♦, make sure to explain this superpower to them and support their entrepreneurial ideas. Moreover, they are both nimble and confident in how best to move forward, managing or scaling a business in the most advantageous way. Even if life brings financial setbacks, a 10♦ holds the power to bounce back. Martha Stewart, a 10♦, is a perfect example of this. You might be familiar with Stewart through her popular cookbooks or magazine, *Martha Stewart Living*. Over the span of about forty years, Stewart built her own business and media empire. Then, a single bad decision set her back. In 2004, Stewart was convicted of securities fraud and obstruction of justice. She was sentenced to prison for five months. After serving her time, Stewart jumped right back into reconstructing her business. Today, Stewart is back on top. While it is rare for a person to be able to pull that off, 10♦ hold the power to do just that!

Keep in mind, 10♦ maintain sound judgement around what holds value in life and financial interactions. Sound judgement around relationships is another matter. If a 10♦ is leaning into *materialism*, they may act only in ways that benefit them. Be on the lookout for an adolescent 10♦ who takes this too far by exploiting others. They often do this innocently and unconsciously at first. Let's say you are a parent of a seventeen-year-old 10♦ daughter named Jill. Recently, you found it strange that Jill has taken an interest in a socially awkward freshman. They are spending a lot of time together, especially at the freshman's house. You discover the freshman happens to be the sister of your daughter's latest crush. Hmmm. Now things are making more sense. While your daughter may be commended on leveraging opportunity, she may also be using someone else to get what she wants. It is situations like this that warrant having discussions with a 10♦ about ethics around relationships. Ask them to consider different means to an end; one that does not hurt or exploit others.

Summary of Higher and Lower Personality Traits

Higher: Analytical, ambitious, sound judgement, humanitarian, keen business sense.

Lower: Egocentric, self-doubt, materialistic, opinionated, exploiter, difficult love karma.

Childhood Influence Mercury Cards

It is common knowledge that a child's personality is most malleable during the formative years – from birth to eight years of age. In the Destiny Card system, the Mercury Cards in a Birth Card's Life Spread reveal influences a child with this Birth Card will experience between birth through age 12. As such, a child's Mercury Cards must be considered so an adult can nurture a child from a place of awareness and work with them from where a child is at in their development. A 10♦ child has the following Mercury Cards: **8♠, 4♣, and K♣.** The K♣ may mean there is an influential father who is likely a Club Birth or Planetary Ruling Card. Alternatively, outside of any specific person associated with these three cards, the basic meanings of these cards describe experiences that may be impactful during this child's formative years. These cards suggest a young 10♦ experiences a harmonious home life and good health. They tend to do well in school, especially mastering subjects they deem worthy.

Potential Callings / Vocations by Zodiac Sign

January 17 – Capricorn: 5♥ Planetary Ruling Card

The influence of conservative Capricorn encourages these 10♦ to be more responsible and caring about the well-being of others. They can make an excellent government official or manager, attorney, community activist, or owner of a small business.

February 15 – Aquarius: 3♣ Planetary Ruling Card

Having a 3♣ Planetary Ruling Card instills creativity in these 10♦. As such, they can succeed as an actor/actress, cartoonist, writer, singer, rapper, or teacher. Those who prefer a professional career can excel as an attorney, business owner, physician, scientist, or engineer.

March 13 – Pisces: 3♠ Planetary Ruling Card

With the artistic 3♠ Planetary Ruling Card, these 10♦ can create a financially successful career as an artist, musician, composer, dancer, singer, rapper, writer, or banker. Some are prone to worry and may find relief in sports which can also be leveraged into a career.

April 11 – Aries: A♦ Planetary Ruling Card

Having an A♦ Planetary Ruling Card pushes many of these 10♦ to be competitive. They often enjoy work as sports athletes or within a sports organization. They can also succeed as an entrepreneur particularly if it includes the marketing of physical activity.

May 9 – Taurus: A♥ Planetary Ruling Card

Having an A♥ Planetary Ruling Card instills the need for attention and affection in these 10♦. Careers that tend to attract these individuals are acting, politics, or a sports athlete. If the aesthetic side of their personality is strong, they can do well selling homes or home-related products.

June 7 – Gemini: 8♠ Planetary Ruling Card

The spiritual power of an 8♠ Planetary Ruling Card can be weakened by a lack of self-discipline in these 10♦. They do best in intellectual occupations (e.g., teacher, journalist, lawyer, politician, or physician).

July 5 – Cancer: 10♥ Planetary Ruling Card

With a 10♥ Planetary Ruling Card, these 10♦ tend to be more sensitive and artistic. Some possess a great voice which can be leveraged in a career in singing or a voice-over job. They dislike restrictive jobs or ones that require too much effort. Some can also do well as an investor, day trader of stocks, or banker.

August 3 – Leo: 10♦ Planetary Ruling Card

With the influence of Leo, these 10♦ possess charm and ambition that takes them to the top in any field they desire. They do well as business leaders, sports athletes, producers, actors, directors, models, or movie writers.

September 1 – Virgo: 8♣ Planetary Ruling Card

Appearances are important to these 10♦, so much that, they can make a career out of it as a model, fitness instructor, dietician, cosmetic salesperson, TV personality, sports athlete, professional clothing buyer, or retail owner.

Famous 10♦

Phil McGraw, psychologist/author/TV personality – 9/1/1950
Betty White, actress – 1/17/1922
Tom Brady, football player – 8/3/1977
Michelle Obama, former First Lady of the U.S. – 1/17/1964
Mohammed Ali, boxer – 1/17/1942
Megan Thee Stallion, rapper – 2/15/1995

Welcome to the world of the achieving Ten of Spades!

Ten of Spades = Accomplishment in work and health

According to the Destiny Card system, souls chronologically experience God's lessons across 52 life incarnations. (Think of these as the universe's lessons if this aligns more with your beliefs.) The Birth Card each soul is born into determines the order and type of lessons a soul experiences. When you examine a Birth Card, you will notice it displays a suit of either a Heart, Club, Diamond, or Spade. This suit is significant because it represents the gifts a person born into this suit will possess and how they will direct their energies to learn lessons in their current life incarnation. A Heart Birth Card retains gifts and experiences life lessons around love and relationships. A Club Birth Card holds capabilities and experiences life lessons in their ability to communicate and absorb knowledge. A Diamond Birth Card possesses talents and experiences life lessons around money and values. And finally, a Spade Birth Card manifests gifts and experiences life lessons in work and health. Souls progress through incarnations and life lessons beginning as Hearts, moving on to Clubs, then Diamonds, and finally as Spades. Therefore, individuals born as Heart Cards are the youngest souls and individuals born as Spades Cards are the oldest souls.

In addition, the number on a Birth Card is equally meaningful as souls sequentially experience life lessons beginning as an Ace and culminating with lessons as a King. Because souls reincarnate, a Ten Birth Card's previous life incarnation was as a Nine. Ten Birth Cards have reached a milestone. No longer are they a single digit number. They have cultivated the knowledge and experiences of past lives as an Ace up through a Nine. Think of it as like a climber who has reached the mountain top. Dr. Martin Luther King, Jr, gave his famous mountaintop speech on April 3, 1968, the day before being assassinated. In his speech, Martin proclaimed, "I've been to the mountaintop. And I don't mind. Like anybody, I would like to live — a long life; longevity has its place. But I'm not concerned about that now. I just want to do God's will. And, he's allowed me to go up to the mountaintop. And I've looked over. And I've seen the Promised Land." Being at the mountaintop gives a person a unique perspective. They can see where they have been and what is ahead. Such positionality is power, which is why Ten Birth Cards represent accomplishment. **It makes sense, then, that a 10♠ child's purpose, gifts, and life lessons revolve around how they navigate *accomplishment* in their life. And due to** being a Spade, this child will learn lessons by experiencing accomplishment in *work* and *health*.

How to Nurture the Temperament and Personality of a 10♠ Child

Surely you have heard the phrase, 'stirring up a hornet's nest.' It refers to how a person can actively cause a commotion, like poking a stick in a hornet's nest. A 10♠ is often born into an environment that is like a stirred-up hornet's nest. Such commotion can be caused by different circumstances such as being part of a family who frequently moves or travels or being in an environment with emotional challenges due to death, divorce, or a new marriage. While you might think this kind of early experience for a 10♠ is a disadvantage, in many cases it often helps motivate them to act rather than passively going with the flow. You see, 10♠ are born with an *action-oriented* temperament. Under the age of five, this temperament tends to manifest as restlessness. These are active toddlers that need to be kept busy. By school age, 10♠ often discover they can apply their active and ambitious personality to work through changes and make the best of situations. They learn efforts can pay off. Their success breeds more effort which leads to more success. Some 10♠ even learn to make do with what they have and come up with inventive solutions to problems. For instance, perhaps you jokingly tell your eight-year-old 10♠, "Looks like you'll only get stick and coal for Christmas." They immediately appear unfazed and reply, "Well, I can still use those things for something!" Some 10♠ hold the potential of becoming famous for their inventions or scientific breakthroughs. To this point, Isaac Newton was a 10♠.

According to psychologists, a person is in a *state of flow* when they are so absorbed in an activity that they lose track of time or anything outside of the task itself. You might call it being 'in the zone.' The state of flow concept was coined by psychologist, Mihaly Csikszentmihalyi, who proclaimed, "The best moments in our lives are not the passive, receptive, relaxing times…The best moments usually occur if a person's body or mind is stretched to its limits in a voluntary effort to accomplish something difficult and worthwhile." No other birth card can access a state of flow like a 10♠. This is a 10♠'s greatest superpower – *self-discipline*. For the most part, this ability provides advantages. A 10♠ can be counted upon to start and finish any project. Big or small. The more mentally complicated the project, the better. They can focus on a task, enter a state of flow, and be extremely productive. They rarely procrastinate. They maintain a *strong work ethic*. You would be correct if you think these individuals make superb students. They do. However, some 10♠ expect the same work ethic from their peers. Working collaboratively with team members, a 10♠ may feel held back by others who do not exhibit comparable work speed and effort. Such an environment often frustrates a 10♠. They may feel the need to pick up the slack of others by doing some of their work but then resent them for having to do so. In extreme cases, it may be better for a 10♠ to work independently. All this said, there is a potential drawback to a 10♠'s capacity to achieve a state of flow. So powerful is this gift, some 10♠ may forget or ignore anything outside the task at hand. Their state of flow manifests into tunnel vision. Such vision blocks out other things and people in the process. They become so wrapped up in work, they ignore others. This is the teen so absorbed in a project they repeatedly ignore calls for dinner.

Without the development of self-discipline during their youth, a 10♠ may scatter their energy and diminish their motivation to academically achieve. Interestingly, one significant factor that impacts whether a young 10♠ develops self-discipline is based upon the nature of their relationship with teachers. Did you know that educational researchers have found that out of the numerous factors influencing student achievement, teacher quality is the most influential factor? Indeed, this is true. 10♠ are particularly sensitive to the quality of their teachers. If you are a parent of a 10♠, consider the management style of your child's care providers and teachers. An overly critical teacher, even with the best of intentions, can put too much pressure on a 10♠. 10♠ internally feel the pressure to achieve; so too much criticism or setting the bar too high can stress them out. An indicator that this may be happening is if a 10♠ overly reacts when they make mistakes. An ideal teacher for a 10♠ uses *positive and negative reinforcements* as tools to manage them. 10♠ love to set and achieve goals. Reinforcements help a 10♠ develop self-discipline in goal setting. Positive reinforcement involves using praise and reward to reinforce desired behaviors. Examples in a classroom include a thumbs up or smile from the teacher, or earning stickers, completion certificates, or computer time. The concept of negative reinforcements tends to have a bad connotation because people associate it with punishment. It is not the same thing. Negative reinforcement involves removing a condition to motivate a desired behavior. Examples in a classroom include a teacher giving students a short break or partner time after a specified amount of work has been completed.

Now for the best news if you are a parent of a 10♠. Reinforcements can be effectively used by parents at home, too. For instance, 10♠ respond well to chores that are attached to an allowance or when grades are attached to dollar bills. Try not to be too demanding of them or primarily point out their faults. 10♠ are innately driven and if they falter in achievement, they often beat themselves up enough. No good comes from adults who pile on negativity. In fact, be on lookout for unhealthy *overachievement* in your 10♠. As one example, avoid setting up too much competition between siblings if you have other children. A 10♠ has the power to blow out their competition. Every. Single. Time. This can create disharmony amongst siblings and sets a 10♠ up for developing unhealthy views toward achievement. These 10♠ may become *impatient* when working with others. The inability to have patience with oneself or others can be problematic as a 10♠ matures. As the Chinese proverb advises, "One moment of patience may ward off great disaster. One moment of impatience may ruin a whole life."

When a 10♠ is pressured to achieve, they tend to program themselves to believe they must overachieve. These individuals become *workaholics* and then they may struggle with perfectionism and stress. At an extreme, some may even manifest an *obsessive-compulsive disorder*. Obsessive-compulsive disorder is when a person has persistent fears that compel them to exhibit perfectionism, repetitive behaviors, or attention to detail that is so excessive it disrupts their daily life. If you are a parent and see that your child is showing signs of being a workaholic, encourage them to find ways to balance work and health. As one example, teach them to set a timer for work to schedule breaks. Balancing their work energy with other aspects of their life is imperative. A 10♠ will benefit the most when they take mental breaks that allow them to get thoughts of work out of their mind. Sports activities that require focused attention are great for a 10♠ such as mountain biking, motocross racing, skiing, and tennis to name a few. 10♠ can become so self-disciplined that they can push aside their stress. These individuals may need help getting in touch with their body to become aware of stress. An adult may be able to recognize when a 10♠ is stressed because this child may emotionally overreact to minor incidents or hold excessive fears around schoolwork. One helpful technique to try is *progressive muscle relaxation*. Progressive muscle relaxation involves focusing upon, tightening, and relaxing specific muscles in the body. There are several videos on YouTube that teach a child how to apply this technique.

For older 10♠, consider using various energy healing techniques that target and revitalize specific *chakras* in your child's body. Chakras are energy centers that receive and transmit energy throughout the body. There are seven major chakras running along the spine of one's body that are associated with different nerves, organs, joints, and tissues near a chakra's location. A person may experience negative physical and emotional symptoms when their flow of energy becomes unbalanced – either under or overactive – at a specific chakra site. For instance, chronic stress or poor habits can cause a chakra to become imbalanced. Various healing techniques directed at chakra revitalization include yoga, meditation, toning sounds, acupuncture, affirmations, aromatherapy, light therapy, breathing practices, crystal healing, and massage (especially reiki, shiatsu, and reflexology). Additionally, many 10♠ are sensitive to music. Listening to specific kinds of music can allow a 10♠ to express their underlying feelings that contribute to their stress.

And finally, remember that 10♠ enjoy setting and achieving goals. This is the ideal child to purchase a planner for. They receive so much pleasure from making lists of tasks and then checking them off as they accomplish them. They are open to learning new ways to be efficient or improve themselves. Purchase self-help books to help them deal with unhealthy habits. If your teen struggles with perfectionism I suggest the book, *Never Good Enough: How to Use Perfectionism to Your Advantage without Letting it Ruin Your Life* by Monica Ramirez Basco. For a teen struggling with stress and anxiety, I recommend *The Anxiety Toolkit for Teens: Easy and Practical CBT and DBT Tools to Manage your Stress Anxiety Worry and Panic* by Teen Thrive, an organization that publishes books to help teens manage stress and anxiety. CBT stands for *cognitive behavior therapy* which is a treatment showing promise to help many people manage anxiety. For extreme cases, especially in the event a child is demonstrating obsessive-compulsive behaviors, seek therapy with a professional.

Summary of Higher and Lower Personality Traits

Higher: Action-oriented, strong work ethic, excellent follow through, fast thinking, athletic.

Lower: Loner, aloof, unemotional, obsessive compulsive, workaholic, impatient.

Childhood Influence Mercury Cards

It is common knowledge that a child's personality is most malleable during the formative years – from birth to eight years of age. In the Destiny Card system, the Mercury Cards in a Birth Card's Life Spread reveal influences a child with this Birth Card will experience between birth through age 12. As such, a child's Mercury Cards must be considered so an adult can nurture a child from a place of awareness and work with them from where a child is at in their development. A 10♠ child has the following Mercury Cards: **5♣, 8♦, and 5♥**. Alternatively, outside of any specific person associated with these three cards, the basic meanings of these cards describe experiences that may be impactful during this child's formative years. These cards suggest they experience discontent or emotional uncertainty related to their family circumstances. Even so, they are often financially protected.

Potential Callings / Vocations by Zodiac Sign

January 4 – Capricorn: 7♦ Planetary Ruling Card

With the spiritual energy of a 7♦ Planetary Ruling card, these 10♠ enjoy careers in which they can support others on a large scale. They can accomplish this kind of support by working for a government agency (e.g., commerce department, Homeland security, CDC, CIA, or FBI). Alternatively, some can do well as a scientist, researcher, or business owner.

February 2- Aquarius: 5♠ Planetary Ruling Card

The variety loving aspect of a 5♠ Planetary Ruling card enables these 10♠ to achieve in many different areas such as a writer, publisher, psychologist, computer coder, musician, scientist, or musician.

Famous 10♠

Graham McTavish, actor – 1/4/1961
Shakira, singer – 2/2/1977
Ayn Rand, writer – 2/2/1905
Isaac Newton, scientist – 1/4/1643
Kris Bryant, baseball player – 1/4/1992

Chapter 14

Descriptions of the Jack Birth Cards

Welcome to the world of the fun-loving J♥!

J♥ = Sacrifice in the name of love

According to the Destiny Card system, souls chronologically experience God's lessons within each life incarnation. (Think of these as the universe's lessons if this aligns more with your beliefs.) The Birth Card each soul is born into determines the order and type of lessons a soul experiences. When you examine a Birth Card, you will notice it displays a suit of either a Heart, Club, Diamond, or Spade. This suit is significant because it represents the gifts a person born into this suit will possess and how they will direct their energies to learn lessons in their current life incarnation. A Heart Birth Card retains gifts and experiences life lessons around love and relationships. A Club Birth Card holds capabilities and experiences life lessons in their ability to communicate and absorb knowledge. A Diamond Birth Card possesses talents and experiences life lessons around money and values. And finally, a Spade Birth Card manifests gifts and experiences life lessons in work and health. Souls progress through incarnations and life lessons beginning as Hearts, moving on to Clubs, then Diamonds, and finally as Spades. Therefore, individuals born as Heart Cards are the youngest souls and individuals born as Spades Cards are the oldest souls. In addition, the number on a Birth Card is equally meaningful as souls sequentially experience life lessons beginning as an Ace and culminating with lessons as a King. Jacks are associated with the number eleven. According to the Destiny Card system, when the same number of a Birth Card is doubled, as in the case of an Eleven card, the inherent power of the card is doubled. Eleven cards or Jacks hold double the power in the area associated with their suit.

Having more power makes sense because Jacks are one of the royal court cards. Just as people legitimately born into royalty are associated with various roles, royal court cards hold different roles with different responsibilities. For example, Kings hold more power and more responsibility than a Queen. A Jack is more like a Prince. Still, you are probably wondering what kind of responsibility is associated with each of the royal court Birth Cards. Normal people are not born ruling over subjects they are responsible for. Instead, royal court Birth Cards are tasked with the responsibility of finalizing a soul's path toward spiritual enlightenment. Across life incarnations as a Jack and progressing to a King, a soul exclusively works toward this goal. The specific role of all Jacks is to initiate these final steps by refining their attitude toward responsibility. **It makes sense, then, that a J♥ child's purpose, gifts, and life lessons revolve around powerful experiences of free will and *not having constraints* to learn about personal responsibility. And due to being a Heart, this child will learn lessons of not having constraints around *emotions* and *love*.**

How to Nurture the Temperament and Personality of a J♥ Child

J♥ are often born expressing tremendous love and joy. As a newborn, they will amaze others because they smile a lot. From infancy through preschool, a J♥ will enjoy giving and receiving affection. They love to snuggle. If you are a parent of a J♥, purchase them a fuzzy blanket or stuffed animal as it will soothe them. Throughout their life, a J♥ retains a loving and youthful personality. You can even recognize a J♥ by their youthful appearance. They physically appear boyish or girlish no matter their age. And their youthfulness is more than skin deep. If you are the friend or family member of a J♥, lucky for you! You see, a J♥'s superpower is that they are *sweet at heart*. They easily forgive others and rarely hold grudges. They are often energetic, sociable, and fun to be around. If they are teasing people they care about, there is usually a twinkle in their eye and a silly grin on their face.

This harmonious start to life tends to be helpful because once a J♥ reaches school age some challenges begin to manifest. These challenges typically involve having to make sacrifices that are outside of their control. Perhaps a parent or sibling is in poor health. Or perhaps their parents have divorced, and they must help care for siblings. Whatever their specific circumstances, a J♥ feels an overbearing sense of duty or an unfair number of restrictions for their age. Initially, they may resist making these sacrifices. If you are a parent of a J♥ and understand this situation, you know things are complicated. Sacrifices are required. Be careful in how you talk about these sacrifices with your J♥. They get their feelings hurt more easily than other Birth Cards. Avoid using guilt to try to get a J♥ to take on more responsibility. Saying things like, "How can you be so selfish when I ask you to do something for me? I have given up so much in life to care for you" is not productive. Instead, explain the entire situation with your J♥. Do not hold back any truths or parts of a story because you think they are too young to handle it. It is their destiny to deal with sacrifice and learn from these kinds of situations. Keep in mind, there are different kinds of sacrifice: time, money, social, emotional, physical, spiritual, and intellectual. For a J♥, *emotional sacrifices* are the hardest.

Remember that Jacks hold double the power associated with their suit. Being a Heart card, J♥ are born feeling emotions more intensely and for longer periods of time when compared to children associated with other Birth Cards. This temperament is intensified by a J♥'s tendency to only see their own perspective. You see, a J♥ is one of twelve face cards and one of three face cards that show only one side of the person's face. This visual representation is why a J♥ is described as a *one-eyed Jack*. Such a depiction accurately represents them because their perception is limited. They hold a fixed and one-dimensional point of view – their own point of view. When a J♥ is unable to consider the viewpoints or emotions of others, they are less capable of compromising with others, and they tend to take things personally. A key life lesson for all J♥ is that they must learn to manage their intense emotions. Some J♥ learn to manage emotions on their own, but they do so by adopting unhealthy habits. For example, they soothe their emotions by eating pleasurable foods. This behavior may cause a young J♥ to develop issues with their weight which in turn, can invite bullying. Clearly, it is better to encourage a J♥ to find healthier avenues for managing their emotions. While sports can provide emotional release for a J♥, competitive sports may not be the best option. You see, J♥ can become overly emotional when they lose. Therefore, encourage less-competitive sports such as martial arts, aerobics, dancing, skateboarding, biking, skiing, running, hiking, and surfing. Creative expression is likely the best and healthiest way for a J♥ to release their intense emotions. Numerous J♥ are *artistically gifted*. If your J♥ demonstrates artistic talent, sign them up for art classes. The arts include a wide range of activities such as painting, sculpture, theater, music, architecture, dance, literature, and cinema. Purchase arts and crafts kits for them as a gift and watch them shine.

Another unhealthy behavior a J♥ may adopt to manage their considerable emotions is *giving too much*. For instance, imagine you are the parent of a fifteen-year-old J♥ daughter. She has an important Language Arts paper due at the end of the week. On Wednesday, you ask about the paper and find she has barely started it. Your J♥ is very artistic and loves creative writing. What is going on? You discover that same week, your daughter's best friend broke up with her boyfriend. Your daughter decided to devote her time and energy toward soothing her friend's heartache. While she does finish the paper at the last minute, it is far from great work. With a J♥, these types of scenarios can happen repeatedly to the extent that their sacrifices interfere with work and school. Granted, this is the destiny of a J♥, but as stated, they can take these practices too far. These J♥ grow up conditioned to save others. At an extreme, they may manifest a *martyr complex*. The word martyr typically refers to a person who is willing to die for their beliefs. The way a martyr complex reveals itself in a J♥ is that they go a bit overboard to rescue friends or family members. These individuals seek out and attract broken people. Their sense of purpose and identity gets too wrapped up into making sacrifices. Over time, when interventions and sacrifices do not have good consequences, they blame others, failing to see their own personal responsibility in the situation. If you are a parent of a J♥ and you see signs of a martyr complex taking place within them, it's important to talk to them about their level of involvement with others. When someone else has an emotional problem, they need to learn that the problem is not theirs to fix. Reason with them. Ask them to consider the following questions: What are the disadvantages of rescuing the same person repeatedly? If a parent were to fix every problem a child had, how would that child cope in the real world without the parent? Is there a better approach? Is there a more balanced approach to helping others?

According to child psychologists, between the ages of three to five most children learn some degree of how to manage their emotions. Therefore, it is unusual to discover a child in elementary school who has no capacity whatsoever to manage emotions. Sadly, a J♥ child may find themselves in this situation. As such, they can stand out in a classroom by exhibiting *emotional dysregulation*. A child in a state of emotional dysregulation is unable to control or regulate their emotions in a socially acceptable manner. And an adult can unexpectedly trigger the emotions of a J♥. Let's consider an example. Imagine you are a parent of a five-year-old J♥ named Vanessa. You tell Vanessa you are taking her to the kiddie pool at the local aquatic center. Vanessa has a meltdown screaming, "No, no, don't do that to me!" She refuses to put on her bathing suit and instead throws it into your face. After calming down, Vanessa explains she is afraid the 'cats' will scratch her while she is in the 'kitty' pool. When a J♥ is in a state of uncontrollable emotions, they can be overly dramatic and emotionally immature. If an adult directs more negative than positive comments toward them when they are in such a state, they will likely fuel a J♥'s inclination to be *dramatic*. Instead, an adult should allow a J♥ to calm down before discussing any given emotional situation. Also, it may be helpful to express a J♥'s potential for acting better. Going back to Vanessa, you could say, "When you threw your bathing suit at me, it hurt my eye. I know you can treat me better because you usually do so."

A J♥ who is struggling with emotional dysregulation must be taught how to monitor and self-regulate a wide range of emotions. The first step is to teach them how to monitor their positive and negative emotions. A great way to introduce this topic to a child is to read them the book, *How Full is Your Bucket? For Kids* by Tom Rath and Mary Reckmeyer. This book explains that everyone carries around an invisible bucket that contains positive emotions. Throughout a given day, one's bucket is emptied or filled based upon the negative or positive interactions they experience. An adult can use this metaphor to check in with a child, asking them how their bucket is doing. Then, a child can be taught that they have control over their own bucket, filling it through kindness and self-care. I suggest reading the book, *Have You Filled a Bucket Today? A Guide to Daily Happiness for Kids*, by Carol McCloud. This book not only describes ways a child can fill or empty their own bucket, but it also explains how a child can fill or empty other people's buckets. On the Internet, an adult can find ideas, videos, songs, and activities to help teach and implement this bucket concept.

In addition, J♥ benefit from being taught techniques to self-regulate their emotions. Initially, this involves exposing them to activities that calm them down. In any given emotional situation, an adult might be unable to reason with a J♥. *Sensory bins* or *calming corners* are great tools an adult can provide to help a child calm down. Sensory bins are typically large containers filled with materials that stimulate the sense to distract or calm negative emotions. Bins can contain kinetic sand, various types of pasta, water with ice cubes and various sizes of funnels, or soil with plastic snakes and insects. Calming corners are areas in a bedroom or classroom that contain calming furniture and objects, such as a bean bag chair, stuffed animals, and headphones to listen to soothing music. Some J♥ physically need to release negative energy. In school, a J♥ often reveals this need by constantly shaking or tapping their legs at their desks. *Fidget bands* for chairs can offer support for these children. A fidget band is a strap of stretchy material that is attached around the legs of a chair. A child can move the band with their feet to release physical energy without making noises that distract others. As a child becomes aware that calming techniques work, they can begin to choose their own way to calm down, thereby promoting their own ability to self-regulate emotions.

Without intervention, a J♥ suffering from emotional dysregulation can become *volatile* or easily provoked into strong emotions and reactionary behaviors. Obviously, these J♥ can have difficulty maintaining healthy relationships with friends, family members, and teachers. In school, this kind of behavior can invite bullying. A bully will likely perceive the volatile nature of a J♥ as a weakness they can exploit. When a J♥ is consumed with emotions, they become unable to listen to others, which means they may be perceived by adults as being defiant. Such behavior may cause them to be labeled with *oppositional defiant disorder* (ODD). While the causes of ODD are unknown, symptoms include physical and /or verbal aggression, hostility, and defiance toward authority figures which negatively impacts a child's ability to achieve in school. Extreme cases of emotional dysregulation may require a child to receive therapy.

Once a J♥ learns to manage their intense emotions, they tend to discover one of their greatest superpowers – they are *emotionally perceptive* to others. These J♥'s can be counted upon by their friends to show up follow through with plans because they respect the emotions of others. Some J♥ apply this gift to a profession like teaching, counseling, ministry, or nursing as they feel called to support the emotional needs of others. Another way some J♥'s may apply this gift is by taking up causes to fight for the underdogs of the world. These J♥ feel a strong sense of social justice. They are particularly perceptive to the needs of marginalized groups of people. As such, they may pursue law or politics to serve their community.

Are you familiar with Mother Goose nursery rhymes? Perhaps you recall the one that professed, "Jack be nimble, Jack be quick, Jack jumped over the candlestick." Or how about the rhyme that declared, "Jack and Jill went up a hill to fetch a pail of water. Jack fell down and broke his crown and Jill came tumbling after?" Like me, you may be asking yourself two questions. First, why is the name Jack used so much? You can even find the name Jack in fairy tales. Remember Jack who climbed a beanstalk? Secondly, why is the Jack character often depicted as youthful and enthusiastic? The answer to both questions is related to the same inside story. The name Jack originated from the Celtic language to mean one who is healthy and full of vital energy. Over time, the name Jack became a generic reference for any young and energetic person. Authors use the name Jack to represent and invite all young readers, regardless of gender, to their story. The name Jack fits the Jack Birth Cards because they all possess the traits of being *youthful*, *gender-neutral*, and *carefree*. And remember that J♥ are born not feeling constraints around love and relationships. A J♥ may lean into their gender-neutral part of their personality and prefer to view themselves as non-binary, where they do not identify as male or female. And then there are some J♥ who label their identity within a spectrum of all genders and sexualities such as lesbian, gay, bisexual, trans, queer, questioning, intersex, asexual, aromantic, pansexual, or polysexual (LGBTQIAA+). Alternatively, a heterosexual J♥ may express their free will in love by acting like a playboy or playgirl.

Summary of Higher and Lower Personality Traits

Higher: Dedicated, energetic, artistic, emotionally perceptive, sociable, sweet at heart.

Lower: Immature, dramatic, fixed, unhealthy eating, martyr complex, emotionally volatile.

Childhood Influence Mercury Cards

It is common knowledge that a child's personality is most malleable during the formative years – from birth to eight years of age. In the Destiny Card system, the Mercury Cards in a Birth Card's Life Spread reveal influences a child with this Birth Card will experience between birth through age 12. As such, a child's Mercury Cards must be considered so an adult can nurture a child from a place of awareness and work with them from where a child is at in their development. A J♥ child has the following Mercury Cards: **9♠, 10♠, and Q♥**. The Q♥ may mean there is an influential mother who is likely a Heart Birth or Planetary Ruling Card. Alternatively, outside of any specific person associated with these three cards, the basic meanings of these cards describe experiences that may be impactful during this child's formative years. These cards suggest a J♥ child may experience distractions, disappointments, or sacrifices needed in the home. These disappointments may pressure them to work hard. They often need to learn how to master their emotions otherwise they can stifle their potential.

Potential Callings / Vocations by Zodiac Sign

July 30 – Leo: J♥ Planetary Ruling Card

With a J♥ Planetary Ruling Card, these J♥ are doubly prone to exhibit extremes in emotions. This can be channeled into a career in acting. They can also be quite successful in a career in manufacturing, law, business, or journalism if their emotions or ego do not get in the way.

August 28 – Virgo: 9♣ Planetary Ruling Card

Having a 9♣ Planetary Ruling Card provides these J♥ with a blend of sexual charm and mental brilliance that can be used to excel in business, sales, acting, or writing.

September 26 – Libra: 9♠ Planetary Ruling Card

The influence of Libra instills a sense of charm and diplomacy in these J♥, making them a wonderful attorney, diplomat, ambassador, or other government worker. Those who prefer artistic work can succeed as an artist, actor, composer, musician, or writer. A sports career is also possible.

October 24 – Libra or Scorpio: 9♠, or 2♥ and 2♦ Planetary Ruling Card

The Libra affiliated J♥ prefer to support the well-being of others in a career through teaching, counseling, social work, or alternative medicine healing. The Scorpio affiliated individuals prefer to make money through work as an attorney (e.g., in the field of contract or corporate law), real estate broker, or salesperson.

November 22 – Scorpio: 2♥ and 2♦ Planetary Ruling Card

The energy of Mars is strong in these J♥, making them excel in male-dominated professions that include ministry, sports, or executive leadership.

December 20 – Sagittarius: K♥ Planetary Ruling Card

With double the charm from the influences of Sagittarius and a K♥ Planetary Ruling Card, these J♥ are best suited working with people. Suitable careers include ministry, teaching, counseling, alternative medicine healing, acting, law, and politics.

Famous J♥
Scarlett Johansson, actress – 11/22/1984
Drake, rapper – 10/24/1986
Serena Williams, tennis player – 9/26/1981
LeAnne Rimes, singer – 8/28/1982
Sheryl Sandberg, COO of Face Book – 8/28/1969
Billie Jean King, tennis player – 11/22/1943

Welcome to the world of the fun-loving J♣!

J♣ = Mental creativity

According to the Destiny Card system, souls chronologically experience God's lessons within each life incarnation. (Think of these as the universe's lessons if this aligns more with your beliefs.) The Birth Card each soul is born into determines the order and type of lessons a soul experiences. When you examine a Birth Card, you will notice it displays a suit of either a Heart, Club, Diamond, or Spade. This suit is significant because it represents the gifts a person born into this suit will possess and how they will direct their energies to learn lessons in their current life incarnation. A Heart Birth Card retains gifts and experiences life lessons around love and relationships. A Club Birth Card holds capabilities and experiences life lessons in their ability to communicate and absorb knowledge. A Diamond Birth Card possesses talents and experiences life lessons around money and values. And finally, a Spade Birth Card manifests gifts and experiences life lessons in work and health. Souls progress through incarnations and life lessons beginning as Hearts, moving on to Clubs, then Diamonds, and finally as Spades. Therefore, individuals born as Heart Cards are the youngest souls and individuals born as Spades Cards are the oldest souls. In addition, the number on a Birth Card is equally meaningful as souls sequentially experience life lessons beginning as an Ace and culminating with lessons as a King. Jacks are associated with the number eleven. According to the Destiny Card system, when the same number of a Birth Card is doubled, as in the case of an Eleven card, the inherent power of the card is doubled. Eleven cards or Jacks hold double the power in the area associated with their suit.

Having more power makes sense because Jacks are one of the royal court cards. Just as people legitimately born into royalty are associated with various roles, royal court cards hold different roles with different responsibilities. For example, Kings hold more power and more responsibility than a Queen. A Jack is more like a Prince. Still, you are probably wondering what kind of responsibility is associated with the royal court Birth Cards. Normal people are not born ruling over subjects they are responsible for. Instead, royal court Birth Cards are tasked with the responsibility of finalizing a soul's path toward spiritual enlightenment. Across life incarnations as a Jack and progressing to a King, a soul exclusively works toward this goal. The specific role of all Jacks is to initiate steps on the path toward spiritual enlightenment by refining their attitude toward responsibility. **It makes sense, then, that a J♣ child's purpose, gifts, and life lessons revolve around powerful experiences of free will and *not having constraints* to learn about responsibility. And due to being a Club, this child will learn lessons related to not having constraints around *communication* and *knowledge*.**

How to Nurture the Temperament and Personality of a J♣ Child
In the early 1980's, The National Enquirer magazine came up with the slogan, "enquiring minds want to know," which became a pop culture catchphrase. This slogan is the perfect motto for a

J♣. Their need to know is as essential as needing air to breathe. J♣ are busy toddlers who get into everything. To best nurture a young J♣, an intellectually stimulating environment is a top priority. If possible, they need preschool and not day care. Once they reach school age, a creative and rigorous form of education often works best. A J♣ will literally lose their vitality if they attend a school that is focused on *rote learning*. A school that practices rote learning often does so to prepare students for standardized testing. As a J♣ grows older, if their schooling is not providing adequate challenge, they will need extracurricular activities. Encourage mental activities such as computer coding, robotics, drama, music or foreign language lessons, band, book, or chess club. If you are a parent of a J♣ with financial limitations, try to find alternative or low-cost ways to mentally stimulate a J♣. Visit a local Goodwill and purchase board games, especially games that require strategic thinking. Games that involve strategy include Chutes and Ladder, Scrabble, Chess, Settlers of Catan, and Azul. Play these games with your J♣. However, be prepared to lose. You see, a superpower of a J♣ is that they are excellent *strategic thinkers*. A strategic thinker can analyze a topic or goal from multiple perspectives. This means they are gifted at seeing the big picture and understanding all aspects of a situation, including failure points in a plan or idea. Because J♣ are gifted at seeing dual sides of the same issue, they easily win debates. For the debate loving J♣, you may to suggest they join the debate team at school. Also, J♣ love academic competitions, too, so they enjoy being a member of Knowledge Bowl, Math or Science Olympiad, or High School Quiz Bowl, Mock Trial, Doors to Diplomacy competition, and Model Congress or United Nations. With these traits, it is no wonder that many J♣ become successful attorneys, professors, writers, and politicians.

Because J♣ possess a strategic mind, it is imperative for adults to use reason when interacting with them. As a parent or teacher working with a J♣, it is not okay to tell them to do something, "because I said so." They must know why. While child psychologists agree that the age of reasoning with children begins around age seven, J♣ are more advanced and can begin to understand reason as a toddler. You are probably thinking that explaining the whys to a child can be time consuming. Indeed. But, without the *why*, a J♣ may be argumentative. If the situation does not allow the time for reasoning, then it is okay to promise to provide it later. Just be certain to follow through with that promise.

Young J♣ can amaze adults with their creative mental insights. For instance, this is the six-year-old child who says, "I like the number twenty-half. It's not ten, it's just twenty-half!" When a J♣ expresses their insights, they discover another superpower – the *gift of gab*! As such, many J♣ grow up and become successful actors or TV personalities. As an example, Oprah Winfrey is a J♣. However, this same gift affords a young J♣ the ability to *make up stories*. You will marvel at the stories a four-year-old J♣ can come up with. This behavior is amusing until your J♣ directs this gift into telling lies to manipulate others or to get out of trouble. As an example, pretend you are a parent of a four-year-old J♣. One day, you discover drawings with colored markers on the dining room wall. When you ask your J♣ about it, they claim a visiting friend did the deed. Yet, that friend visited yesterday, and you did not see the marks until after they left. It is clear your J♣ is lying. In a moment like this, if an adult gets emotional and makes accusations, the J♣ will not fess up. It is better to wait and talk about the situation when you are calmer. Think through what you will say. Perhaps explain the importance of honesty and possible consequences when a person is not completely honest. Remember that J♣ respond well to reasoning. If possible, apply a *logical consequence*. In parenting, a logical consequence is a reasonable consequence that is related to the child's misbehavior. For instance, cleaning the marker drawings off the dining room wall would be a logical consequence for the scenario given above.

For older J♣, it is far better to allow them some input toward a consequence or provide them with a choice between two consequences. For minor lies, it may be best to tell them they will not be punished if they tell the truth. Praise them when they do tell the truth. Additionally, be on the lookout for an adolescent J♣ to direct their mental creativity in findings ways to talk a parent out of implementing a consequence. They often deploy tactics they know will trigger a parent. If you are a parent of a J♣ and this is happening to you, you may want to try a technique called *gray rocking*. As its name implies, you respond like a rock during your child's mental attacks, acting as neutral and unresponsive as possible to deflect their behavior. This method involves keeping your face calm, avoiding eye contact, and acting like nothing out of the ordinary is going on while your child has a meltdown. While some psychologists have found this method to be effective with manipulative behavior, it may not work with some children. Try it a few times and prepare for the manipulation to get worse before it gets better. If the behavior escalates over time, then stop using it.

If another Birth Card could peek inside the brain of a J♣, they would immediately notice a higher level of mental processing than what they are used to. They would compare it to something like drinking water out of a fire hose. Most J♣ begin to recognize this distinction between themselves and others during adolescence. They may feel abnormal. This may cause a J♣ to get so wrapped up into mental thoughts they forget to express their feelings. Some J♣ build up mental frustrations and then release them by venting out toward others. Like a volcano, their outbursts may be hot and burn those around them. Help a J♣ manage these types of episodes by paying attention to nonverbal signs of anger, such as a clenched jaw or impatient responses to others' questions. Then, ask them to check in with their feelings and express them. You can search the Internet to find emotion charts that can help a younger J♣ to identify emotions they are feeling. For older J♣, ask them to close their eyes and tune into their body. Ask: "Do they feel tense in any areas? How do they feel?" Have them describe their feelings and brainstorm possible causes. Finally, ask what actions need to be taken to alleviate these feelings. Give them choices of activities if they cannot think of any. Encourage your J♣ to immediately take some time to engage in an activity to release their bottled-up feelings.

Have you ever heard of or watched the movie, "The Secret Life of Walter Mitty?" Walter, played by Ben Stiller, endured his boring job and life by daydreaming. That is, excessive daydreaming. Daydreaming represents another kind of behavior a J♣ might display due to their overactive mind. Sure, you are thinking, most people have experienced daydreaming and they have grown up to be just fine. In fact, there are benefits to daydreaming, such as increases in one's creativity and problem-solving skills. But, like so many other good things, too much of one thing can lead to problems. Excessive daydreaming, otherwise known as *maladaptive daydreaming*, is unhealthy. For example, maladaptive daydreamers tend to disassociate from relationships, which only amplifies relational issues when they are engaging in immature and irresponsible behaviors. Alternatively, a J♣ may try to relieve mental pressure through *escapist behaviors*. For example, imagine you are the parent of a thirteen-year-old J♣ boy named Jason. Jason has weekly chores at home which includes taking out the garbage and recycling. Lately, you have had to complete this chore because your J♣ is too busy playing video games. All. The. Time. You are tired of having to constantly nag and argue with him about this responsibility. This is not to say you should prevent a J♣ from playing video games. On the contrary, they need avenues through which to direct their vast mental powers. Wasting some time in frivolous mental pursuits is okay because they possess so much mental energy. Instead, reason with them. They understand the logic of timing associated with garage pick up. Brainstorm solutions together. For instance, they could set an alarm on their phone to remind them of this chore.

To cope, a J♣ must learn how to manage all their mental energy. Going back to the fire hose metaphor, it is not like they can simply turn off or readjust the hose to reduce the water pressure. Rather, they need to learn different and healthy ways to direct their mental energy. Without this coping mechanism, the mental pressure inside their brain can build up and create *anxiety*. Or they will release their mental energy by taking advantage of opportunities to yank an adult's chain just to see how they'll react. These J♣ verbally express themselves and can wear a parent down. Remember J♣ learn lessons around not feeling constraints around communication. This means they may be disrespectful to adults. If you are a parent of a J♣, you may need to reign in this behavior. Establish pre-agreed upon expectations and consequences for disrespectful communication. If they break the rules, hold your J♣ accountable with a consequence. Dare I mention that taking away video playing time might be an effective logical consequence.

Summary of Higher and Lower Personality Traits

Higher: Intellectual, strategic thinker, creative storyteller, progressive thinker, resourceful.

Lower: Irresponsible, dishonest, argumentative, impatient, daydreamer, anxious.

Childhood Influence Mercury Cards

It is common knowledge that a child's personality is most malleable during the formative years – from birth to eight years of age. In the Destiny Card system, the Mercury Cards in a Birth Card's Life Spread reveal influences a child with this Birth Card will experience between birth through age 12. As such, a child's Mercury Cards must be considered so an adult can nurture a child from a place of awareness and work with them from where a child is at in their development. A J♣ child has the following Mercury Cards: **9♦, 5♥, and Q♦**. The Q♦ may mean there is an influential mother who is likely a Diamond Birth or Planetary Ruling Card. Alternatively, outside of any specific person associated with these three cards, the basic meanings of these cards describe experiences that may be impactful during this child's formative years. These cards suggest a J♣ may experience an ending involving something valued, such as a separation from a loved one through divorce or having to give up a valued activity due to a health issue. There also may be financial limitations and they must learn to be resourceful.

Potential Callings / Vocations by Zodiac Sign

January 29 – Aquarius: 4♥ Planetary Ruling Card
With a 4♥ Planetary Ruling Card, these J♣ enjoy work that has a humanitarian aspect to it. They can do well as a professor, scientist, writer, attorney, political leader, or television talk show host.

February 27 – Pisces: 4♦ Planetary Ruling Card
These J♣ may be conflicted in work choices. Having a 4♦ Planetary Ruling Card instills a need for financial stability, but these J♣ dislike routine work. They need creativity in their work which can be accomplished through a career as a writer, attorney, politician, journalist, or a position in the entertainment industry.

March 25 – Aries: 2♣ Planetary Ruling Card
The strong aspect of Mars energy in these Aries combined with the argumentative 2♣ Planetary Ruling Card packs a triple punch in these J♣. They can be quarrelsome and expressive to an extreme. They can successfully redirect this energy into being an excellent trial attorney, writer, military officer, community or political activist, singer, or songwriter.

April 23 – Taurus: 7♠ Planetary Ruling Card
The 7♠ Planetary Ruling Card suggests some health issues may impact these J♣ which can make them high-strung. Artistic expression can help these individuals. Therefore, they do well when they pursue writing, music, art, or careers in the entertainment industry.

May 21 – Taurus or Gemini: 7♠ or 9♦ Planetary Ruling Card
The Taurus affiliated J♣ prefer artistic occupations such as acting or other forms of entertainment. The Gemini affiliated J♣ prefer communicative occupations (e.g., writing, language interpreter, journalism, and teaching).

June 19 – Gemini: 9♦ Planetary Ruling Card
The 9♦ Planetary Ruling Cards instills a bit of financial dissatisfaction in these J♣. Therefore, they are not well suited for financially risky jobs. They do better in professions as a writer, journalist, publisher, scientist, or researcher.

July 17 – Cancer: Q♠ Planetary Ruling Card
The influence of Cancer imparts a sensitivity in these J♣ that makes them well suited for success in theater or politics. Some apply this sensitive attribute into business and can make an excellent manager, director, or executive.

August 15 – Leo: J♣ Planetary Ruling Card

With a J♣ Planetary Ruling card, measures of energy and mental creativity are over the top in these J♣. They can succeed in just about any mentally demanding profession (e.g., attorney, politician, actor, writer, musician, artist, or publisher). Some are blessed with an excellent physique and can find success as a professional athlete.

September 13 – Virgo: 9♦ Planetary Ruling Card

The analytical aspect of Virgo combined with a 9♦ Planetary Ruling Card sets these J♣ up well to succeed in jobs where assessing value is needed (e.g., accounting, appraisal, medical or scientific researcher, or economist).

October 11 – Libra: 7♠ Planetary Ruling Card

With a 7♠ Planetary Ruling Card, these J♣ need to direct their emotional and mental energies into work. They can do well as an artist, musician, singer, actor, government worker, or social reformer.

November 9 – Scorpio: 2♣ and 2♠ Planetary Ruling Cards

The emotional intensity aspect of Scorpio allows these J♣ to succeed as actors. And due to the communicative gifts associated with a 2♣ Planetary Ruling Card they can also do well as an attorney, politician, writer, researcher, physician, or architect.

December 7 – Sagittarius: K♣ Planetary Ruling Card

With a K♣ Planetary Ruling Card, these J♣ hold so much power they may reject responsibility because it seems so overwhelming. Working under the rule of others does not suit them. They often thrive working independently as an artist, attorney, politician, writer, journalist, or in a job in the entertainment industry.

Famous J♣

Nick Lachey, singer – 11/9/1973
Oprah Winfrey, TV personality – 1/29/1954
Danica Patrick, race car driver – 3/25/1982
John Cena, wrestler/ actor – 4/23/1977
Jennifer Lawrence, actress – 8/15/1990
Tyler Perry, actor/ director/ producer – 9/13/1969

Welcome to the world of the fun-loving J♦!

J♦ = Financial creativity

According to the Destiny Card system, souls chronologically experience God's lesson plans within each life incarnation. (Think of these as the Universe's lesson plans if this aligns more with your beliefs.) The Birth Card each soul is born into determines the order and type of lessons a soul experiences. When you examine a Birth Card, you will notice it displays a suit of either a Heart, Club, Diamond, or Spade. This suit is significant because it represents the gifts a person born into this suit will possess and how they will direct their energies to learn lessons in their current life incarnation. A Heart Birth Card retains gifts and experiences life lessons around love and relationships. A Club Birth Card holds capabilities and experiences life lessons in their ability to communicate and absorb knowledge. A Diamond Birth Card possesses talents and experiences life lessons around money and values. And finally, a Spade Birth Card manifests gifts and experiences life lessons in work and health. Souls progress through incarnations and life lessons beginning as Hearts, moving on to Clubs, then Diamonds, and finally as Spades. Therefore, individuals born as Heart Cards are the youngest souls and individuals born as Spades Cards are the oldest souls. In addition, the number on a Birth Card is equally meaningful as souls sequentially experience life lessons beginning as an Ace and culminating with lessons as a King. Jacks are associated with the number eleven. According to the Destiny Card system, when the same number of a Birth Card is doubled, as in the case of an Eleven card, the inherent power of the card is doubled. Eleven cards or Jacks hold double the power in the area associated with their suit.

Having more power makes sense because Jacks are one of the royal court cards. Just as people legitimately born into royalty are associated with various roles, royal court cards hold different roles with different responsibilities. For example, Kings hold more power and more responsibility than a Queen. A Jack is more like a Prince. Still, you are probably wondering what kind of responsibility is associated with the royal court Birth Cards. Normal people are not born ruling over subjects they are responsible for. Instead, royal court Birth Cards are tasked with the responsibility of finalizing a soul's path toward spiritual enlightenment. Across life incarnations as a Jack and progressing to a King, a soul exclusively works toward this goal. The specific role of all Jacks is to initiate the final steps on the path toward spiritual enlightenment by refining their attitude toward responsibility. **It makes sense, then, that a J♦ child's purpose, gifts, and life lessons revolve around powerful experiences of free will and *not having constraints* to learn about personal responsibility. And due to being a Diamond, this child will learn lessons related to not having constraints with *money* and *values*.**

How to Nurture the Temperament and Personality of a J♦ Child

During infancy, J♦ are a joy to watch as they play because they are naturally *creative* and *free-spirited*. Put them in a tub of water with toys and you will notice their face lights up. Bath time is dramatic as a J♦ verbally and non-verbally interacts with their toys, role-playing real life scenarios, producing authentic sounds, and generating amusing commentary. Do not be surprised when your J♦ refuses to leave the tub even though their skin is deeply wrinkled, and the water has long gone cold. Because they enjoy the playfulness of their early years, a J♦ may be hesitant to go off to daycare, preschool, or kindergarten. Give them extra attention and care during this time because this attitude is temporary. Once a J♦ cultivates friendships – and they will in large numbers – they will be in their element. When they discover their new environment has more friends and resources to play with, they will soon forget their fears. In elementary school, a J♦ will continue to enjoy school but more for the access to friends and fun activities than for the mental challenge.

Throughout elementary school, J♦ are clever enough to easily earn excellent grades. This dynamic may change in middle school. This is not to say a J♦ does not possess the mental gifts to do well. They simply do not want to put in the extra work when there is no immediate payoff. Moreover, if a J♦ does not perceive value in the work they are asked to complete, they will rush through it or claim they are finished when they really are not. At an extreme, these students are classroom slackers and clowns. *Witty* by nature, the attention they receive from peers by acting out far surpasses the satisfaction they would earn by completing their assignments. At select times, a teacher working with a J♦ may want to make deals with them by leveraging some form of payoff. As an example, perhaps a math worksheet has been assigned that consists of 25 problems to solve. The J♦ agrees to do their best quality work for a specific amount of time and the teacher only grades the problems they were able to finish. If a J♦ demonstrates an agreed upon proficiency toward the math concept, they can earn some free time. In addition, a teacher may boost achievement of a J♦ by assigning alternative projects that better align with their strengths and interests and demonstrates learning. A J♦'s strengths and interests make them better suited to educational activities such as role-playing, play-based learning, debating, educational video gaming, persuasive writing, tinkering, and engineering projects. Some J♦ are blessed with artistic talent, or they retain skills in conducting research or making presentations. Any of these skills can be integrated into academic tasks. If a J♦ develops a problematic attitude toward traditional schooling, contemplate an alternative educational setting. Options could include online learning, an emotional growth boarding school, an art focused charter or magnet school, a wilderness school, or traditional school that offers work-study programs.

During their teen years, you may notice that a J♦ begins to express an *entrepreneurial spirit*. For example, pretend you are a parent of a twelve-year-old J♦ boy. One day a neighbor calls asking to speak to your son about his lawn mowing business which you are unaware that he started. When you ask your son about it, he confidently explains that he made cold calls knocking at the doors of neighbor's houses and has generated a customer base. Knowing your son has issues with responsibility, you are naturally concerned. This said, encourage him while keeping distant supervision. Refrain from micromanaging. Look for opportunities to discuss concepts of responsibility, commitment, and money management. Remember J♦ are destined to learn lessons from not feeling constraints around money. This often means a J♦ will be irresponsible with the money they earn. Avoid lecturing him if some irresponsible behaviors negatively impact their business. Lessons around responsibility will be more powerful when they are learned outside of the home. J♦ need to explore opportunities like this to discover their superpower – *salesmanship*.

Countless numbers of adult J♦ are professional salespeople, successfully selling products, ideas, or lifestyles. Even if a J♦ does not pursue sales as a career, they often are promoting something in their work. For example, pretend a twenty-year-old J♦ creates a successful diet and exercise program. The program is enthusiastically shared with family and friends, who later encourage the J♦ to post videos of it on YouTube. The J♦ creates the content and sets up a YouTube subscription and becomes an instant success. In the mind of a J♦, this work is not sales. They are helping others. When a J♦ sells a lifestyle of *higher truths and values*, they are expressing a higher side of their Birth Card.

It is well-known that when a person is described as acting like a used car salesman, this depiction is not intended as a compliment. A used car salesman has the reputation of being pushy, sleazy, and just down-right dishonest. Unfortunately, these behaviors can characterize some J♦ when they manifest the lowest traits of their Birth Card. Remember that J♦ learn lessons around not having constraints around money and *values*. This means that parenting an adolescent J♦ will often involve managing behaviors that reflect poor values. And sometimes this can mean a J♦ will lie to get what they want. Clear expectations and boundaries are essential. For some parents, this reality will be exhausting. A typical example is a J♦ who throws a party when the parents are out of town. Having so many friends, the J♦'s party is a blowout and things quickly gets out of hand. Property damage results. When told they are grounded, a J♦ will complain that others are to blame. They may lie saying they invited a couple of friends over and didn't know others would show up. They will endeavor to talk their parents out of the grounding. You see, J♦ are also extremely persuasive and they will try to wear a parent down. Parents must stand firm when holding a J♦ accountable for their actions. Make sure to assign realistic consequence and follow through with it. When a parent repeatedly gives in to a J♦, they will be reinforcing their lower personality traits. This also means that parenting styles matter when raising a J♦. If a parent adopts a friend-like parenting style with a J♦, this approach will work short term but then be doomed long-term. In this case, a stricter parent should take over the discipline part of parenting. Likewise, a laisse-faire or inconsistent discipline approach can establish learned behavior that will manifest as irresponsibility in other areas of a J♦ life, making the practice of adulting for them difficult later in life.

When J♦ are repeatedly held accountable for immature or irresponsible behavior, they may develop the perception that all a parent does is nag, nag, nag. These J♦ complain that this parent constantly says, "Why didn't you do this? Why didn't you do that? How many times have we talked about this?" At a certain point, these J♦ stop listening to a parent. All the negative judgement is too much. If this describes your situation, you may want to evaluate the amount of positive versus negative statements that you direct at your J♦. And keep in mind the wise advice of Albert Einstein, who stated, "Insanity is doing the same thing over and over and expecting different results." Therefore, try a different approach. Any given trait of a child can be expressed in a positive or negative manner. Pick a negative behavior and try to redirect it in a positive manner. As an example, let's say a J♦ is clowning around in school and peer pressuring friends to join in. If you are a teacher of this J♦, you can view this behavior in a positive light by seeing them as being gifted with the power of persuasion. This gift should not be suppressed. Instead, it should be redirected. Find a cause that will interest this J♦. As an example, let's say recess is important to this child and school funding issues have reduced the amount of sports equipment at your school. Encourage this child to organize a fundraising event with you to solve this problem. Ask them to persuade their peers to help.

Summary of Higher and Lower Personality Traits

Higher: Highly persuasive, witty, independent, salesmanship, artistic, flirtatious.

Lower: Too proud, lazy, frivolous spender, irresponsible, deceitful, noncommittal.

Childhood Influence Mercury Cards
It is common knowledge that a child's personality is most malleable during the formative years – from birth to eight years of age. In the Destiny Card system, the Mercury Cards in a Birth Card's Life Spread reveal influences a child with this Birth Card will experience between birth through age 12. As such, a child's Mercury Cards must be considered so an adult can nurture a child from a place of awareness and work with them from where a child is at in their development. A J♦ child has the following Mercury Cards: **4♥, 5♦, and 4♣**. Alternatively, outside of any specific person associated with these three cards, the basic meanings of these cards describe experiences that may be impactful during this child's formative years. These cards suggest the early years for a J♦ are harmonious. They are born into a loving family and experience good health. This said, there is some possibility of discontent related to changes in their family's financial or living situation.

Potential Callings / Vocations by Zodiac Sign

January 16 – Capricorn: 6♣ Planetary Ruling Card
With a 6♣ Planetary Ruling Card, these J♦ may play and procrastinate during their early years. Conventional Capricorn instills a strong patriotic belief in them that attracts them to government or military work. Artistic leaning individuals can make a career out of their creative self-expression.

February 14 – Aquarius: 6♠ Planetary Ruling Card
The visionary aspect of Aquarius allows these J♦ to pursue entrepreneurial ideas and succeed as a salesperson. They can even sell their ideas as a writer, especially if they are critiquing or recommending ideas or places to travel.

March 12 – Pisces: Q♥ Planetary Ruling Card
With a Q♥ Planetary Ruling Card, these J♦ possess an abundance of charm that ensures financial success. They can do well as an actor, politician, church leader, writer, chef, or pharmaceutical salesperson.

April 10 – Aries, 2♠ Planetary Ruling Card
With a 2♠ Planetary Ruling Card, these J♦ work well with others. The influence of Aries tends to promote them quickly into leadership. They make excellent promoters and salespeople, particularly selling their ideas to the public (e.g., speaker, writer, or politician).

May 8 – Taurus: 4♦ Planetary Ruling Card

The need for stability in finances associated with Taurus coupled with a 4♦ Planetary Ruling Card motivates these J♦ to work hard. They make an excellent real estate broker, home builder, salesperson, writer, politician, or civic leader.

June 6 – Gemini: 4♥ Planetary Ruling Card

With the communicative gifts of Gemini and charm connected to their 4♥ Planetary Ruling Card, these J♦ can do well selling ideas to the public. They can successfully make a career as an attorney, teacher, public speaker, journalist, television commentator, comedian, actor, or research scientist.

July 4 – Cancer: K♣ Planetary Ruling Card

The leadership qualities inherent with a K♣ Planetary Ruling Card makes these J♦ wish for, but also fear the responsibility associated with leadership. When they accept these qualities there is nothing they cannot do well. They can find much success across a spectrum of careers such as military leader, politician, actor, or leader in entertainment to name a few.

August 2 – Leo: J♦ Planetary Ruling Card

Creativity runs strong in these double J♦ which allows them to achieve in professions that apply creativity such as a screen writer, play wright, actor, financial planner, or business owner.

Famous J♦

Lin-Manuel Miranda, singer/ composer – 1/16/1980
Tammy Duckworth, politician/military veteran – 3/12/1968
Mitt Romney, politician – 3/12/1947
Carole Baskin, big-cats rights activist – 6/6/1961
Post Malone, rapper – 7/4/1995

Welcome to the world of the fun-loving J♠!

J♠ = Artistic creativity

According to the Destiny Card system, souls chronologically experience God's lessons within each life incarnation. (Think of these as the universe's lessons if this aligns more with your beliefs.) The Birth Card each soul is born into determines the order and type of lessons a soul experiences. When you examine a Birth Card, you will notice it displays a suit of either a Heart, Club, Diamond, or Spade. This suit is significant because it represents the gifts a person born into this suit will possess and how they will direct their energies to learn lessons in their current life incarnation. A Heart Birth Card retains gifts and experiences life lessons around love and relationships. A Club Birth Card holds capabilities and experiences life lessons in their ability to communicate and absorb knowledge. A Diamond Birth Card possesses talents and experiences life lessons around money and values. And finally, a Spade Birth Card manifests gifts and experiences life lessons in work and health. Souls progress through incarnations and life lessons beginning as Hearts, moving on to Clubs, then Diamonds, and finally as Spades. Therefore, individuals born as Heart Cards are the youngest souls and individuals born as Spades Cards are the oldest souls. In addition, the number on a Birth Card is equally meaningful as souls sequentially experience life lessons beginning as an Ace and culminating with lessons as a King. Jacks are associated with the number eleven. According to the Destiny Card system, when the same number of a Birth Card is doubled, as in the case of an Eleven card, the inherent power of the card is doubled. Eleven cards or Jacks hold double the power in the area associated with their suit.

Having more power makes sense because Jacks are one of the royal court cards. Just as people legitimately born into royalty are associated with various roles, royal court cards hold different roles with different responsibilities. For example, Kings hold more power and more responsibility than a Queen. A Jack is more like a Prince. Still, you are probably wondering what kind of responsibility is associated with the royal court Birth Cards. Normal people are not born ruling over subjects they are responsible for. Instead, royal court Birth Cards are tasked with the responsibility of finalizing a soul's path toward spiritual enlightenment. Across life incarnations as a Jack and progressing to a King, a soul exclusively works toward this goal. The specific role of all Jacks is to initiate steps on the path toward spiritual enlightenment by refining their attitude toward responsibility. **It makes sense, then, that a J♠ child's purpose, gifts, and life lessons revolve around powerful experiences of free will and *not having constraints* to learn about personal responsibility. And due to being a Spade, this child will learn lessons related to not having constraints around *work* and *health*.**

How to Nurture the Temperament and Personality of a J♠ Child

If one were to take notes on the behavior of a young J♠, they would find them an interesting mix of contrasts. For instance, imagine that you are a coach of a soccer team that has made the playoffs. One of your key players is a male J♠ named Jack. During pregame practice for a playoff game, Jack is upsetting you because he is goofing off. Fifteen minutes later, the official game is being played and Jack is the most focused and disciplined player. Later, at a celebratory pizza party, you observe Jack being reserved, quiet, and thoughtful. Minutes later you see him acting like an extrovert. The reason these behaviors can coexist in a J♠ is because they are old souls. Because they have experienced so many previous lives, a J♠ can subconsciously tap into many different behaviors and spectrums of personality. This explains why many J♠ have become successful actors or actresses. Therefore, encourage a J♠ to take drama or art classes that can showcase their talents. The arts include a wide range of activities such as painting, sculpture, theater, music, architecture, dance, literature, and cinema. While a J♠ can be lazy in certain areas of their life, they tend to be most industrious when they follow their artistic interests. And because they are gifted with the ability to perceive the motives of many different personalities, J♠s can do well in business. These J♠ can effectively tell a client or customer exactly what they want to hear. Because J♠ have similar aspects as a 3♠, you may want to read about the personality traits of this Birth Card.

From a very young age, J♠ exhibit an affinity toward learning. Being an old soul, they are born knowing that knowledge is power. They embrace both informal and formal educational opportunities. They can do well in traditional school settings even if they are diagnosed with a learning disability. The reason I mention a learning disability is because some J♠ are diagnosed having one or two. Conditions that can manifest include autism (high-functioning Asperger's syndrome), attention-deficit disorder, and obsessive-compulsive disorder. Although these conditions are viewed as deficits by many adults, for a J♠ they are often assets. Environmental activist, Greta Thunberg, is a J♠ and an excellent example of this. As a person diagnosed with high functioning Asperger's syndrome, it is not surprising that Thunberg comes up with unconventional ideas. In addition, Thunberg has been diagnosed with obsessive-compulsive disorder. Clearly, this condition explains Thunberg's dogged determination and hyper focus in spreading her message about climate change Even if a J♠ does not display learning disabilities, they will still express some wild, out-of-the-box ideas. You see, because J♠ are to learn lessons around not having constraints in work, their minds do not work the same as most people. Their superpower is that they are *original thinkers*. Writer, J.R.R. Tolkien was a J♠. Did he not invent a fantastical world when he wrote *The Lord of the Rings* trilogy? As a parent or teacher of a J♠, try not to suppress or express disdain toward their wild and crazy ideas. Take their unconventional ideas seriously and support them any way you can.

Speaking of unconventional; a unique parenting style may be required to effectively raise a J♠. Even if you have successfully raised other children, the same tried and true techniques will not always work with a J♠. Bear with me as I explain the reason for this. The J♠ is one of twelve face cards and one of the three face cards that show only one side of the person's face. This visual representation is why a J♠ is described as a *one-eyed Jack*. Such a depiction accurately represents them because their perception is limited. They hold a one-dimensional point of view – their own point of view. This temperament is intensified by a J♠'s tendency to feel no constraints around work. This may mean they may act without the ability to consider how their behavior impacts others. These J♠ tend to take short cuts. At an extreme, they may con others or rip them off to get what they want. And, when a two-eyed adult with depth perception interacts with a one-dimensional child, conflicts are sure to arise. Let's consider an example. Imagine you are a parent of a three-year-old J♠ named Colter. Helping Colter in the bathroom, you pull several pieces of toilet paper off the roll and hand it to him. Colter immediately starts yelling, "Put it back! Put it back!" This scenario describes the one-dimensional nature of a J♠ who is feeling the need for independence. In such a situation, it is best to allow Colter to get his own toilet paper rather than insisting he use what you pulled off.

One of the best ways to nurture a J♠ is to expose them to the concept of *multiple perspectives*. This involves exposing a child to multiple and varying viewpoints around a single context. Child psychologists agree this approach can be started at a young age, say around kindergarten age. For this age, I recommend reading the book, *Fish is Fish* by Leo Lionni. This book tells the story of a friendship between a tadpole and a minnow. The friendship changes when the tadpole develops into a frog. After leaving the pond, the frog adopts a new perspective that is different from the minnow. This book can help jumpstart a conversation about how different perspectives can create problems in relationships. I also love *The Story of Ruby Bridges* by Robert Coles because it portrays multiple perspectives through a lens of prejudice. Whether you are a parent or teacher, you can find a lot of other children's books and videos that can be used to teach about multiple perspectives. Using role play can also help teach this concept. During these lessons, ask a J♠ to try to imagine themselves in the shoes of other individuals. On the Internet, you can find problem-solving charts that consider different points of view as part of the process of solving a problem. This kind of activity can help a J♠ consider the positive and negative repercussions their actions can have on others. The objective is to get a J♠ to internalize the process of considering different viewpoints, so they automatically incorporate it into their thinking when they are older.

Additionally, a more relaxed or non-confrontational parenting style may be necessary to adopt with a J♠ to avoid power struggles. Remember, J♠ are tempted to lie and they are most likely to experiment with this lower trait when they are young. A J♠ will engage in anything between white lies, half-truths and outright lies. For a parent who values truth, this behavior can drive them crazy. A preschool aged J♠ will begin to test boundaries around honesty in small ways. For instance, imagine you are a parent of a four-year-old J♠ daughter. One afternoon, she asks for Oreo cookies as a snack. You say, "Yes, but no more than three." From another room you see her take six Oreos out of the cookie jar. Minutes later you ask your daughter how many cookies she ate. She insists she took and ate three. In this instance, avoid labeling your daughter a liar. Instead, ask for clarity, "Perhaps you misunderstood me. How many cookies did I say you could eat? How many did you eat?" Give your daughter a second chance to tell the truth. Nudge her toward the truth by looking inside the cookie jar and saying, "That sounds a bit unrealistic. I know there were more Oreos in this jar. Take a few minutes and think about what happened. Then tell me what really happened." Make certain this child knows they will be in less trouble if they tell the truth. Be sure to follow through with this stance. At another time, start a discussion about the importance of honesty and the harmful effects of lying. For an older J♠, initiate conversations when a television show or movie provides a good example of lying. And don't forget that some personality deficits can be reframed into assets. Encourage your J♠ to direct their inclination to tell fantastical stories by urging them to journal and write creative stories. Without some intervention, a J♠ may continue to test their boundaries with lying in more extensive ways. Pick your battles if this is the situation with your J♠. If you find lying increases to the level of being compulsive, perhaps seek therapy or family counseling.

Summary of Higher and Lower Personality Traits

Higher: Industrious, artistic, inventive, independent, humble, successful with people.

Lower: Con artist, liar, untrustworthy, unfaithful, take shortcuts, irresponsible.

Childhood Influence Mercury Cards
It is common knowledge that a child's personality is most malleable during the formative years – from birth to eight years of age. In the Destiny Card system, the Mercury Cards in a Birth

Card's Life Spread reveal influences a child with this Birth Card will experience between birth through age 12. As such, a child's Mercury Cards must be considered so an adult can nurture a child from a place of awareness and work with them from where a child is at in their development. A J♠ child has the following Mercury Cards: **8♣ and 9♣**. Alternatively, outside of any specific person associated with these two cards, the basic meanings of these cards describe experiences that may be impactful during this child's formative years. These cards suggest a J♠ is blessed with mental power that ensures early educational achievement. Also, they may be impacted by a personal illness or by a death in the family.

Potential Callings / Vocations by Zodiac Sign

January 3 – Capricorn: 10♦ Planetary Ruling Card

With a 10♦ Planetary Ruling Card, these J♠ are tempted toward materialism which has the potential of dissipating their power. They can succeed as a writer, actor, scientist, engineer, or healer (especially as a naturopathic doctor).

February 1 – Aquarius: 8♠ Planetary Ruling Card

The individualistic aspect of Aquarius and the power inherent to having an 8♠ Planetary Ruling Card propels these J♠ in any artistic-based career they decide to follow (e.g., actor, writer, singer, public speaker, athlete, musician, or any other kind of performer).

Famous J♠

J. R. R. Tolkien, writer – 1/3/1892
Florence Pugh, actress – 1/3/1996
Harry Styles, singer/ songwriter – 2/1/1994
Greta Thunberg, environmental activist – 1/3/2003
Mel Gibson, actor – 1/3/1956
Lisa Marie Presley, singer – 2/1/1968

Chapter 15

Descriptions of the Queen Birth Cards

Welcome to the world of the motherly Q♥!

Q♥ = Serve through love and relationships

According to the Destiny Card system, souls chronologically experience God's lessons within each life incarnation. (Think of these as the universe's lessons if this aligns more with your beliefs.) The Birth Card each soul is born into determines the order and type of lessons a soul experiences. When you examine a Birth Card, you will notice it displays a suit of either a Heart, Club, Diamond, or Spade. This suit is significant because it represents the gifts a person born into this suit will possess and how they will direct their energies to learn lessons in their current life incarnation. A Heart Birth Card retains gifts and experiences life lessons around love and relationships. A Club Birth Card holds capabilities and experiences life lessons in their ability to communicate and absorb knowledge. A Diamond Birth Card possesses talents and experiences life lessons around money and values. And finally, a Spade Birth Card manifests gifts and experiences life lessons in work and health. Souls progress through incarnations and life lessons beginning as Hearts, moving on to Clubs, then Diamonds, and finally as Spades. Therefore, individuals born as Heart Cards are the youngest souls and individuals born as Spades Cards are the oldest souls. In addition, the number on a Birth Card is equally meaningful as souls sequentially experience life lessons beginning as an Ace and culminating with lessons as a King. Queen playing cards are associated with the number twelve. Holding a higher value than most other cards is inherent to Queens because they are one of the royal court cards. As such, they possess considerable power and responsibility. Just as people legitimately born into royalty are associated with various roles, royal court cards hold various roles and responsibilities. Kings and Queens co-rule their kingdom, while Jacks are more like a Prince holding less responsibility.

You are probably wondering what kind of responsibility is associated with royal court Birth Cards. In the real world, average people are not born ruling over subjects in their community. A person associated with a royal court Birth Card is tasked with the responsibility of benefiting humanity by applying wisdom from incarnations as an Ace through a Ten in their suit. While a King rules, a Queen serves. This role of service is depicted in the Queen playing cards. When you examine these cards, you will notice the Queen is holding a flower. Look closer at how the flowers are being held. The Queen holds the flower like a scepter to symbolize the area of their power and responsibility. Now you are probably wondering: what do flowers represent? You may be aware of the individual meanings of specific flowers. For instance, roses symbolize love. Red roses express deep love and desire, while yellow roses symbolize friendship. However, more broadly speaking, flowers represent feminine energy and the possibility of new life as they are part of the reproductive cycle of plants. **It makes sense, then, that a Q♥ child's purpose, gifts, and life lessons revolve around a powerful mothering energy that inspires them to *serve* humanity. And due to being a Heart, this child will learn lessons on how to serve humanity by modeling higher principles in *love* and *relationships*.**

How to Nurture the Temperament and Personality of a Q♥ Child
Every parent can tell you stories about their child when they were deep into the "mine" stage. For example, imagine a five-year-old boy comes home from kindergarten and asks his mom for a snack of goldfish crackers. His two-year-old sister, upon hearing this, chimes in that she wants goldfish crackers too. Mom discovers there is only one small pack of crackers left so she explains they will need to share. After receiving half of the crackers, the two-year-old refuses to accept this decision. Screaming "Mine! Mine! Mine!" the toddler grabs the five-year-old's crackers. While this is normal behavior for a toddler, it can look different if your child is a Q♥. In fact, this stage is often a breeze for parents to get through with a Q♥. A parent of a Q♥ can simply explain to them how to share and why they should do it. Then, a parent can ask them to practice sharing and praise them to reinforce their behavior. Of course, all bets are off if your child has missed a nap or has skipped a meal. But, generally, a Q♥ will easily learn how to share. You see, Q♥s are born with a *generous* and *loving* temperament. This is also why you may notice how young Q♥ love playing roles in which they can *mother others*. They enjoy hosting tea parties, playing house, overseeing pretend school, or babysitting their siblings. And, by all means, they love to take the role of the one who is in charge. Encourage these tendencies in your Q♥. If your Q♥ does not have siblings, support their nature by purchasing them a pet to care for or by teaching them how to garden, cook, bake, or any other nurturing activity. For older Q♥, urge them to sign up for a CPR class or a lifeguard training program, or to volunteer at a local soup kitchen to feed the homeless.

With such superpowers, it is no wonder Q♥ children are well loved by their elementary school teachers and classmates alike. Q♥ also stand out in school as they are *bright* and *inquisitive*. Notably Q♥ tend to achieve higher proficiency scores in language arts when compared to students of the same age. This makes sense because language arts curriculum tends to be prioritized in elementary education and Q♥s are highly motivated to earn the love and affection of their teachers. If you are a parent of a Q♥, do not be surprised if they come home from school and want to regale you with stories of learning something that emotionally impacted them. Be an active listener during these times and encourage your Q♥'s enthusiasm. Some Q♥ may discover they are emotionally drawn to the arts. The arts include a wide range of activities such as painting, sculpture, theater, music, architecture, dance, literature, and cinema. Purchase arts and crafts kits for them as a gift and watch them shine.

With such early achievement in school, it is common for Q♥ to be guided into leadership opportunities between middle and high school. Keep in mind the leadership of a Queen looks different from the leadership of a King. Queens reign through service to their community in the area associated with their suit. Q♥ reign, or perhaps it would be more accurate to say they 'rain' love in their role as a leader. Have you ever watched the TV show, *Dog Whisperer*, starring Cesar Millan? Millan is a highly skilled dog trainer. Within a 30-minute episode of his show, Millan would demonstrate his ability to transform the behavior of a dog. How easily he could win over the hearts and minds of the most aggressive and ill-disciplined dogs seemed magical. Watching him work, you cannot help but wonder: what is his secret? In a 2016 interview with Meredith Vieira, Millan was asked to share his secret. He said he approached each dog with two intentions. First, he presented himself as an authority figure. Because dogs socialize in packs, this means a dog owner should act like a pack leader. Second, he interacted with dogs from a place of love. What is remarkable about this process is that it resembles what a Q♥ instinctually knows how to treat all living things. Of course, Millan understands this because he is a Q♥. Therefore, Q♥ should be encouraged to take on leadership roles that leverage their relational gifts. If you are a teacher of a Q♥, recommend them to serve as a member of their school's *restorative justice team.* Restorative justice teams consist of adults and student-leaders who facilitate conflict resolution situations for students in the school. Through such a role also get a Q♥ will likely expose another superpower. Q♥ are gifted in *seeing the best in others.* You see, Q♥ have experienced many past lives as other Heart Birth Cards; and they can subconsciously draw upon the emotions from these past lives. It is as if they can emotionally walk in other people's shoes and understand their feelings, motivations, strengths, and weaknesses. Such a trait allows a Q♥ to love others without much bias or judgement. In addition, they tend to model higher principles in love by showing respect for diversity in all its forms – other people's culture, history, and life experiences. They refrain from expressing harsh criticism and prefer to see the best in others no matter their mistakes in life. They model forgiveness and are all about giving people second chances in life. Consider yourself blessed if you have a Q♥ in your life!

Mothering is not an individual experience though. Hence, from a young age, a Q♥ will be tested in how they manage *relational boundaries.* Relational boundaries are behaviors that separate people and help a person distinguish their unique identity from that of another person. It is especially important for a Q♥ to advocate for their own needs when relating with others. Let's consider an example. Amanda, Ellen, and Samara are close friends who attend the same high school. They particularly enjoy hanging out together and listening to music. When Amanda hears that one of their favorite duos, Dan and Shay, will be appearing at a local venue she asks her friends if they want to go. Because her mother works at the venue, she promised her two friends that she could get tickets. However, the event sells out quickly and Amanda's mother is only able to get two tickets. Amanda tells her mom she plans to give both tickets to her friends. You see, Amanda is a Q♥. Amanda's mom disagrees with this idea and suggests that she pick a random number between one and 100 and whichever friend can guess a number closest to it wins one of the tickets. Amanda ends up giving both tickets to her friends. The day after the concert, Amanda feels heartbroken. When Amanda complains to her mom about it, her mother has no sympathy. While Amanda's behavior represents an act of kindness, this kind of behavior may be problematic if a person repeatedly allows the needs of others to supersede their own.

The underlying issue in scenarios like Amanda's is that Q♥s believe in the golden rule: *treat others as you would want to be treated.* The problem is that a Q♥ also expects others to follow this same rule. When a Q♥ continues to follow this rule and others do not reciprocate, resentment toward others may manifest. If you are a parent of a Q♥ and observe this kind of behavior, try to get your child to process these situations. Encourage them to express their own needs and wants. Perhaps help them role play what to say to others. They must perceive that their own needs are equally as important and respected as other people's needs. They also need to understand that others cannot read their mind. They are responsible for not only communicating their needs, but also advocating their importance. Without this realization and practice, a Q♥ may grow into adulthood continuing to suppress their needs and refusing to ask for help. These Q♥ often embrace an identity in which they make sacrifices for others. This identity develops a false sense of satisfaction when they overly nurture others. Yet, internally, they sacrifice a peaceful mind. Over time, some Q♥ may manifest co-dependent relationships when making sacrifices for others is tied to feeling worthless unless they are needed by others. Because this behavior can be generationally passed along to other family members, family therapy may be warranted.

Summary of Higher and Lower Personality Traits

Higher: Attractive, charismatic, sensual, marriageable, generous, leader, compassionate.

Lower: Lazy, moody, self-indulgent, blind to the fault of others, over-nurturing.

Childhood Influence Mercury Cards
It is common knowledge that a child's personality is most malleable during the formative years – from birth to eight years of age. In the Destiny Card system, the Mercury Cards in a Birth Card's Life Spread reveal influences a child with this Birth Card will experience between birth through age 12. As such, a child's Mercury Cards must be considered so an adult can nurture a child from a place of awareness and work with them from where a child is at in their development. A Q♥ child has the following Mercury Cards: **10♣, J♦, and J♠**. The Jacks may mean there is an influential father and/ or brothers who are likely a Diamond or Spade Birth or Planetary Ruling Card. Alternatively, outside of any specific person associated with these three cards, the basic meanings of these cards may be impactful during this child's formative years. These cards suggest a Q♥ shines in early educational experiences. They tend to be born into a highly creative family that encourages independence in their children.

Potential Callings / Vocations by Zodiac Sign

July 29 – Leo: Q♥ Planetary Ruling Card
Having a Q♥ Planetary Ruling Card, doubles the emotional sensitivity in these individuals. They can direct this sensitivity into theater, writing, music, teaching, or art. Care should be taken if they are compelled to direct these energies into spiritual ministry or politics because these occupations may emotionally drain them.

August 27 – Virgo: 10♣ Planetary Ruling Card
The critical aspect of Virgo blends well with these Q♥. They make an excellent business manager, executive, teacher, publisher, politician, life coach, or writer.

September 25 – Libra: 8♦ Planetary Ruling Card

The 8♦ Planetary Ruling Card instills a wonderful sense of value and money power in these Q♥. They can succeed in sales (especially beauty products), entertainment, law, and politics.

October 23 – Libra or Scorpio: 8♦ or K♠ and 5♣ Planetary Ruling Cards

The Libra affiliated Q♥ prefer careers in business or selling home-related or beauty products. Scorpio affiliated individuals possess strong leadership qualities. Many of these individuals pursue positions in medicine, law, politics, or the entertainment industry.

November 21 – Scorpio: K♠ and 5♣ Planetary Ruling Cards

With a K♠ Planetary Ruling Card, it would be far better for these Q♥ to find a position whereby they are calling the shots. They can do well as a writer, teacher, artist, actor, musician, or minister.

December 19 – Sagittarius: 3♥ Planetary Ruling Card

A 3♥ Planetary Ruling Card manifests some emotional obstacles in life for these Q♥. Even so, they can succeed in an assortment of careers (e.g., scientist, engineer, nurse, business leader, musician, writer, or artist).

Famous Q♥

Ryan Reynolds, actor – 10/23/1976
Criss Angel, magician – 12/19/1967
Ken Burns, documentary filmmaker – 7/29/ 1953
Meghan McCain, TV host – 10/23/1984
Sanjay Gupta, neurosurgeon / journalist – 10/23/1969

Welcome to the world of the motherly Q♣!

Q♣ = Serve through communication and knowledge

According to the Destiny Card system, souls chronologically experience God's lessons within each life incarnation. (Think of these as the universe's lessons if this aligns more with your beliefs.) The Birth Card each soul is born into determines the order and type of lessons a soul experiences. When you examine a Birth Card, you will notice it displays a suit of either a Heart, Club, Diamond, or Spade. This suit is significant because it represents the gifts a person born into this suit will possess and how they will direct their energies to learn lessons in their current life incarnation. A Heart Birth Card retains gifts and experiences life lessons around love and relationships. A Club Birth Card holds capabilities and experiences life lessons in their ability to communicate and absorb knowledge. A Diamond Birth Card possesses talents and experiences life lessons around money and values. And finally, a Spade Birth Card manifests gifts and experiences life lessons in work and health. Souls progress through incarnations and life lessons beginning as Hearts, moving on to Clubs, then Diamonds, and finally as Spades. Therefore, individuals born as Heart Cards are the youngest souls and individuals born as Spades Cards are the oldest souls. In addition, the number on a Birth Card is equally meaningful as souls sequentially experience life lessons beginning as an Ace and culminating with lessons as a King. Queen playing cards are associated with the number twelve. Holding a higher value than most other cards is inherent to Queens because they are one of the royal court cards. As such, they possess more power and responsibility. Just as people legitimately born into royalty are associated with various roles, royal court cards hold various roles with various responsibilities. Kings and Queens co-rule their kingdom, while Jacks are more like a Prince holding less responsibility.

You are probably wondering what kind of responsibility is associated with royal court Birth Cards. In the real world, average people are not born ruling over subjects in their community. A person associated with a royal court Birth Card is tasked with the responsibility of benefiting humanity by applying wisdom from incarnations as an Ace through a Ten in their suit. While a King rules, a Queen serves. This role of service is depicted in the Queen playing cards. When you examine these cards, you will notice the Queen is holding a flower. Look closer at how the flower is being held. The Queen holds their flower like a scepter to symbolize the area of their power and responsibility. Now you are probably wondering: what do flowers represent? You may be aware of the individual meanings of specific flowers. For instance, roses symbolize love. Red roses express deep love and desire, while yellow roses symbolize friendship. However, more broadly speaking, flowers represent feminine energy and the possibility of new life as they are part of the reproductive cycle of plants. **It makes sense, then, that a Q♣ child's purpose, gifts, and life lessons revolve around a powerful mothering energy that inspires them to *serve* humanity. And due to being a Club, this child will learn lessons on how to serve humanity by modeling higher principles around *communication* and *knowledge*.**

How to Nurture the Temperament and Personality of a Q♣ Child
Young Q♣ are like mental sponges. They grasp things quickly and will work hard to satiate their curious mind. If you are a parent of a Q♣, purchase them preschool workbooks to feed their appetite for knowledge. Once they are in school, make sure they have a planner and encourage them to think about their own short and long-term goals. You see, one Q♣ superpower is that they are highly *organized planners*. They are easy to incentivize and enjoy the organizing part of the goal-setting process. If their goals do not work out as they expected, help talk them through lessons learned and opportunities for new approaches. You see, Q♣ are also optimists at heart and will embrace self-improvement. To nurture a Q♣, adults should implement *positive reinforcement* strategies. Positive reinforcement is when an adult rewards a child for positive behavior. In school, rewards can include praise (e.g., thumbs up, cheering, clapping, high five, or hug), stickers, special awards, free time, certificates, books, or small toys. At home, rewards can include praise, allowance, or special treats (e.g., going out to dinner, playing a game they want to play, or providing an extra privilege like staying up later than their normal bedtime). A Q♣ is the ideal child to assign weekly chores and then reward them for accomplishing them.

Q♣ children are creative, but not in the same way as other creative Birth Cards. Their creativity stems from their ability to *synthesize* information which involves bringing together different ideas from various materials or resources, combining them into common themes, and then creating an inventive product. Synthesis is considered a higher order thinking skill. Most often the product for a Q♣ is a presentation or creative writing. This trait explains why many Q♣ make excellent teachers and writers. They can mentally absorb and synthesize complex information. Then, they can communicate information in an innovative, logical, and kid-friendly way. In education, this teaching ability is called *pedagogical content knowledge*. Pedagogical content knowledge is the ability of a person to take and synthesize content and student knowledge in such a way as to make instruction of information understandable to students. If you are a teacher of a Q♣, you count on them to help tutor other children in the classroom.

Because Q♣ are *life-long learners* know that any money spent developing their mental gifts is money well spent. Sign your Q♣ up for extra-curricular activities, such as coding classes, robotics, summer camp, drama, or theater classes. If money is an issue, get them a library card and sign them up for free activities like scouting, a community gardening club, or online clubs (NASA kids club, Science Explores STEM, Scholastic Book Club, or National Geographic Kids Club). Be aware that Q♣ are generally born with a *higher-than-average information processing speed*. Therefore, a Q♣ tends to comprehend better when there are no distractions. They should focus on learning one thing at a time, rather than multi-tasking. Know that this same trait may initially manifest as a learning disability. You see, because their brains are working faster than their mouth, some Q♣ develop a *fluency disorder*, which is difficulty speaking in a fluid way. What is also happening is that their minds are synthesizing, going off in different directions of thought. If this is the case for your Q♣ child, discourage teachers from putting them into a lower reading group or labeling them with a learning disability. Support them by encouraging them to read at their own pace and to focus on comprehension. Negative comments about their fluency can produce a child who stutters or holds fears of being cold called upon to read out loud in class. Difficulties with fluency may also cause a Q♣ to have difficulty learning a new language. This is because acquiring a new language initially relies heavily upon oral language development. An impatient Q♣ will want to quit language classes.

Speaking of patience, as a rule, Q♣ tend to be *impatient*. This is the four-year-old child in the back seat of a car who repeatedly asks, "Are we there yet? Are we there yet?" As a Q♣ grows older and more confident in their cognitive gifts, they may exhibit impatience when working with others. The slower mental processing pace of others may be frustrating to them, and they can develop intolerance. As an example, a Q♣ may interrupt others when they are talking if the other person is not getting to the point fast enough. Also, a Q♣ may dislike cooperative learning assignments or projects in which students work together as a group. A Q♣ may feel like they are always pulling the weight, others are holding them back, or others are being lazy. Again, encourage patience and emphasize the importance of learning to work with others. If you are a teacher, you will know this problem is happening if a Q♣ asks if they can work independently from the group. A good solution may be to assign roles within the group with each role having individual expectations and assessment.

Finally, and most importantly, a Q♣ should be taught to tap into and trust their excellent *intuition* – another Q♣ superpower. Beginning at a young age, ask your Q♣ to engage in a moment of silence to think about a troubling situation. Ask them to listen for an inner voice to guide them. This process can become a form of channeling for a Q♣. Channeling for a Q♣ often involves gaining intuitions from a spiritual guide. When working with an older Q♣, encourage them to *free write* or journal. Freewriting is an informal kind of writing whereby someone automatically writes. They should write without worrying about content or grammar. The purpose is simply for them to pull out ideas. Again, make sure your Q♣ gets into the habit of practicing these activities free from distractions. If a Q♣ feels their intuition is blocked, stress may be an issue. You see, some Q♣ do not manage stress well. When a Q♣ is in a stressed state, urge them to engage in physical exercise. Ideally, exercise should entail a Q♣ having to focus on the activity at hand. Physical activities that require focused concentration work best such as aerobics, mountain biking, skiing, tennis, and racquetball to name a few. When a Q♣ becomes aware of their intuitive gifts and starts to apply them, watch out. For example, this is the child who accurately tells a parent where to 'find' their 'missing' keys. Keep in mind this same gift may also mean it is difficult to talk a Q♣ out of their perceptions. They subconsciously know their knowledge comes from a higher source and they will resist you or others telling them their perceived truths are incorrect.

Summary of Higher and Lower Personality Traits

Higher: Intuitive, highly organized planner, hard worker, high processing speed, synthesizer.

Lower: Demanding, impatient, opinionated, fluency issues, bossy, intolerant.

Childhood Influence Mercury Cards
It is common knowledge that a child's personality is most malleable during the formative years – from birth to eight years of age. In the Destiny Card system, the Mercury Cards in a Birth Card's Life Spread reveal influences a child with this Birth Card will experience between birth through age 12. As such, a child's Mercury Cards must be considered so an adult can nurture a child from a place of awareness and work with them from where a child is at in their development. A Q♣ child has the following Mercury Cards: **10♠, 10♣, and 4♥**. Alternatively, outside of any specific person associated with these three cards, the basic meanings of these cards may be impactful during this child's formative years. These cards suggest Q♣ shine in early educational experiences so long as they are not bored. Not only are they extremely bright, but they will work hard to acquire knowledge. They tend to be born into a stable home environment.

Potential Callings / Vocations by Zodiac Sign

January 28 – Aquarius: 7♦ Planetary Ruling Card

The aspect of Aquarius in these Q♣ makes them want to explore avant-garde ideas. As such, they can do well as a professor, scientist, writer, musician, minister, attorney, or socially minded activist.

February 26 – Pisces: 5♠ Planetary Ruling Card

Due to the energy of Pisces, these Q♣ possess double the intuition. Therefore, they do well in inventive careers such as a writer, designer, composer, or producer. Those who prefer travel are inclined toward acting, singing, or playing music.

March 24 – Aries: 3♦ Planetary Ruling Card

With a 3♦ Planetary Ruling Card, these Q♣ are attracted to creatively working with money as a business owner, financial advisor, or real estate broker. Those who follow the value aspect of their 3♦ can do well as a military or police officer, athlete, or firefighter.

April 22 – Taurus: 5♣ Planetary Ruling Card

With a 5♣ Planetary Ruling Card, these Q♣ dislike routine jobs. They prefer careers in music, acting, writing, designing, or landscaping. For those who can manage their restless energies, a job in public or government service might be a good fit.

May 20 – Taurus or Gemini: 5♣ or 10♠ Planetary Ruling Card

The Taurus affiliated Q♣ can succeed in various mental fields (e.g., engineer, scientist, attorney, or counselor). The Gemini affiliated prefer communicative jobs (e.g., business owner, teacher, artist, actor, or singer).

June 18 – Gemini: 10♠ Planetary Ruling Card

Fast-paced Gemini combined with the workaholic aspect of a 10♠ Planetary Ruling Cards suggest these Q♣ will excel in a mental profession such as an attorney, politician, teacher, researcher, accountant, or writer. Some individuals can leverage creative expression into a career as a musician or actor.

July 16 – Cancer: Ace of Clubs Planetary Ruling Card

The nurturing aspect of Cancer compels these Q♣ toward careers in which they can support humanitarian or social justice causes. They are often interested in journalism, social work, teaching, painting, writing, or politics.

August 14 – Leo: Q♣ Planetary Ruling Card

Double the Q♣ energy in these individuals directs many of them into sharing knowledge with a broader community as a comedian, professor, writer, business leader, or organizational leader.

September 12 – Virgo: 10♠ Planetary Ruling Card

With the analytical aspect of Virgo combined with the hardworking 10♠ Planetary Ruling Card, these Q♣ are often found in behind-the-scenes mental jobs (e.g., laboratory technician, scientist, engineer, architect, librarian, or counselor).

October 10 – Libra: 5♣ Planetary Ruling Card

The restless energy implicit to having a 5♣ Planetary Ruling Card make these Q♣ prefer work that allows personal freedom. They can do well as a composer, director, actor, travel writer, or sports player.

November 8 – Scorpio: 3♦ and J♥ Planetary Ruling Cards

Having a 3♦ as a Planetary Ruling Card instills financial creativity in these Q♣, allowing them to do well as a business leader, banker, insurance broker, corporate attorney, mortgage broker, or property manager.

December 6 – Sagittarius: Ace of Spades Planetary Ruling Card

Compassionate Sagittarius inspires these Q♣ to help others through a career as a teacher, counselor, nurse, or physician. Some artistic leaning individuals can succeed in the theater, music, or as a psychic.

Famous Q♣

Pierce Brown, writer – 1/28/1988
Mila Kunis, actress – 8/14/1983
Machine Gun Kelly, rapper – 4/22/1990
Halle Berry, actress – 8/14/1966
Edith Randall, Destiny Card writer and astrologer – 10/10/1897
Jennifer Hudson, singer – 9/12/1981

Welcome to the world of the motherly Q♦!

Q♦ = Serve through values and money

According to the Destiny Card system, souls chronologically experience God's lessons within each life incarnation. (Think of these as the universe's lessons if this aligns more with your beliefs.) The Birth Card each soul is born into determines the order and type of lessons a soul experiences. When you examine a Birth Card, you will notice it displays a suit of either a Heart, Club, Diamond, or Spade. This suit is significant because it represents the gifts a person born into this suit will possess and how they will direct their energies to learn lessons in their current life incarnation. A Heart Birth Card retains gifts and experiences life lessons around love and relationships. A Club Birth Card holds capabilities and experiences life lessons in their ability to communicate and absorb knowledge. A Diamond Birth Card possesses talents and experiences life lessons around money and values. And finally, a Spade Birth Card manifests gifts and experiences life lessons in work and health. Souls progress through incarnations and life lessons beginning as Hearts, moving on to Clubs, then Diamonds, and finally as Spades. Therefore, individuals born as Heart Cards are the youngest souls and individuals born as Spades Cards are the oldest souls. In addition, the number on a Birth Card is equally meaningful as souls sequentially experience life lessons beginning as an Ace and culminating with lessons as a King. Queen playing cards are associated with the number twelve. Holding a higher value than most other cards is inherent to Queens because they are part of the royal court. Just as people legitimately born into royalty are associated with various roles, royal court cards hold various roles with various responsibilities. Kings and Queens co-rule their kingdom, while Jacks are more like a Prince holding less responsibility.

You are probably wondering what kind of responsibility is associated with royal court Birth Cards. In the real world, average people are not born ruling over subjects in their community. A person associated with a royal court Birth Card is tasked with the responsibility of benefiting humanity by applying wisdom from incarnations as an Ace through a Ten in their suit. While a King rules, a Queen serves. This role of service is depicted in the Queen playing cards. When you examine these cards, you will notice the Queen is holding a flower. Look closer at how the flower is being held. The Queen holds a flower like a scepter to symbolize the area of their power and responsibility. Now you are probably wondering: what do flowers represent? You may be aware of the individual meanings of specific flowers. For instance, roses symbolize love. Red roses express deep love and desire, while yellow roses symbolize friendship. However, broadly speaking, flowers represent feminine energy and the possibility of new life as they are part of the reproductive cycle of plants. **It makes sense, then, that a Q♦ child's purpose, gifts, and life lessons revolve around a powerful mothering energy that inspires them to *serve* humanity. And due to being a Diamond, this child will learn lessons on how to serve humanity by modeling higher principles related to *values* and *money*.**

How to Nurture the Temperament and Personality of a Q♦ Child

In the early 1970's, the cosmetic company L'Oréal, published an advertisement with a tagline that has lasted for generations. The tagline stated, "Because I'm worth it." The original intention behind the statement was to reflect the women's right movement that was gaining popularity. Later, the "I'm" language was changed to "You're" making the tagline, "Because you're worth it." As such, the tagline has been associated with the idea that a woman should spend money on high quality cosmetics because they are worth it. This sentiment is relevant to a Q♦ because they are born feeling they possess worth. Afterall, they are Queens! As the ultimate Queen within the Diamond suit, Q♦ bring a tremendous amount of financial knowledge and *business acumen* from past lives. The flip side to their many past lives is that Q♦ tend to carry a lot of negative karma. For this reason, the path of a Q♦ is one, if not the most difficult, life path of all the Birth Cards. This is particularly true for a female Q♦. This karma shows up as challenges in the homelife of a young Q♦. These challenges may involve frequent moves, abandonment, abuse, or dysfunctional family relationships. When a Q♦'s internal perception of high worth conflicts with the reality of how they are treated in their home life, *insecurity* can result. How a Q♦ manages these early karmic experiences will greatly impact their future mindset. Will they lean into the mothering and philanthropical side of their card and develop a positive mindset? Or will they drown in their insecurity and cynicism, and develop a fearful mindset?

Most Q♦ respond to difficulties in the home by tapping into their innate superpowers – *competence*, *resourcefulness*, and *independence*. This is the infant who will begin walking at a younger age. Adults raising these children should avoid over nurturing them. Such treatment would likely trigger a rebellious response. This is the toddler who gets frustrated and claims, "I can do it" if an adult does not embrace their independent spirit. Within reason, allow these children to take on *independent* activities at an earlier age than you would for the average child. For instance, toddlers first learn to feed themselves using a spoon. A Q♦ may insist upon using a fork. Grant these types of requests and praise your Q♦ even if they make mistakes. As a Q♦ grows older, they will desire more and more independence. They will want to spend more time with their friends than their family. Make compromises to keep the peace. If an adult refuses to make some allowances for a Q♦, they may rebel. They may engage an adult in a power struggle. An older and rebellious Q♦ may flee the nest before it is healthy for them to do so.

The positive side of a Q♦'s nature is that they possess an independent drive to succeed. Q♦ are easily motivated by money. Have them analyze needs in the family home, local or broader community, and try to come up with innovative business ideas. Encourage them to make a business plan and pitch it. Even if this exercise results in simply negotiating chores and an allowance, it will be beneficial to the Q♦ because they will feel they have more control over their life. Do not be surprised if a Q♦ wants to start their own business before graduating from high school. Hear them out and support them as much as possible. If they struggle in their efforts, refrain from intervening. When it comes to business, they tend to possess *sound judgment* and are highly resilient. The Roman philosopher Seneca stated many years ago: "Throw me to the wolves and I will return leading the pack." In business, a Q♦ can fail and come back stronger than other. This said, make sure a Q♦ does not primarily focus on acquiring money. They should strive to acquire values outside of money. Q♦ who lean into their higher traits are philanthropic, sharing their wealth with others. Some go beyond sharing money. They serve humanity by mentoring others and sharing their financial wisdom. Q♦ financial advisor, Suze Orman, is a perfect example of this. She has empowered people from all socioeconomic walks of life to gain control over their financial life.

An obsession with money can be a Q♦'s Achilles heel. These Q♦ may develop different priorities from their parents or family. For instance, a parent may believe eating Easter dinner together as a family to be a high priority. A sixteen-year-old Q♦ may disagree. They would prefer to work during this time because they get double the pay. If this is an issue with your Q♦, please remember they are wired differently in what they value. Additionally, as a parent or teacher of a Q♦, it is important to understand that they feel a lot of internal pressure to succeed. In fact, when they make mistakes, they tend to beat themselves up quite a bit. Some Q♦ suffer hard blows to their self-esteem when they are criticized by others. These Q♦ may become perfectionists and then demand others do things their way. When others do not conform to their thinking, they may voice their own criticism of them and be cruel in what they communicate. In cases like this, a Q♦ may need *socio-emotional learning* lessons. Socio-emotional learning is an approach used to help children understand their own emotions, the emotions of others, and how to communicate with others. For many Q♦, they need lessons in how to communicate with kindness and empathy. I recommend reading to them the children's book titled, *Taste Your Words*, by Bonnie Clark. The book portrays a girl who hurts others with her mean words. The book teaches children about the consequences of mean words and how one should think before speaking.

Part of the reason why a Q♦ is likely to engage in criticism is because they have exceptional *analytical minds*. Analytical thinkers can focus on a problem, extract, and evaluate relevant details, and find a viable solution. Teach your Q♦ to apply this superpower in positive, rather than negative ways. In educational settings, analytical thinkers love authentic learning experiences where they are figuring out solutions to problems that are relevant and based upon real-life. This means they are ideal students to be exposed to problem-based and project based learning approaches. Problem-based learning is a teaching methodology that uses real-life problems to drive student learning of concepts that are related to solving problems. Likewise, project-based learning uses real-life problems, but students are also expected to demonstrate learning through the development of a product or presentation. Q♦ are bright and *self-reliant* learners. A teacher can give them alternative assignments and they will follow through in accomplishing them without much oversight. If your Q♦ is not getting enough stimulation in school, it would be a good idea to provide extra-curricular activities and ones that hone their analytical skills. Perhaps sign them up for chess, debate club, coding, or STEM activities (Science, Technology, Engineering, and Mathematics).

The "because I'm worth it" tagline can also be applied to a Q♦'s behavior in spending money. You see, some Q♦ obsess over money and then hold fears around not having enough money even though this tends to be more of a perception than a reality. These Q♦ are not generous. They may overspend and/or use their money to manipulate others. One can recognize these Q♦ because they have very few to no close friends. The root of the issue for these Q♦ is that they have not dealt with the insecurities from their childhood. Their self-worth is based upon how they look or what they can buy. They cover up their *insecurity* by blindly attempting to buy love and self-worth. At an extreme, these Q♦ can be mean-spirited and narcissistic.

Summary of Higher and Lower Personality Traits

Higher: Shrewd in business, analytical, resourceful, competent, charitable, self-reliant.

Lower: Hypercritical, narcissistic, overspending, insecurity, lack of empathy.

Childhood Influence Mercury Cards
It is common knowledge that a child's personality is most malleable during the formative years – from birth to eight years of age. In the Destiny Card system, the Mercury Cards in a Birth

Card's Life Spread reveal influences a child with this Birth Card will experience between birth through age 12. As such, a child's Mercury Cards must be considered so an adult can nurture a child from a place of awareness and work with them from where a child is at in their development. A Q♦ child has the following Mercury Cards: **5♥, 6♦, and 4♦**. Alternatively, outside of any specific person associated with these three cards, the basic meanings of these cards may be impactful during this child's formative years. These cards suggest a young Q♦ experiences emotional obligations and challenges to be dealt with due to serious karmic debts. Such pressures cause them to rebel and want to escape. They are often protected financially during childhood. They tend to be born into a family which is financially stable.

Potential Callings / Vocations by Zodiac Sign

January 15 – Capricorn: 7♠ Planetary Ruling Card
The spiritual wisdom of a 7♠ Planetary Ruling Card combined with the responsible nature of Capricorn drives these Q♦ toward promoting spiritual values. They can do well as a religious leader, government leader, politician, entrepreneur, or business leader (particularly in a merchandising role).

February 13 – Aquarius: 5♦ Planetary Ruling Card
Free-spirited and inventive Aquarius in these Q♦ make them attracted to artistic careers. Their ambition allows them to succeed as an actor, television or radio personality, musician, artist, or writer.

March 11 – Pisces: Q♠ Planetary Ruling Card
Even though the Q♠ Planetary Ruling Card suggests these Q♦ will remain behind the scenes, their power to promote ideas is tremendous. They can work for the government as a speech writer, be a social activist, or represent a company or political interest group as a lobbyist. Some may succeed as a musician or dancer.

April 9 – Aries: 3♠ Planetary Ruling Card
With the artistic 3♠ as their Planetary Ruling Card, these Q♦ are more likely to be found acting, entertaining, or writing music. Some possess a strong drive to change the values of others and are often called into politics, activism, or leading social movements.

May 7 – Taurus: 3♣ Planetary Ruling Card
Instilled with a Taurus' fondness for beauty, these Q♦ have a keen eye for art. They can do well as an art dealer, director, producer, composer, fashion designer, or painter. They can also succeed in sales, particularly if their products adorn people (e.g., clothing, jewelry, shoes, and other accessories).

June 5 – Gemini: 5♥ Planetary Ruling Card

The combined influence of stimulus-seeking Gemini with the emotional restlessness of a 5♥ Planetary Ruling Card makes these Q♦ prefer jobs that include travel, flexibility, variety, and freedom. They can do well as an actor, writer, or in a sales-related profession.

July 3 – Cancer: A♦ Planetary Ruling Card

Cancer blends well with these Q♦, motivating them to make money through humanitarian efforts. They can do well as a teacher, charity fundraiser, non-profit leader, or public servant. Those more inclined to the sciences often make an excellent physician or nurse.

August 1 – Leo: Q♦ Planetary Ruling Card

With a Q♦ Planetary Ruling Card, these Q♦ have double the charm and expensive tastes. They demand a career that can support their tastes (e.g., actor, clothes designer, architect, musician, or attorney).

Famous Q♦

Jason Momoa, actor – 8/1/1979
Suze Orman, financial advisor – 6/5/1951
Martin Luther King, Jr., civil rights activist – 1/15/1929
Regina King, actress – 1/15/1971
Rupert Murdoch, media mogul – 3/11/1931
Jodie Comer, actress – 3/1//1993

Welcome to the world of the motherly Q♠

Q♠ = Serve through humility

According to the Destiny Card system, souls chronologically experience God's lessons within each life incarnation. (Think of these as the universe's lessons if this aligns more with your beliefs.) The Birth Card each soul is born into determines the order and type of lessons a soul experiences. When you examine a Birth Card, you will notice it displays a suit of either a Heart, Club, Diamond, or Spade. This suit is significant because it represents the gifts a person born into this suit will possess and how they will direct their energies to learn lessons in their current life incarnation. A Heart Birth Card retains gifts and experiences life lessons around love and relationships. A Club Birth Card holds capabilities and experiences life lessons in their ability to communicate and absorb knowledge. A Diamond Birth Card possesses talents and experiences life lessons around money and values. And finally, a Spade Birth Card manifests gifts and experiences life lessons in work and health. Souls progress through incarnations and life lessons beginning as Hearts, moving on to Clubs, then Diamonds, and finally as Spades. Therefore, individuals born as Heart Cards are the youngest souls and individuals born as Spades Cards are the oldest souls. In addition, the number on a Birth Card is equally meaningful as souls sequentially experience life lessons beginning as an Ace and culminating with lessons as a King. Queen playing cards are associated with the number twelve. Holding a higher value than the majority of other cards is inherent to Queens because they are part of the royal court. Just as people legitimately born into royalty are associated with various roles, royal court cards hold various roles with various responsibilities. Kings and Queens co-rule their kingdom, while Jacks are more like a Prince holding less responsibility.

You are probably wondering what kind of responsibility is associated with royal court Birth Cards. In the real world, average people are not born ruling over subjects in their community. A person associated with a royal court Birth Card is tasked with the responsibility of benefiting humanity by applying wisdom from incarnations as an Ace through a Ten in their suit. While a King rules, a Queen serves. This role of service is depicted in the Queen playing cards. When you examine these cards, you will notice the Queen is holding a flower. Look closer at how the flower is being held. The Queen holds a flower like a scepter to symbolize the area of their power and responsibility. Now you are probably wondering: what do flowers represent? You may be aware of the individual meanings of specific flowers. For instance, roses symbolize love. Red roses express deep love and desire, while yellow roses symbolize friendship. However, broadly speaking, flowers represent feminine energy and the possibility of new life as they are part of the reproductive cycle of plants. **It makes sense, then, that a Q♠ child's purpose, gifts, and life lessons revolve around a powerful mothering energy that inspires them to *serve* humanity. And due to being a Spade, this child will learn lessons on how to serve humanity by modeling higher wisdom related to *health* and *work*.**

How to Nurture the Temperament and Personality of a Q♠ Child
If you closely examine a Q♠ playing card, you will notice the Queen holds a scepter under her left arm. The scepter is positioned as if the Queen is trying to hide it. This depiction is significant because it reveals an important mission for all Q♠ – to acquire wisdom by cultivating *humility*. Humility is achieved when a person demonstrates modesty toward one's own gifts while simultaneously valuing the gifts of others. A Q♠ often fosters humility by being born into a family of old souls and powerful personalities who influence the trajectory of this child's life path. Let's consider one example of how such an influence can impact a Q♠. Imagine a sixteen-year-old Q♠ named Katherine is applying for colleges. A domineering family member pushes their own alma mater and career interests on to Katherine. Aggressive pressure from this family member creates a dilemma for Katherine. Ultimately, Katherine chooses the path of least resistance and pursues a career that does not instill a sense of purpose or self-worth for her. In adulthood, she develops apathy toward her work. She underachieves, promotions pass her by, and she finds herself serving others in a behind-the-scenes kind of manner. Katherine cultivates humility as the adversity she experiences tempers her ego and makes her aware of her limitations. You may be wondering why a Queen, gifted with great power, would be tasked with this lesson. Why is it their mission to cultivate humility? Remember that souls reincarnate in a specific order. A Q♠'s previous life incarnation was as a J♠. More pertinent is that a Q♠'s next life incarnation will be as a K♠. Because the K♠ represents the final life incarnation, a person

born to this card holds more power than any other Birth Card. As such, learning the lesson of humility is a prerequisite to earning the power and position of a K♠.

To help a Q♠ navigate lessons in humility, it is beneficial to expose them to this topic as early as possible. There is a wonderful assortment of books that aim to teach humility to young children. One book is the classic, *The Emperor's New Clothes*, by Hans Christian Anderson. It is the story of a vain emperor who spent his time and money on purchasing expensive clothing. Later, the emperor paraded outside wearing no clothing, having been fooled that his new clothing was invisible. When the townspeople laughed at the emperor, he experienced a lesson in humility. I would also suggest reading *The Tower: A Story of Humility*, by Richard Paul Evans. The main character desires to be great. He achieves this goal, but not in the way he plans. When he engages in an act of kindness toward a young child, he discovers humility and inadvertently attains his goal. If you are the parent of a Q♠, read these books and discuss the concept of humility using age-appropriate examples within everyday life. Alternatively, an adult can teach a Q♠ about humility by discussing the life of a worker bee. In a bee colony, worker bees are females who are unable to reproduce. They utilize their feminine energy to nurture the Queen bee and feed her newly born larvae. Worker bees complete numerous housekeeping chores in the hive, from cleaning and building the hive to guarding the hive from intruders. Use the important role of worker bees to encourage a Q♠ to understand the benefits of serving others.

As a rule, Q♠ are born with an *introverted* temperament. If you are a parent of a Q♠, you will find them to be *reserved* and *easy to discipline*. In school, Q♠ are viewed by their teachers as *steadfast* and *hard workers*. They are highly intelligent and can be expected to pursue higher education. Because all Q♠ have a K♣ Planetary Ruling card, they enjoy mastering a field of study and then serving others with their vast fund of knowledge. As a Q♠ grows older, it is common to observe them immersed in deep thought. During these moments, they may portray a flat expression or a scowl on their face. You might wonder if they are upset. What is likely happening is that they are processing their feelings. They are practicing their superpower – *self-awareness*. Self-awareness involves the ability to focus on one's feelings and be in touch with one's strengths and limitations. It allows a person to consider their actions and evaluate how those actions align with their internal values. Such analysis allows a person to recognize how their behavior affects others and then consider ways they may need to adjust their behaviors. For example, imagine an eight-year-old Q♠ girl has completed her work in class and is allowed some choice time. Choice time is a designated time in which students can assert independence by choosing to engage in a preferred activity. The girl sees a classmate playing at the arts and crafts table and chooses to work there. The classmate not only refuses to share materials, but she also grabs all the red markers. In this situation, a Q♠ tends to act passive and goes into *self-awareness processing mode*. Soon after, the Q♠ decides to leave the arts and crafts table without confrontation, recognizing her classmate is having a hard day. She heads over to the science magnet station and happily plays with magnets. If you are an adult working with a Q♠, help them foster this ability. If your Q♠ acts like a *whiner*, this is a sure sign they have yet to master their gift of self-awareness. There are numerous children's books to read to a Q♠ to discuss this concept. I would suggest the book, *Your Fantastic Elastic Brain* by JoAnn

Deak because it touches upon how one's brain holds the capacity to improve. Once a Q♠ learns to hone their gift of self-awareness, there are no limits to how they can apply it. Moreover, they are better prepared to achieve their goal of cultivating humility.

One type of adversity all Q♠ are sure to face in life is *drudgery*. If a young Q♠ experiences drudgery and responds by adopting a *passive* attitude, they are expressing the low side of their Birth Card. These children obsess over the grind of life and whine about the unfairness of every troubling situation. They may adopt *apathy* toward their work or physical activity. For instance, when asked to clean their room, this is the child that says, "I have a passion for NOT cleaning my room!" As such, they can attract more struggles and remain on the proverbial hamster wheel of mental struggle. At an extreme, a Q♠ can manifest *learned helplessness*. Learned helplessness is when a child quits trying to change their circumstances even though they can because they have repeatedly faced negative situations outside of their control. Let's consider an example. Amanda is an eleven-year-old Q♠. Viewed by her middle school teachers as being bright, a hard worker, and mature for her age, they encourage her to run for a student council position. The objective of student council is to provide leadership and implement projects and activities that help the school. Each year of middle school, Amanda runs for a position on student council. And each year she fails in her efforts. In high school, when someone suggests she run for student council, Amanda feels she should not try anymore when the outcome never changes. In other words, Amanda feels powerless. She has learned to be helpless.

To nurture a Q♠, help them develop an inner mastery over their attitude. Another great book to read to a Q♠ is titled, *Baditude! What to Do When Life Stinks!* by Julia Cook. In this book, the main character realizes how his negative attitude alienates others. The reason this message is so important to a Q♠ is that they must recognize how their attitude impacts life. They must learn to have faith, stay upbeat, and believe things will get better. Such an attitude adjustment can literally set them free. When they focus on their spiritual side, the external circumstances in their life improve. They inadvertently attract happiness and well-being. These higher expressing Q♠ do not try to change or complain about their external circumstances. They apply their gift of self-awareness and manage their attitude towards health and work. This is amazing because this means a Q♠ has the power to manifest the landscape of their life.

Summary of Higher and Lower Personality Traits

Higher: Introvert, self-awareness, intelligent, easy to discipline, steadfast, hard worker, humble.

Lower: Too passive, jealous, whiner, apathetic, unenthusiastic, learned helplessness.

Childhood Influence Mercury Cards
It is common knowledge that a child's personality is most malleable during the formative years – from birth to eight years of age. In the Destiny Card system, the Mercury Cards in a Birth Card's Life Spread reveal influences a child with this Birth Card will experience between birth through age 12. As such, a child's Mercury Cards must be considered so an adult can nurture a child from a place of awareness and work with them from where a child is at in their

development. A Q♠ child has the following Mercury Cards: **J♣, Q♦, and J♦**. The Q♦ may mean there is an influential mother who is likely a Diamond Birth or Planetary Ruling Card. Likewise, the Jacks may mean there is an influential father and/ or brothers who are likely a Club or Diamond Birth or Planetary Ruling Card. Alternatively, outside of any specific person associated with these three cards, the basic meanings of these cards may be impactful during this child's formative years. These cards suggest Q♠ children are creative, inquisitive, willing to learn and work hard. They tend to be born into a family with powerful personalities who expect their child to be self-sufficient.

Potential Callings / Vocations by Zodiac Sign

January 2 – Capricorn: K♣ Planetary Ruling Card

Only one date Is associated with a Q♠. Responsible Capricorn blends well with this Birth Card. While they can achieve success in any area, they are better suited to serve others as a teacher, preacher, elder care worker, homemaker, science researcher, physician, office administrator, or government servant.

Famous Q♠

Jim Bakker, televangelist – 1/2/1940
Christy Turlington, model – 1/2/1969
Dax Shepard, actor – 1/2/1975
Kate Bosworth, actress – 1/2/1983
Tia Carrere, actress – 1/2/1967

Chapter 16

Descriptions of the King Birth Cards

Welcome to the world of the commanding K♥!

K♥ = Rule through love and relationships

According to the Destiny Card system, souls chronologically experience God's lessons across 52 life incarnations. (Think of these as the universe's lessons if this aligns more with your beliefs.) The Birth Card each soul is born into determines the order and type of lessons a soul experiences. When you examine a Birth Card, you will notice it displays a suit of either a Heart, Club, Diamond, or Spade. This suit is significant because it represents the gifts a person born into this suit will possess and how they will direct their energies to learn lessons in their current life incarnation. A Heart Birth Card retains gifts and experiences life lessons around love and relationships. A Club Birth Card holds capabilities and experiences life lessons in their ability to communicate and absorb knowledge. A Diamond Birth Card possesses talents and experiences life lessons around money and values. And finally, a Spade Birth Card manifests gifts and experiences life lessons in work and health. Souls progress through incarnations and life lessons beginning as Hearts, moving on to Clubs, then Diamonds, and finally as Spades. Therefore, individuals born as Heart Cards are the youngest souls and individuals born as Spades Cards are the oldest souls.

In addition, the number on a Birth Card is equally meaningful as souls sequentially experience life lessons beginning as an Ace and culminating with lessons as a King. King playing cards are associated with the number thirteen. Thirteen is not only the highest value any single playing card can possess, but it also represents the final incarnation a soul will experience within a specific suit. As such, King Birth Cards retain the most power and responsibility in the area associated with their suit. **It makes sense, then, that a K♥ child's purpose, gifts, and life lessons revolve around having a tremendous amount of *power and responsibility* in their life. And, due to being a Heart, this child will learn lessons by experiencing tremendous power and responsibility around *love* and *relationships*.**

How to Nurture the Temperament and Personality of a K♥ Child

K♥ are born with a sweet natured temperament. Even strangers are often drawn to them. With such a temperament, a young K♥ may adopt one of two opposite dispositions: extreme shyness or an attention demanding personality. While shy K♥ tend to outgrow their shyness, attention seeking K♥ may maintain their demanding personality throughout their life. If you are a parent of a K♥ who demands attention, give into this need to a certain extent. This is not to say you should spoil a K♥. But, because they are a King, these children need to feel special. The best way an adult can make them feel special is through demonstrative displays of affection such as hugging, kissing, and cuddling. Verbal expressions of love also nurture them. Try to provide individualized quality time with a K♥. If you have other children, try to plan an activity that just you and your K♥ can do together. Are you pressed for time? No worries. A young K♥ will happily enjoy helping a parent complete mundane tasks like preparing dinner together so long as the interaction is loving. Most importantly, model loving practices in the home. If you make a mistake that involves a K♥, own up to it. Apologize. They are forgiving souls. One of their greatest superpowers is that they subconsciously understand that love is not a transactional experience. They believe in *unconditional love* and strive to moel that to everyone in their sphere of influence.

Remember, a K♥ child is to learn lessons by experiencing tremendous power and responsibility around *love* and *relationships*. You may be wondering then, what is the nature of a K♥'s power and responsibility? Let's unpack each of these topics separately, starting with a description of a K♥'s power. As the final incarnation of the Heart Birth Cards, a K♥ has accumulated lessons around love and relationships from twelve past life incarnations. These past lives and lessons provide a K♥ with a superior *emotional power* over others. Let's consider an example. Have you ever watched the 1990's movie, *Meet Joe Black*? After a fatal car accident, Joe Black's body comes back to life having been inhabited by Death. In the role of Death, Joe visits a successful businessman named Bill to prepare him for his upcoming death. During his visit, Joe falls in love with Bill's daughter, Susan. If you watched this movie, you could not help but think it was odd the way in which Joe stood still throughout the entire movie. Also, Joe did not talk very much. However, in the romantic scenes, Joe's non-verbal communication was off the charts, packed with sensuality. The sexual chemistry between Joe and Susan was powerful. Only one card has that level of sensuality – the K♥. A K♥'s *sensuality* is heightened due to their tremendous emotional power. The intense sensuality of Joe's character makes sense because Joe was played by Brad Pitt, a bona fide K♥!

With such power, K♥ have the responsibility to use it to rule over others in loving ways. A young K♥ can show early signs of this behavior in a home or classroom. For example, imagine a situation in which you are a parent of three children. Your youngest child is a five-year-old K♥. You purchase a play structure for the backyard to provide independent outdoor time for your children. As a family, you have discussed the expectations of sharing the play structure. One day a dispute arose over whose turn it is to use the slide. Eavesdropping from a nearby window, you hear one of your children manage the situation with love and compassion. That child is not your oldest child. It is your youngest child. Your K♥ child. K♥ truly possess heart-warming gifts around love and relationships. Having experienced past lives as an Ace through Queen in the Hearts suit, they are emotionally more mature than you may imagine. Respect this maturity. If there are arguments in the home or emotionally difficult discussions to be had, be frank in communicating with your K♥. They are not too young to understand emotions and the complicated situations that create them. The best way to nurture them is to allow them to lead others with love so long as they are doing so in a positive way.

If you are a parent of a K♥, make sure you have discussions with them from a young age about their emotional superpower. Being proactive will go a long way in ensuring that a K♥ uses their power in healthy ways. First, help a K♥ child recognize their power when you see them exercise it. Perhaps you observe them engage in a small act of kindness that has a powerful effect on someone else. Ask them to reflect upon the experience: "How did their small act of kindness make the other person feel? In turn how did that make them feel?" As they grow older, ask them to consider situations in which people abuse others with emotional power. This can easily be achieved while watching TV shows or movies with your K♥. As an example, perhaps you are watching the TV show *Malcolm in the Middle*. One character named Jason is a middle school student who decides to hang out with friends instead of finishing a Language Arts essay due the following day. A week later Jason receives his incomplete essay and finds he earned a D grade. Jason, being a charming person, decides to persuade his Language Arts teacher to change the D to a higher grade. After he is successful, he boasts to his friends about it. Using their charm to *emotionally manipulate* others is exactly the kind of temptation a K♥ may experience in life. Therefore, it is important to bring out the higher angels in a K♥. Going back to the TV show and Jason, this situation would be ideal time to ask a K♥, "What would you do in a similar situation? What are the long-term consequences of behaving like this?" Remind them that individuals ultimately hold the power to make choices; to use their love power in good or not so good ways. Throughout a K♥'s teen years, try to continue dialoguing with them about their emotional power as they navigate relationships with others. It is common for a K♥ to transfer their rule over relationships in the home to rule over the love dynamics between their closest friends. If they are helping a friend manage challenging emotions, ask them to explain what lessons they are learning. Refrain from telling them how to handle the situation. All Kings dislike being told what to do. Just ask good questions and praise them when they offer healthy advice.

The Greek philosopher Aristotle stated, "Educating the mind without educating the heart is no education at all." This statement is a great rule of thumb for a K♥. K♥ are *intelligent* and capable of doing extremely well in school. However, some K♥ may have difficulty focusing upon their work when there is disharmony in classroom relationships. Harmony with others may need to be reinstated before they can apply themselves to academics. If they are involved in an emotional conflict, teach them how to resolve it using their emotional power. I recommend using a strategy designed by Dr. Becky A. Bailey called *a conflict resolution time machine*. As its name implies, students are asked to go back in time to the conflict and they are guided to work through it using helpful rather than harmful words. You can check out examples of this strategy being effectively implemented on YouTube. Not only does a K♥ hold the potential to master this strategy, but they can become a valuable role model for others. Additionally, a K♥ benefits from a teacher who builds a loving relationship with them. If not, a young K♥ may come across as *moody* or needy. As a K♥ grows into adolescence, they can even to lose respect for people in authority positions who they perceive as not being fair or kind in relationships. An adult who is dismissive of the emotions of a K♥ may inadvertently be contributing to a K♥s decision to underperform. Therefore, a great way to nurture a K♥ is to build a sense of community in the classroom. This can be accomplished by establishing morning check-in meetings and connecting rituals. An example of a connecting ritual is where students can choose a special greeting with their teacher as they enter the classroom (e.g., high five, hug, fist bump, or dance move). Remember, K♥ rule through love. As such, they should be given leadership roles. A teacher can assign a K♥ to a classroom job of noticing and encouraging others who are having a hard day. Or invite them to lead activities intended to build classroom rapport.

One potential life challenge for a K♥ is that they may experience some form of emotional betrayal as a child. As one example, some experience abandonment by a father figure. Abandonment is the worst form of punishment for an affection-seeking K♥. If a K♥ is left to process this kind of a situation on their own, they are more likely to lean into the lower traits of their Birth Card. Often these behaviors first reveal themselves during adolescence when they emotionally lead others in negative ways. These experiences can teach a K♥ that they can emotionally manipulate others. This realization is often reinforced when a K♥ discovers they possess another superpower: the ability to *seduce* others. Let's consider an extreme example. Perhaps a thirteen-year-old male K♥ overhears a huge fight between his parents. The next day, his father abandons the family, never to be heard from again. Initially, this K♥ is angry at his father. Then the anger is redirected at his mother who he blames for the abandonment. Furthermore, let's say this K♥ does not receive counseling or family therapy. Over the next few years, this mother-son relationship deteriorates. The K♥ loses respect for his mother which in turn, leads him to disrespect other females. During his time in high school, this K♥ leans into his ability to seduce others and goes on to breaks many hearts, viewing female peers only as sexual conquests.

If a young K♥ has experienced an emotional disappointment or betrayal, they would benefit from being taught about *empathy*. Empathy is the ability of a person to understand the emotions of others. Developmentally a K♥ can be taught to describe their own emotions between the ages of three to five. Next, they can be taught to notice and describe the emotions of others. Once a K♥ reaches elementary school age, an adult can teach them how to create *empathy maps*. Empathy maps are visual tools that leverage empathy to build healthy relationships between people. They can be used in a classroom or a home that contains multiple children. The process involves children describing a situation, considering everyone's emotions and possible hurt feelings, and identifying how each child involved could have reacted in a more loving and healthy manner. In addition, it can be helpful to encourage a K♥ to build relationships with empathetic role models. Going back to the example of a K♥ who has experienced abandonment by a father, such a child might benefit from spending time with a loving grandfather, uncle, or other male relative. And do not forget that male coaches and teachers can make excellent mentors. There are also numerous organizations such as the Boys and Girls Club of America that can help provide healthy role models for a K♥.

Another way to support a K♥ is to teach them *coping skills* for when they are struggling with intense emotions. Interestingly, some K♥ learn to cope by sleeping a lot. Needing more sleep is natural for a K♥ because they are constantly dealing with powerful emotions. Be careful not to confuse this need with laziness. Allow some latitude with this behavior. Have you not experienced exhaustion when you had an emotionally draining day? Another way to help a

K♥ cope with their emotions is to urge them to participate in physical activity or creative forms of expression. Do not be surprised if a K♥ decides to direct a lot of their time engaging in creative expression. This may be frustrating for an adult. As an example, perhaps a K♥ decides to spend more time writing their own songs, rather than working on schoolwork. Alternatively, they may have periods of time when they want to put more energy into their friendships. Overall, have some trust in them. Know that the relationships or artistic skills they cultivate do have a purpose. And have trust they will become a successful adult. Afterall, they are a King.

Summary of Higher and Lower Personality Traits

Higher: Leader, tender-hearted, protective, sensual, artistic, friendly, unconditional love.

Lower: Self-indulgent, anger issues, emotionally manipulative, seductive.

Childhood Influence Mercury Cards

It is common knowledge that a child's personality is most malleable during the formative years – from birth to eight years of age. In the Destiny Card system, the Mercury Cards in a Birth Card's Life Spread reveal influences a child with this Birth Card will experience between birth through age 12. As such, a child's Mercury Cards must be considered so an adult can nurture a child from a place of awareness and work with them from where a child is at in their development. A K♥ child has the following Mercury Cards: **K♦, 7♥, and 3♣**. The K♦ may mean there is an influential father who is likely a Diamond Birth or Planetary Ruling Card. This father may instill values and attitudes (good or bad) in a K♥. Alternatively, outside of any specific person associated with these three cards, the basic meanings of these cards describe experiences that may be impactful during this child's formative years. These cards suggest a K♥ is financially protected in youth. An early emotional betrayal or abandonment may blindside them. To manage their strong emotions, they often turn to creative expression through writing, music, or art.

Potential Callings / Vocations by Zodiac Sign

June 30 – Cancer: 2♥ Planetary Ruling Card
With the caring aspect of Cancer coupled with a sensitive awareness toward the needs of others due to a 2♥ Planetary Ruling Card, these K♥ feel called to preach, counsel, or teach others. By channeling their highly emotional inclinations into creative work, they can also do well as an actor, director, or musician.

July 28 – Leo: K♥ Planetary Ruling Card
Magnetic charm and sex appeal may be off the charts in these double K♥. Therefore, many succeed in the artistic fields as an actor, musician, or director. Those with humanitarian leanings can enjoy a career as a writer, publisher, politician, or social reform leader.

August 26 – Virgo: K♦ Planetary Ruling Card

With a K♦ Planetary Ruling card, these K♥ are tempted to embrace materialism and adoration. They may do their best in a lucrative profession that helps others (e.g., physician, veterinarian, scientific researcher, counselor, spiritual leader, or teacher).

September 24 – Libra: 6♥ Planetary Ruling Card

With the diplomatic influence of Libra combined with the peacemaker 6♥ Planetary Ruling card, these K♥ can make an excellent attorney, judge, politician, or spiritual leader. Some are equipped to shine through their artistic expression as a writer, architect, designer, actor, or singer.

October 22 – Libra: 6♥ Planetary Ruling Card

The beauty loving aspect of Libra instills much artistic sensitivity in these K♥. They can make a successful musician, artist, or actor. For those wanting to serve, they can do well as a politician or spiritual leader.

November 20 – Scorpio: 4♣ and 4♠ Planetary Ruling Cards

Having two Planetary Ruling Cards with the number Four energy imparts much stability and organizational abilities within these K♥. Some feel compelled to protect others as a business, spiritual, or political leader. They can also make a fine scientist, judge, musician, or artist.

December 18 – Sagittarius: 2♦ Planetary Ruling Card

With the wheeler dealer aspect of a 2♦ Planetary Ruling card, these K♥ can sell products created from their emotions to the public through singing and song writing, dramatic performances, movie directing or producing, publishing, or through their political views.

Famous K♥

Billie Eilish, singer/ songwriter – 12/18/2001
Brad Pitt, actor – 12/18/1963
Christina Aguilera, singer/ songwriter – 12/18/1980
Michael Phelps, Olympic swimmer – 6/30/1985
Liz Cheney, politician – 7/28/1966
Joe Biden, President of the United States – 11/20/1942

Welcome to the world of the commanding K♣!

K♣ = Rule through communication and knowledge

According to the Destiny Card system, souls chronologically experience God's lessons across 52 life incarnations. (Think of these as the universe's lessons if this aligns more with your beliefs.) The Birth Card each soul is born into determines the order and type of lessons a soul experiences. When you examine a Birth Card, you will notice it displays a suit of either a Heart, Club, Diamond, or Spade. This suit is significant because it represents the gifts a person born into this suit will possess and how they will direct their energies to learn lessons in their current life incarnation. A Heart Birth Card retains gifts and experiences life lessons around love and relationships. A Club Birth Card holds capabilities and experiences life lessons in their ability to communicate and absorb knowledge. A Diamond Birth Card possesses talents and experiences life lessons around money and values. And finally, a Spade Birth Card manifests gifts and experiences life lessons in work and health. Souls progress through incarnations and life lessons beginning as Hearts, moving on to Clubs, then Diamonds, and finally as Spades. Therefore, individuals born as Heart Cards are the youngest souls and individuals born as Spades Cards are the oldest souls.

In addition, the number on a Birth Card is equally meaningful as souls sequentially experience life lessons beginning as an Ace and culminating with lessons as a King. King playing cards are associated with the number thirteen. Thirteen is not only the highest value any single playing card can possess, but it also represents the final incarnation a soul will experience within a specific suit. As such, King Birth Cards retain the most power and responsibility in the area associated with their suit. **It makes sense, then, that a K♣ child's purpose, gifts, and life lessons revolve around having a tremendous amount of *power and responsibility* in their life. And, due to being a Club, this child will learn lessons by experiencing tremendous power and responsibility related to *communication* and *knowledge*.**

How to Nurture the Temperament and Personality of a K♣ Child

From an early age, a K♣ will want to assert their *independence* and need for self-determination. This is the toddler who uses their voice to demand autonomy by insisting, "You are not the boss of me. Don't tell me what to do!" Moreover, this is not a young child who will be satisfied with a request from an adult and then told, "because I said so." A K♣ child may demand that adults provide a rationale, an explanation of why they need to do something or act a certain way. And as they grow older, they will desire flexibility and choices in the decisions that affect them. As such, a *democratic* teaching or parenting style is most effective to use with them. A democratic style involves joint decision-making between an adult and child. Although this kind of management is time consuming for an adult working with or parenting a K♣, it will pay off in the long run. It will likely prevent arguments. If you are disciplining a K♣, provide choices that are acceptable to you and then let the K♣ have the final choice. Let's consider an example. Imagine you are the teacher of an eleven-year-old K♣ girl. You love teaching math and are excited when you discover she is an exceptional math student. One day you observe her, having successfully finished her math quiz ahead of her classmates, forcefully turn the quiz over and slam her pencil down. Non-verbally she is claiming she holds the power to achieve, and you feel satisfied in being part of that success. Weeks later you are teaching Common Core or what is known as the 'new math.' You assign a task in which students must write out more steps in solving a problem to show conceptual understanding along with the right answer. Your K♣

outright rejects this task. Why should she take five minutes to solve one problem when she can produce the right answer in one minute? Your best student has now morphed into a challenging student. Again, the best way to nurture a K♣ is to provide flexibility and choice. Explain to this K♣ that your goal is for her to demonstrate competency. If the assignment contains 10 problems, she can choose to solve all 10 her way and receive a low grade. Or she can pick five to solve using the new way and if she shows competency, she can receive full credit.

Because K♣ are exceptional *analytical thinkers*, many of them excel in math and finance. Analytical thinkers can focus on a problem, extract, and evaluate relevant details, and find a viable solution. Such a skill can be applied or transferred to many different subjects and careers. Additionally, a K♣ possess a tremendous capacity to acquire knowledge. As an example, let's say you are a parent of a ten-year-old K♣ boy who is learning the geography of the United States. You probably recall these lessons when you were in elementary school whereby you learned the names of states and their capitals. The night before your son has a test on this information, you discover he has not only memorized the names of all 50 states and their capitals, but he also knows the state birds, flowers, and trees. You ask your son how he was able to achieve this knowledge. He says it was simple. He got a book from the library that contained visual representations of all the information. He absorbed the information. When he closes his eyes, he can visualize everything in his head. Wow, you are impressed with his visual learning. However, do not assume a K♣ is primarily a visual learner. K♣ can also grasp information by actively listening. One of their superpowers is that they can comprehend complex systems at a deeper level and more than any other Birth Card. Of course, this would involve them wanting to listen to whomever was speaking. You see, if a K♣ does not respect the information presented or the person who is presenting it, they will tune out. When they do listen, they comprehend everything. Remember, a K♣ is born with inherent knowledge having experienced many past lives as an Ace through a Queen in the Club suit. Learning for a K♣ is more of a recall and associative process; they can tap into memories from past lives. Do not read this and be fooled into thinking they will learn whatever you put in front of them though. They will decide what they want to learn. Therefore, follow and support their interests. Do they love facts about the solar system? Buy astronomy books or get them from the library. Do they love animals? Take them to the zoo.

During their teen years, K♣ tend to walk to the beat of a different drum. Their mature sense of humor may go over the head of their peers. They may come across as an odd duck. While they tend not to be popular in school, they do attract some close friends who appreciate them. If you are a parent of a K♣, do not be surprised if your child is accused of not respecting an authority figure. As an example, a K♣ may lose respect for a teacher who is telling them something that is in opposition to their own truths. Or perhaps they take exception when a teacher accuses them of doing something wrong when they did not. By and large, K♣ possess *high integrity*. These kinds of situations may cause them to rebel. Some will be *argumentative*, and they will arm themself with a lot of information as to why they are correct. These K♣ are *stubborn* and will not back down from their point of view. As such, they need to be heard and taken seriously or they will lose respect for the authority figure managing them.

Similar behavior can manifest in the home. The majority of K♣ do not respond well to being told what to do or how to think. The popular tweeter, Kevin the dad, proclaimed, "Parenting is like a circus. Sometimes you are the ringmaster. Most of the time you're the clown." Most K♣ adolescents tend to view their parents as clowns. If you are a parent of a K♣ who has this attitude, you may be frustrated because you ask them to do something, and they refuse to comply. For instance, perhaps you ask them to do their homework before rather than after dinner. When you confront them with their lack of follow through, they can be argumentative. At an extreme, they lash out by criticizing you. Most often the parent that receives criticism from a K♣ is the mother. And this scenario is more likely if the K♣ is a male. In these instances, and if possible, it may be better for discipline to be administered by a father or father figure.

Have you ever watched the animated TV show, *The Simpsons*? Recognized as the longest running American sitcom, you have probably watched an episode or are somewhat familiar with the main characters. The character, Bart, is a particular fan favorite. Bart is clever, mischievous, and misunderstood. Bart is misunderstood in a similar way that some K♣ are misunderstood. Bart is famously known for saying he was an "underachiever and proud of it." One of the greatest life challenges for a young K♣ is that they need to accept their power and responsibility to lead others with their knowledge. Such responsibility may be overwhelming for them. As such, countless K♣ respond to this pressure by *underachieving* in their youth. And some of these K♣ direct their intelligence into troublesome behavior, just as Bart Simpson did.

Speaking of Bart, Bart's famous proclamation is equally a statement about the status of the American educational setting. Early public schooling is tightly structured, giving students little choice in what content they are to learn. This kind of learning is not always the best for male students or a K♣. As previously stated, K♣ need more choice in their learning. If a particular form of learning is not satisfactory to a K♣ and they are pressured to achieve, some will manifest underachievement. Additionally, a K♣ will be selective in what subjects or teachers they will or will not put effort towards. If you are the teacher of a K♣, try to engage them in cooperative learning and assign them leadership duties. They love telling others what to do. Schools that support problem or project-based learning may also be a better educational approach for a K♣ student because students are put in the driver's seat of their learning environment. Problem-based learning is a teaching methodology that uses real-life problems to drive student learning of concepts that are related to solving problems. Likewise, project-based learning uses real-life problems, but students are also expected to demonstrate learning through the development of a product or presentation. Plus, these approaches to learning tend to showcase the analytical skills of a K♣.

Deep down a K♣ subconsciously understands they are required to achieve big things. They are destined to be a *leader* in a specific field of study. This perception puts a lot of academic pressure on a K♣. When the pressure is too much, a K♣ may respond by acting *indifferent* or like they do not care about academics. These K♣ do not respond well to adults trying to manage them. This is a signal to adults that they need some space. While an adult may assume a K♣ is being lazy, what may be happening is that they are overwhelmed. Applying more pressure will likely only worsen the situation. If you are a parent of a K♣, urge them to release some of their stress through physical activity or creative expression such as playing music, playing sports, or listening to music. Provide intellectual stimulation not connected to academics. K♣ enjoy friends who can intellectually keep up with them and with their unique sense of humor. Support time with friends. K♣ especially love mental games they can play with their friends. Purchase board games that simultaneously boost their analytical skills such as Codenames, Chess, Settlers of Catan, Coup (The Dystopian Universe), Dominion, or Stratego. Perhaps, set up a family game night of Trivial Pursuit. However, be prepared to lose. K♣ are not only competitive, but they also retain an impressive breadth of knowledge. This explains why some K♣ become college professors later in life.

Summary of Higher and Lower Personality Traits

Higher: Leader, intelligent, libertarian, analytical, futuristic, high integrity, systems thinker.

Lower: Intense, indifferent, unmanageable, stubborn, underachiever, bossy.

Childhood Influence Mercury Cards

It is common knowledge that a child's personality is most malleable during the formative years – from birth to eight years of age. In the Destiny Card system, the Mercury Cards in a Birth Card's Life Spread reveal influences a child with this Birth Card will experience between birth through age 12. As such, a child's Mercury Cards must be considered so an adult can nurture a child from a place of awareness and work with them from where a child is at in their development. A K♣ child has the following Mercury Cards: **J♦, 7♣, and 3♠**. The J♦ may mean there is an influential father and/or brother who is likely a Diamond Birth or Planetary Ruling Card. Alternatively, outside of any specific person associated with these three cards, the basic meanings of these cards describe experiences that may be impactful during this child's formative years. These cards suggest a K♣ demonstrates gifts of artistic talent, creativity, and wit at a young age. They can talk adults into doing things their way. Negativity may be directed at them particularly if they are underachieving.

Potential Callings / Vocations by Zodiac Sign

January 27 – Aquarius: 6♣ Planetary Ruling Card

Having a 6♣ Planetary Ruling card, these K♣ are more susceptible to procrastinating and underachieving. Tapping into their humanitarian Aquarius nature, they can do well as a politician, teacher, counselor, physician, musician, or actor.

February 25 – Pisces: 6♠ Planetary Ruling Card

With a 6♠ Planetary Ruling card, these K♣ feel destined to serve more behind the scenes to heal and support others. They can do well as a physician, artist, teacher, preacher, musician, government official, or administrator.

March 23 – Aries: 4♦ Planetary Ruling Card

The influence of Aries in these K♣ instills ambition to achieve. While they can achieve in any career (even sports or acting), they may prefer running a business, publishing, creating art, or exploring scientific research.

April 21 – Aries or Taurus: 4♦ or 4♥ Planetary Ruling Card

The Aries affiliated K♣ possess an innate drive for financial stability. They generally work in business. The Taurus affiliated K♣ are more interested in careers that provide a more harmonious work environment (e.g., landscape architect, scientist, artist, or actor).

May 19 – Taurus: 4♥ Planetary Ruling Card

With a Taurus' fondness for beauty, many of these K♣ prefer to pursue careers in music, singing/ song writing, art, or acting. Some prefer to provide for their family and do so in a well-paying job as a physician or business leader. Some want to give voice to others through writing or activism.

June 17 – Gemini: J♦ Planetary Ruling Card

Extroverted Gemini in these K♣ helps them achieve whatever their heart desires. Most prefer general professions (e.g., attorney, writer, teacher, language interpreter, mathematician, or scientist). Having both King and Jack energies, these individuals have double the male energy so they can also excel as an athlete, or in a male dominated business.

July 15 – Cancer: 2♣ Planetary Ruling Card

Having a 2♣ Planetary Ruling card, these K♣ hold superb communication skills which can propel them to succeed as a writer, journalist, teacher, counselor, minister, or physician. Those with artistic leanings can communicate feelings through their paintings or music.

August 13 – Leo: K♣ Planetary Ruling Card

With double the K♣ energy, these individuals truly enjoy working with facts as a statistician, mathematician, business, or government leader. The extroverted aspect of Leo may sway some into the limelight as an actor, director, producer, or athlete.

September 11 – Virgo: J♦ Planetary Ruling Card

The influence of Virgo instills an attention to detail like no other in these K♣. They are drawn to meticulous jobs such as a scientific researcher, technician, economist, or writer. Some enjoy local government jobs in which they can make a difference, such as county commissioner, major, or secretary of state.

October 9 – Libra: 4♥ Planetary Ruling Card

The entertaining and cooperative aspect of Libra steers these K♣ into careers such as acting, film directing, singing, composing, or playing music. Those with political leanings can do well as a diplomat, ambassador, politician, or speech writer.

November 7 – Scorpio: 4♦ and Q♥ Planetary Ruling Cards

The inquiring mind of Scorpio is strong in these K♣. They are sure to achieve as a physician, scientist, surgeon, researcher, or professor. Those interested in film can succeed as a screenwriter, director, or producer.

December 5 – Sagittarius: 2♠ Planetary Ruling Card

With a 2♠ Planetary Ruling card, these K♣ excel when they partner with others, particularly in business or sales. Partnering can also reduce the intense pressure they feel to achieve. Those wanting to serve can do so as a minister, politician, government, or military leader.

Famous K♣

George Harrison, musician – 2/25/1943
Taraji Henson, actress – 9/11/1970
Ludacris, rapper – 9/11/1977
Venus Williams, tennis player – 6/17/1980
Harry Connick, Jr, singer/ actor – 9/11/1967
Louise Eriksen, female football player – 9/11/1995

Welcome to the world of the commanding K♦!

K♦ = Rule through money and values

According to the Destiny Card system, souls chronologically experience God's lessons across 52 life incarnations. (Think of these as the universe's lessons if this aligns more with your beliefs.) The Birth Card each soul is born into determines the order and type of lessons a soul experiences. When you examine a Birth Card, you will notice it displays a suit of either a Heart, Club, Diamond, or Spade. This suit is significant because it represents the gifts a person born into this suit will possess and how they will direct their energies to learn lessons in their current life incarnation. A Heart Birth Card retains gifts and experiences life lessons around love and relationships. A Club Birth Card holds capabilities and experiences life lessons in their ability to communicate and absorb knowledge. A Diamond Birth Card possesses talents and experiences life lessons around money and values. And finally, a Spade Birth Card manifests gifts and experiences life lessons in work and health. Souls progress through incarnations and life lessons beginning as Hearts, moving on to Clubs, then Diamonds, and finally as Spades. Therefore, individuals born as Heart Cards are the youngest souls and individuals born as Spades Cards are the oldest souls.

In addition, the number on a Birth Card is equally meaningful as souls sequentially experience life lessons beginning as an Ace and culminating with lessons as a King. King playing cards are associated with the number thirteen. Thirteen is not only the highest value any single playing card can possess, but it also represents the final incarnation a soul will experience within a specific suit. As such, King Birth Cards retain the most power and responsibility in the area associated with their suit. **It makes sense, then, that a K♦ child's purpose, gifts, and life lessons revolve around having a tremendous amount of *power and responsibility* in their life. And, due to being a Diamond, this child will learn lessons by experiencing tremendous power and responsibility around *values* and *money*.**

How to Nurture the Temperament and Personality of a K♦ Child

Born with tremendous power around *values* and *money*, you may be wondering then, what is the nature of a K♦'s power? Studying the images of King playing cards can shed some light. When you examine each of the King playing cards, you will notice they contain weapons. The image of weaponry represents the aggressive power Kings hold to rule over others. However, a K♦ playing card reveals a weapon that is different from all other King Birth Cards. While other King Birth Cards display swords, the K♦ holds a battle-ax. This weapon associated with a King is also different from what you have seen in film or on TV programs. In those representations, many kings wore swords, but that was more of a fashion statement. Nevertheless, you typically do not see images of a King wearing or holding a battle-ax. A battle-ax is a serious weapon with its capacity to both bludgeon and make deep cuts into a person's body. Why, then, does the K♦ card include a battle-ax? Clearly, the battle-ax is a symbol. It symbolizes the fact that all K♦ are unafraid of intense battle. In daily life, they do not turn away when faced with conflict or confrontation. They appear confident and will stand their ground in a dispute.

Ambition and *fearlessness* show up early in a K♦ child. This is the infant who crawls and walks earlier than children of a similar age. Or the toddler who climbs up and along narrow and high concrete ledges outdoors, jumps down from a scary height, and frightens their parents. During early childhood, if a K♦ values something like a specific toy, they can be incentivized to do something to obtain that toy. On the other hand, if they want a specific toy and you or someone else takes it away, they will rebel. They will demand their toy. Therefore, if you are a parent of a K♦, expect the typical 'mine' stage to be amped up a notch. After all, they are Kings! While they are in elementary school, leverage a K♦'s competitive nature by challenging them to win at activities such as earning good grades, playing in sports, and achieving academic certificates or badges. *Reverse psychology* can work well with a K♦ at this age. Reverse psychology is a strategy that involves someone compelling a person to behave in a certain way by advocating they behave in an opposite way. Applied to a K♦, an adult can simply imply doubt that they can achieve or win something. Then, you will discover that message becomes an amazing motivator. As a K♦ grows older, reverse psychology will no longer be effective. An adolescent K♦ will insist upon autonomy toward what they accomplish. An adult should help guide and not micromanage an adolescent K♦ to apply their ambition in positive ways. Regardless of gender, a K♦ can excel in competitive sports such as football, wrestling, softball, baseball, volleyball, swimming, and basketball. Sports that recognize top players or involve one-on-one competition can be particularly exhilarating for a K♦. Remember, they are warriors and will work hard to achieve recognition as such.

K♦ often succeed at competition because they are gifted at *controlling their emotions*. Even if they internally are feeling fearful, they will not expose this to their competitor. Rather, they will appear confident and in total control. While the ability to control emotions can give a K♦ an advantage in sports, it potentially has the opposite effect when applied to relationships. A K♦ who overly controls their emotions, can come across as callous and *unsympathetic*. These K♦ may not be capable of admitting their mistakes or flaws. Such behavior can lead to intense break-ups with people close to them. What is interesting is that deep down K♦ are sensitive souls. Therefore, a good way to nurture a K♦ is to teach them not to be afraid to communicate their own emotions. And this is not a child who should be told, "Don't be a baby" or "Man up" when they cry or display emotions. If you are a parent of a K♦, make sure to always validate their feelings. If this foundation is not established early on, some K♦ will have difficulty communicating later in life when their partner wants to discuss feelings. Later in life, these K♦ may implement strict rules on their own children in relation to their inability to express their emotions and thereby promote a cycle of family dysfunction.

A young K♦ can be *bossy*. Some are outright demanding and cocky. Let's consider an example. Picture a middle school aged K♦ girl named Alisha who has physically matured ahead of her peers. She is popular, confident, and intimidating. One day, Alisha is running late to her science class. When she arrives to class, she discovers the chairs next to her friends have all been taken. She assesses the situation quickly, presents a confrontational pose to the least popular nearby student, and says, "Move." Although Alisha has spoken one word, her non-verbal communication is clear and powerful. The student responds by immediately moving to a different chair. Sadly, this K♦ may fail to perceive the unfairness of her actions. Moreover, this K♦ may fail to even consider the other student's feelings or perspective. The reason behind this behavior is depicted on the K♦ playing card. You see, the K♦ is a face card and one of three royal court cards that show only one side of the person's face. This visual representation is why a K♦ is described as a one-eyed King. Such a depiction accurately represents them because their perspective is *short-sighted*.

With a propensity to be blind to the perspectives of others, K♦ can benefit from being exposed to *multi-perspectivity*. Multi-perspectivity is a strategy by which a topic or problem is analyzed by considering the needs and feelings of everyone involved. In school this practice can be implemented when analyzing real-world problems. For example, let's say a social science teacher explains to students that the state's legislators are considering banning teen drivers from having other teens in their car within the first year of obtaining a driver's license. The teacher asks students to consider the advantages and disadvantages of this law through different people's viewpoints. The teacher asks students to answer several questions: What groups of people will be impacted by this law? What might be the points of view held by each of these groups of people? What emotions may be expressed by each group of people? What potential conflicts may exist between these different points of view? Are there areas for compromise? Multi-perspectivity can be taught across different content areas in school. In a science classroom, conundrums represent another example of an activity that asks students to consider multiple perspectives when analyzing a scientific problem. Likewise, Language Arts curriculum offers numerous opportunities for students to discuss multiple viewpoints by way of exploring different characters in books.

If you are a parent of a K♦, encourage an older K♦ to participate in activities that provide practice in considering multiple perspectives. These activities can include being a member of a debate team or joining clubs that support diversity. And don't forget K♦ have *leadership* skills. Encourage them to serve as a member of their school's restorative justice team. Restorative justice teams consist of adults and student-leaders who facilitate conflict resolution situations for students in the school. This position would not only enhance a K♦'s leadership skills, but it would also teach them a valuable lesson around active listening to others. Some K♦ enjoy the power that comes with a position within student government. Urge them to run for such a position but challenge them to consider how they might support all students and viewpoints if elected. Another way to teach multi-perspectivity is to discuss current events while eating dinner together as a family. For instance, pick a current controversial issue to discuss and ask each family member to share their point of view. Make sure to establish ground rules for these discussions as a K♦ can over-power others. Model respect toward multiple viewpoints and refrain from having to pick one side. And you may need to remind a passionate K♦ it's okay to agree to disagree.

If a K♦ does not learn to consider other people's perspectives and feelings, they are susceptible of becoming a *bully*. If you are a teacher witnessing a K♦ bully, you know this is unacceptable behavior and requires intervention. Engage this child in a private discussion about their behavior. Listen to their side of the story. Then explain the other side to the story in terms of how others feel when they are bullied. If more incidents arise, discuss bullying as a whole class without calling them out for their behavior. Show the movie, *Wonder*, to the class to prompt discussion. This movie tells the story of fifth grader, Auggie Pullman, who experiences bullying due to facial differences. Use role play around specific situations that include bullying. Look on the Internet for resources on bullying and teach them to the class. Seek the help of support staff, counselors, and administration. If you are the parent of a K♦ and have other children, you may notice similar bullying behaviors at home. Use this book to read about the Birth Cards of your other children. A child with lower self-esteem or tendency toward negativity may be an easy target for bullying by a K♦. Be on the lookout for your K♦ to act like a *tyrant* toward siblings. Remember, K♦'s are warriors, and they may not be aware of how intimidating they can be to someone with less power.

Another important way to nurture a K♦ is to support them in enacting higher values. For example, if you are a parent of a K♦, encourage philanthropic activities from a young age. Perhaps, your child has outgrown certain toys. Challenge this K♦ to find a way to get rid of their toys in a manner that benefits others. Older K♦ may be interested in starting their own business. Support them but stipulate you will do so if they adopt a humanitarian or environmentally favorable aspect to it. The desire to acquire money may be so strong in a K♦ that they may lose ambition toward doing homework and making good grades. Their attention and efforts may shift to playing sports or working a part-time job. Negotiate with a K♦ on these matters. Perhaps, a different school model would better suit them such as one that provides a work/ study program or work internships. You may also want to consider alternative schools such as a High School for Arts and Business.

Summary of Higher and Lower Personality Traits

Higher: Leader in business or finance, fearless, ambitious, emotional control, strong values.

Lower: Arrogant, stubborn, tyrant, aggressive, bully, short-sighted, unsympathetic.

Childhood Influence Mercury Cards

It is common knowledge that a child's personality is most malleable during the formative years – from birth to eight years of age. In the Destiny Card system, the Mercury Cards in a Birth Card's Life Spread reveal influences a child with this Birth Card will experience between birth through age 12. As such, a child's Mercury Cards must be considered so an adult can nurture a child from a place of awareness and work with them from where a child is at in their development. A K♦ child has the following Mercury Cards: **6♥, 7♦, and 4♣**. Alternatively, outside of any specific person associated with these three cards, the basic meanings of these cards describe experiences that may be impactful during this child's formative years. These cards suggest a K♦ may experience some betrayal connected to spiritual values that needs to be brought into harmony. They are blessed by an organized and stable mind that allows them to do well in school.

Potential Callings / Vocations by Zodiac Sign

January 14 – Capricorn: 8♣ Planetary Ruling Card

Having the mental power of an 8♣ Planetary Ruling card, these K♦ possess a lot of ambition. They tend to embrace materialism. Their versatility ensures achievement across various careers (e.g., banker, politician, government leader, actor, musician, or entertainer).

February 12 – Aquarius: 6♦ Planetary Ruling Card

The humanitarian aspect of Aquarius helps these K♦ lean toward the values side of their card. They can do well as a politician, attorney, writer, appraiser, and in jobs that require diplomacy or mediation skills.

March 10 – Pisces: 4♣ Planetary Ruling Card

Having a 4♣ Planetary Ruling card instills a hard work ethic in these K♦. It also tends to bring forth the spiritual values side of their card. They can do well as an artist, musician, singer, writer, or actor. They can also run their own business or succeed as professional athletes.

April 8 – Aries: 2♦ Planetary Ruling Card

Having a 2♦ Planetary Ruling card heightens the ability for these K♦ to assess people, situations, and products. Therefore, they can do particularly well as a recruiter, real estate broker, attorney, appraiser, physician, researcher, or business leader.

May 6 – Taurus: 4♣ Planetary Ruling Card

The 4♣ Planetary Ruling card instills enjoyment of the home and friends in these K♦. Blessed with a pleasant speaking voice, they can do well as an actor, attorney, politician, singer, or preacher.

June 4 – Gemini: 6♥ Planetary Ruling Card

With a 6♥ Planetary Ruling card, these K♦ can be susceptible to falling into ruts and lacking motivation at times. When they do apply themselves, they can do well as an attorney, stock or real estate broker, sports commentator, athlete, or business leader.

July 2 – Cancer: K♥ Planetary Ruling Card

Nurturing Cancer when combined with the tender-hearted K♥ Planetary Ruling card causes these K♦ to prefer people or service-oriented jobs such as a teacher, preacher, coach, tour guide, business or project manager, group or team leader.

Famous K♦

George Clooney, actor – 5/6/1961
Angelina Jolie, actress – 6/4/1975
Brent Kavanaugh, Associate Justice of the Supreme Court of the U.S. – 2/12/1965
Carrie Underwood, singer/ songwriter – 3/10/1983
LL Cool J, rapper – 1/14/1968
Evan Spiegel, CEO of Snap Inc. – 6/4/1990

Welcome to the world of the commanding K♠!

K♠ = Rule through will and wisdom

According to the Destiny Card system, souls chronologically experience God's lessons across 52 life incarnations. (Think of these as the universe's lessons if this aligns more with your beliefs.) The Birth Card each soul is born into determines the order and type of lessons a soul experiences. When you examine a Birth Card, you will notice it displays a suit of either a Heart, Club, Diamond, or Spade. This suit is significant because it represents the gifts a person born into this suit will possess and how they will direct their energies to learn lessons in their current life incarnation. A Heart Birth Card retains gifts and experiences life lessons around love and relationships. A Club Birth Card holds capabilities and experiences life lessons in their ability to communicate and absorb knowledge. A Diamond Birth Card possesses talents and experiences life lessons around money and values. And finally, a Spade Birth Card manifests gifts and experiences life lessons in work and health. Souls progress through incarnations and life lessons beginning as Hearts, moving on to Clubs, then Diamonds, and finally as Spades. Therefore, individuals born as Heart Cards are the youngest souls and individuals born as Spades Cards are the oldest souls.

In addition, the number on a Birth Card is equally meaningful as souls sequentially experience life lessons beginning as an Ace and culminating with lessons as a King. King playing cards are associated with the number thirteen. Thirteen is not only the highest value any single playing card can possess, but it also represents the final incarnation a soul will experience within a specific suit. As such, King Birth Cards retain the most power and responsibility in the area associated with their suit. **It makes sense, then, that a K♠ child's purpose, gifts, and life lessons revolve around having a tremendous amount of *power and responsibility* in their life. And, due to being a Spade, this child will learn lessons by experiencing tremendous power and responsibility around *work* and *health*.**

How to Nurture the Temperament and Personality of a K♠ Child

Have you ever watched the movie, *The Curious Case of Benjamin Button*? Or perhaps you read the book with the same title, written by F. Scott Fitzgerald. The main character, Benjamin, ages backwards. As a newborn, Benjamin looks more like a withered old man. Over time, his physical appearance changes, each year becoming younger and younger. This story is relevant to a K♠ because any person born to this Birth Card possesses the wisdom of an old person. You see, K♠s are the *oldest souls*. Hence, as a young child they may come across to others as odd because they may act more like an old person. For instance, let's say you are visiting a friend who is a parent of a two-year-old female K♠. While interacting with your friend's child you are gossiping about another friend. Your tone of voice is negative and critical. You look down at the child and find her scowling at you. You and your friend laugh because it is as if she is disapproving of your comments. And, indeed, she may be doing just that! From the time a K♠ begins to crawl or walk, they will demonstrate *independence*. And adults around them will be impressed by their *strong will power.* As a toddler, their emphatic "No!" to a simple request will make an adult think twice of pushing them too hard to comply. If you are a parent of a K♠, provide structure and routines with eating and napping times. An upset K♠ can disrupt the home environment like no other Birth Card.

A K♠'s *persistence* is so strong that they often have more will power than their siblings and parents. When a young child or adolescent has more power than others around them, there is bound to be conflict. Additionally, a K♠ is born with a *fixed or inflexible* temperament. This means they will resist conforming to the beliefs of others when their views do not align with them. Conflicts with a K♠ can easily evolve into *power struggles*. Therefore, adults would be wise to tread lightly with a K♠ when implementing discipline. Do not be surprised when traditional approaches to discipline may not be effective. For example, imagine you are a parent of a three-year-old K♠ named Lucy. Lucy shares a bedroom with her sister, Rebecca, who is four years older. Often, you are frustrated in having to constantly remind your daughters to clean up their bedroom. On one such occasion, Rebecca blames Lucy for the mess. Both of your daughters get into an argument and their fighting is driving you crazy. You decide to implement a timeout as it's a technique that has successfully worked with your older child. Both girls are to sit quietly for fifteen minutes; one in the dining room and the other in the kitchen. You explain that the timeout serves as a time to cool off and is not meant as a punishment. However, Lucy does not calm down during timeout. Rather, Lucy stews over how she has been wronged. Fifteen minutes later, you bring the girls back together to discuss the incident. Lucy is even more furious than before and verbally attacks Rebecca. Such a reaction can happen when a K♠ is accused of doing something wrong when they did not. A better approach for a K♠ in this scenario would be to engage them in an activity that will calm and distract them such as drawing, painting, or listening to music. Then, after they have calmed down, deal with each child separately versus together to address the issue at hand.

A K♠ responds best to a *democratic* parenting and classroom management style. In education, a democratic classroom management style involves establishing mutual respect and collaboration when solving behavioral problems. This does not mean that a child makes the rules. Rather, a child has input and the ability to make choices within the process. Likewise, a K♠ would benefit from a democratic parenting style in which they are encouraged to be independent, make their own decisions, and learn from mistakes. What is interesting is that some K♠ are born into a family with a father or father figure who tends to implement an *authoritarian* style of parenting. An authoritarian style of parenting is a strict form of parenting in which an adult expects control and obedience. Such a style often involves an adult using corporal punishment when a child makes mistakes. This style tends to backfire with a K♠ for several reasons. First, as a rule, Kings dislike being told what to do. Second, as the oldest soul, a K♠ tends to possess more wisdom than their parents! Lastly, if a young K♠ is parented with a 'my way or the highway' approach, they will likely lean into the lower traits of their Birth Card. If you are a parent of a K♠ and this is happening, tread carefully. Perhaps, seek family therapy. Left under the influence of an authoritarian approach, an older K♠ may mimic authoritarian behaviors and direct them at others. At an extreme, these K♠ may grow up to act like a bully.

A K♠ will likely lean into their higher personality traits when they tap into and follow their innate spiritual values and wisdom. As an adult working with or caring for a K♠, you can assist them in this undertaking by helping them connect to their inner wisdom. This can be facilitated by engaging them in *mindfulness* activities. Mindfulness exercises allow a person to focus on the present moment and listen to their inner wisdom. Such activities can be used at home or in a classroom. There are countess ideas on the Internet, including videos on YouTube that guide children through the process of mindfulness. In addition, urge a K♠ to participate in forms of creative expression possibly through art, music, knitting, dance, or journaling. And by all means, allow them to act like a King. Challenge them to take on positions of responsibility and *leadership*. If you are a teacher of a K♠, appoint them as caretaker for the class pet or group captain for a collaborative project. Ask them to share their deepest thoughts and beliefs. And make certain that you show respect for their innate wisdom.

Another good way for an adult to nurture a K♠ is to help support their achievement of short and long-term goals. Guide rather than micromanage a K♠ through the process of making and achieving goals of their own making. Keep in mind that if they are pressured to pursue goals not of their making, a K♠ may be pushed toward mediocrity. If you are a parent of a K♠, you have good intentions in wanting your child to be successful in life. Therefore, find what interests them and support them in pursuing it. If a K♠ manifests mediocrity, refrain from adding more pressure or making goals for them. Let them be. Seriously. Let them be. It is the destiny of a K♠ to be successful in life. They key is that a K♠ should be allowed to decide what success looks like for them. A K♠ can master any topic or profession. The only limitations for a K♠ are self-made ones. Some may be intimidated by their internal power. These K♠ may fear taking on the responsibilities that come along with such great power. While it is possible that some K♠ may fear their power and refuse to accept it, most K♠ accept it over time and then use it to lead others. As a leader, they literally hold the power to lead humanity in its own evolution. They hold the capacity to deconstruct and reconstruct institutions, systems, policies, and structures. You see, a K♠'s greatest superpower is that they hold the potential to be a *change-maker*. As its name suggests, a change-maker is someone who creatively takes action to solve a social problem.

Albert Einstein was quoted as saying, "There are two ways to live. You can live as if nothing is a miracle. You can live as if everything is a miracle." Because K♠ are change-makers, they can foster a miraculous impact on society. Much of this has to do with the fact that the life of a K♠ represents not only a soul's last incarnation of the Spades suit, but also the final life incarnation. As such, their final life lesson and potential is momentous. They are to lead and inspire changes that push humanity to evolve. Having experienced 51 past life incarnations and lessons, a K♠ subconsciously understands the concept of *spiritual transmutation* and its role in human evolution. Think of spiritual transmutation as a mechanism like biological adaptation and its role in evolution. Let's consider an example. In Finland, tawny owls have changed in color to adapt to a warmer climate with less snow. Generations ago, most tawny owls were pale gray in color to camouflage with the snow. Currently, most tawny owls are brown in color. This change did not happen in one generation. It was a slow process, over many generations. Tawny owls adapted to ensure survival of the species. Likewise, humanity slowly evolves through the process of spiritual transmutation. Now, let's consider a real-life example of how a K♠ can have a role in this process. During elementary school, like most Americans you probably read about Paul Revere and his part in history. Prior to the American Revolutionary War, Revere was a goldsmith by trade; a business economically hit hard by British taxes. Revere joined up with other locals gathering intelligence on the movements of the British soldiers. He is most famous for his midnight ride in which he warned American patriots that "the British were coming." His one action was the start of a domino effect that changed the course of history. Scholars believe that without Revere's action, the Battles of Lexington and Concord could have gone much differently. America might have capitulated to the British and not be the free country it is today if not for the actions of Revere. Being a bona fide K♠, Revere was an agent of change and played a role in America's spiritual transmutation.

Summary of Higher and Lower Personality Traits

Higher: Leader, independent, persistent, humble, high integrity, strong will, change-maker.

Lower: Despot, inflexible, discontent, huge ego, bully, political or religious extremist.

Childhood Influence Mercury Cards

It is common knowledge that a child's personality is most malleable during the formative years – from birth to eight years of age. In the Destiny Card system, the Mercury Cards in a Birth Card's Life Spread reveal influences a child with this Birth Card will experience between birth through age 12. As such, a child's Mercury Cards must be considered so an adult can nurture a child from a place of awareness and work with them from where a child is at in their development. A K♠ child has the following Mercury Cards: **3♥, 6♣, and A♥**. Alternatively, outside of any specific person associated with these three cards, the basic meanings of these cards describe experiences that may be impactful during this child's formative years. These cards suggest a young K♠ experiences emotional indecision with a close relationship, possibly because they perceive a lack of love from a father or father figure. Meanwhile, they often experience an affectionate relationship with a different family member. During their youth they may procrastinate in school.

Potential Callings / Vocations by Zodiac Sign

January 1 – Capricorn: 5♣ Planetary Ruling Card

Only one birthdate is associated with a K♠. Many Capricorns prefer to be the boss and not be bossed around. This trait is intensified in the commanding K♠, making them best suited to lead. They can lead as a musician, artist, actor, politician, teacher, business executive, government official, or preacher. Some prefer leading behind the scenes as a psychologist, psychiatrist, or counselor.

Famous K♠

Sifan Hassan, Olympic runner – 1/1/1993
Christine Lagarde, President of the European Central Bank – 1/1/1956
Frank Langella, actor – 1/1/1938
Betsy Ross, maker of first American Flag – 1/1/1752
J. D. Salinger, writer – 1/1/1919
Noor Inayat Khan, female British spy during World War II – 1/1/1914

Chapter 17

Descriptions of the Joker Birth Card

Welcome to the world of the chameleon Joker!

Joker = The wild card

According to the Destiny Card system, souls chronologically experience God's lessons across 52 life incarnations. (Think of these as the universe's lessons if this aligns more with your beliefs.) The Birth Card each soul is born into determines the order and type of lessons a soul experiences. Souls progress through life incarnations beginning as Hearts, moving on to Clubs, then Diamonds, and finally as Spades. Therefore, individuals born as Heart Cards are the youngest souls and individuals born as Spades are the oldest souls. When you examine a Birth Card, you will notice it displays a suit of either a Heart, Club, Diamond, or Spade. This suit is significant because it represents the gifts a person born into this suit will possess and how they will direct their energies to learn lessons in their current life incarnation. A Heart Birth Card retains gifts and experiences life lessons around love and relationships. A Club Birth Card holds capabilities and experiences life lessons in their ability to communicate and absorb knowledge. A Diamond Birth Card possesses talents and experiences life lessons around money and values. And finally, a Spade Birth Card manifests gifts and experiences life lessons in work and health.

When you examine all playing cards in a deck, you will notice one card contains all four suits. This is the Joker playing card. When you look closer at this card, you will see there is also no indication of a value or number associated with it. So, what gifts and energies does a Joker possess in their life incarnation? The answer is simple. Jokers hold the privilege to choose their own Birth Card for their current life incarnation. If you have played the game of poker, you are likely familiar with the role the Joker plays as being a *wild* card. A wild card is a card that can be used to represent any other playing card based upon the desire of the player. **A child born a Joker Birth Card is truly a wild card; able to observe their surroundings and morph into whatever suit and number of Birth Card they desire.**

There is only one birthday, December 31, that is associated with the Joker Birth Card. Because it is a mystery as to what playing card a Joker will choose to manifest in their current life incarnation, it is impossible to accurately explain their temperament or extensive personality traits. This said, a couple of traits can be described by analyzing the Joker playing card. Closely examining this card, you immediately notice the Joker resembles a court jester. In the medieval and Renaissance eras, court jesters were responsible for entertaining the royal court. They did so by wearing outrageous clothing, singing, juggling, telling jokes, and storytelling. Jokers also entertained the court by making impressions of the Queen, King, or other important figures in the court. For these reasons, people born associated with the Joker

Birth Card possess a high degree of *creativity*. Certainly, to invent oneself would require such a degree of creativity. This attribute often predisposes Joker Birth Cards to pursue the dramatic arts. Many successful actors and actresses are Jokers. Because they are like chameleons, they can easily study a character and flawlessly imitate the character's personality and mannerisms.

The Destiny Card system is based upon the concept of reincarnation. Such a concept has been embraced by many people and cultures. As an example, the Dalai Lama, proclaimed, "Reincarnation is not an exclusively Hindu or Buddhist concept, but it is a part of the history of human origin." Remember, the Destiny Card system consists of spreads that mathematically adjust to create life lessons for a soul based upon their Birth Card. But what happens to a soul between life incarnations? Numerous psychics and mystical writers have argued that souls, upon death, are met by their spiritual guides. These guides help a soul unpack their past life, and help them to identify and analyze their celebrations, mistakes, and lessons learned. More importantly, they assist them in examining a soul's overall spiritual growth within their most recent and past incarnation. And like any good teacher, a spiritual guide will work with this soul to assess spiritual growth and design plans for this soul's next incarnation. It is my opinion that a soul's life incarnation as a Joker represents a second chance – a do-over at repeating a previous life incarnation. Perhaps a soul reflects upon their prior or several past lives and decides their spiritual trajectory is way off. A repeated life incarnation may be just the right solution to getting back on track toward their journey toward spiritual enlightenment. Whether or not this hypothesis is true is a mystery; a mystery just as enigmatic as the Joker itself!

Famous Jokers
Donald Trump, Jr, political activist – 1/31/1977
Ben Kingsley, actor – 12/31/1943
Gabby Douglas, Olympic gymnast – 12/31/1995
Anthony Hopkins, actor – 12/31/1937
Psy, singer/ songwriter – 12/31/1977
Josh Hawley, politician – 12/21/1979

Made in United States
Troutdale, OR
02/10/2025